BABY BOOMER COMICS

THE WILD, WACKY, WONDERFUL
COMIC BOOKS OF THE 1960s!

by Craig "Mr. Silver Age" Shutt

including illustrations by Jim Mooney

Published by

700 E. State St. • Iola, WI 54990-0001
Telephone: (715) 445-2214 • (888) 457-2873

Please, call or write us for our free catalog of collectibles publications. To place an order or receive our free catalog, call (800) 258-0929.

ISBN: 0-87349-668-X
Library of Congress Catalog Number: 2003105293
Printed in the United States of America

To my wife, Mary Kay,
for her unwavering support
of "Mr. Silver Age."

And also for laughing
in the right places.

WHEN TITANS
THANK!

This book would not have happened without the support and influence of a number of people at different periods leading up to its publication.

I owe a big debt to the staff behind *Comics Buyer's Guide*, where my column *Ask Mister Silver Age* appears in every issue. Thanks go to...

COMICS BUYER'S GUIDE

...**Maggie Thompson**, who gave me a huge thrill when she published my first unsolicited article back in 1992 and has supported "Mr. Silver Age" ever since;

...**Brent Frankenhoff**, for having the patience and good humor to work with my wackiness on a weekly basis;

... and **John Jackson Miller**, for bringing the book to fruition after years of discussions and delays and for seeing it steadfastly through its labor-intensive production.

You can check out what I'm doing now in each issue of *Comics Buyer's Guide* — call (800) 258-0929 to subscribe!

Behind the scenes at Krause Publications, I'd also like to thank **Kim Schierl**, lead designer on the project; **Shawn Williams**, for his design assistance; **Steve Duberstein** for helping generate this edition's price guide; and **Don Gulbrandsen**, **Debbie Bradley**, and **Mark Williams** for helping make it all happen.

I'm thrilled that **Jim Mooney**, Silver Age artist extraordinaire, agreed to create the visual for the "Mr. Silver Age" character for this edition. Jim was one of my first choices to illustrate this book, and I'm thrilled he was able to help out! Thanks, Jim!

I'd also like to thank **Mark Waid**, DC Trivia Geek #1, for his fast and in-depth replies to questions throughout the years and his generosity in sharing his amazing database of DC reprint citations.

Thanks also go to **Kurt Busiek** for his support and help. They may be big-name comics pros, but at heart they're big-time comics fans.

Research assistance also came from the late **Rich Morrissey**, as well as **Edwin Murray, Michael L. Fleisher, Paul Levitz, Bob Hughes,** and **Jon Ingersoll**. All their help is greatly appreciated. I've also learned a lot from the reference works of George Olshevsky.

Thanks also go to two Silver Age comics publishers, **DC Comics** and **Marvel Enterprises,** who are not only going strong today, but actively reprinting many of the tales touched on herein in affordable compilations. We've listed many such compilations here, but you can get the whole list of what's out there from www.dccomics.com and www.marvel.com. You've seen their movies — now buy the comics!

And there's no better place to pick up those collections than at your local comics shop: call (888) COMIC-BOOK to find one near you.

The *Mr. Silver Age* column probably would not exist without the influence of two earlier commentators: **Don Rosa,** who wrote his trivia-based Information Center for many years in several fanzines, and **Fred Hembeck,** who continues skewering Silver Age comics in his *Comics Buyer's Guide* comic strip, showed me it was possible to express a love for old comics while casting a skeptical eye on the details. And thanks to Joe Bowlby, friend and graphics designer, for creating a truly cool column logo for *Mr. Silver Age*.

My enthusiasm for these comics probably would not have become so ingrained without the help of my brothers, **Tom** and **Joel**, who read so many (but probably fewer) right along with me during our formative years. And the book certainly wouldn't have happened without the love and respect of my parents, **Kenneth** and **Gayle**, who never threw away a single one of my comics. I am happy to finally be able to show them that reading all those funny books for so long had a payoff.

You're all aces in my book — and, now, at last, you can finally read it!

Craig "Mr. Silver Age" Shutt
October, 2003

A Hearty Welcome from Mr. Silver Age!

Welcome to the Museum of Baby Boomer Comics! I'm kindly old Mr. Silver Age, your genial tour guide through this shrine to Silver Age wonderment.

By paying an extremely reasonable amount to join us today, you've shown an admirable interest in reliving the excitement and fun embodied in these old comics. My job is to help you wallow in their coolness for a bit. Nice work if you can get it.

As we wander through the museum looking at the covers and contents on display, please feel free to ask any questions you want. That's why I'm here, and, all modesty aside, I'm pretty all-seeing and all-knowing, which is how I snagged this cushy job. Well, that and the fact that I own the museum.

Before we get going, let me answer any general questions you have about comics history, so we all start out on the same page, so to speak. And remember, there's no such thing as a dumb question, so feel free to ask anything. Yes, you in the back?

What's a Baby Boomer?

OK, let me rephrase what I said earlier. While there *are* dumb questions, I'm going to answer them all as if they're equally fascinating, because that's the helpful and nonjudgmental kind of guy I am. Feel free to wander off during the boring parts of this intro and listen in when you need to.

A Baby Boomer is anybody lucky enough to have been born between 1946 and 1964, that post-World War II era when soldiers returned home, settled down, and helped to create babies at a booming rate. As the largest portion of this group hit its prime comics-reading years around 8 years old, some pretty cool comics started to be produced. This era of comics remained cool for so long (all through the 1960s) that it since has come to be called The Silver Age.

Why is it called The Silver Age?

Because the name "Golden Age" was taken by an earlier period of comics coolness. When the late 1950s and 1960s were recognized as the second cool period of comics, Silver seemed the most appropriate name to follow Gold, given its Olympic standing.

So when was The Golden Age?

The Golden Age began when Superman made his first appearance in *Action Comics* #1 (Jun 38). Ironically, creators Jerry Siegel (writer) and Joe Shuster (artist) had been trying to sell their adventure hero as a comic strip for five years with no takers. DC finally accepted it, and the strips were cut up to fit onto comic-book pages. Within several years, Superman not only had his own comic strip but movie serials, cartoons, toys, and a whole mess of comics.

He also had a whole mess of imitators, some so close they got shut down. But publishers soon found a blend of super-heroics and originality that appealed to readers, and the period boomed with the first super-heroes. The popularity of comics was aided by World War II, when young servicemen had lots of time on their hands when they weren't kicking the pants off the Nazis and the Japanese, so they avidly read the adventures of their favorite four-color heroes doing likewise in comic books. As soldiers returned from the war and began to settle down (and have those booming babies), the Golden Age petered out and super-heroes lost their popularity.

Action Comics #1 (Jun 38), the title and issue that launched a thousand (or more) super-heroes.
© 1938 National Periodical Publications, Inc. (DC)

What the heck was that (Jun 38) dealie you put after the comic's name?

That refers to June 1938, the month in which *Action Comics* #1 appeared. Comics are periodicals, so they have dates on them like other magazines (and we always use three letters to indicate the month). But they are unusual periodicals because many fans collect them, and that was encouraged by publishers numbering them to help readers determine if they'd missed any issues.

Ironically, publishers used to avoid numbering comics "#1" because readers in both the Golden and Silver Ages liked the time-tested value of a comic that had been around for a long time (and so did retailers stocking them). In some cases, when one comic was cancelled, a new one continued the numbering of the canceled title even if they had nothing in common. (This was encouraged by Post Office regulations, which required a new Second Class mailing permit for each new title — but not for one that was renamed.) In other instances, Silver Age first issues simply dropped their number from the cover in the hopes that this omission wouldn't be noticeable to buyers.

Nowadays, publishers produce as many new #1s as possible and keep numbers low by restarting titles for no good reason. That encourages fans to think they can collect a complete run of a title and suggests that lots of comics may be "collector's items" that should be put in a plastic bag with a board to protect it. Back in the Golden Age and Silver Age, comics more often than not were folded in half and stuck in a back pocket. In part, that's why they've become so desirable — kids destroyed them while they were reading them.

Tales from the Crypt was just one of E.C.'s horror titles. The comics series inspired the HBO horror anthology of the same name.
© 1951 E.C. Comics

Was there anything between these Ages or did they bump up together?

Most people agree that the Golden Age ended sometime in the late 1940s or early 1950s as super-heroes lost their appeal and other types of comics sprang up. The comics that appeared after the Golden Age and before the Silver Age were dominated by crime and horror comics. The latter were most famously represented by the E.C. Comics line, which included some of the premier horror comics of all time, such as *Tales from the*

Crypt and *Vault of Horror*, plus science fiction comics such as *Weird Fantasy* and *Weird Science* (and *Mad*, which later become a magazine). Some historians give that intervening period an age designation, too, but most fans agree there are spikes on the comics' coolness meter, and only those spikes get named.

What's that seal in the upper right-hand corner on most Silver Age comics?

That's the seal of approval from the Comics Code Authority, which was started in 1954. It indicates that a group of reviewers have approved every page as appropriate to be read by little kids. The Code was a response by a majority of comics publishers at the time to the negative attitude directed at comics by parents and other moral guardians (many self-appointed) who fostered the belief that crime and horror comics caused kids to go bad. One famous book, *Seduction of the Innocent* by Fredric Wertham, used the less-than-scientific approach that since juvenile delinquents read comic books, then comics caused kids to go bad. Nobody pointed out that little brainy nerds and Boy Scouts were reading even more comic books — heck, *all* kids read comic books!

To prevent a governmental imposition of standards (which was a real threat following a disastrous Congressional hearing examining comics), publishers enacted a stringent code that eliminated virtually any chance that anyone would object to a comic that passed its inspection. Many of the publishers skirting — or going over — the line of good taste closed up shop altogether. The Code's tight restrictions significantly limited the types of stories and twists that could be used in a comic, especially compared to the gore and sadism found in some of them previously. But it also forced creators to find imaginative and challenging ways to tell interesting, all-ages stories that made this period entertaining in its own way and extremely kid-friendly.

Although ostensibly a teen, Jimmy Olsen never was quite in step with the rest of his peers, as this 1964 cover illustrates. Were leather-clad biker gangs still a threat in the post-Camelot era?
© 1964 National Periodical Publications, Inc. (DC)

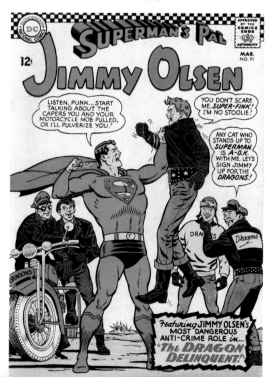

Was anything else fun going on in The Silver Age besides these way-cool comics?

I guess. The Silver Age of comics coincided with the Golden Age of rock 'n' roll, starting with Elvis, Buddy Holly, and doo-wop groups and continuing through beatniks, Dylan, The British Invasion, The Summer of Love, and Woodstock.

Toy fads covered the spectrum from Davy Crockett and Purple People Eater hats to hula hoops, Barbie, G.I. Joe, sea monkeys, and x-ray specs. Those last two were best known to kids who read comics and kept being sucked into sending in cash for the stupid junk that always looked about 10,000 times better all in color for a dime than it did all in a box sitting on their floor.

The Silver Age began shortly before the Russians launched Sputnik, and that Cold War fever produced a fascination for science and science fiction that had a profound effect on comics.

Many of the other fads, music, and cultural aspects of the time were reflected in the comics, too. Sadly, though, Silver Age comics were mostly produced by people old enough to be your dad, so the sighting of a hip and happening artifact or phrase in a comic book usually meant its time had passed about a year earlier. Comics heroes said "groovy" until about 1976.

So which company started the Silver Age?

DC Comics got the ball rolling by introducing a wave of super-heroes that clicked with readers. The first to do so was The Flash, the fastest man alive, who was introduced in *Showcase* #4 (Oct 56). One year earlier, though, DC had introduced a backup strip featuring a super-hero-like character, a Martian named J'onn J'onzz. Disguised as an Earth detective, he appeared as a back-up feature in *Detective Comics* behind Batman stories.

The Flash (Barry Allen) actually was a revival of a similar character from the Golden Age of comics, but the differences made all the difference. The hero's stories were more scientifically couched (if not authentically more scientific) and his costume was sleekly space-age. The stories also tended to be longer and more complicated, with clean, dramatic art.

What other characters were important to DC's Silver Age?

When The Flash proved popular, DC's editors used the same formula in 1959 to introduce Green Lantern, another updated Golden Age hero. He upped the space-age ante substantially. The original GL was a railroad structural engineer with a magical ring. The new guy (Hal Jordan) was a high-tech test pilot given a ring by a group of all-seeing aliens, who used a band of alien warriors scattered throughout the galaxy to maintain justice. GL's adventures involved alien worlds and invasions as much as they did the weird bank robbers that were a staple of these heroes' adventures.

DC Editor Julius Schwartz began his revival of Golden Age characters with a revamped Flash in **Showcase** #4 (Oct 56, above) and followed it three years later with a Green Lantern revival in **Showcase** #22 (Oct 59, below).
© 1956 and 1959 National Periodical Publications, Inc. (DC)

Figuring you can't have too much of a good thing, DC revived The Atom (Ray Palmer) and Hawkman (Carter Hall) in 1961. The Atom was revamped from a small guy with an "atomic" (not really) punch into a scientist who could alter his height and weight. Hawkman changed from an Egyptian king reincarnated as an archeologist into an alien police officer visiting Earth to learn new techniques. Works for me.

The revival concept really struck gold in 1960 when DC revived one of its best ideas, the super-hero team-up. The original Justice Society of America, which gathered most of DC's Golden Age heroes into stirring stories in the fondly remembered *All-Star Comics* back in the 1940s, was updated into The Justice League of America in 1960. It included the revived Flash and Green Lantern plus J'onn J'onzz, Aquaman (who had muddled along as a backup feature through the 1950s), and the three iconic heroes who had been published continuously since their original Golden Age introduction, Superman, Batman, and Wonder Woman.

These three latter heroes were big parts of the Silver Age, too. Superman (Kal-El from Krypton and Clark Kent) began having adventures that added super-girls and super-pets and super-teens from the future and a super-bottle full of Kryptonians and a Phantom Zone jail full of Kryptonian bad guys and so many kinds of kryptonite it was hard to keep track. But kids loved the details and the elaborate plot gimmicks that made the stories function (if not actually work).

With the success of the hero revivals, it wasn't long before they all teamed up as The Justice League of America in **The Brave and the Bold** #28 (Mar 60)

When The Flash was awarded his own series in 1959, the title then picked up the numbering of the Golden Age series, beginning with

DC's Golden and Silver Age finally met and shook hands in **The Flash** #123 (Sep 61).

Batman (Bruce Wayne) had a rougher time of it, first fighting aliens in a burst of science fictiony stories and then focusing on his detective roots — at least until his hugely popular TV show turned him into a "camp" joke that wasn't as sly as the editors (and TV producers) thought. Before the show ran its course, comics fans tired of the "Biff! Pow!" mentality that many heroes at many companies came to embrace.

Wonder Woman (Diana Prince) plugged along in her comic and was beloved by many little girls eager to have a heroine of their own to match up to the big boys. But, frankly, her stories were wildly improbable even by little-girl standards, and the super-boys let her join The Justice League of America only to serve as secretary at meetings. Ah yes, those were the good old days.

Did it take long for the Silver Age to get going?

It sure did. DC's editors were striking out in new directions to find something that worked, and they had to wait for sales results to come back to know if they were on the right track. As a result, The Flash was introduced in *Showcase* #4 in 1956, appeared in #8 in mid-1957, reappeared in two more issues in 1958, and finally got his own title in 1959 (which started with #105, cleverly continuing the numbering from the Golden Age series to avoid the dreaded #1).

It wasn't until 1959 that the second revival, Green Lantern, appeared in *Showcase* #22 (Sep-Oct 59). GL made three straight appearances and then became a charter member of the JLA. (Green Arrow joined in *JLA* #4 — the editors just forgot to include the long-time backup hero in the original team — followed by The Atom and Hawkman.)

Did DC ever have its Silver Age heroes meet its Golden Age heroes?

You better believe it. In fact, the first meeting led to an innovative concept that enthralled readers for years. At least, it did until long after the Silver Age ended, when editors decided that writers had made too big of a mess with their toys and made them put them all back in their box nice and neatly (sort of).

The Silver Age Flash met the Golden Age Flash in *The Flash* #123 (Sep 61), when the new Scarlet Speedster accidentally vibrated his body (he did that a lot) at just the right frequency to pass into another dimension where another Earth existed just like ours. Except, on this world, the comics heroes that the new Flash had grown up reading really existed!

The new Flash, being a bit full of himself, termed his own, newer world Earth-1, while the home to the older heroes became known as Earth-2.

This provided a nice, neat way for the original versions of the new heroes (and plenty of others that hadn't been revamped) to be available for stories without having to account for them on a monthly basis — they were off on Earth-2 doing their own thing.

The concept expanded dramatically when the JLA met the JSA in a two-part extravaganza beginning with "Crisis on Earth-One" in *JLA* #21 (Aug 63). That began an annual, usually two-part, "Crisis" adventure and opened the door to team-ups and more meetings for all types of heroes.

But soon, whenever a writer wanted to revive a hero whose past didn't quite match up with either the Golden Age Earth-2 heroes or the Silver Age Earth-1 heroes, a new Earth was created.

By the 1980s, there were dozens of these Earths — or an infinite number, as the *Crisis on Infinite Earths* mini-series implied. It did away with all the extra Earths, condensing everything to one universe (and killing the superfluous versions of key characters like Superman, Batman, and Wonder Woman that were a major reason for the confusion in the first place). The changes were so dramatic that many fans refer to any DC adventure as taking place in a pre- or post-*Crisis* time frame.

Who were the key creators during DC's Silver Age?

That's a big question. I would hate to try to list them all and leave anyone out, but we can still focus on a few of the key names that will recur time and again during our tour of the museum:

Julius Schwartz: This is the DC editor who got things rolling, when he agreed to put an updated Flash into *Showcase*. He got the job because he'd edited the Golden Age Flash after joining the company in 1944. Originally a literary agent for a number of famous science-fiction writers, Schwartz emphasized science, pseudo-science, and puzzle-solving in his stories. He also was the editor behind all of DC's hero revivals and saved Batman from cancellation in 1964, when he took over the title and returned him to his detective roots. In 1970, he moved over to Superman titles and enjoyed a lengthy tenure there, retiring in the mid-1980s.

Mort Weisinger: The editor of all the Silver Age Superman books, he expanded the legend to include lots of additional Kryptonian natives plus other doo-dads. Known for asking little kids in his neighborhood what they wanted to see Superman do and using that feedback for springboards, his stories were high-concept puzzles that often created implausible (but exciting!) situations that were solved in similarly implausible or highly coincidental ways. He also was known for brow-beating and belittling his stable of writers until he retired and left the Superman books to Schwartz in 1970.

Gardner Fox: The writer of the first 65 Justice League adventures, pulp-magazine author Fox began writing scripts in the Golden Age, co-creating many well-known characters including The Flash, Hawkman, Sandman, and Doctor Fate and writing a number of Justice Society stories. A prolific science-fiction writer, as well, he wrote thousands of stories during his career.

John Broome: The main writer on *Flash* and *Green Lantern*, Broome began his career working for Schwartz in the 1940s and wrote stories of The Justice Society and a host of science-fiction short stories. He retired from comics in 1970. (He did *not* write the first Flash story, though, with that honor falling to editor/writer Bob Kanigher, who edited many of DC's war books and shared an office with Schwartz.)

Carmine Infantino: The designer of The Silver Age Flash and penciller on his early stories, Infantino began working in comics in the mid-1940s and pencilled the Golden Age Flash, Green Lantern, Black Canary, and others (although his favorite strip, he said, was Detective Chimp). He also helped Schwartz reinvigorate Batman in the mid-1960s. In 1967, he was named DC's editorial director and later was named publisher. He returned to freelancing in 1976.

Julius Schwartz

John Broome

Carmine Infantino

Gil Kane

Bob Kane

Gil Kane: The designer of the Silver Age Green Lantern and Atom, Kane began pencilling comics in the 1940s and worked for a number of companies through the 1950s in a variety of genres. He also did work for Marvel Comics in the late 1960s on Spider-Man and others.

Wayne Boring: The best-known Superman artist of the 1950s, Boring imagined a barrel-chested Superman who often was shown flying in a standing position, a Boring trademark. He continued working on the character throughout the Silver Age in lesser amounts over time and later also did work for Marvel.

Curt Swan: Probably the most emblematic Superman artist of the 1960s, Swan's clean art produced a friendly, emotive Superman that appealed to young kids. He worked on the character through the 1970s, teaming with Murphy Anderson to update the hero's look and create a licensing image that has served as the public's face of Superman to this day. He also was a key contributor to The Legion of Super-Heroes, a team with a large fan following.

Bob Kane: The creator (with Bill Finger) of Batman, Kane did only a few stories on his famous character in the Silver Age. Most of the art was assigned to ghost artists, especially Shelly Moldoff, Jim Mooney, and Dick Sprang. Sprang's design is the one best known to fans of the early Silver Age, while versions by Carmine Infantino and later Neal Adams are best remembered by fans of the 1960s Batman.

Were there other companies that were popular during the Silver Age?

One stands head and shoulders above the rest: Marvel Comics. In fact, by the mid-1960s, Marvel became so popular that its comics sales surpassed DC's, and DC editors were scratching their heads over why they were losing the kids' attention.

The reason was that Marvel had its own style of comics story, one that played up action, drama, and soap-opera continuity. But it also had a sly humor that let readers know that it didn't take its over-the-top style of hype too seriously. That combination attracted a lot of college-age readers who'd figured they had outgrown comics. Campus speaking tours kept college kids reading, and their little brothers and sisters followed along. Without Marvel's entrance into super-hero comics in 1961, it's doubtful that the coolness factor of comics would have spiked high enough to have crowned this period as The Silver Age.

What heroes made Marvel popular?

Marvel's earliest heroes included The Fantastic Four (above) and Iron Man (below). While The FF had their own series, Iron Man was a feature in the former horror anthology **Tales of Suspense**.
© 1961 and 1962 Marvel Comics

Marvel entered the Silver Age with *Fantastic Four* #1 (Nov 61), a series about brainy Reed Richards (Mr. Fantastic), his college roommate Ben Grimm (The Thing), Reed's girlfriend Susan Storm (Invisible Girl), and her younger brother Johnny Storm (The Human Torch). They became a team unlike anything seen at DC, with a growing love affair between Mr. Fantastic and The Invisible Girl, a running sibling-like feud between The Human Torch and The Thing, and a tension-filled friendship between Mr. Fantastic (who wanted to cure Ben) and Ben (who vacillated over whether he wanted to be cured). The team at its heart was a family, just one that battled dastardly villains each month.

Marvel had been cranking out a wide range of comics featuring Godzilla-like monsters and *Twilight-Zone*-like (in their dreams) mystery books to try to ride out the 1950s sales slump. They heard that DC's *Justice League of America* was a hit, so they created their own team comic. But their approach didn't give powers to heroic individuals who then lived up to those ideals, it gave powers to regular Joes who had a hard time handling the ups and downs of living daily life while battling major super-villains.

What other characters were important to Marvel's Silver Age?

The Fantastic Four were quickly followed in 1962 by Iron Man, an industrialist (Tony Stark) who was forced to wear an iron chest plate to keep his heart beating but it turned him into a technological super-dude. (And he heeps on ticking: John Jackson Miller, one of my editors on this book, writes the *Iron Man* title for Marvel today!)

A few months later, Dr. Bruce Banner was transformed into The Hulk for the first time. That same month, the thunder god Thor (Dr. Don Blake) took over a mystery series, and he was soon followed by a puny high-school kid who gained arachnid qualities and become a little-known hero called Spider-Man (Peter Parker).

Another misfit team, The X-Men, followed in 1963, consisting of five teen-age mutants (Cyclops, Angel, Beast, Iceman, and Marvel Girl) shunned by society and led by a bald mentor, Professor X.

By then, Marvel had enough home-grown heroes to create a team-up book closer in structure to DC's JLA, and it created *Avengers* to star some of its biggest names. In 1964, the blind lawyer turned crime fighter Daredevil (Matt Murdock) scored his own book.

As with DC, however, Marvel's titles were no slam-dunk successes. *The Incredible Hulk*, in fact, lasted only six issues before being cancelled (he got another shot). Marvel's publisher was so sure that kids would hate the idea of a super-hero based on an icky spider that the character was sneaked into the last issue of an already canceled comic, *Amazing Fantasy* #15. Spider-Man had his own title with his next appearance because his former title no longer existed by the time sales results were in.

Did Marvel have an Earth-2?

No, Marvel's writers and artists were too creative to lift an idea like that directly. They also didn't have as much interest in reviving their 1940s heroes (they weren't that memorable, for the most part). They revived only three concepts, two as the original characters.

The first was Namor the Sub-Mariner. He was found living as an amnesiac bowery bum and regained his memory to claim the titles of King of Atlantis, Pain in the Butt to the Fantastic Four, and Reed's Rival for Sue's Affection. Then, Captain America was found frozen alive in a block of ice, having failed in his final World War II mission. He was de-iced and became The Avengers' leader (and got his own feature).

The Human Torch, ironically an android in the Golden Age, had his name reused by a member of the Fantastic Four (and then was revived himself in a convoluted way as the android The Vision. Long story).

Iron Man was a feature in the former horror anthology **Tales of Suspense**.
© 1962 Marvel Comics

While he started as a throwaway story in the final issue of **Amazing Fantasy***, Spider-Man went on to be Marvel's most-recognized character.*
© 1964 Marvel Comics

Who were the key creators at Marvel Comics in the Silver Age?

Again, the list is too long to do any more than to hit the key names and give a few details.

Stan Lee

Stan Lee: Marvel's sole editor, primary writer, and head cheerleader was the face and personality of The Silver Age. A relative to the publisher of Timely, a forerunner to Marvel, Lee began writing text pieces and scripts in his late teens during the Golden Age, shortening his last name from Lieber so he could save his "real" name for "real" writing later in his career. By the late 1950s, Lee had risen to editor and art director, and it fell to him, with artist Jack Kirby, to create The Fantastic Four in response to The Justice League. The concept of heroes with shortcomings and distinct, argumentative personalities caught on, and fans of all ages started picking up comics.

Lee was able to plot and/or write virtually the entire Marvel line in the early days thanks to an innovative storytelling approach he developed with his artists. Rather than provide a panel-by-panel script complete with dialogue, as writers did at other companies, he supplied a short plot, anywhere from a paragraph to several pages (sometimes talked out over the phone with the artist) and the artist fleshed out the story from there, pacing the pages to suit the story he was telling. Lee then added dialogue, sometimes creating a different interpretation of the action than the artist intended — but also producing a synergy that maximized both creators' talents.

Jack Kirby

Jack Kirby: The moving force behind the artistic look of Marvel's comics as well as a major plotter for many of his books, Kirby began pencilling comics in the 1940s as one half of a creative team with writer/artist Joe Simon. Together they produced a vast quantity of work, including creating Captain America and the first-ever romance comic. At Marvel, Kirby helped create most of the key Silver Age super-heroes, often designing the character and laying out issues for the books he didn't pencil himself. His artistic style was mimicked by artists who followed, often by dictate from Lee to maintain the action and excitement Kirby generated. In 1970, a dissatisfied Kirby left Marvel and moved to DC, where he created a series of books known as The Fourth World that contributed a number of key characters to the DC Universe. He later returned to Marvel, and he also worked for other companies as well right up to his death in 1994.

Steve Ditko: Best known for co-creating Spider-Man as well as the supernatural Doctor Strange, Ditko worked for several companies, notably Charlton, during the Silver Age. A reclusive artist, he seldom was photographed and never gave interviews, preferring his work speak for itself. He also was known for following the teachings of Ayn Rand and used her philosophies about good and evil being a black-and-white question in creating several of his own characters. After pencilling 38 issues of *Amazing Spider-Man* to great acclaim, Ditko left the series in a dispute with Lee and has done only occasional work for Marvel since.

Don Heck: Best known for his penciling on the first few years of The Avengers and Iron Man, Heck worked for both Marvel and DC in later years. A long-time artist in other genres, he had a scratchy style that was not as popular on Silver Age super-heroes as other Marvel artists' styles were. Even so, he played a key role in developing some of the best-remembered characters.

Roy Thomas

Roy Thomas: A former high-school English teacher in the Midwest, Thomas became the first long-time fan to turn comics pro, opening the door for others to follow. He joined Marvel in the mid-1960s, becoming Stan Lee's right-hand man and taking on a variety of series as the company expanded. (Ironically, he'd been brought to New

York for a job at DC, but left after only a couple weeks of working for Mort Weisinger.) He is best known for his long stint on *Avengers* as well as being the instigator for Marvel to license the Conan property, with which he had a long and well-remembered run for several decades.

John Romita: A long-time penciller on DC's romance comics in the 1950s, Romita joined Marvel shortly before Steve Ditko left Spider-Man and, despite his resistance to doing more pencilling, created the design for Spider-Man that is best-known today due to its far-ranging licensing impact. His clean, attractive style produced handsome men and sexy women, gaining him many fans despite his replacement of a well-loved creator. Romita stayed on the strip for many years and later began the *Spider-Man* comic strip with Lee. In the 1970s, Romita became Marvel's art director, laying out covers and doing art corrections, mimicking other styles. He has drawn virtually every Marvel character in his long tenure with the company.

John Buscema: Buscema worked at Marvel (then Timely) during the Golden Age, left to work in the more lucrative field of advertising, and returned to Marvel as its Silver Age comics began growing in stature in the mid-1960s (so he could work at home rather than commute several hours each day to his agency office). Despite his professed hatred for super-hero art, his most popular Silver Age work came on *Avengers* in the late 1960s. He went on to a long run on *Conan*, which he enjoyed more and which became the title he was best known for.

Gene Colan: A Golden Age artist for a variety of publishers including both DC and Marvel (then Timely), Colan worked on adventure strips at DC before rejoining Marvel in the mid-1960s. His moody, atmospheric style worked well on both *Daredevil* and *Iron Man*, for which he was best known in The Silver Age. He later became identified with his 1970s run on *Tomb of Dracula*, which played to his noirish style well.

John Romita

John Buscema

Were there any other companies that were popular in the Silver Age?

There were a bunch. Hey, it was the Silver Age! Part of the reason it was so cool was that there were all kinds of comics from all kinds of publishers aimed at all kinds of kids — and you could get eight to 10 of them for a dollar!

In fact, DC Comics had many kinds of comics besides super-heroes — teen-age humor comics, funny-animal comics, war comics, love comics, and a few others. Marvel also had a Western comic and a teen-age-humor/fashion book. In addition to those other options at the Big Two, there were these others:

Archie Comics was a significant player, producing a wide variety of titles featuring its red-headed teen-ager and his cast of high-school buddies and tormentors.

The company started a super-hero line headlined by The Fly and The Jaguar in 1959.

Then they revamped some of their own Golden Age heroes, including The Shield, The Comet, and The Web, after Batman's TV show made camp super-heroes The Thing To Imitate for about 10 minutes in 1966.

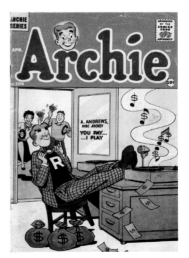

Archie's antics usually involved a get-rich-quick scheme that the red-headed wonder had hatched to impress one of the two loves of his life, Veronica Lodge.

All the comics of the Silver Age — not just the super-hero ones — appear in my price guide on page 203!

To avoid the restrictions of The Comics Code Authority, **Mad** magazine changed its format from a comic book to a magazine in 1955.
© 1955 E.C. Comics

Is anyone else in the running with The Flash to have started the Silver Age? Read on...
© 1962 National Periodical Publications Inc. (DC)

^{TM}**Dell (and later Gold Key)** produced many parent-friendly comics, especially Disney-licensed stories, as well as a wide assortment of movie-and TV-licensed titles. The company was so sure of the quality of its product and name that it didn't join the Comics Code Authority as most other publishers did, instead offering the Dell Comics Pledge to Parents.

Harvey Comics offered a quantity of titles designed for younger kids excited by comics but not yet excited by super-heroes.

The company's titles featured Richie Rich, Casper the Friendly Ghost, Sad Sack, Little Dot, Little Lotta, and many others.

Mad **magazine** was the only E.C. comic to survive the Comics Code Authority — which isn't surprising considering the code forbade the use of specific key words in many E.C. titles. Although not the only reason for the change, *Mad's* revamp into a magazine ensured it avoided oversight by the Code, and it is still warping kids today.

Warren Publishing began publishing black-and-white magazines featuring E.C.-like horror short stories in 1965, using many of the same artists who had become popular with that publisher. Since *Eerie* and *Creepy* didn't fit into a comics spinner rack, their distribution was limited, but their artistic approach had an impact on many fans and creators.

Plus, many other publishers active in previous periods continued to put out comics in the Silver Age. Charlton pumped out a steady stream of romance, racing, war, and humor comics. ACG, also known as the American Comics Group, released a variety of fantasy and romance comics, too. And let's not forget Wham-O, the Frisbee company!

So did Flash's first appearance officially begin The Silver Age?

Ah, I'm glad you asked that. No really, I am. Because there have been some lingering arguments over that point, and that's where our tour of the museum begins. It's a little exhibit just around the bend here that examines the beginnings of those lazy, hazy, silvery days back in the 1950s, when drugstore spinners were crammed with a wide variety of comic books and virtually every one was all in color for a dime.

Let's go in, shall we? Please refrain from drawing mustaches and horns on faces in the comics' panels like you did when you were a kid or I'll be forced to whack you upside the head...

SWIFTLY, THE TINY UNIFORM EXPANDS IN CONTACT WITH THE AIR, AND SPLIT-INSTANTS LATER...

--THE FLASH!!

When Did the Silver Age Start?

"So lay it on the line here, Mr. Silver Age. Does everyone agree that The Flash's first adventure began The Silver Age of comics, that glorious revival of super-heroes that Baby Boomers know and love?"

© 1956 National Periodical Publications, Inc. (DC)

You'll quickly find that, in comic books, it's hard to find any subject on which everyone agrees. But, as with sports, that's part of why it's so much fun! Sadly, though, the beginning of The Silver Age would seem like one of those cut-and-dried facts of life, and yet it just isn't so. In truth, there seem to be more theories about when the Silver Age began as time goes by. Or maybe I just hear more of them.

Keep one point in mind: I don't believe the Silver Age is a label stamped on the cover of specific books that makes them inherently worth more. The Silver Age was a period in time. It's an important period because of the excitement and quality of comics in general, not because each issue was individually greater than any others before or since.

I compare it to an award-winning garden. Some of the flowers bloomed before the garden was winning awards and others kept blooming long afterward. But some really great ones came along and peaked as other flowers were blooming, too, and the garden became an award-winner. Some of the garden's blooms, on their own merits, are pretty so-so. Looking at any one flower might not explain why the garden won awards. It's the combination of their all blooming at once that made it so great. And then, at some point, a majority of the flowers faded and the garden stopped winning awards, even though some flowers kept blooming as well as ever. A few could have even improved. But it wasn't the same any more.

The Silver Age started with *Showcase* #4 (Sep-Oct 56), The Flash's first appearance. The reason for so much discussion on that point is that the revival of fun super-hero comics was a gradual process. It took more than two years for Flash to get his own title after his *Showcase* debut and even longer before Marvel tried out a super-hero comic (in 1960). That leaves lots of room for interpretation. So let's look at the options for where this special period in comics could have begun and why all but one of them is just plain wrong:

*Here it is: The Silver Age began with **Showcase** #4 (Sep-Oct 56), when Flash got the recycled-heroes ball rolling. Then DC recycled the JSA, Stan Lee decided to create his own super-hero team, and the Silver Age was cooking!*

• **Captain Comet** in *Strange Adventures #9 (Jun 51):* Set in the present time, Adam Blake was a librarian born with a mutant futuristic brain that allowed him to have interplanetary adventures while roaming the galaxy in his guise as Captain Comet. His combination of super-powers and a secret identity made him essentially one of DC's few 1950s super-heroes. But his stories were much more science-fiction adventures than stories of a super-hero, and his last adventure took place in 1954. No other super-heroes came along during his run, similar to him or otherwise, so it's hard to claim he created *anything*, much less the entire super-hero revival that was in bloom during the 1960s.

• *Superman's Pal Jimmy Olsen* #1 (Sep-Oct 54): This was the first new super-hero-related title of the new super-hero era, argue proponents, and it continued through the Silver Age with no change in direction. But it was just the response to the popularity of the radio character, not the catalyst for more comics (except possibly the Lois Lane comic four years later). A few fans use this same logic to stretch the beginning of the Silver Age back to *Superboy* #1 (Mar-Apr 49), the first Superman variation after the end of WW II. But, as with Captain Comet, these comics didn't serve as the stimulus for more titles in a similar vein, they were just isolated events. Even a blind squirrel finds a few nuts.

• **The institution of the Comics Code,** with the seal first appearing in March 1955. It's true that the Code did change comics dramatically, but it wasn't responsible for generating the attributes that make the late 1950s and 1960s memorable. It produced a variety of restrictions that probably hamstrung writers in using many dramatic situations — but it also ensured that all the comics coming out had adventures that parents felt safe allowing little kids to read, and little kids read them in abundance because they were a lot of fun on a little-kid level. Writers found creative ways to write within the Code restrictions and produced a generation of all-ages comics in the process. The Silver Age was a thriving, exciting period *despite* the Comics Code, not because of it.

• *Detective #225* (Nov 55): This issue introduced J'onn J'onzz (pronounced, I learned long after my formative years, "John Jones"). The Martian Manhunter was stranded on Earth, so he became a detective, using his alien powers to help solve crimes. The argument in his favor is that he was the first long-running new super-hero of the mid-1950s, complete with a costume and cape. He was significant enough to become a charter member of The Justice League of America, the culmination of the super-hero revival, and, thus, was the first Silver Age hero. But in his early tales, J'onn wasn't a super-hero: He was a detective with enhanced abilities. He used his super-powers in his civilian identity or while invisible. He was just one of a variety of quirky detectives DC was featuring then: TV detectives, Indian detectives, supernatural detectives, even animal detectives. It was only in *Detective* #273 (Nov 59) — more than six months after the Flash gained his own title as a full-fledged super-hero — that J'onn's existence was revealed and he became a "super-hero" with a true secret identity and all the trappings. Had Flash not come along, I doubt that The Martian Manhunter would've led the charge from his back-up position in *Detective* to a new super-hero age. More likely, he would've stayed on the sidelines with Roy Raymond, Pow-Wow Smith, Mark Merlin, Detective Chimp, and all the other second-string detective heroes.

• *Showcase #4:* The Flash was the first super-hero based on reviving an earlier Golden Age hero, the idea that served as the spark for many of the

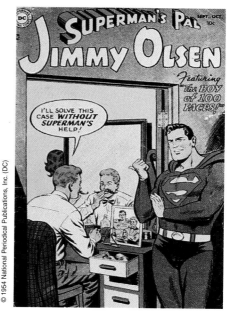

*Did **Superman's Pal, Jimmy Olsen** launch the Silver Age? Nah, this first new super-hero-related title of the new era was a response to the radio character's popularity.*

Did the Comics Code, with a seal which began appearing on comics in March 1955, bring on the Silver Age? Did it end when Spidey dropped the seal in 1971? Nope. The Code isn't what gave the Silver Age its special pizzazz.

The Silver Age was a thriving, exciting period *despite* the Comics Code, not because of it.

For long moments, the robot brain crackles and buzzes—there is a vivid flash—and a strange, awesome figure...

The robot brain... look what it brought—an alien being!

I read your mind well, Earthman—and I understand your every thought and word!

© 1955 National Periodical Publications, Inc. (DC)

Did J'onn J'onzz's first appearance in **Detective Comics** *#225 (Nov 55) start the Silver Age? Nope. He was really a detective with science-fiction powers. He didn't become a "super-hero" until after The Flash was established.*

The Silver Age is something to celebrate and remember.

Mister Silver Age Recommends...

***Showcase* Vol. 1, #4**

DC
Oct 1956
Cover artist:
Carmine Infantino,
Joe Kubert
"Mystery of the Human Thunderbolt"
Writer: Robert Kanigher
Penciller: Carmine Infantino
Inker: Joe Kubert

Then 10¢
Now $26,000

© 1956 National Periodical Publications, Inc. (DC)

Reprints appear in...
• DC Silver Age Classics: Showcase #4
• Essential Showcase 1956-1959
• Flash Archives Vol. 1
• Greatest Flash Stories Ever Told
• Secret Origins Vol. 1 #1
• Secret Origins Annual #1
• Secret Origins HC collection
• Secret Origins TPB
• DC Millennium Edition: Showcase #4

key starts of the Silver Age. His popularity led to revivals of Green Lantern, Atom, Hawkman and, most importantly, The Justice Society of America (as The Justice League of America). The JLA's popularity in turn was the stimulus for Stan Lee to create Marvel's own team, The Fantastic Four. Without Flash's success, we wouldn't have had at least four other key DC heroes, The JLA, or the Marvel Age of Comics. In other words, we wouldn't have had the Silver Age.

• *Fantastic Four* **#1 (Nov 61):** Marvel's line gave the Silver Age additional energy. Until then, the Silver Age was riding on one company's new heroes, and that by itself might not have generated the excitement to attract so many fans and garner so much publicity. And Marvel's comics, with their self-deprecating humor and soap-opera stabs at presenting real people who just happened to have super-powers, expanded the audience and the styles of stories being told. But Marvel's heroes built on what DC started; it wasn't the catalyst for it starting originally.

The way I look at it, this means every comic dated Dec 56 came out during the Silver Age and no comic dated Aug 56 came out in the Silver Age. But would I label every October 1956 comic as that title's "first Silver Age issue"? Nah. That makes it sound like something magical happened that month inside the comic and that it's somehow intrinsically more important (and possibly more valuable). *The Overstreet Comic Book Price Guide* disagrees, to some extent. It notes this "Silver Age" distinction for some but not all titles, apparently those that did then or soon would house super-heroes, such as *House of Mystery* and *Strange Tales*. Fortunately, it doesn't seem to affect their prices. *The Standard Catalog of Comic Books*, meanwhile, goes with my definitions all the way. (Little wonder: It's by the same folks who're bringing you this book!)

Keep in mind, "Silver Age" is different from "Earth-1," the part of the DC multiverse where Silver Age super-heroes lived. We could have been reading Earth-1 Batman stories before the Silver Age started. Or vice versa. Or even at different times in *Batman* and *Detective*. Picking an adventure in each title that clearly shows when Superman, Batman, and Wonder Woman—the major ongoing super-heroes during the 1950s — shifted to tell tales about the Silver Age Earth-1 versions of these heroes and away from the Golden Age Earth-2 versions is more interesting to me than picking the one that shows when they entered "the Silver Age." Earth-1 is a location for a story and character that might be pinpointed by plot continuities; the Silver Age is more of a state of mind.

Why is this "start of The Silver Age" designation important? Well, in all honesty, it probably isn't. The actual specific, carbon-dated starting point is immaterial, because the Silver Age is more than just specific dates on the cover of a comic. It's a period when comics told the first stories of many heroes who still exist today, in tales that could be read and understood by readers of all ages (well, for as much as *anybody* could understand some of the bizarre plot points and coincidences that were used). The excitement of so much new and unfolding material that would continue to thrill new generations of readers has never been captured in comics since The Silver Age ended. It's something to celebrate and remember, no matter when it began.

But it began with *Showcase* #4.

Let there be...
TRIVIA!

One of the highlights of the museum can be found on practically every page of this tome from here on out: The Mister Silver Age Trivia Challenge. While you're having your memory jogged by your visit here, you can match wits with some of comics' greatest fans by checking out the questions at the bottom of each page.

They're a little tougher than the "feature" quizzes in this book (like the one on the following page), in that they aren't multiple choice but really require you to dredge your memory.

The first 80 questions printed below were originally created by Mr. Silver Age with one simple purpose: to frustrate the beejeebers out of two teams of contestants, one made up of pros and one of fans, who vied for the Silver Age trivia crown at the 1996 Chicago Comicon. The Pro team consisted of Kurt Busiek, Tony Isabella, Dan Mishkin, and Mark Waid; fan panelists were Mike Chary, Pete Coogan, Jim Drew and Sidne Gail Ward. Believe me, these people were not easy to fool.

Prior to the 2003 edition of Mr. Silver Age's Trivia Contest at Wizard World Chicago, solitary Pro Mark Waid (left) looks on as Fan panelist Todd Allen (middle) begs for answers … errr, confers with Mr. Silver Age (right).

At the panel, the first of what has become a tradition at the Chicago comics convention, the Pros pulverized the Fans by a score too high to mention—which also has become a tradition. The Pros were particularly good at Criminal Organizations and Evil Teammates, make of that what you will. Sadly, neither team knew enough of Tomahawk's Rangers to score the points. The Pros allowed *Comics Buyer's Guide*'s own Tony Isabella to field that one, and he fell short. But he made up for it right away by naming every Earth-two hero who took part in the first Crisis.

The second 86 questions were asked of Pro and Fan teams of trivia experts at the 1997 Chicago comics convention, following up on the stellar debut challenge from the previous year's event. Kurt Busiek, Tony Isabella, Dan Mishkin and Mark Waid returned to defend their championship as The Deathless Pros. (Get it? Don't blame me; Busiek named them.) The Fan team included returnees Mike Chary and Sidne Gail Ward along with newcomers Matt Holmes and Todd Allen. As happened the previous year, the Pros stomped the Fans big time, winning 850 to 100. Yikes.

But losing this match was no embarrassment, as you'll soon see when you dig into the questions. Waid claims the undisputed title of DC Comics Geek #1, while Busiek is pretty unbeatable on Marvel's history. Throw in Isabella, self-proclaimed to be America's most-beloved comics writer and columnist, plus long-time Silver Age fan Mishkin, and you've got a tough team. Besides, these guys are used to being in front of a crowd and thinking on their feet.

The questions are slightly simplified to fit the format of our pages but, even so, they're plenty tough. How do you measure up? Take the Challenge and see.

TRIVIA CHALLENGE I
Category: **GIRLFRIENDS** Who was the girlfriend of MERBOY?

Answer on page 25

'Legends' of the DC Silver Age: A Pop Quiz

"Hey, Mr. Silver Age, what's so special about 'Gotham Gang Line-Up' from *Detective* #328 (Jun 64)? I thought the big changes in Batman occurred the issue before that!"

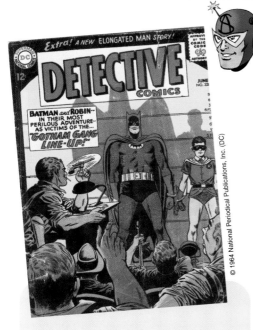

© 1964 National Periodical Publications, Inc. (DC)

*Alfred died in **Detective Comics** #328, the second "New Look" issue. He got better in **Detective Comics** #356, but how did he die in the first place?*

Well, you're right that "Gotham Gang Line-Up" was the second story in Batman's New Look era, when Editor Julius Schwartz added a yellow oval to The Caped Crusader's bat insignia and returned him to his detective roots, leaving behind his science-fictiony battles on alien worlds. As a title, it's not as dramatic or lyrical as "Robin Dies at Dawn!" or "When Titans Clash!" But it was more memorable — and important.

Because "Gotham Gang Line-up!" was the story in which Bruce Wayne's long-time butler, Alfred, bit the dust. In fact, the story is interesting because, not only did they kill off a central character of 25 years' standing, that event wasn't even mentioned on the cover! Back then, that was unusual. Today it would be unthinkable.

Virtually every DC Silver Age series had issues that stood out at least as much as the title character's first appearance. In some cases, the issues featured characters that recurred for years before disappearing. In others, they revolved around shticks that kept getting replayed. And in some, such as *Detective* #328, they were pivotal moments that changed the series — at least until they undid that moment so they could tell more stories using that character.

How well do you remember those characters, shticks, and great scenes from the Silver Age? Not at all? A few? Every single one? Hah! Let's test your knowledge of those bygone days with a little quiz before we go any further on this tour, shall we?

You'd better get used to these, because I like to quiz my visitors from time to time to see how much they know and how much I've got to fill them in so they fully appreciate everything. Don't worry. These quizzes are all multiple-choice, so you've got a good chance of having your memory jogged. That's assuming you have a memory that *can* be jogged, that is. If not, guessing works, too. You can score yourself at the end. Good luck!

1. OK, so you know that Alfred the Butler died in "Gotham Gang Line-up" in *Detective* #328. But *how* did he die?

a. He stopped a bullet meant for Batman.
b. He saved Robin from drowning but was swept away.
c. A rock fell on him.
d. He killed an entire planet full of broccoli people and took his own life to atone for it.

2. When Abin Sur needed someone to replace him as Green Lantern, why did he select Hal Jordan instead of Guy Gardner?
a. Hal Jordan was more fearless than Guy Gardner.
b. Hal Jordan was closer than Guy Gardner.
c. Hal Jordan was a test pilot and more used to flying than Guy Gardner.
d. Hal Jordan was prettier than Guy Gardner.

TRIVIA CHALLENGE I
Category: **GIRLFRIENDS** · Who was the wife of **SUPERMAN-RED**, and where did she live? · Answer on page 26

3. Who were Nightwing and Flamebird?
   a. Batman and Robin.
   b. Superman and Jimmy Olsen.
   c. Superman and Batman.
   d. Dean Martin and Jerry Lewis.

4. Who was Wonder Woman's mentor?
   a. I Ching.
   b. Rama Kushna.
   c. Felix Faust.
   d. Steve Trevor.

5. How did Tadwallader Jutefruce change into Super-Hip?
   a. By spinning in circles.
   b. By touching his wristbands together.
   c. By shouting the magic word, "Psycho-Watusi!"
   d. By taking off his clothes in a phone booth.

6. How did Pete Ross learn Superboy's secret identity?
   a. Clark Kent told him.
   b. At school.
   c. While camping.
   d. From a renegade Superboy robot.

7. What sound did Hawkman make when he talked to birds?
   a. Zee-zee.
   b. Wheet-wheet.
   c. Hawk-aaaa.
   d. Ta-pocketa-pocketa.

*Hawkman could talk to all kinds of birds, not just hawks, as was made clear in **Hawkman** #1. But the sound he made before starting his conversation was the same no matter who he was jawing with. What did it sound like?*

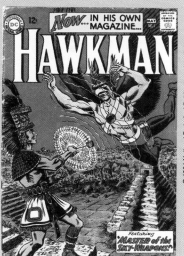

© 1964 National Periodical Publications, Inc. (DC)

8. From what material did The Atom make his costume?
   a. Cloth made of unstable molecules.
   b. Cloth made from dwarf-star matter.
   c. Cloth from the Micro-World.
   d. Cloth from the rocket that brought him to Earth.

9. Why was Brother Power the Geek shot into space in a missile?
   a. A businessman wanted to get rid of him.
   b. He didn't think the world was ready for his message.
   c. He was radioactive and didn't want to contaminate his friends.
   d. He wanted to visit The Inhumans on the moon.

10. What was the terrible secret of Supergirl's friend Lena Thorul?
   a. She was really an alien with E.S.P powers.
   b. She was ashamed of her past.
   c. She was a renegade Supergirl robot.
   d. She appeared on the cover of *Mad*.

11. Who destroyed the arm of Lightning Lad of the Legion of Super-Heroes?
   a. Starfinger.
   b. Zaryan.
   c. Moby Dick.
   d. Proty.

12. What was the source of Barry (The Flash) Allen's super powers?
   a. A lighting bolt.
   b. Hard water.
   c. A scientific formula.
   d. An elf.

Answers on the following page!

TRIVIA CHALLENGE I
Category: **GIRLFRIENDS**   Whose girlfriend was named UNA?   Answer on page 27   Answer from page 23 **WONDER GIRL**

SECRET ORIGIN OF THE SILVER AGE!   **25**

While any one of The Dynamic Duo's arch-villains could have done in the faithful Alfred, it was a force of nature (OK, a big rock) that did the deed in **Detective Comics** #328.

© 1964 National Periodical Publications, Inc. (DC)

ANSWERS

1. How did Alfred die?
Answer c: A rock fell on him.

Oh, sure, it was a little more dramatic than that. But that's basically what happened. The Dynamic Duo was fighting some crooks on a construction site, and one of them climbed into a steam shovel and dropped a boulder on Batman and Robin. Arriving on the scene just in time, Alfred swerved his motorcycle under the rock to push them away, but he fell and took the impact himself. Thus was born Bruce Wayne's benevolent Alfred Foundation.

You can wipe those tears from your eyes, however. As comics fans are wont to say after so much experience with seeing their favorite heroes die, Alfred got better. He was brought back in *Detective* #356 (Oct 66), more than two years later, which (you have to admit) showed admirable editorial restraint.

If you want to know the whole sordid truth, though, Alfred never *truly* was pining for the fjords. No, it appears that The World's Greatest Detective accidentally buried Alfred alive. Oops. Fortunately, a kindly scientist happened to stroll past the Wayne family mausoleum and heard Alfred's weak moans from inside his refrigerated coffin. (These wealthy playboys spare no expense when they bury their servants, do they?)

Unfortunately, the kindly scientist was, as he put it, "a radical individualist always experimenting, always finding new laws of nature and science — laws which orthodox scientists do not yet admit!" He tried to regenerate Alfred's body, which, after all, alive or dead or frozen into an icicle, was crushed under a rock.

But the experiment went awry, the scientist died and took on Alfred's appearance, and Alfred changed into an ugly white monster with white circles all over his body. Revived, he decided he hated Batman and Robin and called himself The Outsider, which was *a propos*, because it's doubtful he was going to be invited to too many cocktail parties looking like that.

In any event, Alfred/The Outsider terrorized The Dynamic Duo in a number of adventures and finally regained his senses (and body) in *Detective* #356, "The Inside Story of The Outsider." It was an exciting adventure that had Batman fighting the evil Alfred, as Robin turned into a coffin. It's full of... What's that? No, that's right, I said *turned* into a coffin, not *put* into a coffin.

All right, in truth, it was a dumb story. But it brought Alfred back to life, which wasn't easy to do, because Julie apparently had intended for him to remain dead. But Alfred received a second chance, once William Dozier, the producer of the new *Batman* TV show, learned that a critical supporting character in the comics he was using for his series was now an ex-supporting character. He asked for Bruce's butler to return to the series, and Julie set to work.

The issue with Alfred's revival also depicted another pivotal moment in the Batman mythos: the first meeting of Alfred and Aunt Harriet! She had come to live with The Dynamic Duo (in their civilian guises, of course), when Alfred bit the dust, adding a small feminine touch that Julie thought might add a few dramatic moments. It didn't really, but she was a regular cast member in the TV show — making this issue a double-bag super-collector's item twice over!

The producer of the Batman TV show was responsible for bringing Alfred back from the dead in the comics.

Mister Silver Age Recommends...

Detective Comics #356

DC
Oct 1966
Cover artist:
Carmine Infantino, Joe Giella
"The Inside Story of The Outsider"
Writer: Gardner Fox
Penciller: Sheldon Moldoff
Inker: Joe Giella

Then 12¢
Now $28

Reprints appear in...
• Detective Comics #440

© 1966 National Periodical Publications, Inc. (DC)

TRIVIA CHALLENGE I
Category: **GIRLFRIENDS**   Who dated JANE FOSTER after she left Don Blake's employ?   Answer on page 28   Answer from page 24   **LOIS LANE; KANDO**

26

BABY BOOMER COMICS

2. When Abin Sur needed a replacement to serve as Green Lantern, why did he select Hal Jordan instead of Guy Gardner?
Answer b: Hal Jordan was closer.

If Abin Sur had picked Guy Gardner to become Green Lantern, Guy would have had to face dastardly foes like The Shark, Sonar, and Sinestro. But he wasn't selected, as we learned in **Green Lantern #59**.

© 1968 National Periodical Publications, Inc. (DC)

Whew! What a close one! Although the Silver Age Guy Gardner was a reasonably decent sort (making his only appearance to tell this tale), the guy who began to appear in the comic in the 1980s was "updated" to fit with modern sensibilities, and he was just this side of a total jerk. On the other hand, when editors decided Hal Jordan was too nice a guy to appeal to 1990s audiences, they had him go insane and kill a huge heaping wad of the other Green Lanterns. So it's hard to say Abin's plan worked out to full success in the end. But we don't care about the end, I'm happy to say; we care only about the Silver Age.

And it was in the Silver Age, specifically *Green Lantern* #59 (Mar 68), when Hal Jordan first learned about Guy Gardner. This twist of fate was revealed by a machine invented by the Guardians, those wacky little blue guys on the planet Oa who gave Hal and all the other billions of Green Lanterns (later deceased) their power rings. In a nutshell, Hal discovered that Abin Sur could just as easily have called on Guy, because they were equally without fear. (The fact that Guy subsequently proved to be without brains doesn't seem to have been considered by Abin's power ring.)

Since Hal was in nearby California and Guy was in East City, Hal got the call. All right! Hard to believe a down-to-earth guy like Hal was out in California, but stranger things have happened. Alfred came back to life, after all. Knowing that it was sheer proximity that gave him, rather than Guy, the chance to get his butt kicked on occasion by Star Sapphire, Sinestro, and all the rest, Hal decided to make friends with Guy next time he was out East (without revealing to Guy how close he came to being The Emerald Gladiator, of course), and the rest is history. An irritating, sad history, if you read comics in the 1990s, but history, nonetheless.

3. Who were Nightwing and Flamebird?
Answer b: Superman and Jimmy Olsen.

This was one of the many bits of business editor Mort Weisinger added to the Superman legend, giving him an endless variety of plot springboards to mix up the vast quantity of Superman stories he told each month. With Superman (or Superboy) appearing in eight or more comics per month, several with three stories per issue, Kal-El and his cast of characters needed as many ways to get a story off to a fast start as they could find.

Superman's adventures in The Bottle City of Kandor, the shrunken town that fortuitously avoided Krypton's demise, offered any number of plot starters and enders. Shrinking to become a non-powered hero with his red-haired sidekick in an alien world he could (sorta) call home was as exciting a setup as there was.

The Man of Steel and The Boy One Brick Short of a Load first gained these identities in *Superman* #158 (Jan 63), when the pals parachuted into Kandor to solve a mystery that interested them. Since they had no powers, they thought of themselves as kind of like Batman and Robin. No, a nightwing and a flamebird didn't come flying through the window and give them Batman-like inspiration. Instead, Nor-Kann, a friend of Superman's parents, happened to

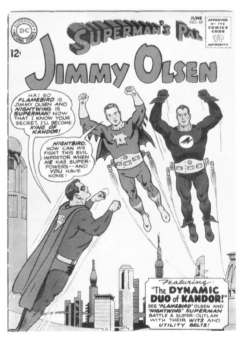

Kandor's Dynamic Duo, Nightwing and Flamebird (aka Superman and Jimmy Olsen), fought crime in the bottle city in several adventures.

© 1963 National Periodical Publications, Inc. (DC)

TRIVIA CHALLENGE I
Category: **WEDDINGS**

Who did IRIS WEST nearly marry by mistake?

Answer on page 29

Answer from page 25
CAPTAIN MAR-VELL

She may not have used him to tell fortunes, but Wonder Woman did rely on I Ching's advice during the non-costumed phase of her career.
© 1968 National Periodical Publications, Inc. (DC)

Wonder Woman's oddly-named karate teacher I Ching has managed to stay dead for a generation. Imagine that!

When things got rough, Tadwallader Jutefruce turned into Super-Hip to save the day in **Adventures of Bob Hope**.
© 1965 National Periodical Publications, Inc. (DC)

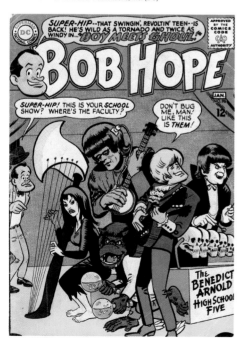

have both birds in his secret underground laboratory (and aviary, apparently). Donning the disguises and handy jet packs, they used their wits and fists to have adventures of derring-do and, oh, yeah, give Supes a breather from being unbeatable.

They suited up countless (at least by me) times, returning for another adventure only a few months later in *Jimmy Olsen* #69 (Jun 63). Why Kandor needed *two* non-super-powered guys to keep pulling their collective fat out of the fire, especially one as trouble-prone as Jimbo, is known only to a few. More specifically, it was known mostly by Weisinger and his writers. That's more than enough.

4. Who was Wonder Woman's mentor?
Answer a. I Ching.

Wonder Woman has had about as many careers as Supergirl has had costumes (and that's a lot), including a reversion to her Golden Age time period (and art style) in the middle of the Silver Age. One of her strangest points began in *Wonder Woman* #179 (Nov-Dec 68), when she gave up her costume altogether and teamed up with the venerable Ching, an Oriental wise man who taught her all kinds of hand-to-hand combat stuff and let her dress like Mrs. Peel from The Avengers. Mr. Ching was created by Denny O'Neil, who has since said he thought the name was a good idea at the time. They can't all be gems.

Artist Mike Sekowsky began writing the stories a few issues later, when O'Neil left the series, and he took it even further into new territory. The stories covered a wide range of genres, including mysteries and spy/romance pieces. They were unusual and interesting in their own way, but most of them didn't really qualify as "Wonder Woman" tales, as far as I was concerned. The New Improved Diana Prince junked this lifestyle in #204, when I Ching went to meet his maker. So far, he's managed to stay bereft of life, an outstanding feat for a Silver Age character. But the new century is still young, so don't count him out.

5. How did Tadwallader Jutefruce change into Super-Hip?
Answer a: By spinning in circles.

Yes, it's true, Bob Hope had a Silver Age, too! DC had a number of licensed humor comics, including *The Adventures of Bob Hope, The Adventures of Dean Martin and Jerry Lewis* (which Jer took over when the partners split), *The Many Loves of Dobie Gillis, Sgt. Bilko,* and *Sgt. Bilko's Pvt. Doberman.*

I had a soft spot in my heart (and maybe head) for these stories. They tried to keep the "comic" in comic books at a time when super-heroes definitely ruled the roost. (Unlike Mort Weisinger, who often was putting the "comic" into his Superman stories without really meaning to.) They also had the annoying tendency of having several words before the key names in their titles, making it tougher to find them in comics boxes — are Jerry's comics under "A", "D" or "J" — or under "Movie Comics?" Arrggh! But they're worth the hunt.

In any event, Tad was a shy, unassuming student at Benedict Arnold High School. When he became upset or enraged, he spun in circles and turned into Super-Hip, something like The Hulk did, only not exactly. He came to live, in his civilian guise, with Bob in *Bob Hope* #95 (Oct-Nov 65).

TRIVIA CHALLENGE I
Category: **WEDDINGS**   Who broke up JANET and HANK PYM's wedding?   Answer on page 30   Answer from page 26

DR. JIM NORTH

His powers consisted of being able to fly and transform any part of his body into anything he felt like — a bucket of tar, a magnet, a giant meatball-maker, *etc.* — much like Plastic Man only with even more variety. A darned handy power, I'd say. And, of course, he was hip. He had long blond hair, dressed in ruffled Edwardian clothes, and carried an electric guitar! If that wasn't hip (to DC in the mid to late 1960s), nothing was!

Changing to Super-Hip took considerable effort. Captions called this whirligig such things as "the psycho-watusi" and the "psychoneurotic frug." Bob, who first witnessed Tad's change in #102, told him, "That's the greatest dance since they combined the Mashed Potato with the Swim and got Fish & Chips!" Please remember: I don't write 'em, I just read 'em.

6. How did Pete Ross learn Superboy's secret identity?
Answer c: While camping.

This is probably the most repeated scene in Silver Age Superman comics after the panel of the rocket blasting off from Krypton and Superbaby lifting that stupid crib. It first appeared in *Superboy* #90 (Jul 61), in a five-panel sequence, and it reappeared in sequences of up to four panels virtually every time Pete showed up thereafter for many years. In *Superboy* #94 (Jan 62), for instance, it took three panels — one to change, one for Pete to watch Superboy fly away, and one to watch him return and change back into Clark. And that was just four issues later!

The key panel always had the same angle: Pete in the foreground lying in a sleeping bag, looking out through an open tent flap as Clark changed clothes *right in front of the open tent facing Pete* as a lightning bolt lit up the area. (Superboy apparently didn't develop his super common sense until later in his career.) If you read a Pete Ross story, and this panel is *not* there, you know that issue was *tightly* edited for space.

7. What sound did Hawkman make when he talked to birds?
Answer b: Wheet-wheet.

I have no idea how this was supposed to work. It seemed to be a shorthand way of telling us that Hawkman wasn't speaking English to the birds, as if we needed that clue. The birds, in reply, just prefaced their remarks with one "wheet" before they started blabbing. Where this talent came from was never really explained. But the implication seemed to be that it was Katar Hol's very own skill, not one picked up from his Absorbascon. That device was a Thanagarian invention that gave The Hawks information about anything they wanted to know about Earth — languages, the location of someone, their history, *etc.* Kind of like Google only shaped like a headband that downloaded stuff into your brain.

But apparently Hawkman didn't need to use this device to talk to birds. In *Hawkman* #1 (Apr-May 64), for instance, he and Hawkgirl were having a contest to see who could capture a crook faster — Hawkman using Earth techniques or Hawkgirl using Thanagarian methods. Hawkman did a great job of dusting for fingerprints and checking computer files, all tried-and-true police procedures. Then he flew off to find the crook.

"I could have applied the standard Earth method of trailing a criminal by

After Pete Ross learned Superboy's true identity in **Superboy** *#90, he tried to help the Boy of Steel by making his own costume and providing excuses for Clark to slip away.*

> "Wheet-wheet" was apparently comics shorthand to tell us that Hawkman wasn't speaking English to the birds.
>
> As if we needed that clue.

TRIVIA CHALLENGE I
Category: **WEDDINGS**   *What royal person did CHAMELEON BOY nearly marry?*   Answer on page 31   Answer from page 27   **PROFESSOR ZOOM**

SECRET ORIGIN OF THE SILVER AGE!   **29**

The Atom of Earth-2 gives Ray Palmer a pop quiz of his own in **The Atom** #36. The one thing he didn't ask Ray (at least on this cover) was what his costume was made out of.

© 1968 National Periodical Publications, Inc. (DC)

Legendary reprints

Here's where to find some of these stories in cheaper reprint editions:

"Gotham Gang Line-Up!" from *Detective Comics* #328 was reprinted in *Detective Comics* #438.

Green Lantern #59 was reprinted in *Green Lantern* #184.

Nightwing and Flamebird's adventures from *Superman* #158 and *Jimmy Olsen* #69 were reprinted in *Jimmy Olsen* #140.

Wonder Woman #179 was reprinted in *Wonder Woman* #191.

The introduction of Pete Ross in *Superboy* #90 was reprinted in *Adventure Comics* #343 and *The Best of DC Digest* #15.

Hawkman #1 was reprinted in *Hawkman Archives* #1

The Atom's origin from *Showcase* #34 was reprinted in *80-Page Giant* #8, *Secret Origins Giant* #2, *DC Blue-Ribbon Digest* #9, the *Secret Origins* hardback collection, and *Atom Archives* #1.

questioning people at gas stations or restaurants where he may have stopped," he explained to the reader. "But sometimes a detective has to improvise — and take advantage of his own special abilities! It's time for some bird talk..." Does that mean that talking to birds *isn't* a Thanagarian Absorbascon trick but rather an ability he developed on his own? That's one talented guy! But then, despite his bare chest, he wasn't a DC super-hero because of his good looks! (Hawkgirl could have been, but that's another story.)

8. Of what material is the Atom's costume composed?
Answer b: Cloth made from dwarf-star matter.

Ray Palmer, a research scientist in Ivy Town, found a fragment of a white dwarf star while picnicking during "Birth of The Atom!" in *Showcase* #34 (Sep-Oct 61). He used it to control his mass and size as The Atom, in an origin story that clearly showed that DC Science and Earth Science are two different animals. Frankly, it wasn't the first or last time that distinction would be apparent.

Ray, seemingly a combination of Einstein and Ralph Lauren, also used the dwarf-star matter to create his costume. This is a process that would have been fascinating to see, but we just have to take writer Gardner Fox's word for it. The best part was that, when this costume made of dwarf-star matter was expanded to Ray's approximate 6-foot size, it was invisible. So Ray could wear it all the time. And when he clicked down to 6-inch Atom size, it appeared out of nowhere.

What I want to know is whether he had to shrink down so he could remove it to take a shower or change clothes? Or maybe, when he was Ray, he could just peel it off even though it was invisible when stretched out. That's a lot of stretching, but it sure would've made it easier to go to the bathroom!

His costume's marvelous properties played a key role in an early adventure, "Trouble at the Ten-Year Club!" in #11 (Feb-Mar 64). At least, I'm pretty sure of that dating. My copy lacks a cover and first-page indicia, no doubt because the sight of Jean Loring dressed in a pirate outfit in the second story, "Voyage to Beyond!" kept me re-reading the issue until it fell apart.

In the story, a crook fighting The Atom suddenly made The Tiny Titan grow to his regular size, at which point the crook decked him. When The Mighty Mite revived, he hypothesized that he didn't *really* grow to his normal size, because he was still wearing his costume! And, as we all knew, when Ray was normal size, his costume was invisible. Sure enough, he was right on the money, and this knowledge helped him capture the crook. It's good to remember these little costume quirks.

9. Why was Brother Power shot into space in a missile?
Answer a: A businessman wanted to get rid of him.

All right, I know this wasn't exactly a *pivotal* moment in the Silver Age, but have a heart! I mean, how many guys will admit to not only buying and reading *Brother Power The Geek* #1, but, after doing so, going back to buy and read *Brother Power The Geek* #2 (Nov-Dec 68), where Sliderule showed up? Well, I'm the guy. I've been waiting more than three decades to justify spending that 12 cents. Using it in this quiz ought to just about do it.

At any rate, our businessman, known as Lord Sliderule, was just your typical

TRIVIA CHALLENGE I
Category: **WEDDINGS**

Who did MERA have to defeat in order to marry Aquaman?

Answer on page 32

Answer from page 28
THE CIRCUS OF CRIME

30

BABY BOOMER COMICS

"industrial genius," as the board of Acme Missile Parts called him — at least, typical for writer/artist Joe Simon. BP was Simon's attempt to capture the hippie culture that was becoming so popular in 1968, but, sadly, it was more akin to watching Howard Cunningham on *Happy Days* try to dress up like Fonzie. Many of DC's attempts at hipness fell excruciatingly short, and this two-issue title has come to epitomize how far short they usually thudded.

"Here is the real-life scene of the dangers in Hippie-land!" #1's cover blared at readers. Pow, in fact, was a ragdoll brought to life by a stray bolt of lightning, in much the same way as The Flash had been given his super-powers — only with none of the strange chemicals that splashed on The Scarlet Speedster to help out. Once brought to life, BP spent time huddled in a science lab. "So this is your hang-up!" one of his hippie friends exclaimed upon finding him. "Chemistry is my bag!" Pow said. "I've been trying to find out what makes me go-go!" 'Nuff said.

Lord Sliderule showed up in #2, dressed like a European ruler from the Dark Ages, complete with baggy shorts, feathered cap, monocle, and flowing cape held by two midgets. Hey, if Malcolm Forbes could ride motorcycles and hang out with Liz Taylor, why not? The rest of Sliderule's team was equally charming.

Sliderule had to increase production in order to take over the factory where Brother Power worked. The industrial genius took an instant dislike to our hero, and that dislike was made even stronger when Pow solved the production problem. This created a *real* problem for Lord Sliderule, since he wanted to take over the factory so he could sell its blueprints to America's enemies. As I said, the typical industrial genius, 1968 style.

Sliderule framed Brother Pow as a saboteur, and Pow tried to escape the authorities by hiding in a missile. But Sliderule saw him and launched the rocket. "Poor Pow!" his friend Cindy mused that night, watching the stars. "I wonder if we'll ever see him again?" Don't we all? As with most things from the Silver Age, The Geekster was revived in a 1993 one-shot, but the less said about that, the better.

10. What was Lena Thorul's terrible secret?
Answer b: She was ashamed of her past.

Lena's past included the fact that she was Lex Luthor's sister, something her parents were able to hide from her and the world through a cunning plan: After Lex went bad, they moved out of town and made an anagram out of their last name. It was one of the many anagrams DC used to disguise people's real names, usually by exactly reversing the order of letters. This produced my life-long habit of reading weird names backward to see who someone *really* is. Sadly, it doesn't work all that well in real life. But it came up aces in The Silver Age!

Lena became best buds with Linda Lee Danvers (aka Supergirl), and they hung out together in the back pages of *Action Comics* in the mid-1960s, beginning

*We all remember Brother Power's origin, so he didn't really need to recap it for us in **Brother Power The Geek** #2, especially since it had just been covered the issue before.*
© 1968 National Periodical Publications, Inc. (DC)

DC trying to be hip with *Brother Power* was like Howard Cunningham trying to dress up like Fonzie.

Painful to watch.

Mister Silver Age Recommends...

TRIVIA CHALLENGE I
Category: **FIRST WORDS**
Whose first Silver Age words were: "That self-inflating balloon should throw them off-guard until I can lasso them with my Bat-rope!"
Answer on page 33
Answer from page 29
PRINCESS ELWINDA

ACTION COMICS

The GREAT SUPERGIRL DOUBLE-CROSS!

Supergirl used all of her super wiles to break up Lena Thorul's romance in **Action Comics** *#317. It's not what you'd expect from your best friend, but Kara thought it was for a good reason.*
© 1964 National Periodical Publications, Inc. (DC)

with issue #295 (Dec 62). Lena had some basic ESP powers, thanks to a terrible experiment that went awry one day when she strolled into her brother's lab. But that doesn't count as a terrible secret, just a terrible power, when your best girlfriend can fly through space and move planets. In fact, considering how many people around Lena had major secrets, her ESP powers must have been mighty basic.

All that wouldn't mean Lena was ashamed of her past, just ignorant of it. But then Lena *discovered* she was Lex's sister in *Action Comics* #313 (Jul 64), and the knowledge so shocked and shamed her that she developed complete amnesia. She later recovered her memory, except for one bit of information — guess which?

Eventually, in *Action Comics* #317 (Oct 64), she married an FBI agent — no thanks to The Maid of Steel, who (in typical Supergirl fashion) misjudged Lena's beau and spent the entire adventure using her super-powers to try to break them up. Makes you wonder why Supergirl's adventures never really caught on with Silver Age fans, doesn't it?

11. Who destroyed Lightning Lad's arm?
Answer c: Moby Dick.

To be precise, it was "The Super-Moby Dick of Space!" as shown in *Adventure Comics* #332 (May 65). Moby was a large (and sometimes gigantic, depending on whether artist John Forte lost his sense of scale in any one panel) whale-like space monster with green scaly skin, red dragon wings, and baby-blue eyes. But, to be even more precise, it was Lightning Lad himself who did it: He blasted Moby with his lightning, it reflected off the whale's scaly hide, and the rays hit Garth's right arm with "some terrific green poison from the monster's body."

LL made it back to the Legion's clubhouse, where noted scientist Dr. Lanphier amputated the limb and installed a robot arm. Lightning Lad was pretty perturbed by this, as you can well understand, and he spent the issue tracking down Moby. (That worked so well for Captain Ahab.) But he overcame his blind hatred, because, after all, he was a Legionnaire.

That didn't make his robot arm go away, but a simple thing like amputation didn't prevent him from having his arm restored. It took all of one panel in *Adventure Comics* #351 (Dec 66), a panel in which Matter-Eater Lad also slimmed down again and Bouncing Boy got fat again, thanks to a doctor who double-crossed Evillo. Don't ask.

You wouldn't call Garth Ranzz Ishmael, but he took on aspects of Captain Ahab in "The Super-Moby Dick of Space," which originally appeared in **Adventure Comics** *#332.*
© 1965 National Periodical Publications, Inc. (DC)

As to the other suggested answers, Starfinger couldn't have destroyed Lightning Lad's arm, because Starfinger *was* Lightning Lad, as the other Legionnaires found out in *Adventure Comics* #336 (Sep 65) after capturing him. He was, of course, hypnotized by the *real* Starfinger and not just having kicks, as those Legionnaire rascals were wont to do sometimes. Zaryan didn't destroy

TRIVIA CHALLENGE I
Category: **FIRST WORDS**

Whose first Silver Age words were: "Bah! Everywhere it is the same! I live in a world too small for me!" Answer on page 34

Answer from page 30
OCEANUS

32

BABY BOOMER COMICS

Lightning Lad's arm; he actually *killed* Lightning Lad back in *Adventure Comics* #304 (Jan 63). Obviously, LL got better. And Proty, who was The Legion's telepathic pet, gave its life so our lightning pal *could* get better, in *Adventure Comics* #312 (Sep 63). Proty never got better, but there was a Proty II. That's almost as good, since Proty didn't have any real features to speak of, being a protoplasmic blob. Life can be harsh in the 30th Century.

12. What was the source of Barry Allen's super powers?
Answer d: An elf.

Hah! You thought I only put joke answers at "d," didn't you? Er, you did realize all the "d" answers were jokes, didn't you? In this case, "d" is still a joke answer; it just happens to be correct, too. The whole sordid mess was explained in *The Flash* #167 (Feb 67), the strongest argument I've ever seen for the Crisis on Infinite Earths needing to wipe everything out.

The elf was Mopee, and he was a "Heavenly Helpmate" who revealed that he had given Barry Allen his powers by directing the lightning bolt that hit the chemicals that gave Bar his super powers. But Mopee had made a mistake, since the chemicals weren't the personal property of Barry (as they were supposed to be if used for a good deed) but belonged to the police department. So Mopee was sent back to correct his mistake and take away The Flash's powers. The Flash suggested that, instead, he go buy his own chemicals so they could splash on him appropriately. Mopee agreed but insisted that Flash buy the chemicals with money earned in his super-hero identity. So Flash had to hire himself out for quick cash, stumbling into an exciting adventure in the process.

This "make the money as Flash" deal makes no sense, of course, since he wouldn't even *be* The Flash without the chemicals he had to buy. But that's OK, because none of those specific plot points mentioned above really matter. You'll never hear a single fan mention them, no matter how elaborate an origin he describes for The Silver Age's very first hero. And this story isn't alone in the Land of the Conveniently Forgotten.

The truth is that, on rare occasions, DC's editors went just a tad overboard in creating an exciting story, writing themselves into a corner or producing a cover that ultimately required too much fudging of facts that we little kids considered fundamental to the hero's existence. So we'd just pretend that story never happened.

No Silver Age Flash fan will ever tell you that Mopee gave Barry Allen his powers. By an unspoken universal decision, we simply decided that story had never taken place. It was a convenient way to ensure the world of Silver Age comics stayed the way we wanted it to be, at least at some level. Sure, heroes died and lived again and sometimes they did screwy things for the sake of a dramatic scene. But goofy guys like Mopee aren't responsible for the #1 hero's dramatic origin. We may have been dumb little kids eager to read about our favorite super-heroes and their legends and origins and geegaws and gimcracks, but we did have *some* standards.

Legendary Scoring:

11-12: Excellent! You deserve the Silver Cross for Outstanding Comic Book Knowledge! You're so well-versed in high-quality literature, you no doubt got question #7 correct because you knew that "zee-zee" was the sound made by Jimmy Olsen's Superman signal watch, "hawk-aaaa" was the battle cry of The Blackhawks, and "ta-pocketa-pocketa" was the favorite sound of James Thurber's Walter Mitty, who sadly didn't have his own Silver Age comic book.

8-10: Darn good! You deserve a Silver Star, which you can paste onto your forehead. You're *so* good, you probably knew that in question #4, Rama Kushna was Deadman's other-worldly mentor, Felix Faust was an evil magician who battled The Justice League and Steve Trevor was Wondie's main squeeze, who died, got better, died, got better, and then was written out of the series altogether. Of course you did!

5-7: Pretty good. You receive a Silver Bell, even though it's not Christmastime in the city. You probably got question #8 right because you knew that The Fantastic Four's Reed Richards created cloth from unstable molecules, while The Atom visited the Micro-World with the Justice League but didn't bring back any souvenirs. And, of course, it was Superman who had a costume from cloth left in his rocket ship. Smart work!

3-5: Not good. Maybe you just don't test well. These standardized pop quizzes never pick up a person's true ability (or their geekiness). Still, after the tour is over, it wouldn't hurt for you to head to your local comics shop and dig through the bargain bins to find a few comics with Go-Go Checks on the top. That's a sure sign of quality entertainment.

0-2: Awful. Whoa, baby, you've got a Crisis on your hands! You've come to the right place to learn far, far more than this test indicates you're remembering about the glorious Silver Age right now. Unless your excuse is that you were hit on the head by a falling acid-free box and promptly lost your memory. If that's the case, who knows? Maybe you're really related to Lex Luthor!

TRIVIA CHALLENGE I
Category: FIRST WORDS

Whose first Silver Age words were: "Good! I've switched on the invisibility and the anti-detector devices to shield our presence from the inhabitants of the planet!" Answer on page 35

Answer from page 31
BAT-GIRL

'Legends' of the Marvel Silver Age: A Pop Quiz

"So, is this big display for the cover of *Fantastic Four* #1 here because it's the biggest and most important comic book of Marvel's Silver Age?"

© 1961 Marvel

Nope, although it certainly was the book that got things moving, and the title continued to be one of the greatest of the Silver Age, right up until co-creator Jack Kirby left after #102. It's possibly the best long run of any comics series ever. No, it's hanging there because it has another distinction: It's probably the most parodied and "homaged" cover from The Silver Age.

It's hard to substantiate a claim like that, of course, and certainly key Golden Age comics such as *Action* #1 or *Detective* #27 (Batman's debut) have had their fair share of homages (and they've had 20 more years to accumulate them). But that basic Jack Kirby combination of old-fashioned Godzilla-sized monster and weird super-heroes has spoken to many artists trying to invoke the feeling of old-time 1960s comics.

Oddly enough, it's nowhere near the most dramatic or inspiring cover from Marvel — it doesn't even show the villain they actually fought in their first issue! But it still captures the thrills and serves as an in-joke for those who know their comics history. And if you didn't know it before, you do now. (For examples of homage covers, see page 41.) But do you know what villain The FF battled in their first issue, even if he's not shown, right? Right?

In fact, how much do you know about the rest of Marvel's early history, hmm? Maybe we ought to check you out on The House of Ideas before we go any further in this tour, too. So here's a pop quiz — trust me, it won't be the last one you get to take — to see how much you know about some of Marvel's heroes' first days.

1. What super-villain did our super-heroic team battle in *Fantastic Four* #1?
   a. Dr. Doom.
   b. Mole Man.
   c. The Skrulls.
   d. Lex Luthor.

2. Where did Tony Stark create his Iron Man costume?
   a. In his laboratory at Stark Industries.
   b. At a small workshop in Southeast Asia.
   c. At a secret Army base in Europe.
   d. In his garage.

TRIVIA CHALLENGE I
Category: **FIRST WORDS**   *Whose first Silver Age words were: "Go away, you puny flea."*   Answer on page 36

Answer from page 32
THE THING

3. What triggered Bruce Banner's changes to The Hulk in his first issues?

  a. Stress.
  b. Nighttime.
  c. A gamma ray gun.
  d. A mask.

The Hulk certainly did change from his earliest appearance in **Incredible Hulk** *#1, where he was colored gray, but what initially triggered the change?*

4. After show biz didn't pan out, for what job did Spider-Man apply in *Amazing Spider-Man* #1?

  a. Police officer.
  b. The fifth member of The Fantastic Four.
  c. *Daily Bugle* photographer.
  d. *Daily Bugle* window washer.

Aunt May gave Peter some serious career counseling (yeah, right) in **Amazing Spider-Man** *#1, but, like most other teenagers, Peter didn't listen and applied for a job anyway. What was it?*

5. Who released Loki from his eons of imprisonment?

  a. Thor.
  b. Odin.
  c. Heimdall.
  d. Xena.

If a Norse god is imprisoned in a tree, and no one is around to hear, does he make a sound? Or, for that matter, can he be freed? How did Loki manage that feat?

6. Who was the first X-Man to kiss Jean Grey, the only female among the original teammates?

  a. Hank McCoy, The Beast.
  b. Scott Summers, Cyclops.
  c. Warren Worthington III, The Angel.
  d. Professor Xavier, the lecher.

Three of the four male X-Men attempted to woo their newest teammate, Jean Grey, in **X-Men** *#1, but who eventually kissed her?*

7. Which super-hero wanted to hire Matt Murdock (Daredevil) to be his lawyer in *Daredevil* #2?

  a. Namor the Sub-Mariner, to represent him to surface people.
  b. The Hulk, to prove him innocent of murder.
  c. The Thing, to help the FF sign a better lease.
  d. Batman, to help him sign a good merchandising deal.

Even early in their careers, the law firm of Nelson and Murdock was used to unusual clients. Who paid the firm a visit in **Daredevil** *#2?*

8. Where was Captain America's shield when The Avengers found him frozen in Arctic ice?

  a. Frozen onto his arm.
  b. Strapped to his chest.
  c. Hidden on an Army base.
  d. Hidden in a comics fan's attic.

When he was revived in **Avengers** *#4, Cap was more concerned with Bucky's fate than where his shield was stored, but we're more concerned with his fashion sense. Where was that darn shield stored?*

TRIVIA CHALLENGE I
Category: **COSTUMES**

Who created the second costume worn by KID FLASH?

Answer on page 37

Answer from page 33
HAWKGIRL

SECRET ORIGIN OF THE SILVER AGE!

35

ANSWERS

THAT WAS TO BE THE LAST OF MY MISFORTUNES! MY LUCK BEGAN TO TURN IN MY FAVOR! I MASTERED THE CREATURES DOWN HERE -- MADE THEM DO MY BIDDING -- AND WITH THEIR HELP, I CARVED OUT AN UNDER-GROUND EMPIRE!

The Mole Man was the first villain The Fantastic Four faced, with Marvel not straying far from its monster-based stories that had proven so popular in the late 1950s. Even Moley himself had the typical monster-movie origin.
© 1961 Marvel

The Mole Man was a classic Lee-Kirby villain: He wasn't evil, just misunderstood.

Mister Silver Age Recommends...

Fantastic Four Vol. 1, #1

Marvel
Nov 1961
Cover artist:
Jack Kirby

"The Fantastic Four"
Writer: Stan Lee
Artist: Jack Kirby

Then 10¢
Now $16,000

Reprints appear in...
• Marvel Masterworks #2
• Essential Fantastic Four #1
• Fantastic Four Annual #1 and #7

© 1961 Marvel

1. What super-villain did our team battle in *Fantastic Four* #1?
Answer b. Mole Man.

That big galoot on the cover belonged to Moley, but you'd still think a guy with a catchy name like that would get some kind of cover billing. But when *Fantastic Four* #1 appeared, Marvel was known for its long line of short-story monster comics, starring such plug-uglies as Fin Fang Foom, Tim Boo Ba, Zzutak, and The Blip. Showing MM's little pet managed to retain that continuity while also introducing Marvel's new super-hero concept.

To emphasize that, The FF didn't wear costumes until *FF* #3, retaining more of a "normal person" look to their adventures.

By the time they added costumes, fans were accustomed to this idea of super-heroes starring in comics from their favorite monster publisher. (The Thing's costume consisted of a full-length shirt and pants, plus a helmet. It took him only a few panels to ditch the shirt and helmet. The pants were replaced with the blue bathing suit he's worn ever since, keeping his rocky, monstrous appearance evident all the time.)

The Mole Man was a classic Lee-Kirby villain — he wasn't really evil, just misunderstood. When The FF finally caught up with Moley in his subterranean lair, he explained that he had abandoned mankind, because his short stature and rat-like appearance made people ridicule him.

When he decided to isolate himself to avoid the taunts, he fell into a cavern that tumbled him into the center of the Earth. (It could happen.) The fall caused him to lose most of his eyesight, making it difficult for him to return to the surface even if he'd wanted to (which he didn't).

Fortuitously, he discovered a race of subterranean people and became their master, carving out an empire and taming underground monsters like our cover pal. But, just when we'd built up our sympathy for him, he let slip that his next plan was to dig tunnels under every city on Earth, wreck their atomic plants and other sources of power, and destroy everything above ground. Not really what you want to hear from a guy looking for your sympathy.

Ultimately, The FF sealed him back underground, where they agreed he was better off — and they hoped he thought so, too. (Of course, he didn't.) Such perspective was common for Marvel's major villains.

Dr. Doom, for instance, was a disfigured genius who became ruler of a European nation, thereby gaining diplomatic immunity that protected him from the ramifications of his (always unsuccessful) schemes.

Magneto, the X-Men's main villain, simply disagreed with Professor Xavier's idea that mutants should help protect human beings. He thought mutants should take over the world before the humans destroyed them — and humans' usual reaction to The X-Men indicated Magneto may have had a point.

Of course, there were villains who were evil just because they felt like it, too. But some of Marvel's evil-doers made you stop to think about just how close they came to not being such pains in the butt.

TRIVIA CHALLENGE I
Category: COSTUMES — Who gave those red-and-green outfits to the **BLACKHAWKS?** — Answer on page 38 — Answer from page 34 **NAMOR**

2. Where did Tony Stark create his Iron Man costume?
Answer a: At a small workshop in Southeast Asia.

Why would he do that? More importantly, *how* could he do that? The first question is easy enough – he had no choice, as he was a prisoner of a South Vietnamese warlord. He arrived at this predicament in *Tales of Suspense* #39 (Mar 63), when, as armament inventor Tony Stark, he had gone to Vietnam to scout out the terrain to learn how his "miniature transistors" could help the U.S. beat the overwhelming numbers that favored the Commies. Unfortunately, Tony tripped over a booby-trap wire, was caught in an explosion, and was captured by guerillas.

In addition to being merciless and numerous, the guerillas were skilled diagnosticians and knew that the shrapnel lodged near Tony's heart meant he had only one week to live. So the warlord decided to trick Tony into building him a powerful weapon. Tony agreed but he knew they were tricking him and that he had only days to live. The logic he used to reach this conclusion may have been a bit faulty, but he was a multi-millionaire genius, so let's just chalk it up to "intuition" and move on.

Knowing he had only a few days to live, Tony worked feverishly with Professor Yinsen, a great physicist who also was a prisoner. Together, they created a chest plate that could keep Tony's heart pumping despite the shrapnel. And, to accessorize the plate, they created an iron suit that covered his entire body and outfitted it with lots 'n' lots of Tony's magical transistors, which Stan used to explain any power Iron Man might need. That was some jungle workshop, wasn't it?

The initial gray suit lasted only until the next issue, when one of Tony's many, many girlfriends suggested that Iron Man would look way cooler, if his armor was gold. A quick coat of untarnishable gold paint spiffed up IM quickly. That clunky (but pretty) suit was replaced in *TOS* #48 with a lighter-weight, more powerful red and yellow version. Ever the tinkerer, Tony hasn't left the suit along for long ever since.

A life-saver in more ways than one, Tony Stark's original gray armor first clanked onto the scene in **Tales of Suspense** *#39. The clunky battle-suit also kept the wounded inventor's heart beating. Stark has been upgrading the armor ever since, replacing the original suit with a sleeker (and lighter) red and yellow version.*
© 1963 Marvel

3. What triggered Bruce Banner's change to The Hulk in his first issues?
Answer b: Nighttime.

After saving teen-ager Rick Jones and being bombarded with gamma radiation in *The Incredible Hulk* #1 (May 62), Banner was taken with Jones to a secure area to recover from his exposure to the gamma rays. As the sun set, Banner changed into the (gray) Hulk, telling the startled Jones, "Get out of my way, insect."

The Hulk created havoc on the base until sunrise, when he reverted. "Soon the sun will set again," he told Rick. "And here I sit, helplessly fearing I may again become — The Hulk!" Sure enough, when the sun set, ol' Greenskin returned for another nocturnal engagement.

That formula continued until #3 (Sep 62), when Banner rocketed into space thanks to a General Thunderbolt Ross trap, and was bathed by a radiation belt that held, as Stan wrote, "those powerful rays about which so little is truly known!" It certainly wasn't known by Stan, who used radiation for all kinds of funky Silver Age fun. This time, they allowed Hulk to change during the day.

Change was the order of the day in **Incredible Hulk** *#1, with Bruce Banner metamorphosing into The Gray Goliath every time the sun went down.*
© 1962 Marvel

TRIVIA CHALLENGE I
Category: **COSTUMES**   Who gave ENLONGATED MAN his new orange costume?   Answer on page 39   Answer from page 35
BARRY ALLEN

After trying to turn The Fantastic Four into a quintet, Spider-Man got a quick lesson in non-profit organizations from Marvel's first super-team in **Amazing Spider-Man** #1.

The IRS put an abrupt end to Spidey's show-biz career.

The series died (gasp!) with the sixth issue, but The Hulk returned 19 months later for a co-starring role in *Tales to Astonish* #60 (Oct 64). In that ish, Banner quickly told readers that the change "only happens when I'm the most worried…when the pressure becomes unbearable!" No doubt Stan found it made far more sense to allow Banner to change at random times when it was most dramatic.

4. After show biz didn't pan out, for what job did Spider-Man apply in *Amazing Spider-Man* #1?
Answer b: The fifth member of The Fantastic Four.

Hey, at least they would've still been The FF, right? It may seem a bit ridiculous for someone to suggest joining the family-oriented Fantastic Four, but this was early in their career, before that family dynamic was quite so established.

Besides, the truth of the matter is that The Fantastic Four later *would* change its roster. First, its members added Johnny Storm's girlfriend, Crystal of The Inhumans, when Sue was pregnant with son Franklin around *FF* #81 (Dec 68). Later, all heck would break loose with people coming and going, and Spider-Man actually *did* become a member for a while. But that's another story. *This* story is about the notion of Spider-Man joining this family team isn't a far-fetched as it may sound. But his reasons for joining were pretty loopy.

Peter's early career as a professional Spider-Man was not all peaches and cream. Heck, there were *no* peaches *or* cream! But that's why we loved the guy so much. In *ASM* #1's opening tale, he smartly signed up a manager who found him all kinds of bookings that earned him good bread. But his manager explained that, no doubt for tax reasons, he had to pay the wall-crawler with a check. Spidey agreed but was dismayed to learn that a bank wouldn't cash his check without identification — which Spidey didn't have as Spidey and couldn't give as Peter. Oh, the irony!

Before he could figure a way out of this dilemma, his manager dropped him, because J. Jonah Jameson began his smear campaign that turned public sentiment against him. That's show biz.

Undaunted, Spidey crawled by FF HQ in *ASM* #1's second story, where he immediately was attacked by the foursome for breaking in unannounced. After they smacked each other around for a while, Reed finally had the brilliant idea of asking Spidey why he'd dropped by. Peter suavely explained that he'd come to join the team and had given them a demonstration of his powers to convince them that he deserved their top salary. They explained they were a non-profit organization and received no salaries, top or otherwise. So Spidey left, sadder but wiser in the ways of professional super-heroing.

5. Who released Loki from his eons of imprisonment?
Answer c: Heimdall.

But it wasn't his fault, really! In fact, I'm thinking the gods need to check the loopholes in their spells, because this one didn't quite work right. Loki coincidentally escaped imprisonment inside an Asgardian tree just days (technically, two issues) after The Mighty Thor returned to the fabled realm himself in *Journey into Mystery* #83. What a coincidence.

TRIVIA CHALLENGE I
Category: **COSTUMES**   Who was **IRON MAN** battling when he decided to replace his clunky, yellow armor?   Answer on page 40   Answer from page 36
Mr. CIPHER

The gods (no names, please) had sunk ol' Loki inside the tree because, to use the technical term, he was a major pain in the butt. And they decided he wouldn't be freed until someone shed a tear over his plight — which wasn't too likely. But that changed in *JIM* #85, when Heimdall, the warder of the Rainbow Bridge, happened to stroll by, apparently on his day off. I dunno, had *I* been the god who'd imprisoned Loki, I might've put up a sign or something to alert passersby, but that's just me.

Loki made a leaf fall and hit Heimdall in the eye, causing his eye to produce tears. That resulted in The God of Mischief being freed, with him explaining, "Because of my plight, I was able to gain control of this tree! And thus I was able to affect Heimdall's eye! Therefore my plight did indeed cause him to shed a tear!" Uh-huh. To my way of thinking, if the law believes that, then the law is a ass, to coin a phrase. In any event, Loki was free to wreak havoc on his half-brother for a good long time.

6. Who was the first X-Man to kiss Jean Grey, the only female among the original teammates?
Answer a: Hank McCoy, The Beast.

Hah! A sneaky question. You would expect the answer to be Cyclops or The Angel, as they vied for Jean's attention in the team's early days of adventuring. Their approach was completely opposite, of course, in keeping with their personalities and Stan's desire to enhance the drama. Cyclops had a long, silent (and obsessive) crush on Jean that he refused to reveal for fear that his mutant eye blasts would come between them. Angel, on the other hand, was a happy-go-lucky rich guy (albeit one with wings) and he worked constantly to charm the pants off Jean (not literally, of course — heroes didn't do that kind of thing to their sweeties in the Silver Age, at least not on-panel).

The rest of the team was already in place and had taken a few runs through the Danger Room, when Jean Grey arrived at Professor Xavier's mutant school in *X-Men* #1 (Sep 63). The guys (including Bobby Drake, who didn't get listed 'cause he was just a kid) spiffed themselves up to greet the newest pupil. Jean showed off a few ways her telekinetic powers could be used, and the prof left them to get better acquainted. Seeing his chance, Hank leaned over and planted a welcoming wet one right on Jean's cheek. His efforts got him lifted in the air, spun around and dropped unceremoniously onto the couch. Needless to say, none of the others tried their luck — at least not then. But Scott and Warren didn't give up quite that easily. (Scott, ultimately, won out — those strong silent types are hard to beat.)

7. Which super-hero wanted to hire Matt Murdock (Daredevil) to be his lawyer in **Daredevil** #2?
Answer c: The Thing, to help The FF sign a better lease.

One of the keys to Marvel's early popularity was that Stan created a consistent universe in which the heroes who lived together in New York City tended to run into each other, if only for a one-panel cameo or a scene.

These weren't team-ups, simply appearances by other heroes who naturally would encounter other heroes. And these heroes often had the same basic problems that everyone else in the country had — such as having to sign a lease.

Essential Reprints

These early adventures have been reprinted countless times in comics and book collections. Hey, they're classics! Here are the easiest places to find them today:

Fantastic Four #1 was reprinted in *Marvel Masterworks* #2, *Essential Fantastic Four* #1, and *Fantastic Four Annuals* #1 and 7.

Tales of Suspense #39 was reprinted in *Marvel Masterworks* #20 and *Essential Iron Man* #1.

The Incredible Hulk #1-6 were reprinted in *Marvel Masterworks* #8 and *Essential Hulk* #1.

Amazing Spider-Man #1 was reprinted in *Marvel Masterworks* #1, *Marvel Tales* #138, *Spider-Man Classics* #2, and *Essential Spider-Man* #1.

Journey into Mystery #85 was reprinted in *Marvel Masterworks* #18, and *Journey into Mystery Annual* #1.

X-Men #1 was reprinted in *Marvel Masterworks* #3.

Daredevil #2 was reprinted in *Marvel Masterworks* #17 and *Essential Daredevil* #1.

Avengers #4 was reprinted in *Marvel Masterworks* #4, *Essential Avengers* #1, *Avengers Annual* #3, and *Captain America* #400.

The Fireside trade paperback *Origins of Marvel Comics* reprinted *FF* #1 and *Hulk* #1, while *Son of Origins* reprinted *TOS* #39 and *X-Men* #1.

The 2002 Marvel trade paperback *Fantastic Firsts* reprinted *FF* #1 and *X-Men* #1.

TRIVIA CHALLENGE I
Category: **BAD GUYS** **Where did DR. DOOM attend college (according to FF Annual #2)?** Answer on page 41

Answer from page 37
SUE DIBNY

SECRET ORIGIN OF THE SILVER AGE!

Legendary Scoring

8: Excellent! You were such a true-blue Marvel fan, you no doubt knew that, in question #1, The FF battled The Skrulls for the first time in #2 and Dr. Doom didn't show up to bedevil the team until #5. Lex Luthor hasn't shown up yet, but I wouldn't put it past him to be plotting against them even now.

6-7: Very Good! You didn't score on every question, but you no doubt snagged question #3 because you knew that it was in *The Hulk* #4 that Bruce created a gamma-ray machine and that the process went awry in #6, when it accidentally joined The Hulk's body with Banner's head, requiring Banner to wear a mask to disguise his real identity! Good job!

4-5: Pretty Good! Don't worry, you'll know a lot more about The House of Idea's beginnings when you finish this tour. You'll no doubt find lots of cool stuff to check out when you head to your local bookshop or online seller to score some of the handy reprints Marvel is making available to fill in the gaps in your databank of geeky trivia.

0-3: Not So Good! Yikes! You need a serious injection of Stan Lee-brand bombast and excitement! Take plenty of notes during your tour and then snag as many back issues and reprint collections as you can find. I envy your reading list, because you've got a lot of fine super-hero enjoyment ahead of you! Excelsior, effendi!

In this case, The FF apparently had heard of the new hotshot lawyer in town (as if there were only one), so The Thing stopped by to see him. Unfortunately, he didn't know his own strength and pulled the door to Nelson & Murdock's office off the hinges on his way in. Then, he discovered that Matt, the guy who handled leases for the firm, wasn't available, and Foggy couldn't help.

Disappointed but not discouraged, The Thing asked Foggy to have Matt stop by their headquarters to check out their space and the lease. He was given a photo of Murdock to feed into their security system so Matt wouldn't be stopped (don't ask how) and hopped out the window — where the rest of the team was waiting in the Fantasti-Car. "My, what an attractive hairdo!" Susan (Invisible Girl) Storm thought upon seeing the lawyers' secretary, Karen Page, looking out the window. "I'll have to try that sometime!" "C'mon Reed!" whined Johnny (Human Torch) Storm, "Why won't you let me drive this buggy??!"

Such appearances kept readers feeling as if they'd stepped into a complete new universe in a Marvel comic. It also just happened to ensure that all the kids reading *Daredevil* were aware of the wacky characters populating *Fantastic Four*. Stan seldom missed a chance to mention that kind of thing.

8. Where was Captain America's shield, when the Avengers found him frozen in ice in the Arctic?
Answer b: Strapped to his chest.

The discovery of Captain America's frozen body in *Avengers* #4 (Mar 64) was a dramatic moment in the Marvel universe. Cap had been a big star in the Golden Age, with his iconic costume and slam-bam approach to adventures, courtesy of Joe Simon and Jack Kirby. When Stan Lee and Kirby revived him, they decided to keep the original character, saving them the intricacies of DC's approach to reviving heroes while also creating some dramatic difficulties for this man out of time.

Cap's return began when The Sub-Mariner encountered a tribe of Eskimos worshipping a man encased in a block of ice. Subby threw the giant ice cube into the sea and scattered the tribe. The cube drifted south and thawed, at which point The Avengers pulled the body from the sea while tooling past in their undersea craft. They discovered that, beneath a khaki suit, the man was wearing the costume of Captain America!

When he revived, he explained that, in the waning days of World War II, he and his sidekick Bucky had tried to stop an explosive-filled drone from being launched to strike an Army base. They arrived too late, but they both jumped onto the rocket to attempt to defuse it. Bucky managed to explode the bomb early, killing him and throwing Cap into the icy water, where he was frozen.

It was a neat way to bring a WW II character into the 1960s (and leave him feeling guilty about his partner's death, another Stan trademark). The only question is: Why were Cap and Bucky dressed in their Army uniforms, rather than their costumes? It was explained they were acting as guards but why not in costume? The villain certainly knew who this blonde Army motorcyclist was when he burst into the room.

And how the heck could Cap drive a motorcycle with a shield strapped to his chest under his shirt — and why didn't it stick out on both sides? This question recurred throughout the Silver Age, as Cap tended to disguise himself

TRIVIA CHALLENGE I
Category: **BAD GUYS**   Where was LUTHOR sent for killing Superman in an imaginary story? Answer on page 42   Answer from page 38 **MISTER DOLL**

40   **BABY BOOMER COMICS**

by strapping his shield to his back and putting a suit coat over it. There's no way a guy could manage that with a shield that size! But there's no way Batman could put a rubber mask over his cowl and fool a hoodlum for two seconds, either, and we'd accepted that for decades. So it's probably too late to be asking about it now.

Putting Cap and Bucky into mufti didn't serve any purpose in the story, it was just one of those weird moments that never was explained. But it's easy to overlook such a quirk in such a great story, one that revived a key figure who represented an America long since past in a time when comics were becoming as great as they'd been in Cap's original hey-day.

*How Cap's shield became neatly laid on his chest when he fell from the sky into the freezing Arctic waters is a mystery for the ages and not one that The Avengers were anxious to investigate in **Avengers** #4.*
© 1964 Marvel

And They Call It "Original Art"...

Homages to the cover of *Fantastic Four* #1 have appeared on these comics, and probably others, too:

Avengers West Coast #54 (Jan 90)
© 1990 Marvel

Danger Unlimited #4 (May 94)
© 1994 Dark Horse Comics

Fantastic Four #126 (Sep 72)
© 1972 Marvel

Fantastic Four #264 (Mar 84)
© 1984 Marvel

Married With Children: Quantum Quartet #1 (Oct 93).
© 1993 Now Comics

Marvel Age #14 (May 84)
© 1984 Marvel

Ren & Stimpy Show Special: Four Swerks (Jan 95)
© 1995 Marvel

Simpsons Comics #1 (93)
© 1993 Twentieth Century Fox Film Corp..

What If? #36 (Dec 82)
© 1982 Marvel

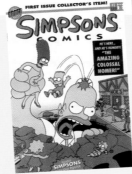

TRIVIA CHALLENGE I
Category: **BAD GUYS**   What did LUTHOR give the people of Lexor to make them love him? Answer on page 43   Answer from page 39
STATE UNIVERSITY

When Titans Clashed!

"As a devout Marvel Zombie*, I really like the long-running series of stories entitled 'When Titans Clash!' Can you tell me which story was the very first to use that cherished name?"

Sadly for Marvel fans, the House of Ideas can't really stake a claim to the idea of that catchy, senses-shattering title—although it certainly wins the award for the most usages. In fact, you really ought to be talking to Mr. Silver Age's big brother, Mr. Golden Age, to get the skinny on this one.

Whoa! What the heck is Mr. Silver Age doing talking about a story that appeared in Superman *#17? Does his older brother, Mr. Golden Age, know his comics are being messed with?*

It turns out that "When Titans Clash!" made its debut as the title of the first story in *Superman* #17 (Jul-Aug 42). The title titans were Kal-El (of course) and Lex Luthor. Our bald baddie tricked Supes into handing over a piece of jewelry called the Powerstone. Lex's lust for that hefty gem, which gave its owner enormous power, began in *Action* #47 (Apr 42). So even back then, there occasionally was continuity between titles and stories.

In this later issue, Lex finally got his slimy hands on the stone and gained super-powers. Our two super-strong dudes proceeded to bash each other's brains out with most of Metropolis' infrastructure during the course of this 13-page epic. That was about the extent of it — heck, that's the extent of *most* stories with this title!

"When Titans Clash!" has become something of the standard-bearer for two key Silver Age Marvel concepts: the writers' penchant for overly dramatic, somewhat-stilted language in their titles and their obvious way of dressing up long slugfests to seem to be more than what they really were — a way to kill some pages. Marvel used this title about a half-dozen times during the Silver Age, and it since has become an in-joke to express the period's giddy attitude.

But it was far from the most bombastic title to appear in a Marvel comic book during the Silver Age. Stan Lee liked rearranging typical sentence structure to give it more drama and replicate the English used in days of yore, particularly Biblical times. He also wasn't shy about lifting book titles or Shakespearean phrases, adapting them for the story at hand. That was heightened when he hired Roy Thomas, a former English teacher, as his right-hand man.

For example, take this stretch of *X-Men* issues from #17 to #23: "And None Shall Survive!" "If Iceman Should Fail!" "Lo, Now Shall Appear The Mimic!" "I, Lucifer!" "From Whence Comes Dominus!" "Divided, We Fall!" and "To Save a City!" You know you want to go read every one of those!

* Marvel Zombie (n): A 1980s term (usually derogatory) for readers who buy all the Marvel Comics, even ones they don't like. There are "DC Zombies," too.

To be sure, sometimes the titles were a bit over the top, such as the one for Iceman's origin in *X-Men* #44 (May 68), a backup tale called "The Iceman Cometh!" And sometimes they weren't quite as original as they no doubt thought. For instance, Roy Thomas titled *Daredevil* #59 (Dec 69) "The Torpedo Will Get You if You Don't Watch Out!" which is kind of a long way around to

TRIVIA CHALLENGE I
Category: **BAD GUYS**   What was **DR. DOOM** trying to contact when his college experiment blew up?   Answer on page 44   Answer from page 42 **PHANTOM ZONE**

42   **BABY BOOMER COMICS**

say, "The Torpedo is the villain this month." A couple years later, Steve Englehart drew on the same poetic inspiration for *Amazing Adventures* #16 (Jan 73), (in a story edited by Roy the Boy) to write, "And The Juggernaut Will Get You if You Don't Watch Out!"

DC's titles tended to be a big more straightforward in their structure, often using sentence subjects as titles ("The Planet That…"), but that approach also produced memorable lines. As the second wave of Silver Age writers began to infiltrate DC in the late 1960s, their titles, too, began to become more literary based. Many of these writers had grown up reading comics, a first for the industry. Some had been big Marvel fans (as indicated by the letters they'd had published in the letters columns), and DC was actively trying to emulate the success Marvel was having.

So it's not really surprising that *Justice League of America* #104 (Feb 73), in which a gigantic, hairy beast returned to battle the team again, was titled, "The Shaggy Man Will Get You if You Don't Watch Out!"

Meanwhile, don't despair if you want to relive this epic original titanic clash but can't shell out the bucks for a Golden Age issue. You can check it out in *Superman Archives* #5 or, for the more frugal hunters and gatherers among you, in *Superman* #252 (Jun 72), which is close enough to the Silver Age to count in my book. That issue also includes the earlier *Action* story. What a deal!

In fact, lots of great Golden Age and early Silver Age stuff was reprinted in comics during the Silver Age and 1970s. I particularly recommend most Silver Age *80-Page Giant* annuals, the DC *100-Page Super Spectacular*, and the 100-page comics that were slipped into many titles' runs. Mighty fine reading.

In addition, DC and Marvel both have produced an incredible variety of hardback collections of their Golden Age and Silver Age comics, in DC's *Archive* and Marvel's *Masterworks* series, as well as Marvel's black-and-white paperback *Essentials* collections. All of these can be found at your local comic store, and it in turn can be found by calling 888/COMIC-BOOK (888/266-4226) or checking the Yellow Pages under "Comic Books."

© 1965 Marvel

© 1968 Marvel

Titans clashing!

It's not all that surprising that "When Titans Clash!" became one of Marvel's favorite titles. Early on, Stan Lee not only wrote most of the stories, he had a lot of titans who clashed when he couldn't think of much else for them to do. Here's where the title (or a variation) was used:

"When Titans Clash!" Iron Man fights a villain using his old costume in *Tales of Suspense* #65 (May 65).
"When Titans Clash!" Thor and Hercules square off in *Journey into Mystery Annual* #1 (65).
"When Titans Clash!" The X-Men battle The Super-Adaptoid in *X-Men* #29 (Feb 67).
"When Mutants Clash!" The X-Men fight Quicksilver and The Scarlet Witch in *X-Men* #45 (Jun 68).
"A Clash of Titans!" The Hulk tussles with The Sub-Mariner in *The Incredible Hulk* #118 (Aug 69).
"When Titans Collide!" and "A Clash of Titans!" are two of the three chapters in the epic Captain Marvel-Thanos duel in *Captain Marvel* #28 (Sep 73).

The title has become shorthand for the way Marvel titled its Silver Age comics and has been used a number of times since as a homage to those issues. It has graced two *Fantastic Four* stories, #200 (Nov 78) and #260 (Nov 83). Neil Gaiman also used it as the title for the story of his pivotal arch-foes' battle in Eclipse Comics' *Miracleman* #24 (Aug 93). It won't surprise you a bit to learn that the story arc overall was called "The Silver Age."

TRIVIA CHALLENGE I
Category: BODY PARTS What part of the body held the weapon of KLAW? Answer on page 45 Answer from page 41 WATER & SCIENCE

SECRET ORIGIN OF THE SILVER AGE! 43

Everything I Need to Know I Learned from The Justice League

"I always thought Silver Age super-hero comics were just a bunch of guys in skin-tight suits doing a lot of yelling and hitting. Was there any more to them than that?"

You better believe there was, bunky. Sometimes, comics offered more than just dramatic battles, weird science facts, amazing coincidences, and elaborate death traps. Sometimes, they provided lessons that even little kids could understand and relate to. And they were lessons that today's kids — and adults — would still be wise to heed.

Take the Justice League of America, for example. With editor Julius Schwartz and writer Gardner Fox at the helm, you knew the team's adventures were going to feature scientific gadgets and explanations that occasionally even made sense. But their adventures also implied that, to be an adult super-hero, you needed more than muscles. You needed to think unconventionally to outwit your foe and you had to work together for the betterment of all.

Supporting this underlying code was the art. True, Mike Sekowsky didn't draw super-heroes the way most kids wanted them drawn and certainly not as they are today. He didn't draw them with washboard stomachs and so many muscles in their armpits that you wondered if they could put their hands in their pockets. Instead, he drew them as if they were just a bunch of guys in snug costumes. Yes, they were in good shape, but they looked like guys in good shape, not Mr. Universe with a coat of paint.

The Justice League of America spent a lot of time behind the table at their HQ. Unfortunately, not once did anyone remember to send out for Chinese food.

TRIVIA CHALLENGE I
Category: **BODY PARTS** What part of METAMORPHO's body is brown? Answer on page 46 Answer from page 42 THE NETHERWORLD

Whether it was intentional or not, Sekowsky's art, with inking by Bernard Sachs, made the JLA just about the most accessible group of heroes you could ask for. Not only were they pretty smart and not overly muscled, probably a good description of most of their fans, but they sat around and talked about their cases!

Inside their secret cavern HQ, they'd plot strategies, go over what happened to each other, and just generally chew the fat and have a good time, sitting at their round conference table. You don't see much of that in today's comics, because you don't really have to sit around and discuss who punched who in the face during the big fight. But sitting around talking about adventures is something Silver Age fans could do easily and still feel like a super-hero.

But more than that made The JLA great. In the very best adventures, the readers learned simple truths about life that the super-heroes learned right along with them. These were ideas that any kid could apply to his life as soon as he put down the comic book. Best of all, the ideas weren't tacked onto an adventure — good thing, too, because kids are always on the alert for some hokey moral that could ruin a perfectly good story. Instead, the morals were integral parts of the story. Take a look:

"When Gravity Went Wild."
Justice League of America #5 (Jun-Jul 61)

Our story opened, of course, with The JLA sitting around the clubhouse table. Everyone was morose, because the evidence seemed to show that Green Arrow had betrayed them! "It's absolutely incredible!" J'onn J'onzz thought to himself. "No one's ever betrayed us before!" As if there had been much time for betrayal after only a half-dozen or so adventures. Across the table, Wonder Woman was getting a little paranoid. "I wonder what villainy he's dreaming up right now?" she stewed. Yep, they were morose.

The final bit of evidence came from the fact that GA wasn't at HQ. The members were on the verge of convicting him of treason on the basis of that alone when, right on cue, Green Arrow showed up. In response, the world's greatest super-heroes (it said so right on the cover) flung a few venom-tipped barbs at the "silent and tight-lipped" Amazing Archer.

"Wait!" he cried. "You call yourselves Champions of Justice! Is it justice to deny me what any accused person in America enjoys...a fair trial! Hear my side of the story before you judge me!" His stirring words had their effect. Superman, Batman, and Snapper agree to sit as judges while the others told their tales.

What we learned was that six JLA foes escaped from prison, so the team split up to capture them. Flash, Wonder Woman, and Green Arrow went after Captain Cold, Professor Menace, and King Clock, while The Martian Manhunter, Green Lantern, and Aquaman headed off to capture "those master evil-doers" Electric Man, Monty Moran, and The Puppet Master.

After escaping a few traps, the Flash team had the master evildoers on the run. Suddenly, The Emerald Archer fired three arrows, our heroes were stunned by "an explosion of sheer light," and GA and the crooks disappeared. "It'll be interesting to hear how he tries to squirm out of this charge," The Amazon Princess told The Scarlet Speedster, looking daggers into

Mister Silver Age Recommends...

Justice League of America #5

DC
Jun 1961
Cover artist:
Mike Sekowsky, Bernard Sachs

"When Gravity Went Wild"
Writer: Gardner Fox
Penciller: Mike Sekowsky
Inker: Bernard Sachs

Then 10¢
Now $375

© 1961 National Periodical Publications Inc. (DC)

Reprints appear in...
• Justice League of America #39
• Justice League Archives Vol. 1

The JLA confronted their newest member, Green Arrow, who they thought had gone hinky on them, in *Justice League of America* #5, "When Gravity Went Wild!"
© 1961 National Periodical Publications Inc. (DC)

TRIVIA CHALLENGE I
Category: BODY PARTS   What color was the left arm of ULTRA, the multi-alien?   Answer on page 47

Answer from page 43
HIS RIGHT HAND

© 1961 National Periodical Publications Inc. (DC)

Green Arrow let his teammates (and the reader) know that things were not always the way they seemed in **Justice League of America** *#5, "When Gravity Went Wild!"*

Sometimes DC created a cover gag and tried to come up with a story to fit it.

GA's turned back. OK, so they weren't always the worlds most *forgiving* super-heroes.

The Aquaman team also escaped some traps and were fighting huge puppets and a space vessel in mid-air, when GA arrived in his Arrow Plane. "Green Arrow sure must be excited about being a Justice League member!" noted Green Lantern. "Yes, he's probably finished his chore with Flash and Wonder Woman and has come to give us a hand," agreed J'onn. As if Flash and Wonder Woman, who were at least as speedy as GA, couldn't have cared less about helping their compatriots.

Just then, the archer fired three arrows at the ship, and a huge explosion (this one so big it went Varoom! Blam! Varoom!) knocked the three heroes out of the air. When they gained consciousness on the ground, they knew the sad truth: Green Arrow had double-crossed them!

Now it was GA's turn — and he admitted everything they had said was true! But it wasn't the way it looked, he claimed. In fact, his actions were part of his cunning plan to save them all from death! To prove it, he showed Aquaman, GL, and J'onn the holes in the backs of their costumes where he used his arrows to lower them to the ground after the explosion. (How did they, particularly Aquaman, think they'd landed intact, anyway?).

The reason he hadn't revealed his intentions earlier was that he'd discovered that one of the heroes in the room was an impostor! And GA had to hear all their stories to learn which one! Upon being unmasked by GA's clever deductions, the impostor quickly explained the elaborate method he'd used to make his powers work, which was what gave him away to GA.

So the JLA members carted the imposter off to jail — just as Gravity Goes Wild! Remember Gravity from the title? It finally showed up on page 19 of our 24-page epic.

That's what happened sometimes, when they created a cover and then tried to come up with a story to fit it, as was Julie's way of creating exciting covers that would sell. Gravity going wild didn't have anything to do with our moral, though, which we'd already learned from GA's courageous solo efforts.

MORAL: *Don't judge a person's actions without looking at it from his or her point of view. Maybe you don't have all the information.*

"One Hour To Doomsday"
Justice League of America #11 (May 62)

This time out, our horrifying cover scenario actually was central to the story. The five-page battle with The Time Trapper that led off the issue, however, wasn't. It was a mopping-up action from last month's battle with the wizard Felix Faust, which, in itself, is a great story and sets the stage for this issue. (DC often created two-part adventures in this manner, knowing that there were many readers who would never find two issues in a row, thanks to spotty distribution.)

TRIVIA CHALLENGE I
Category: **BODY PARTS**   **Who was the CHIEF battling when he lost his legs?**   Answer on page 48   Answer from page 44
HIS RIGHT LEG

To make a long story short, The JLAers became stuck in the future while trying to return to their own time and had to battle the three demons that Felix Faust had managed to free from an ancient enchantment last issue. Now, 100 years in the future (in 1962, of course; now it's only about 60), these three tall, pink refugees from a dermatology clinic had been freed right on Faust's schedule.

They used their magic to render The JLA helpless, then imprisoned each hero in his or her own personalized beakers as mist:

"Against Superman I now conjure
The spirits of darkness, black and
    sure.
No bone, no hair, no flesh remain,
Your body now as mist contain.
Upward into the jar you go
With the others, row upon row."

AFTER A BRIEF DISCUSSION, THE EMERALD GLADIATOR LIFTS HIS POWER RING...

© 1962 National Periodical Publications Inc. (DC)

IN THE NEXT INSTANT, THE GLOWING RING TRANSFORMS FLASH INTO "GREEN ARROW," GREEN ARROW INTO "FLASH," SUPERMAN INTO "AQUAMAN," AQUAMAN INTO "SUPERMAN," WONDER WOMAN INTO "J'ONN J'ONZZ," J'ONN J'ONZZ INTO "GREEN LANTERN," AND BATMAN INTO "WONDER WOMAN"...

Each hero apparently had his own nifty little stanza, but sadly the only other one we heard was part of the one for The Amazon Princess. ("Wonder Woman, change your guise, as mist, as cloud, you shall arise!") Not that the name's were exactly critical to the rhyming scheme or anything — they were demons, not Elizabeth Barrett Browning.

The JLA made quick hash of this dastardly trap, of course, courtesy of a cunning plan by Green Lantern. (In a weird quirk that Schwartz used on occasion, the story suddenly was interrupted with a panel that challenged: "Dear Reader: Match your wits with those of Green Lantern before reading on! Figure out what The Emerald Warrior did — unseen by the demon Ghast — which helped The Justice League escape his magical trap!" As if we could have actually come up with it.)

Now that they'd been freed, it was Aquaman, showing no ill effects of having been out of water for a hundred years, who devised a strategy. He suggested they disguise themselves as each other. Since the demons' spells apparently needed to use the individual's name, he reasoned that they wouldn't work on the wrong person.

"After a brief discussion" the caption box said (no doubt, something along the lines of, "Nuh-uh, I'm not going to be Wonder Woman, *you* be Wonder Woman!" "No way, I want to be The Flash!"), the change took place. Naturally, they don't change costumes — GL just power-ringed everybody to look different. Whether capes and cowl ears and such turned invisible or evaporated wasn't mentioned, nor was the way GL maintained the changes while he was off battling somewhere else. I never did understand how his ring worked.

Green Lantern saved somebody the embarassment of having to fit into Wonder Woman's costume by willing the heroes into new identities in **Justice League of America** *#11, "One Hour to Doomsday!"*

AGAINST SUPERMAN I NOW CONJURE THE SPIRITS OF DARKNESS, BLACK AND SURE !

SUPERMAN   BATMAN

© 1962 National Periodical Publications Inc. (DC)

Felix Faust's demons captured the Justice League and made up catchy little poems in order to imprison them all in **Justice League of America** *#11, "One Hour to Doomsday!"*

TRIVIA CHALLENGE I
Category: **EVIL TEAMS**   The FRIGHTFUL FOUR consisted of Trapster, Medusa, and who else? Answer on page 49   Answer from page 45 BLUE

(By the way, Batman got to be The Amazon Princess. Aquaman, who was transformed into Superman, asked, "How can I ever perform the feats of the famous Man of Steel?" indicating he must've been outvoted on his first choice, whoever that might have been.)

The League then split into three teams, and each hero used his own incredible powers to perform an amazing simulation of the hero he was impersonating — being sure to think out each element of his actions clearly so readers could follow along.

Did they capture the demons, imprison them, and return to the present safe and sound? You'll either have to read the story or find someone who knows and beg him to tell you, as Snapper does in the final panel, "Please, ease the knees, somebody! Give me the word!" Snapper offered another chance for DC to show off its hip teen lingo, and it didn't disappoint.

MORAL: *Don't judge a person by appearance.*

"The Last Case of The Justice League"
Justice League of America #12 (Jun 62)

Our tale opened with an epic struggle — between Snapper Carr and a fish in the annual fish-catching championship. Before he could land what surely would be the prize-winner, his JLA emergency signal summoned him to a meeting. Oh, sure, he was across the country from their headquarters. But he had a special button installed in his car by The JLA (no doubt by Batman, who has designed and built about a jillion different Batmobiles since the 1940s) that whisked him to their secret cave HQ through the air.

Inside, Snapper was shocked to have Dr. Light greet him. The villain boasted that he'd sent the JLA members to disastrous ends, which he then had Snapper record for posterity. In his dictation, he introduced himself and spent an extra panel detailing what happens when the electrons of an atom are stimulated (finally breaking off with, "But so much for technical details." You gotta love a Schwartz story for adding a little education to the entertainment).

Dr. Light's goal, of course, was to take over the world. But he was no fool, he assured us — I mean, Snapper. He knew The JLA had to be disposed of first. To prove the point, he was depicted standing in his laboratory, clearly having a brainstorm: "Those champions of justice will never permit me to use my powers to dominate the Earth!" It's no wonder Dr. Light became the master criminal he did, with such incredible insight at his command.

So he captured Aquaman (as if that took a criminal mastermind), then used The Sea King's signal device to lure the other JLAers to their HQ. One by one, he beamed them to worlds specially selected to seal their dooms. Aquaman landed on a desert planet; J'onn J'onzz was put on a world of fire (his one kryptonite-like weakness); Flash was stranded on a world that made him too dizzy to stand, much less run; and GA went to a world where wood was magnetic, so his arrows didn't work.

GL and Superman, of course, went to planets that respectively were all yellow and had a red sun. Batman was sent to a planet where trees grew upside down and rocks were made of water. This

Everybody's got a weakness, but it doesn't count if you're not who your enemy thought you were, as Dr. Light discovered in **Justice League of America #12,** *"The Last Case of The Justice League!"*

WHEN AQUAMAN IS PLACED ON A WATERY WORLD, "BATMAN" REVEALS WHAT HAS HAPPENED...

YOU'LL HAVE TO RESCUE THE REAL BATMAN, J'ONN J'ONN! ANY PLANET WITH A NON-YELLOW SUN ROBS ME OF MY SUPER-POWERS!

GLAD TO! AND ON THE WAY I'LL PICK UP WONDER WOMAN AND FLASH!

© 1962 National Periodical Publications Inc. (DC)

TRIVIA CHALLENGE I
Category: EVIL TEAMS

Who, with M. Mallah and The Brain, made up the BROTHERHOOD OF EVIL? Answer on page 50

Answer from page 46
GENERAL IMMORTUS

48

BABY BOOMER COMICS

obviously rendered him powerless — as if being sent to another world didn't make him pretty helpless under any circumstances.

Last but certainly not least, Wonder Woman found that, on her planet, her body didn't respond to her brain. So she climbed a tree, for example, when she intended to ride the air currents. Where she intended to go I have no idea, but that's beside the point. The point is, rolling over on the ground when you wanted to run would be the kind of problem that would make me sit quietly in a corner and try not to think too much. It's also where I would have sent just about all the other heroes, too, but, then, I'm not a master criminal who had scoped out enough worlds to find just the right ones to banish these heroes to.

How did they escape? Easy: Batman removed his mask and became Superman! Well, not exactly. It seemed Superman, being nobody's fool, had used his telescopic vision to see why he and Batman (off on a mission together) were being called back to HQ. So he saw Dr. Light capture the others. Even though he had no idea what happened to the others, he suggested that he and his pal Batman exchange costumes. "It may give us some advantage later on!" he explained. Hey, it worked last issue, didn't it?

As luck would have it, it gave them the absolutely exact advantage they need. Superman remained unharmed by the upside-down trees and water rocks that would have so stymied The World's Greatest Detective. He promptly rescued The Martian Manhunter, and they extricated the others.

They then turned their full attention to foiling Dr. Light's plans. Fortunately, these required Light to steal three light-related objects before dominating the world, so the heroes could divide into teams to battle him. Did they do it? Did the world's light-related mementos remain safe? Did Dr. Light end up ruling the world? I'm not telling, because they've already left us with a valuable lesson this issue.

MORAL: *Everyone has strengths and weaknesses. What makes one person fail may not affect another, but that doesn't make the second person better or stronger. He has weaknesses of his own.*

EVERY TIME I TRY TO RUN--I LOSE MY BALANCE...

© 1962 National Periodical Publications Inc. (DC)

*The Flash fell down every time he went looking for his lost chest logo, thanks to the master plan of Dr. Light in **Justice League of America** #12, "The Last Case of The Justice League!"*

"The Riddle of the Robot Justice League"
Justice League of America #13 (Aug 62)

This story opened with the members off on their own, catching crooks, talking with their sidekicks, or showing off their amazing powers to normal-type civilians. Suddenly, they all disappeared! Two panels later, they were pretty mystified when they ended up among "the gleaming, glittering instruments of a super-scientific civilization."

Luckily, a ball of blue energy was there to enlighten them. It explained in an elaborate scenario that its people had brought The JLA there to battle another group, the Skarns. To make a long story short, if The JLA didn't defeat the Skarns' champions in combat, everyone everywhere in the universe would be blown up. Unfortunately, the Skarn's champs were robot duplicates of whoever they fought, and, though they were supposed to be exact replicas, the robots always won. So the other guys' universes always were blown up.

"We'll go, of course," Green Lantern assured the little blue ball. "And find a way to defeat ourselves," added Wonder Woman, clearly seeing the irony. Not to be

Mister Silver Age Recommends...

Justice League of America #13

DC
Jul 1962
Cover artist:
Mike Sekowsky

"The Riddle of the Robot Justice League"
Writer: Gardner Fox
Penciller: Mike Sekowsky
Inker: Bernard Sachs

Then **12¢**
Now **$210**

© 1962 National Periodical Publications Inc. (DC)

Reprints appear in...
• Justice League of America #93
• Justice League Archives Vol. 2

Everyone seemed to benefit from Aquaman's encouragement and helpful suggestions except that sluggard Superman in *Justice League of America* #13, "The Riddle of the Robot Justice League!"

© 1962 National Periodical Publications Inc. (DC)

Aquaman sometimes didn't have much to do. In the middle of one crisis, Green Lantern created a swimming pool for him so he could root for the other heroes in battle.

topped in the clever-riposte department, The Flash chimed in, "We'll do our best — and if that isn't enough — we'll do even better!" Were these guys the best or what?

So each JLAer was duplicated, except for Aquaman, who theorized that it was due to there being no water on this planet. Did he get upset and pout? Did he gang up with another hero for an unfair advantage? No! GL power-beamed Aquaman a swimming pool so he could be their "coach" and "one-man rooting section," according to The Martian Manhunter and Superman, who escorted the Atlantean to his floating tub. And with that kind of an escort, who was going to argue?

Our heroes didn't fare so well in their battles with themselves, at least at first. And Aquaman's coaching was less than insightful. It consisted of yelling such motivational sayings as "Superman, you're losing...Get with it!" Needless to say, with that help, the robots were beating JLAers every which way. It made a pretty darn impressive cover, one that even had something to do with the main thrust of the story.

"Roused to desperation," the caption told us, The Sea King shouted at The Scarlet Speedster, "Snap out of it, Flash! Turnabout is fair play!" OK, so it's not exactly "Win one for the Gipper." It's not even, "If you screw this up, our entire universe will blow up." But it gave Flash the insight he needed to win, and that's what's important, right? As The Flash noted, "Sometimes a little encouragement will enable a man to get up off his back and battle back to victory."

And a little encouragement was about all Aquaman could offer. For example, he told GL, "A man who won't be beaten can't be beaten!" The Emerald Gladiator turned that advice to his advantage and won. To Wonder Woman, he bellowed, "Remember your Amazon heritage! Yank harder!" The Amazing Amazon wasted no time wondering if he was making a pun on Yankees and Amazons, she just did as told, inspired by her ancestors.

Aquaman offered Batman the sage advice, "You can't let a metal man beat a human!" That's not exactly out of Bartlett's or Dale Carnegie, but it's all the encouragement The Dark Knight needed. Then Aquaman opined to GA, "All you need is a break." Sure enough, The Emerald Archer was spurred to victory. Flush with these wins, Aquaman sized up The Martian Manhunter's battle and shouted, "Hit him at his weak point!" Ooh, clever. J'onn thought this over while he flew end over end backward from a metallic right cross and came up with the right strategy.

"Thanks to that unwitting suggestion of Aquaman's, I defeated my metal self!" J'onn gloated. Unwitting?! Do these incisive comments from The Sea King

TRIVIA CHALLENGE I
Category: **EVIL TEAMS**   Who were Johnny Quick, Power Ring, and Superwoman's **CRIME SYNDICATE** partners?   Answer on page 52   Answer from page 48
MADAME ROUGE

sound unwitting to you? Well, OK, maybe they do — but you can't argue with success!

As proof of this, Aquaman had been watching Superman fall further behind in the race he was running against his duplicate. (Why they raced instead of the Flashes is anybody's guess, but — coincidentally, I'm sure — it aided the upcoming plot twist with Superman.)

Receiving little response to his insightful note to Supes, Aquaman suggested that Superman run faster and not let them down. That bit of pithy advice didn't do the job, either. "Give it a little something extra!" he encouraged The Man of Steel. *That* finally was the phrase that paid for the Last Son of Krypton, who not only beat his duplicate but figured out why the robots always won.

As Aquaman jumped triumphantly from his water tub, the other JLAers crowded around. "Your cheers and helpful suggestions helped me win, Aquaman!" Supes exulted. "Me too!" Wondie chimed in. "And me!" added J'onn, no doubt reluctantly.

So The JLA won and went home happy? Hardly! These were despicable aliens! They decided to blow up our universe anyway! I won't tell you what happened, but I'll give you a hint: You're still around to read this, and you have Aquaman to thank yet again. And not even that green galoot from Mars could claim that The Sea King's comments this time were unwitting!

MORAL: *Encouragement from others and perceptive coaching can help turn the tide of battle, if you're willing to listen and profit from it.*

"Journey Into the Micro-World!"
Justice League of America #18 (Mar 63)

This is one of my all-time favorite JLA morals! Snapper once again flew cross-country to JLA HQ in a roadster that would have trouble running on the road, much less flying, only to find the mountain clubhouse empty. Unlike Snapper, however, raeders could go back in time to see that, in fact, The JLAers had suddenly shrunk out of sight, right past The Atom! Fortunately, The Atom saw them go and followed, joining them in front of three gladiators in the micro-world.

These three guys protected their world's earth, sea, and starways, they explained. But radiation in their helmets was shortening the populace's life spans. Since they couldn't defeat themselves or each other, they wanted The JLA to beat them and remove their helmets. But they warned The JLA that they were invulnerable (a word used so many times in this issue that if you didn't know it going in, you had to go look it up to know what was going on and you knew it going out).

As usual, the heroes split into three teams to battle the gladiators. But, even though the protectors didn't look all that tough, they won. Superman, GL and Wonder Woman were put in a cage, which the protector assured them was escape-proof. Sure enough, Superman couldn't bend the bars. The others arrived and wanted to free them. Superman, trying to be modest, explained to The Martian Manhunter, "While I respect you tremendously — if I can't budge these bars, neither can you!"

Mister Silver Age Recommends...

Justice League of America #18

DC
Mar 1963
Cover artist:
Murphy Anderson

"Journey Into the Micro-World!"
Writer: Gardner Fox
Penciller: Mike Sekowsky
Inker: Bernard Sachs

Then **12¢**
Now **$175**

© 1963 National Periodical Publications Inc. (DC)

Reprints appear in...
• Justice League of America #93
• Justice League Archives Vol. 3

THEN... IT OCCURRED TO US YOU MIGHT LIKE TO SHARE OUR LATEST ADVENTURE, SNAPPER! YOU HAVEN'T TAKEN AN ACTIVE PART IN THE LAST FEW CASES...

YOU'RE NOT JUST PULVERIZING ME, ATOM? THIS *IS* THE REAL DEAL?

© 1963 National Periodical Publications Inc. (DC)

Atom enlisted Snapper Carr to help beat the bad guys because he was still positive he could pound on them in Justice League of America #18, "Journey into the Micro-World!"

TRIVIA CHALLENGE I
Category: **LETTERS** Whose letter column was called "Sock it to Shell-Head?" Answer on page 53 Answer from page 49 **ELECTRO, KRAVEN**

As you probably have figured out by now about J'onn J'onzz from past adventures, he ignored the Man of Steel's advice and tried anyway. But he failed. So did all the others, after hearing from the previous hero who tried that if he couldn't do it, nobody else could, either.

*Batman did what nobody else could do after he got them all to shut up and keep their negativity to themselves in **Justice League of America** #18, "Journey Into the Micro-World!"*

Finally Batman, seemingly fed up with all the negative vibes from these supposed teammates, told them to shut up. "Don't any of you say a word — not a single word — about my not being able to bend those bars! I want a chance at these bars — while you remain silent! Keep silent at all costs!" I was about to suggest that anyway, the way they were getting on each other. That's the way Silver Age *Marvel* heroes bickered, not DC's true-blue pals!

Sure enough, before their amazed eyes, The Caped Crusader bent the bars wide open, apparently gaining strength on this world that he didn't have at home, where iron bars were still pretty darned hard to bend. Bats explained that something in the air seemed to "brainwash" them into pulling their punches and make the predictions of failure come true.

> ## The way DC's heroes sometimes bickered, you'd have thought they were Marvel characters!

To win the battles, The JLA needed someone who hadn't already heard how invulnerable the protectors were. So The Atom shot up through the molecules and brought back Snapper. GL will-powered The Titanic Teen-ager (or something like that) not to hear the protectors, and off they all went. Did Snapper beat the protectors now that he couldn't hear their negative predictions? You'll have to read it to find out, but you might be able to guess.

MORAL: *Don't believe others when they tell you that your goal can't be reached. You won't know until you try.*

Fabled reprints

Want to read these fine moralistic tales in reprint form? Here are the best places to find them:

Justice League of America #5 was reprinted in *Justice League of America* #39 and *Justice League Archives* #1.

Justice League of America #11 was reprinted in *Justice League of America* #85 and *Justice League Archives* #2.

Justice League of America #12 was reprinted in *Justice League of America* #76 and *Justice League Archives* #2.

Justice League of America #13 was reprinted in *Justice League of America* #93 and *Justice League Archives* #2.

Justice League of America #18 was reprinted in *Justice League of America* #93 and *Justice League Archives* #3.

TRIVIA CHALLENGE I
Category: **LETTERS**

Whose letter column was called his "Mail Chute?"

Answer on page 54

Answer from page 50
OWLMAN, ULTRAMAN

Gorillas!

"So I'm looking around at all these DC covers, Mr. Silver Age, and I've gotta know: What's the deal with DC and gorillas? It seems as if back in the Silver Age, there was a gorilla on one cover or another every month or something!"

There's a good reason it seems like that—there *was* a gorilla on one cover or another almost every month. To get to the bottom of this weird obsession, I went straight to The Living Legend himself, Julius Schwartz, and laid it on the line. And he gave me the straight poop.

The catalyst came from "Evolution Plus!" in *Strange Adventures* #8 (May 51). In that cover story, a man wound up in a gorilla's body and landed in a cage at the zoo. Hey, it happens. The cover showed the gorilla holding out a chalkboard between with the bars with the message, "Ruth—Please believe me! I am the victim of a terrible scientific experiment! Ralph."

A few months after the issue came out, Julie's boss, Irwin Donenfeld, came into Julie's office and showed him that sales had jumped 25% on that issue. They guessed it was because of the gorilla on the cover, Julie said. So they put another gorilla on another one of their covers. "It did very well, too."

So what would any good publisher do, if a gorilla on the cover gooses sales? You got it. Julie said that, soon, DC was publishing one cover per month featuring a gorilla. And they had to *limit* the editors to that, or there would've been more. I'm sorry I missed the discussions of who got to use the gorilla each month.

Donenfeld discovered something else: Sales also shot up when fire and/or jail cells were pictured, as well as a person weeping. He kept a small card listing these elements to remind himself to encourage his editors to feature them or some variation as much as possible. After all, that first cover had two of the key ingredients.

"It drove us nuts," Julie said. "It's hard enough to come up with cover ideas. But to have to feature gorillas, jail cells, or fire really made it tough!"

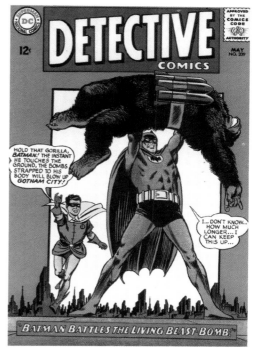

Batman may have had to keep a gorilla villain aloft, but he knew who he was fighting. Do you?
© 1965 National Periodical Publications Inc. (DC)

Can you figure out which of our favorite heroes each of these simians got to make a monkey out of? No fair asking for help from Sam Simeon, Solovar, or Congorilla! But, if you can't remember, check the answer key on the next page.

Gorilla Boss	**Monsieur Mallah**	**Gorilla Wonders**
Titano	**Super-Ape**	**Mikora**
Grodd	**Priscilla**	**Bruna**
Karmak	**King Krypton**	**Gorilla King**

TRIVIA CHALLENGE I
Category: **LETTERS**   What comic book's letter column was called "Via Rocket Mail?"   Answer on page 57

Answer from page 51
IRON MAN

Gorilla answers:

Gorilla Boss – Batman

Titano – Superman

Grodd – Flash

Karmak – Batman

Monsieur Mallah – Doom Patrol

Super-Ape – Superman
(actually, he *was* Superman)

Priscilla – Jerry Lewis

King Krypton – Superman

Gorilla Wonders – All Americans!
(*The Brave and the Bold*'s Strange Sports Stories)

Mikora – Tomahawk

Bruna – Jimmy Olsen

Gorilla King – Wonder Woman

PLUS:

Sam Simeon – The Ape of Angel & The Ape

Solovar — Flash's friend from Gorilla City Congorilla – Pal (more or less) to Congo Bill

Priscilla

Solovar

Grodd

Gorilla King

Needless to say, by the time the Silver Age rolled around, the gorilla craze was in full roar. Virtually every hero got his or her share of gorilla villains. A few of my favorites included: The Gorilla Boss of Gotham City; Titano; Grodd the Super Gorilla; Karmak the Living Beast Bomb; Monsieur Mallah; the Giant Super-Ape; Priscilla the Gorilla; King Krypton the Gorilla of Steel; the Gorilla Wonders of the Diamond; Mikora the Gorilla Ranger, Bruna the Bride of Jungle Jimmy, and the Gorilla King of Amazon Island.

Unfortunately, I wasn't able to learn when the fans started to lose their affection for big apes. But I think it's safe to say the craze has died down by now. I also didn't learn whose idea it was to feature so many covers with bodiless costumes or purple backgrounds. Those are secret origins for another day.

*Some strange compulsion made Mr. Silver Age buy **Superman** #158 featuring "Titano, the Super-Ape!" This time, he explains why; maybe some other time, he'll tell you the big ape's own story. It's a wowser.*
© 1960 National Periodical Publications Inc. (DC)

TRIVIA CHALLENGE I
Category: **LETTERS**

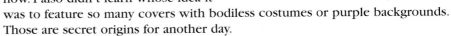
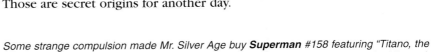
"Look at all the Letters from Our Readers" was whose letter column? Answer on page 58

Answer from page 52
GREEN LANTERN

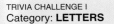
54

BABY BOOMER COMICS

Enter...
THE RELATIONSHIP!

Marvel's Silver Age was a Many Splendored Thing

"There was lots of punching and yelling in The Silver Age (and yes, maybe even a few morals being told), but what about the babes? Did Marvel super-heroes ever get to make love, not mayhem?"

It's true that Marvel is famous for the action and adventure it loaded into its Silver Age comics. Page after page was devoted to our heroes chasing villains and beating the pulp out of them—and vice-versa. Even when two heroes met, they often would paste their peer first and ask questions later. Hey, when you've got Jack Kirby doing so many of your comics, you make use of his talents for non-stop action!

But there was something else Marvel could do better than anybody else back then: romance. Almost every hero had a love life of some kind, even if it only consisted of thinking "Oh, Jane/Jean/Janet/Karen/Betty, if you could but love a poor wretch like me instead of being nice to me only out of pity." And sometimes, the path of true love actually ended in wedding bells.

Of course, a Marvel wedding was not exactly your run-of-the-mill nuptials. Seldom did a coosome twosome tie the knot without a few interruptions to pound the beejeebers out of whichever villains crashed the party. But the deed usually got done, giving all those other poor wretches pining after Jane/Jean/Janet/Karen/Betty hope for the future—and making the readers realize that sometimes, things really *did* work out all right, after all.

It wasn't accidental, either. As Stan the Man himself said in his Soapbox on the Bullpen Bulletins page in the June 1969 issues: "For many years, we've been trying, in our own bumbling way, to illustrate that love is a far greater force, a far greater power, than hate… The power of love—and the power of hate. Which is most truly enduring? When you tend to despair, let the answer sustain you!"

How well do you remember the power of love from those early days of Marvel? Let's just see if your answers will sustain you, shall we? As always here in the Museum of Baby Boomer Comics, don't worry about whether any of these scenarios have changed since the Silver Age ended. You're living on the planet Earth-Silver, a land where The Punisher and Wolverine won't ever exist. I know, I know, what a shame. Now dry your eyes and test your knowledge on these senses-shattering romantic questions. The answers are clear, so don't be slow. It's hip, hip, hip, and away we go:

POP QUIZ

1. Which of the following duos were among the horde of super-villains who attacked Sue Storm and Reed Richards during their wedding?
a. Magneto and Titanium Man.
b. Namor and The Hulk.
c. Attuma and The Human Top.
d. Paste Pot Pete and The Sonic Sponge.

2. Which identity did Daredevil decide he would use to propose to Karen Page?
a. Daredevil.
b. Matt Murdock.
c. Mike Murdock.
d. Pol Manning.

3. Where did Peter Parker first meet Mary Jane Watson?
a. At Anna Watson's house.
b. At Mary Jane's apartment.
c. At Aunt May's house.
d. On *The Dating Game*.

4. Why couldn't Dr. Don Blake (a.k.a. The Mighty Thor) marry nurse Jane Foster?
a. He was really a Norse god, not a human.
b. He was afraid his enemies would hurt her.
c. He didn't think she loved him as Blake.
d. He didn't think she'd like her brother-in-law.

Peter Parker must've kicked himself a few times for putting off meeting Mary Jane Watson for fear she was an unattractive wallflower — two words that never come up in describing MJ, as evidenced by *Amazing Spider-Man* #59. Where did he first meet MJ?

7. What did a lover of Marvel Comics have to do to be awarded the title Real Frantic One?
a. Win a no-prize.
b. Buy three Marvel comics a month.
c. Get a letter printed.
d. Return a page of Jack Kirby's artwork to him.

5. What initially attracted Henry Pym (a.k.a. Ant-Man) to Janet Van Dyne?
a. She was young and vivacious.
b. She was a research scientist like him.
c. She reminded him of his first wife.
d. She didn't mind having wings sprout out of her back.

6. Whom did Namor the Sub-Mariner marry?
a. Lady Dorma.
b. Llyra.
c. Namora.
d. Mera.

Face front, pilgrim! Look at the groovy goodies you could've received for joining Marvelmania International, as shown in its second catalog! Even if a lover of Marvel comics didn't join up, he could still be an R.F.O. How?

TRIVIA CHALLENGE I
Category: **JOBS**

What was the occupation of GUY GARDNER?

Answer on page 59

Answer from page 53
MYSTERY IN SPACE

ENTER: THE RELATIONSHIP!

ANSWERS

Reed and Sue finally got hitched after being attacked by just a few of Marvel's most awesome fiends in **Fantastic Four Annual #3**.

© 1965 Marvel

1. Which of the following duos were among the horde of super-villains who attacked Sue Storm and Reed Richards during their wedding?
Answer c: Attuma and the Human Top.

Talk about having a hectic day! Not only did Sue and Reed have to manage all the wedding details, take care of all their guests, and plan their honeymoon, but they had to fend off virtually every Marvel villain ever created! I'm not exaggerating—well, only a little, as is evident by the fact that a few of the pairs in the answers didn't join in on the fun. But virtually everyone else *except* those few showed up! It was the work of their good buddy Doctor Doom, who decided that the best revenge for not being invited to his college pal's big shindig would be to cause "Bedlam at the Baxter Building" in *Fantastic Four Annual #3* (1965).

Victor reasoned that a team of super-powered foes would be able to defeat The FF during the wedding, when their guard was down. But he wasn't happy gathering up a few past sore losers. No, he put together, as he called it, "a veritable army of the most deadly villains alive!" By skillfully manipulating his high-frequency emotion charger (just something he put together one weekend), he fanned the flames of hatred in the heart of every evil menace in existence. As if it really needed to be fanned. The result was one of the biggest free-for-alls you've ever seen in comics — and in only 23 pages to boot!

A short list of those disrupting things includes Puppet Master, The Red Ghost, Mole Man, Mandarin, Kang, Super Skrull, the hordes of Hydra, Cobra, Executioner, Enchantress, Mr. Hyde, Electro, Mad Thinker, and his Awesome Android, and, yes, The Human Top and Attuma. Whew!

Fortunately for Reed and Sue, a few of the good guys had been invited to the wing-ding, and they proved to be more than a match for the villains (as usual). For example, it took Quicksilver two panels to catch up to The Human Top and punch his lights out, while Attuma and his entire army were beaten by Daredevil.

Mister Silver Age Recommends...

Fantastic Four Annual Vol. 1 #3

Marvel
1965
Cover artist:
Jack Kirby, Mike Esposito

"Bedlam at the Baxter Building"
Writer: Stan Lee
Penciller: Jack Kirby
Inker: Vince Colletta

Then 25¢
Now $100

© 1965 Marvel

Reprints appear in...
• Fantastic Four Annual #9
• Fantastic Four Annual #10
• Marvel Masterworks #25

TRIVIA CHALLENGE I
Category: **JOBS**

What was PROFESSOR HALEY's job before he became a Challenger? Answer on page 60

Answer from page 54
SUGAR & SPIKE

Although this latter battle might seem to be a slight mismatch in favor of the villain, this time it wasn't. On the street outside the wedding, Daredevil took control of a truck onto which the hordes of Hydra had strapped a Vortex Bomb, with which they planned to blow up the Baxter Building. Daredevil and the truck careered through the city until they reached the docks. And there, "by the most dramatic coincidence of the year," as Stan himself admitted, Daredevil dropped the Vortex Bomb right onto Attuma's blue noggin.

Although Doctor Doom tried to get Namor and the Hulk involved, both were out of range of the emotion charger and much too busy in the pages of *Tales to Astonish* #72, in which they co-starred, to come to the wedding. At least, that's what Stan told us in his helpful footnote. I think Magneto and Titanium Man were off recording a Paul McCartney song that weekend. And it's a good thing Paste Pot Pete and the Sonic Sponge didn't show up, or all bets would've been off.

2. Which identity did Daredevil decide he would use to propose to Karen Page?
Answer b: Matt Murdock.

As if being a blind lawyer and a dashing super-hero weren't enough for one guy, Matt Murdock created yet another identity for himself. His swinging twin brother Mike lasted for 16 issues beginning in *Daredevil* #25 (Feb 67). During his stay, he developed into such a wild and crazy guy that DD couldn't decide which identity he liked better—and he obviously figured Karen couldn't decide either. What a testament to his own personality, honed for several decades!

It came to a head in "Unmasked!" in *DD* #29 (Jun 67), when The Man Without Fear decided it was time to pop the question. "Now the only thing left to decide," he said, "is — do I propose to her as Matt Murdock — or as my own 'twin brother', Mike?" Gee, Matt, that's a tough question: Propose to the love of your life as the man she works with every day or as a guy you fabricated for no sane reason. But maybe trying to explain that one will take her mind off the fact that she's marrying a blind guy who swings around the city in tights.

The Man Without Sense…er, I mean, Without Fear didn't make up his mind until he'd swung across town as DD, stopping on his way to say hi to Stan the Man. In the end, the decision was easier than expected: He'd left his loud Mike Murdock clothes back at the apartment, so he had to propose as Matt. In this case, clothes really did make the man. Of course, if Karen turned down Matt, he could always retrieve his Mike Murdock clothes and try again. Ditto for his Daredevil suit. Sooner or later, there had to be *some* identity she liked.

But before DD/Matt/Mike could propose in any identity, Karen was kidnapped so she could be used as bait to trap Daredevil. Ol' Hornhead saved her, of course, but he realized that she would be in constant danger if he married her, so he didn't. Where have we heard that one before? As with Superman, it apparently didn't occur to DD that the fact that he hadn't yet even proposed to Karen, much less married her, didn't seem to stop her from being kidnapped simply because she knew DD. Marrying Matt (or Mike) wasn't going to increase her chances in that regard. I think he was secretly breathing a sigh of relief.

Stan Lee got the brush-off again, this time from ol' Hornhead as he headed across town to propose to Karen Page in Daredevil #29.
© 1967 Marvel

Mister Silver Age Recommends...

Daredevil Vol. 1, #29

Marvel
Jun 1967
Cover artist:
Gene Colan, Frank Giacoia

"Unmasked!"
Writer: Stan Lee
Penciller: Gene Colan
Inker: John Tartaglione

Then 12¢
Now $34

© 1967 Marvel

TRIVIA CHALLENGE I
Category: **JOBS**

What was the name of **CARTER HALL'S** assistant, the museum naturalist? Answer on page 61

Answer from page 57
GYM TEACHER

ENTER: THE RELATIONSHIP!

The final answer, Pol Manning, was not a secret identity used by Daredevil, of course. What a ridiculous thought! No, Pol Manning was the second secret identity of Green Lantern. But that's another story altogether.

Mary Jane Watson comes out from behind that lampshade in **Amazing Spider-Man** *#42.*
© 1966 Marvel

3. Where did Peter Parker first meet Mary Jane Watson?
Answer a: At Anna Watson's house.

"Face it, tiger...you just hit the jackpot!" Has there ever been a more memorable entrance line for a character? That panel, the last one in *Amazing Spider-Man* #42 (Nov 66), remains one of the two most dramatic images I retain of Mary Jane. The other appeared as the final panel of *Amazing Spider-Man* #122 (Jul 73). There, interestingly enough, she didn't say anything at all: She just shut the door so she could console Peter, who was grief-stricken over the death of Gwen Stacy, his one true love (at least then).

That latter panel was the beginning of the long process of turning Mary Jane into a more interesting character, one worthy of being Peter Parker's sweetheart (and wife). The former panel was her introduction, the first time we saw her face after a long build-up. We caught our first view of MJ, *except* for her face (and hair, which was done up in a scarf), in *Amazing Spider-Man* #25 (Jun 65). She was the niece of Aunt May's next-door neighbor and co-bon vivant, Anna Watson.

Peter, alas, didn't meet her then. Mary Jane had stopped by to see him when he was out — as had Betty Brant and Liz Allan. Although MJ's face was hidden from us, Peter's two gal pals could see it clearly, and they were stunned by MJ's beauty. Of course, we just had to take their word for it, but the repercussions of that little get-together showed up in the next issue, to Peter's detriment. It then took until #42 for the mystery of MJ's appearance to be revealed. That first face-to-face pow-wow between our future lovebirds finally occurred on a sunny Sunday, when Peter had no excuse not to accompany Aunt May to dinner at Mrs. Watson's house.

"Aunt May managed to out-maneuver me at last!" he sighed, tying his tie. "Oh well...I guess I might as well meet her and get it over with! She may not be as bad as I expect! She'll probably be worse!" MJ had her own apartment, so she didn't show up at her aunt's house until after the Parkers had arrived. So there was Peter, sitting on the couch daydreaming about whether Gwen liked him or not, when the doorbell rang.

"Peter Parker," Mrs. Watson said, "I'd like you to meet my niece..." "You mean," Peter sputtered, "That's Mary Jane?!!" And there she was, surrounded by comic-book speed lines and drawn by that new guy on the book, John Romita, who had taken over with issue #39, just in time to use his well-honed ability to draw gorgeous babes.

Mister Silver Age Recommends...

Amazing Spider-Man Vol. 1, #42

Marvel
Nov 1966

Cover artist:
John Romita

"The Birth of a Super-Hero!"
Writer: Stan Lee
Penciller: John Romita
Inker: John Romita

Then 12¢
Now $150

© 1965 Marvel

Reprints appear in...
• Marvel Tales #31
• Marvel Tales #182
• Marvel Treasury Edition #1
• Marvel Masterworks #22
• Essential Spider-Man #2

TRIVIA CHALLENGE I
Category: **JOBS**

What was the job of the RED SKULL before he became the Red Skull? Answer on page 62

Answer from page 58
OCEANOGRAPHER

60

BABY BOOMER COMICS

Ironically, Romita says that he and Stan had considered making MJ unattractive, but, at the last minute, they decided she should be pretty. It was a good thing, or we would have had to wonder about Liz and Betty's standard of beauty — and it would have changed the dynamic of the Spider-Man series from then on.

*Thor took his intended home to meet The All-Father in **Thor** #136, a meet-the-parents trip that didn't work out well.*
© 1966 Marvel

4. Why couldn't Dr. Don Blake (a.k.a. The Mighty Thor) marry Jane?
Answer a: He was really a Norse god, not a human.

When fans read those early issues of *Journey into Mystery* for the first time, they're often struck by one amazing fact: Dr. Blake sure got into the swing of hanging out in Asgard pretty quickly. He knew all about Loki, he called Odin "father," the whole bit. Yet this was a guy who, until he stamped that gnarled stick on the ground, was just a little scrawny doctor! What gives?

The answer at last was revealed by Stan and Jack in "The Answer at Last!" in *Thor* #159 (Dec 68). Many years earlier, Thor had been a young, headstrong god of thunder. You know the type: cocky, powerful, feeling his immortality. He got into brawls with other gods, trespassed in far-off Niffelheim where the storm giants lived, and had big parties that woke the neighbors when Odin was gone for the weekend. Typical stuff.

Finally, Odin had had enow, as Odin tended to say. He decreed that Thor was lacking in humility and banished him to Earth. Odin wiped away Thor's memory, turned him into Don Blake, and made him appear at the State College of Medicine, ready for his first day of school. When The God of Thunder had studied hard, earned his degree, and learned some humility, Odin let him find the stick in the cave and get back to doing godlike things.

"Then that was why my marriage to Jane Foster could never be!" Dr. Blake said, as Odin finished the tale. "That was why I could never renounce my godly heritage!" I yam, in other words, what I yam.

> **"Going home to 'meet the folks' means something different when you're dating a Norse God."**

5. What initially attracted Henry Pym (a.k.a. Ant-Man) to Janet Van Dyne?
Answer c: She reminded him of his first wife.

Hank has had neither a smooth super-hero career nor love life. He's had a series of super identities, even more costumes, and two wives. Janet, you see, was his second wife, as was explained in *Tales to Astonish* #44 (Jun 63).

He wasn't married to his first wife for long, since Maria Trovaya was killed during their honeymoon. Maria and her father had escaped the dirty Commies and fled to America, where she met and married Hank. On their return to Hungary for their honeymoon, she was kidnapped. Her body later was found with a note attached to it saying that this was what happened to those who attempted to escape from behind the Iron Curtain. I *told* you they were dirty Commies. They always were in Marvel Comics.

Distraught, Henry remembered Maria telling him he should be more industrious, like the ant. So he worked night and day to create a formula that let him become an ant! Too bad she hadn't told him to fly like an eagle or roar like a lion or something. At least a bat didn't fly in his window.

In any event, soon after becoming Ant-Man, he met Dr. Vernon Van Dyne, who failed to interest Hank in a project he was working on. He also was unable to

*Henry Pym decided that Janet Van Dyne was just the kind of woman he wanted to have join him in his super-doing in **Tales To Astonish** #44.*
© 1963 Marvel

TRIVIA CHALLENGE I
Category: REAL NAMES | What did the initials stand for in A.I.M.? | Answer on page 63 | Answer from page 59
MAVIS TRENT

ENTER: THE RELATIONSHIP!

Cheap Wedding Albums

Here's where to relive these sentimental moments without coughing up the bucks for the real deal:

- *Amazing Spider-Man* #25 was reprinted in *Marvel Tales* #20 and #159, *Essential Spider-Man* #2, and *Marvel Masterworks* #10.
- *Amazing Spider-Man* #42 was reprinted in *Marvel Tales* #31 and #182, *Essential Spider-Man* #2, and *Marvel Masterworks* #22.
- *Amazing Spider-Man* #122 was reprinted in *Marvel Tales* #99.
- *Thor* #159 was reprinted in *Thor* #254 and 1987's *Best of Marvel Comics* collection.
- *Tales to Astonish* #44 was reprinted in *The Superhero Women* trade paperback collection, while #44 and #56 were reprinted in *Essential Ant-Man* #1.
- *Avengers* #59 was reprinted in *Marvel Super Action* #59 and the *Avengers British Annual*.

*Namor finally put on his marrying duds to commit matrimony in **Sub-Mariner** #36, but things didn't go as smoothly as he'd hoped.*

© 1971 Marvel

rouse much interest in Hank for his daughter, Janet, who had tagged along. "She...she looks somewhat like Maria!" Hank thought. "But she's much younger! Not much more than a child." The lack of strong attraction was mutual. "Hmmmm, he's quite handsome," Jan thought. "But scientists are such bores! I prefer the adventurous type, not those dull, intellectual bookworms!"

To make a long story short, Dr. Van Dyne got himself murdered, Janet vowed revenge, her beauty and determination reminded Ant-Man of those qualities in his late wife, and so Hank offered her the chance to join him in his battle against evil-doers as a little teeny-tiny bug known as The Wasp. By the end of the adventure, of course, they were in love with each other. And also, of course, this being a Marvel mag, they were afraid to express their true feelings to each other. So they spent a lot of time over the course of their adventures ruing the fact that the other didn't return the love they felt so strongly. What a bunch of maroons.

It may have been this romantic frustration that kept Hank experimenting. Not content to be a teeny-tiny adventurer, he soon created capsules that let him grow to giant size in addition to shrinking down to ant size. So Ant-Man became Giant-Man. And, when that name started grating on his nerves, he became Goliath and stopped shrinking down to itty-bitty size.

Hank's love life actually improved before his super-hero life settled down. In *Tales to Astonish* #56 (Jun 64), Hank bought an engagement ring for Janet. But before he could give it to her, she told him she was going to a party with her society friends. She was only doing it to get him jealous, but Hank, as always, figured otherwise. She liked to adventure with him, he decided, "but when it comes to romance, she wants someone as wealthy as she!" So he threw the ring away.

At the end of the story, though, Jan thought Hank had died, and she loudly bemoaned the loss of the only man she had ever loved. Hank, who naturally wasn't dead, overheard and professed his own love. "Now I know there can never be anyone else for me!" Janet said, throwing herself into his arms. "There never will be, Jan!" Hank replied. "I promise you that!"

So imagine everyone's surprise in *Avengers* #59 (Dec 68) when Janet agreed to marry the obnoxious Yellowjacket! Especially when Yellowjacket claimed he'd killed Hank Pym! But that's another story altogether.

6. Whom did Namor marry?
Answer a: Lady Dorma.

But it was a close one! And, sadly, it didn't last long. Lady Dorma was a playmate of Namor's during his childhood in Atlantis and grew up alongside him. She was but one of many females vying for the Sub-Mariner's heart, even as Subby set his cap for Sue Storm.

Female jealousy and desire to attract Namor's attention got Subby into a lot of trouble through the years. In *The Incredible Hulk* #118 (Aug 69), for instance, Lady Dorma found Bruce Banner floating in the sea after The Hulk had stopped The Leader one more time (long story). She took him to Atlantis to recover, where Mistress Fara saw her return. Fara was jealous of the attention Namor showed to Lady Dorma, so she told Namor that Dorma had brought a

TRIVIA CHALLENGE I
Category: **REAL NAMES** What was the real first name of PEPPER POTTS? Answer on page 64 Answer from page 60 **HOTEL BELLBOY**

62 BABY BOOMER COMICS

surface-dweller to Atlantis to plot his downfall.

The bad-tempered (not to mention gullible) Namor broke into Dorma's room, where his accusations roused the sleeping Banner next door. Bruce became excited, transformed into The Hulk, and all heck broke loose. Lady Dorma was knocked unconscious while the two future Defenders battled, and Fara snuck up to kill Dorma so she could have Namor for herself. But just then, a nearby wall collapsed on Fara, killing her, and her body cushioned Dorma from the same deadly fate. What a cruel twist of fate!

Jealousy also brought about the sad consequences of Namor's wedding to Lady Dorma, which took place in *Sub-Mariner* #36 (Apr 71). It's a little past the Silver Age in my book, but it was a rousing tale, anyway — despite the sad fact that it wasn't attended by any of those surface-dwelling super-heroes who always make these events such crowd-pleasers.

No sooner had the marriage taken place than Lady Dorma changed shape to reveal she actually was Llyra, the former empress of Lemuria! She had kidnapped Dorma and taken Namor's queen-to-be to her hideout and now claimed to be queen of Atlantis instead! And, unless Namor acknowledged her claim, Dorma would be killed! After a few pages of taunts and chases, it was revealed that, since Dorma had earlier been the one to take the vow of fealty and have her name inscribed on the scroll of sovereigns, she actually was Namor's wife, no matter who was standing next to him during the ceremony.

I wonder what a lawyer would say about that one? He'd probably say the same thing he would say about the legality of Janet's marriage to Yellowjacket, a man who had no idea what his real name was. (It was, in fact, Hank Pym, suffering from amnesia. Long story.) But, since I'm not a lawyer, I won't try to guess what that would be. In any event, Llyra vowed to kill Dorma as soon as she returned to evil-doer headquarters, so the chase was on. Namor tracked her down, but it was too late. Llyra smashed the water cage imprisoning The Sub-Mariner's mate, exposing her to life-taking oxygen. And Lady Dorma died moments later in Namor's arms.

Scoring:

7: Excellent! If you weren't an F.F.F., you certainly merited one, effendi! Such devotion deserves a reward! (Just don't give your answer sheet to Mr. Silver Age looking for one — 'nuff said!)

5-6: Pretty darn good! It's obvious you weren't skipping over all the mushy stuff just to read those pulse-pounding, sense-shattering battle scenes!

2-4: Less than good! OK, so you thought all that boy/girl junk got in the way of a good action story! Maybe you ought to take another look now, since your attitude may have changed since that first reading.

0-1: Not good at all! Hey, if you had wanted to read icky love comics when you were a kid, you'd have been buying back issues of *Wedding Bells*! Besides, you were probably saving up to join F.O.O.M., right?

7. What did a lover of Marvel Comics have to do to be awarded the title Real Frantic One?
Answer b: Buy three Marvel comics a month.

What price love — for a Marvel fan? Well, For those of us who didn't have the shekels to spring for membership in the Merry Marvel Marching Society (M.M.M.S.), Marvelmania International, or Friends Of Ol' Marvel (F.O.O.M.) — or who just got tired of these guys starting up a new fan club every few years — there was still hope.

Beginning in 1967, Stan and the gang adopted the six levels of Marvel fandom originally suggested by fan Mark Evanier, who later gained even more impressive credits as a comics pro, if you can imagine anything more impressive. The final group of options from his suggestions were posted at the bottom of letters pages for many months:

"Know ye these, the hallowed ranks of Marveldom," the headline proclaimed. Beneath were listed the six rankings: "Real Frantic One (R.F.O.), a buyer of at least three Marvel mags a month; Titanic True Believer (T.T.B.), a divinely-inspired 'No-Prize' winner; Quite 'Nuff Sayer (Q.N.S.), a fortunate frantic one who's had a letter printed. Keeper of the Flame (K.O.F.), one who recruits a newcomer to Marvel's rollickin' ranks; Permanent Marvelite Maximus (P.M.M.), anyone possessing all four of the other titles; Fearless Front Facer (F.F.F.), an honorary title bestowed for devotion to Marvel above and beyond the call of duty."

A number of letter writers tacked on their hard-earned initials after their names, and all had a good time with the ranks. They stopped appearing in early 1973, just about the time Marvel introduced F.O.O.M. Since Marvel never revoked our standings, I imagine there are quite a few R.F.O.s still running around out there, and probably a lot of K.O.F.s, too — or at least guys who claim to be K.O.F.s. I don't remember anyone ever being honored with an F.F.F., but there probably was.

TRIVIA CHALLENGE I
Category: REAL NAMES What was the real name of the Blackhawks' LEAPER? Answer on page 65 Answer from page 61 ADVANCED IDEA MECHANICS

ENTER: THE RELATIONSHIP!

Getting Personal: DC's Silver Age Team-Ups

"Mr. Silver Age, super-heroes always seemed to fight each other during their team-ups. Did they *ever* get along well?"

There admittedly was a standard ploy, used more at Marvel than DC back in The Silver Age: Heroes meet and have a misunderstanding that makes each of them think the other is an outlaw, mind-controlled or obstructing the true course of justice. This resulted in mayhem until the confusion was straightened out and the two went on to accomplish their goal—unless, of course, their goal for the issue had been to brawl with each other. In that case, mission accomplished!

On one level, Marvel's creators were giving fans what they wanted. Some readers were obsessed with who would win in any match-up, despite the obvious fact that the *title character* was going to win, even when Millie the Model went up against the guest-starring Hulk (and I would've bought that issue of *Millie* in a heartbeat). At the same time, typing up a plot that says, "The Hulk guest-stars in *Millie* and they fight" *(see sidebar at left)* sure saved a lot of time in the plot-writing department, keeping the issue on schedule.

DC seldom took that approach, if only because its heroes were all upstanding and valiant through and through. Oh, sure, there was the occasional mind-controlling brouhaha, but DC's editors tended to prefer to show how the heroes could fit together, comparing and contrasting powers to solve some puzzle or defeat a villain with this issue's Science Fact of the Month. As a result, team-ups in DC's comics could be a real special event.

I'm not talking about the everyday team-up of Superman and Batman in *World's Finest* or the contrived Batman soirees in *The Brave and the Bold*. Nor do I mean the one-shot appearance of some JLAer or another just to add some variety to a story. I'm talking about team-ups between heroes who hit it off together — guys who teamed up often, as if it were the natural thing to do.

In the best ones, the heroes not only interacted as righters of wrongs and protectors of Earth, but as guys out to have some fun together. They would change into their alter egos only when trouble arose (but it always did). These team-ups made the heroes seem more human and gave us a quick glimpse into their lives beyond their super-powers. Even better, they made it clear that our heroes really *did* have lives besides being costumed cut-ups — we just didn't get to see as much of them as we might like. Even in those rare instances in which the plot wasn't up to the occasion, you still put down the book having learned a little bit more about what made these guys tick.

There were several such team-ups running through those early years of DC's new wave of super-heroes. They gave us a chance to see what happened when friends got together for a few brews before going off to foil the occasional alien invasion...

© 1970 National Periodical Publications (DC)

Why they fight

DC heroes tended to cooperate, right off the bat.

Why, then, was it so easy to manuever two Marvel super-heroes into a battle against each other?

This was made relatively easy because so many Marvel characters were misunderstood. Some were considered at worst outlaws and at best a bit shady, so the chance that a true hero would have to battle one of these guys made for a plausible situation.

Well, at least it was plausible to kids who wanted to see two heroes whale the tar out of each other. And, when that didn't work, villains were always finding new ways to mind-control a hero to take on another.

TRIVIA CHALLENGE I
Category: **REAL NAMES**   What was the real name of TITANO?   Answer on page 66   Answer from page 64 VIRGINIA

64   BABY BOOMER COMICS

Flash & Green Lantern

This was a natural team-up. They were, after all, the first two super-heroes to be resurrected by Julius Schwartz during the Silver Age, and they both had John Broome writing some of their stories. Their personalities also fit together. Both were bachelors with long-time girlfriends who played key roles in their series — unlike Lois Lane and Vicki Vale, who, let's face it, were plot devices that changed personalities according to the author's needs that month.

Barry Allen and Hal Jordan both had scientific bents, holding jobs as, respectively, a police scientist and a test pilot (at least at first). Hey, they were Schwartz characters — what did you expect, something low-class like being a reporter or millionaire? They also meshed well as a visual: The Flash ran along in a streak of red on the ground, while GL flew overhead in a flash of green. It was a natural (especially at Christmastime).

They first teamed up in *Green Lantern* #13 (Jun 62) during the "Duel of the Super-Heroes." Incorporating that long-since-forgotten motif of meeting in their civilian identities before trouble broke out, they didn't appear as super-heroes until page 12, nearly halfway through the adventure! Instead, they were introduced as Barry and Hal. They had accompanied their main squeezes, Iris West and Carol Ferris, to a seashore resort.

The meeting wasn't a coincidence, although the fact that they both had secret identities was. Barry and Iris were on vacation on the West Coast, during which Iris had agreed to interview "the famous test pilot" Hal Jordan for her magazine, *The Picture News*. They arranged to meet at the Sea Palace resort, where Hal took Carol for the weekend (with separate rooms, no doubt, since she was only *possibly* his girlfriend but *definitely* his boss). They were accompanied by Hal's friend Thomas Kalmaku and his wife, Terga (who actually *could* share the room bill).

The get-together didn't go smoothly, however, since Hal was edgy. The only time he perked up was when Barry mentioned his hometown of Central City, because Hal knew The Flash also lived there. Hal's intensity over this trivia fact surprised Barry. "Hmmm!" The Flash thought, "I'm beginning to think this Hal Jordan is an odd one!" Hal's strange actions were noticed by Tom, too. He finally pulled Barry aside to express his concern, and they agreed to keep an eye on their buddy.

Barry and Hal prepared to face off in an archery match while Iris, Carol, and Tom cheered them on during yet another of the group's get-togethers, this time before the heroes become "Captives of the Cosmic Ray!" in **The Flash** *#131.*

Mister Silver Age Recommends...

Green Lantern (2nd series) #13

DC
Jun 1962
Cover artists:
Gil Kane, Joe Giella

"The Duel of the Super-Heroes"
Writer: John Broome
Penciller: Gil Kane
Inker: Joe Giella

Then **12¢**
Now **$185**

Reprints appear in...
• Flash #232
• Green Lantern Archives Vol. 1

TRIVIA CHALLENGE I
Category: LAST WORDS — Whose last words were, "I'm coming, Dinah!" — Answer on page 67

Answer from page 63
OLAF

ENTER: THE RELATIONSHIP!

PIEFACE, HAL AND I ARE NOW READY TO DECIDE WHICH OF US IS THE *SPORTS CHAMPION* OF THIS WEEK-END!

GREAT! I'VE GOT THE TARGET ALL SET UP!

56

IT'S EXACTLY EVEN BETWEEN THEM SO FAR, ISN'T IT, THOMAS?

YES, CAROL! BARRY HAS BEATEN HAL IN TENNIS AND SWIMMING...

There was good reason for Hal's quirky behavior, of course. Before the couples met, aliens had hypnotized him into capturing The Flash for them so they could use The Scarlet Speedster to help them invade Earth. Nice trick if you can pull it off. It'd be a better trick if they had picked a super-hero who actually would accomplish this task rather than going on vacation thousands of miles from the hero's stomping grounds, but space aliens probably can't be that choosy.

The next day, Barry followed Hal and watched as he changed to GL to call his alien masters, no doubt reporting on his failure to have The Flash run past him while he was sitting by the pool, darn the luck. Barry couldn't hear what he was saying, though, so he changed to The Flash to help out — and as soon as he did, GL tried to capture him. So Hal's brilliant strategy worked out after all!

Now, I realize that this plot is beginning to sound like a slight variation on the "super-heroes are mind-controlled and fight each other" storyline I touted as a Marvel specialty. But it wasn't like that, really. Yes, the two were on opposite sides. Yes, one had been brainwashed into being a villain so they could fight. But, no, it wasn't a hero slugfest for two reasons. First, the fight wasn't the story's main plot. Second, it wasn't your typical super-hero punchout — because not one punch was thrown!

As The Flash raced in, GL tried to trap him in a power-ring net; The Scarlet Speedster evaded it and zig-zagged off at super-speed. As GL chased after him, The Flash spun up a whirlwind to hide from the Emerald Gladiator; GL countered it. The Flash changed to Barry Allen; GL created a mirage of a huge tidal wave to draw The Flash out; Flash discovered he'd been tricked and used a yellow beach umbrella to flash away.

Realizing they had a stalemate going, The Flash allowed GL to trap him so he could figure out what was going on. And so we got our cover scene, showing GL distorting The Flash's body so he was top-heavy and couldn't run. What a cunning plan! (Hey, if I'm lying, I'm buying! Back then, it seemed to be a favorite theme to distort The Flash's body as often as possible. Kind of like that fascination DC had with incredibly intelligent gorillas and bodiless uniforms. But that's another story.)

Allowing GL to capture him turned out to be a real stupid thing for The Flash to do. That wasn't because he'd have to go through life with a gigantic forehead but because The Scarlet Speedster couldn't escape the aliens, and they learned everything they needed to know from him about his powers so they could invade Earth. Oops.

Needless to say, it took some pretty exciting adventuring on the parts of both heroes to keep the aliens from taking over our planet, but they did. Afterwards, Flash admitted that he saw GL changing identities. In return, Barry revealed his identity. What a guy! As if GL couldn't have just used his ring to look under Flash's mask on his own. Then the buds went back to their vacation, becoming the first two JLAers (besides Superman and Batman, natch) to know another member's identity.

Julie had big things in mind for his two heroes from the start, for the story ended with a plea to the readers. "This is the first of a proposed series of stories featuring Green Lantern and The Flash working as a team!" we were told. "If you would like to see more of this dynamic duo in action, let us know!" They next met only three months later in "The Captives of the Cosmic

TRIVIA CHALLENGE I
Category: LAST WORDS — Whose last words were, "I'll be lonely no more. For I'm going to join my beloved Mary." Answer on page 68 — Answer from page 64 **TOTO THE CHIMP**

66 — BABY BOOMER COMICS

Ray" in *The Flash* #131 (Sep 62). That's probably a little too quick for Julie to actually have heard from any of those readers he purportedly wanted to hear from and commission a story based on the feedback, but let's not split hairs.

In addition to *The Flash* #131, these team-ups appeared in issues #143, #168 and #191. Flash's guest-appearances in *Green Lantern* occurred in issues #13, #20, and #43.

Good examples of how these team-ups brought out the personal side of our heroes can be seen in "Captives of the Cosmic Ray" in *The Flash* #131 (Sep 62) and "Catastrophic Crimes of Major Disaster" in *Green Lantern* #43 (Apr 66). In both, as in their first meeting, the two were spending time together hanging out as Barry and Hal when all heck broke loose.

In "Captives," our heroes were sitting in the park discussing people who knew their secret identities. (It wasn't a long list.) Then they strolled to a department store to buy arrows, because they were in the middle of a contest to see who could win the most sporting events. Barry had won tennis and swimming, while Hal had claimed golf and billiards. Archery was the final event. Each wanted nothing more than to beat the other, and Carol, Iris, and Thomas were watching avidly to see which of these competitors would take the final prize win.

Just then, an alien space ship landed, and mayhem ensued. When the adventure concluded — am I giving away a big surprise if I mention that the aliens didn't take over Earth this time, either? — Barry and Hal returned to their contest. Only now, they both shot so badly that neither could even hit the target!

"Can't call either of us the winner, Hal!" Barry said, clapping Hal on the shoulder. "I guess our sports contest ended in a tie!" "Suits me, Barry," Hal replied. "I don't get it," Carol mused. "It's as if they suddenly became so friendly toward each other that each was trying to let the other win!" What a couple of pals!

In "Catastrophic Crimes," the story opened with Carol telling Hal they were going on a trip. Hal was thrilled, because Carol called him "darling," a name she had reserved in the past only for Green Lantern. But that was the trouble: Carol had received a sheaf of papers outlining details of GL's life — who he was, where he kept his power battery, the words to his oath, and on and on. Maybe she found a copy of *Showcase* #22. Whatever it was, Hal was thunderstruck. In Central City, the same scenario was playing out between Iris and Barry. She knew about the costume, the ring, the whole shooting match.

Our heroes flew/ran their dates to a fashionable club in Pineaire City, wherever that is, where they apparently were planning to meet that evening despite living half a continent apart. Iris and Carol told each other what they'd learned (bigmouths), as Flash and Green Lantern stood by dumbfounded. Then the heroes went off to lunch — as Flash and Green Lantern.

Now, GL occasionally had had dates with Carol — in fact, he more or less had one with her in his first appearance in the aforementioned *Showcase* #22 (Oct 59). But I doubt that two heroes double-dated for lunch

Facing page and this page: There was more calm before the storm hit Hal and Barry in "Captives of the Cosmic Ray!" in **The Flash** *#131.*

TRIVIA CHALLENGE I
Category: **LAST WORDS** Whose last words were, "Fire away!" Answer on page 69 Answer from page 65 **LARRY LANCE**

ENTER: THE RELATIONSHIP! **67**

before or since in their costumed identities! Unfortunately, before they could even order, all heck broke loose again.

But in this case, we cared less about heck being loose and more about what was going to happen in the relationship between our heroes and their main squeezes. And we got our money's worth here. For instance, there was a great scene about halfway through, after GL and Flash lost their powers (long story). Discovering this fact, Iris said, "I don't care — really! It's the man I love — not the uniform!" Just to rub it in a little more, she added, "Actually, I never loved Flash at all! It's Barry Allen I love — and I still do!"

This little speech put Carol in something of a bind. After all, she had always loved GL, not Hal, no matter how Hal tried to convince her otherwise — even though they were the same person without that mask and the form-fitting uniform. "Hmmm!" she finally replied. "It's true I loved Green Lantern, but now that I know you are Green Lantern, Hal — I love you just as much as when you had your powers!" What a trouper.

What do you do when the woman you love discovers your most closely guarded secret? The Flash and Green Lantern decided to get a bite to eat before having to face the "Catastrophic Crimes of Major Disaster!" in **Green Lantern** *#43.*

© 1966 National Periodical Publications (DC)

To cut to the chase, GL and Flash regained their powers, discovered the slipshod way GL had given away both dual identities, and battled Major Disaster. (Hey, it was a novel-length adventure!). Then they faced their *real* dilemma — what to do about Iris and Carol knowing their identities. Heck, we certainly couldn't allow the two women we hoped to marry someday to be entrusted with the kind of knowledge that might help them make that decision and that also might make our double-identity lives a whole lot easier, could we, guys? After all, girls are icky, slimy blabbermouths! So let's power-ring that information right out of their brains, like the way we always do in these situations! Do it!

The only drawback to this cunning plan was that, well, GL was just too darn *bored* with using his mighty ring to solve this continual problems! "I hate to use that corny routine of power-ringing them to forget our secret identities," he told Flash. "Even I'm getting tired of that! I'd like to pull off something different..." Ah, the troubles of the all-powerful.

No, he didn't try kissing Iris and Carol to see if that would make the girls forget their secrets. You can get away with that only in a big-budget super-hero movie sequels. But I'm not going to tell what he *did* do, either, because that would spoil the ending — and these comics actually had endings! Right there in the same issue where the story started! And I can't think of a better reason to buy a Silver Age comic books than to find out how it ends.

Even with these occasional lapses into DC's patented let's-treat-our-loved-ones-like-dirt school of plotting, these meetings solidified Flash and GL's position as buddies as well as colleagues in the readers' minds — or, at least, in *this* reader's mind.

Allies in Avocado

Another regular Green Lantern partner, of course, was Green Arrow, who co-starred in *Green Lantern/Green Arrow.* But in the first place, it wasn't really a team-up, since they both starred in the book each issue. Second, it didn't begin until The Silver Age was ending, according to my calculations. Third, with all the reprintings that have been done of *GL/GA* #76-89, you can easily check out those stories yourself without my telling you what a great team-up they made.

Green Lantern and Green Arrow had one of their occasional heart-to-heart talks to discuss current affairs and their role in society, this one while learning "Ulysses Star Is Still Alive!" in **Green Lantern & Green Arrow** *#79.*

© 1970 National Periodical Publications (DC)

TRIVIA CHALLENGE I
Category: **LAST WORDS**   Whose last words were, "Run, girls, run!"   Answer on page 70

Answer from page 66
FRANKLIN STORM

Atom & Hawkman

This may be surprising, but I found this team-up to be a natural too. The Atom, of course, is the World's Smallest Super-Hero. Hawkman, by the same token, is one of the biggest — at least, when you include his wings and winged helmet.

This combination of mini and maxi wasn't all they had going for them, of course. These two not only had scientific backgrounds, but they had academic interests, too. Ray Palmer was a research scientist at Ivy Town University, while Carter Hall was curator of The Midway City Museum.

They both had strong female support. Carter (Katar Hol) was married to Shiera (Shayera Hol), who saved his bacon whenever needed as Hawkgirl. And lawyer Jean Loring spent a considerable amount of her time fending off Ray Palmer's insistent marriage proposals (before finally giving in during the 1970s). In addition, they were both major babes.

These mutual interests created natural motivation to bring them together. An additional one, no doubt, was writer Gardner Fox, who provided the early team-up stories in both heroes' books (as well as some Flash/Green Lantern stories, too). Carter and Ray spent more time in costume than did Barry and Hal, no doubt at least in part because their size differences made for more interesting visuals than two guys in suits.

Hawkman and Atom first met in "The Case of the Cosmic Camera" in *The Atom* #7 (Jun-Jul 63), just one year after Barry and Hal teamed up. The impetus was the same as the one often used in today's comics: a disruption in the migratory paths of birds.

Ray Palmer and Carter Hall knew each other in their civilian identities, so why should masks separate them as heroes? Once they'd revealed their secrets and handled the "Master Trap of The Matter Master!" they all went out to dinner in **Hawkman** *#9.*

Mister Silver Age Recommends...

The Atom #7

DC
Jun 1963
Cover artist:
Murphy Anderson, Gil Kane

"The Case of the Cosmic Camera"
Writer: Gardner Fox
Penciller: Murphy Anderson
Inker: Gil Kane

Then 12¢
Now $125

Reprints appear in...
• Atom Archives Vol. 1

© 1963 National Periodical Publications, Inc. (DC)

TRIVIA CHALLENGE I
Category: TITLES
Who was introduced in the story "The Girl from Superman's Past?" Answer on page 71

Answer from page 67
DOOM PATROL

ENTER: THE RELATIONSHIP!

69

GOOD MAN BAD MAN--TURNABOUT THIEF! PART 2

NEXT DAY, AS THE CARTER HALLS SHARE A BEACH PICNIC WITH RAY PALMER AND HIS FIANCÉE JEAN LORING...

mmmm, THOSE LOBSTERS AND CLAMS SMELL GOOD!

HONEY, WHY DON'T YOU AND JEAN TAKE A DIP NOW? RAY AND I WILL WATCH THE FOOD!

THIS'LL GIVE ME A CHANCE TO TELL RAY ABOUT THE STRANGE OCCURRENCE IN THAT BARN LAST NIGHT!

Ray and Carter were each anxious to ask the other about a mystery they'd become involved in, but they promised Jean and Shiera they wouldn't talk shop during a beach picnic in "Good Man, Bad Man, Turnabout Thief!" in **The Atom** *#31...*

Only in comics could birdwatching lead a detective to discover an alien invasion.

Mister Silver Age Recommends...

Hawkman Vol. 1, #9

DC Comics
Aug-Sep 1965

Cover artist:
Murphy Anderson

"Master Trap of The Matter Master"
Writer: Gardner Fox
Penciller: Murphy Anderson
Inker: Murphy Anderson

Then 12¢
Now $65

No, honest, that was the cause. Ray and Jean were out birdwatching and noticed a number of bird species overhead that shouldn't have been there. Many miles away, Hawkman noticed the same thing, as well he should, but none of his bird buddies could explain (wheet! wheet!) why they were doing what they were doing.

While tracking down the answers, The Atom became stranded at sea and tried to ride the air currents home. Hawkman, also working the case, scooped him out of the air, showing that he possessed the eyes of a hawk as well as the wings. "Hawkman!" Atom exclaimed. "I recognize you from pictures I've seen in the papers!" As if the hawk mask and wings wouldn't have clued him in. They swapped stories and worked together to keep the aliens from conquering Earth. (You knew it was going to be aliens trying to conquer Earth, didn't you?)

When the dust settled, Jean and Ray returned to birdwatching, only to meet up with Carter and Shiera, who asked to join them. "Shayera," Carter said, using the Thanagarian spelling of his wife's name in his word balloon right there in front of Ray and Jean. "There's something familiar about that fellow Ray Palmer! Whatever it is — I like him!"

Their new buds felt likewise. "They're a nice couple, Ray," said Jean. "Yes, they are," Ray agreed. "I'm glad they came along! I've a feeling we will be seeing a lot of each other in the days to come!"

I don't know that the operative word was "days," since their next meeting came two years later in "Master Trap of The Matter Master" in *Hawkman* #9 (Aug-Sep 65). In that adventure, the Hawks were shrunk down to teeny-tiny size before defeating The Matter Master, and they needed The Atom's help to regain their regular size. The Atom took them to Ray Palmer's lab and did the deed.

The Hawks, being trained police officers and all, deduced the reason that The Atom was so familiar with Ray's lab. Ray revealed his identity, and they followed suit. "Now that we're all together again," Shiera suggested, "why not call up Jean and have dinner with us? Jean and I have a lot of girl-talk to catch up on!"

Here's hoping that girl-talk didn't include too many super-heroics, considering Jean was the one of the quartet still in the dark about that secret identity thing.

TRIVIA CHALLENGE I
Category: **TITLES**

What story saw a **THING** impersonator sacrifice his life to save Reed? Answer on page 72

Answer from page 68
TRIPLICATE GIRL

70

BABY BOOMER COMICS

They waited yet another two years before teaming up again, this time for a beach picnic in "Good Man, Bad Man, Turnabout Thief" in *The Atom* #31 (Jun-Jul 67). On this occasion, Ray tried to help his lab's cleaning lady by finding her son — who turned out to be the leader of a gang Hawkman was chasing down. The gang leader suddenly became remorseful, saved Carter's life, and vowed to become a good guy. But of course he didn't. Or did he?

Ray and Carter happened to discuss their own side of the perplexing case during a day at the beach with their honeys. They discovered they were talking about the same guy and they headed off together on another rousing adventure.

The next year, Hawkman supplied some professional advice to The Atom, when they both got to "Meet Major Minah!" in *The Atom* #37 (Jun-Jul 68). After Ray returned from an archeological dig in Cambodia with a pet mynah bird (don't ask), he took it to Carter because the bird's wings weren't healing well after battling Viet Minh invaders in Cambodia (don't ask, again).

Our boys changed to their super identities and flew to Hawkman's spaceship, where he outfitted Major with special wings made of a Thanagarian material that would make him fly really fast. But he also warned The Atom that Major knew his secret identity, and his ability to talk could get them into trouble. Oh, you just know where this is going, once Major meets Jean Loring, don't you?

The Powers That Be decided our two heroes got along so well that, when Hawkman's mag was cancelled with #27 (Aug-Sep 68), it was merged into The Atom's book, which became *The Atom & Hawkman* with #39 (Oct-Nov 68). You would think this would have afforded them the opportunity to hang out together all the time, or at least on a bi-monthly basis.

The sad truth, however, is that our heroes appeared together only in three of the seven issues that remained in the series.

Ray and Carter played only minor roles in these adventures, but they were still fun guys. The opening scene of "When Gods Make Madness" in #42 (Apr-May 69), for instance, showed the two walking down the street, with Ray complaining to a sympathetic Carter that "those old fossils" at the science convention wouldn't listen to his newest theory.

But by this point, the emphasis was on plot and adventure, not on seeing Ray and Carter hang out. (In fact, #42 reversed the colors of Ray and Carter's hair, so it's probably just as well we didn't see much of them without their hero hoods on.)

The Atom and Hawkman weren't every reader's favorites, as indicated by their bi-monthly publication status, the ultimate merging of the two books, and their subsequent fade-out. But some influential people read them. At least, they became influential to long-time comics fans.

In just the issues above in which I mentioned the story's title, there were letters published from soon-to-be comics pros Marvin Wolfman, Bill Mantlo, Mike Friedrich, Klaus Janson, and Martin J. Pasko.

So, for you guys trying to break into comics, here's a suggestion: Don't worry about how many pages long your proposals are. Go read some old issues of *Atom* and *Hawkman*! Or am I confusing cause and effect here?

...so, naturally, they waited until the instant the girls' backs were turned!

TRIVIA CHALLENGE I
Category: **TITLES**   What was the name of the story that introduced **THE VISION**?   Answer on page 73   Answer from page 67 **LORI LEMARIS**

ENTER: THE RELATIONSHIP!   **71**

FLASH HAS TAKEN THE LEAD BY VIBRATING THE MOLECULES OF HIS BODY SO HE CAN PASS RIGHT THROUGH THE SAND DUNES, WHILE I MUST *BORE* THROUGH!

The Man of Steel expositorily made it clear how his powers differed from The Flash's in "Superman's Race with The Flash!" in **Superman** *#199, although why he sometimes (but not always) was allowed to fly rather than run wasn't especially clear.*

Superman & Flash

The most famous of these stories featured less of our heroes' civilian identities than those of the teams cited earlier, because they highlighted a natural set-up: determining who was faster, Flash (ostensibly The Fastest Man Alive) or Superman (The Man of Steel and Generally Best Guy at Everything).

A series of three races took place in the Silver Age, which kicked off in the cleverly named "Superman's Race with The Flash!" in *Superman* #199 (Aug 67). Sadly, it didn't resolve much of anything.

A rematch was held four months later in "The Race to the End of the Universe" in *The Flash* #175 (Dec 67), which again left the result debatable. A third competition took place three years later in the two-part "Race to Save the Universe" and "Race to Save Time" in *World's Finest* #198 and #199 (Nov and Dec 70). It promised to resolve things once and for all, but so much mayhem ensued along the race track that calling it "definitive" would be a real stretch.

Particularly after the first one had shown us what little there was to establish about how their super-speed powers differed (The Flash vibrated through things, while Superman ran around them or smashed them down), the stories weren't all that memorable. If these had been their only team-ups, they wouldn't really be worth mentioning beyond the idea that, once again, DC found a way to team up heroes

SOON... MY AURA PROTECTS ME FROM THE HEAT OF *AIR FRICTION*, BUT NOT FROM THESE SCORCHING-HOT *SAND DUNES*! I MUST SLOW DOWN... COOL OFF!

FLASH IS FALLING BACK!

BUT SECONDS LATER, AS THE TWO RACERS SPEED TOWARD *GIZEH*, IN EGYPT!

THE *GREAT PYRAMID* OF *CHEOPS*, FLASH *VIBRATED THROUGH*, WHILE I HAD TO GO *OVER THE TOP!* WE'RE EVEN AGAIN!

TRIVIA CHALLENGE I
Category: TITLES
What plan did LOIS put into action in "The Irresistable Lois Lane?" Answer on page 74

Answer from page 70
"This Man, This Monster"

72

BABY BOOMER COMICS

to compete without having them hit each other.

But my favorite Superman-Flash team-up took place independent of this race trilogy. It appeared in *Superman* #220 (Oct 69) and was called, "Who Stole My Super-Powers?" The story began with Superman lying unconscious on a South Pacific island. He didn't know who he was — or why he was wearing a red suit with a lighting bolt on it. He decided he must be The Flash and discovered, sure enough, he did have super-speed.

Then we switched to "the middle of nowhere," as Barry Allen called it after awakening in a field wearing a Superman costume to find he was being menaced by a bull. Barry discovered he also had super-speed, but he had no other powers. But he *did* have Clark Kent's clothes and wallet! The mystery deepened, as Barry used makeup to make himself look like Clark's driver's license photo and went to *The Daily Planet.* And this was where things started getting interesting.

Let's overlook the fact that Barry was wearing store-bought makeup and that Lois, Jimmy, and Perry didn't notice anything odd. Instead, let's focus on the fact that Barry had absolutely no idea how to do Clark's job. He couldn't write his way out of a paper bag, and this ticked off Perry. Barry, of course, figured he'd just forgotten how to write. (He also decided that for some reason he wore a mask as Superman — which, come to think of it, probably would've worked better than just putting on glasses.) Meanwhile, Superman wasn't having much better luck, as he quickly learned he couldn't vibrate through walls, as The Flash did. But he *could* smash them down and remain unhurt.

Perry sent Barry to cover an easy assignment: a society wedding. When Barry returned to *The Planet* with the news that there was no story because the groom hadn't shown up, Perry bounced Barry out on his ear. (Later, Perry had a change of heart and told Barry/Clark to take a few days off and get his head straightened out. We should all have bosses like Perry.)

Finally, Barry/Clark and Superman/Flash met and discovered what was happening (but I'm not telling what — *nyah nyah*). It was a typical DC team-up story, because it gave the reader a little insight into the real lives of the heroes (or, at least, Superman). We knew it had to take brains to be a police scientist, even though we seldom saw Barry at work. But who would have thought that it actually took talent to be Clark as well as Superman? It also left you wondering just how well Superman would have done as Barry Allen. Superman may know science (doesn't he?), but he wouldn't know police procedures. So maybe being the smartest guy around and doing a good job are two different things.

It would be an even better story except for two really goofy parts. First, Superman/Flash decided to disguise himself while he figured things out. Rather than take off his cowl to see what he looked like (something you would think a guy with amnesia might have tried long ago, in any event), he pulled a hat down over his masked face!

Second, to save our planet from catastrophe, Superman slammed his body against the ground again and again to make the Earth stand still. Oh, sure, he checked first to make sure nobody was around to get hurt and he fused the ground solid so he had a firm surface to push against. So they were really giving this one more thought than usual. But Superman would have had to fuse Isaac Newton's grave solid to keep him from spinning.

Barry Allen, thinking he was Clark Kent, didn't know a scoop when it bit him in the butt, as seen above. Meanwhile Superman, thinking he was The Flash, showed why he wasn't called the World's Greatest Detective when the two heroes asked, "Who Stole My Super-Powers?" in **Superman** *#220.*
© 1969 National Periodical Publications, Inc. (DC)

Mister Silver Age Recommends...

Superman Vol. 1, #220

DC
Oct 1969
Cover artist:
Curt Swan, Murphy Anderson

"Who Stole My Super-Powers?"
Writer: Uncredited
Penciller: Curt Swan
Inker: George Roussos

Then 15¢
Now $20

© 1969 National Periodical Publications, Inc. (DC)

TRIVIA CHALLENGE I
Category: **TEENS**   What were the last names of PATSY and HEDY?   Answer on page 75   Answer from page 71 "Behold, The Vision!"

Were Hal Jordan and Alan Scott meeting on Earth-One to discuss ways to foil evil on their two Earths? No, they were plotting a surprise birthday gift for Doiby Dickles in "Our Mastermind, The Car!" in Green Lantern #52.

© 1966 National Periodical Publications, Inc. (DC)

Green Lantern & Green Lantern

I'll mention it before you do: This is the second team-up I've discussed that features Green Lantern. And this one features two Green Lanterns!

I don't think Green Lantern pops up on the list so much simply because I liked the character. On the contrary, I've never understood how his power worked or how long its effects lasted, because it's never really been defined. It's one of the strangest powers ever possessed by a major character — let alone two (or several thousand, counting The GL Corps). Rather, I think these team-ups were so memorable because of an element that *GL/GA* writer Denny O'Neil once mentioned.

GL was an intergalactic cop with unimaginable powers (as long as you didn't throw a yellow lamp at him). It took some doing to bring his stories down to Earth, so to speak. So he had more "humanizing" elements than most heroes: He had siblings, an unrequited love, a sidekick as Hal Jordan, not GL, and a variety of friends he could teamup with that brought out his human side.

The other element GL offered was a creative team that knew how to make the most of a team-up. John Broome, in both Flash and GL, wrote some great stories, and artists Carmine Infantino and Gil Kane made the most of it. And, of course, GL and Flash, along with Hawkman and Atom, had another running thread: Editor Julius Schwartz. With his science-fiction background, he knew that the key to successful stories starring science-oriented heroes was strong characterization.

Earth-1/Earth-2 team-ups were naturals, of course, and there were several, including The Flashes and Atoms as well as The GLs. But the Green Lanterns were my favorite. True, there was nothing more down-to-Earth than seeing Barry Allen sitting in the Garricks' living room with his cowl off, about to partake of Joan's coffee and sandwiches, as he caught up with Jay. But Alan Scott and Hal Jordan always seemed to have a better and more inspiring time when they got together.

Their first meeting outside The JLA occurred in *Green Lantern* #40 (Oct 65), when we learned the "Secret Origin of the Guardians!" They later got together in *GL* #45, #52, and #61. There was so much going on in that first team-up, what with getting Alan and his sidekick Doiby Dickles established and explaining the title to us, that there was little room for real camaraderie. The two GLs did have a sly chuckle at the end, though, and Hal left us with the thought, "The sun is shining now and all is peaceful! How beautiful everything

I've never really understood how Green Lantern's powers worked. Have you?

TRIVIA CHALLENGE I
Category: **TEENS**   **Who was the high-school attended by SUPER-HIP named for?**   Answer on page 76   Answer from page 72   **PLAN L**

74   **BABY BOOMER COMICS**

is now that the menace is over!" That sounds like a wrap-up to me.

My favorite adventure of the two Emerald Gladiators was their last in The Silver Age, in "Thoroughly Modern Mayhem!" in *GL* #61 (Jun 68). Trust me, it was much better than its title. In essence, crime was rampant on Earth-2, and Alan Scott was being run ragged keeping up with all the crooks. He finally returned home from another day of baddie-bashing, one in which he himself had nearly been beaten to death.

He turned on the radio to hear that the death toll had reached an all-time high in Vietnam (a war apparently not restricted to our Earth) and riots were tearing apart Motor City. And, as he settled into a chair, he realized his home had been ransacked by burglars! Alan was pretty peeved. Changing identities, he screamed his oath into his battery ("And I shall shed my light over dark evil...") and raised his ring high. "Power ring," he commanded. "I order you to get rid of all evil on Earth that is plaguing mankind!"

And with that, he and everyone else on Earth-2 disappeared.

They reappeared on Earth-1, in the desert salt flats of Utah, where Hal happened to be flying by and noticed millions of people in suspended animation packed together like sardines. "There's only one conceivable answer," decided our incredibly insightful hero. "They are from Earth-Two!" He located Alan in the crowd and awoke him. "I failed," Alan despaired. "It didn't work. Leave me alone!" "Come on, Alan, it's never that bad!" Hal suggested. "Tell me about it."

"Can't you see?" Alan asked. "I've failed — miserably! I overlooked the basic human fact that *everyone* by nature has some evil in him. The only way my ring could obey my command was to remove the entire population off Earth and immobilize them! The ring itself stayed behind so I couldn't countermand the order, because I, too, am partially evil. In other words," he summed up, "I can't possibly stop it! Evil will always be present!"

Alan Scott got mad as heck and wasn't going to take it any more, so he fired up his battery and wiped out all of Earth-2's evil in one fell swoop with his power ring in "Thoroughly Modern Mayhem!" in **Green Lantern #61**.

Hal could have suggested that Alan try setting the ring's Evil meter a bit higher and try again — being sure to send the truly evil Earth-2 people someplace more helpful to Hal than the desert salt flats of Earth-1. But, instead, Hal took him by the shoulder. "Listen to me, Alan!" he urged. "You've got to go on..." "Why?" Alan asked. "What's the use? It's beyond me..." "You're wrong!" Hal interrupted. "Despite what's happened, you can't stop resisting evil once you've committed yourself to this goal.

"Listen: I, too, once wanted to give up when my hopes were destroyed! When Carol Ferris told me she was marrying someone else! But I found out you can't stop being what you are — what you should be — because of even the greatest setbacks! Once a Green Lantern, always a Green Lantern!

"You've got to keep plugging away at the little things!" he urged. "Don't get a hang-up over the big problems! Maybe it's a hassle, but they work themselves out if you give 'em a try!" Alan pondered this. Then he shook Hal's hand and clapped him on the shoulder. "I-I'm sorry Hal! I never realized — you're right! Now how about we do something about it — together!"

That's why I liked seeing Alan and Hal get together. That's why I like a lot of the more personalized, recurring team-ups from DC's Silver Age. That's why, in a nutshell, I like DC's Silver Age.

TRIVIA CHALLENGE I
Category: **TEENS**   *Who was BINKY's girlfriend?*   Answer on page 77   Answer from page 73 **WALKER, WOLF**

ENTER: THE RELATIONSHIP!

Zatanna's Magical Mystery Tour

"I remember that when the sexy magician Zatanna was introduced, she was hunting for her missing father, The Golden Age hero Zatara. Did she ever find him?"

She sure did—but it wasn't easy, and it took a whole bunch of Silver Age super-heroes to help, first individually and then together. It was an extraordinary adventure, for the Silver Age or any other period. The story covered a half-dozen guest appearances over a three-year span, as Zatanna bounced from comic to comic (all edited by Julius Schwartz). In each, she gained another clue leading her to her father's ultimate whereabouts.

*Readers saw Zatanna for the first time on the splash page to **Hawkman** #4. Amazingly, her debut wasn't the cover feature, even though it was the first story in the issue. There's just no accounting for taste.*

© 1964 National Periodical Publications, Inc. (DC)

Zatara was, indeed, missing. He hadn't appeared in comics for 13 years, after bursting onto the scene in *Action Comics* #1 (Jun 38), which also starred another hero whose name escapes me at the moment. The star of one of the first series written by legendary writer Gardner Fox, Zatara had a pretty stellar career before vanishing in 1951. (For more, see the sidebar on page 79.)

Fortunately, Zatara had a daughter who grew up to also become a magician and fight crime between stage engagements, using the reverse-spelling spell-casting approach he'd perfected. We'd just never seen her before, because she didn't get a lot of publicity (an odd thing for a person making a living as a stage magician and foiling criminals in her spare time, but there you go).

She burst into the DC universe in "The Girl Who Split in Two!" in *Hawkman* #4 (Oct-Nov 64). The story opened with Carter (Hawkman) Hall and Shiera (Hawkgirl) Hall being mystified about the sudden appearance of two artifacts in their museum. So Hawkman flew to the city of Yin in China's Hunan province to discover the secret origin of a Shang Dynasty statue, while Hawkgirl winged to the Hill of Tara ruins in Ireland to do the same for a Celtic ceremonial cup. Boy, we kids sure learned fascinating stuff reading comics back then.

What The Hawks each found was an immobilized woman dressed in top hat and tails and those unforgettable (at least for us boys) fishnet stockings. Meeting at their orbiting spaceship, Katar and Shayera realized they each had one-half of the same woman. They joined her together after translating her directions (which consisted of each body half saying half of each word—Zatanna has always spoken strangely).

Our magical miss explained that she had been casting a spell to

TRIVIA CHALLENGE I
Category: **TEENS**

Who was the best friend to SCOOTER?

Answer on page 78

Answer from page 74
BENEDICT ARNOLD

76

BABY BOOMER COMICS

find her lost father and found clues that led her to an evil Oriental lama and a sinister druid. Not having been taught that haste makes waste, Zatanna had split herself in two to track both clues at once and wound up immobilized at each location. (It wouldn't be the last time her magic went so screwy she needed help to extricate herself from a fix, either.) Frozen in place, she'd magically caused the artifacts to appear in the Halls' museum to attract their hawkish yet curatorial interest.

The Hawks used that always-helpful absorbascon—kind of a way-before-its-time and way-more-powerful Internet search engine—to learn that no one on Earth knew anything about Zatara. (I do Web searches that end like that, too.) Zatanna was dismayed but undaunted and left to continue her search. Not a bad intro—especially since we still had the 11-page cover story for the issue left to go!

Readers had to wonder about Father and Daughter Z until "The World of the Magic Atom!" in *The Atom* #19 (Jun-Jul 65). After accidentally aiding bank robbers with some stray magic (oops) and then helping Atom magically catch the thieves, Zatanna explained her plight to Ray (The Atom) Palmer. She asked Ray to help her journey into a magical book, where she believed her father was being held prisoner in a sub-atomic world.

Zatanna flashed those fishnetted gams at Ray (the Atom) Palmer while she introduced herself in **The Atom** #19. Take a quick look at that outfit and guess whether Ray helped her out...

Ray declined, since he couldn't shrink anything but himself without making it explode. Bummer. But she overcame his objection by flashing those fishnets, batting her eyes, and magically creating a special shrinking outfit out of dwarf-matter cloth sitting around. (Frankly, that's a lot easier to believe than the idea that physicist Palmer had sewn his costume from a white-dwarf meteorite in the first place, as he had allegedly done. Don't think about that one too long).

Down they went to face the aforementioned Druid in a cool battle of magic and mayhem in an ancient castle. Ultimately, Zatanna learned that the Druid had exiled her father to another world, but the Druid refused to reveal which one. So she waved bye-bye to Ray and went off again.

She next showed up in *Green Lantern* #42 (Jan 66) and asked The Emerald Gladiator for help in searching for "The Other Side of the World." Technically, she did this only because (once again) her magical searches caused a real headache for our hero. Her magicks this time unlocked a portal from the aforementioned Other Side, which allowed the devilish-looking Warlock to gain access to Earth. So she got GL to help stop him.

(By the way, the "Other Side" was explained as being created by a "steady state" flow of primal matter in the form of a cosmic cloud, as opposed to our own universe, which was said to have been formed by a "big bang" of a colossal primal atom. These were, in fact, the two commonly debated theories among cosmologists at the time about how our universe had been created. Would something like that have shown up anywhere besides a Silver Age Schwartz comic? I think not. As you may know without having read as many comics as I have, the "big bang" theory won out, at least for now. But I digress.)

...and it was a cinch that Hal would help out in **Green Lantern** #42.

TRIVIA CHALLENGE I
Category: **SPIES**
What was the code-name for **SHARON CARTER?**
Answer on page 79
Answer from page 75
PEGGY

ENTER: THE RELATIONSHIP!

Zatanna and Ralph Dibny, the Elongated Man, teamed up for a quick adventure in the back of *Detective Comics* #355, which later led to EM taking part in the wrap-up in JLA.
© 1965 National Periodical Publications, Inc. (DC)

Justice League of America Vol. 1, #51

DC Comics
Feb 1967

Cover artist:
Mike Sekowsky

"Z — As in Zatanna — and Zero Hour!"

Writer: Gardner Fox
Penciller: Mike Sekowsky

Then 12¢ **Now** $20

Reprints appear in...
• Justice League of America #110

Zatanna coyly watched the amazed reaction of The JLA, as she thanked them for helping her find her father without their knowledge in *Justice League of America* #51.
© 1967 National Periodical Publications, Inc. (DC)

More magical battles ensued, this time against an army of demons, incubi, djinns, imps, fiends, and familiars. Ultimately, Zatanna learned that Zatara had indeed been banished there. But he escaped, taking with him the crystal ball The Warlock had been working on to open the Earth portal. Zatara went somewhere he couldn't be detected, so The Warlock couldn't retrieve the crystal, which was why he'd been so happy to see Zatanna show up and give him a means to get there. Fortunately, that didn't happen, but Zatanna didn't get there, either.

So Lady Z packed her traveling bag again, looking for this new hiding place. To help her, she needed a magical tripod for sale in a knick-knack shop, but it was stolen before she could get it. Undaunted, she magically caused the thieves to return to the shop. That's what led The Elongated Man to discover "The Tantalizing Troubles of the Tripod Thieves!" in the back-up story in *Detective* #355 (Sep 66).

Ralph Dibny caught the robbers at another crime, but, before he could put them away, they floated off. He couldn't stop them, so he followed them to the shop. There, he saved Zatanna from her jam and learned about her quest. No doubt dazzled by those fishnets, he volunteered to help. But Zatanna probably figured that a guy who could stretch his body into goofy shapes didn't offer much support against imps, djinns, *etc.* So she turned down his offer, he went back to Sue, and Zatty went back to questing.

The quest came to an end in "Z — As in Zatanna — And Zero Hour!" in *Justice League of America* #51 (Feb 67). All the aforementioned heroes plus Batman magically appeared in the JLA headquarters without knowing why they were there. Suddenly, Zatanna appeared and gave them all big hugs for helping her find her father. Protesting that they'd failed in their efforts, the heroes took a seat and listened to Zatanna's happy tale. Don't you just love how so many JLA stories featured them sitting around talking about what they'd already done? I sure did. Sitting around talking was something I was good at pretending to do as a super-hero. But I digress again.

The gist of Zatanna's tale was that she had tracked her father to yet another magical world, where she was about to be overwhelmed. Instead, she summoned all the heroes who previously had helped her, and they went into battle with her.

Batman objected, of course, since he'd never met Zatanna. But it was now late 1966, and any comic book with Batman in it sold like gangbusters due to his TV show. So, to include him, Editor Schwartz concocted a scheme by which Zatanna had actually been the witch that The Outsider had used against The Caped Crusader in "Batman's Bewitched Nightmare!" in *Detective Comics* #336 (Feb 65).

TRIVIA CHALLENGE I
Category: **SPIES**

What was the code-name for JIMMY OLSEN?

Answer on page 80

Answer from page 76
SYLVESTER

78

BABY BOOMER COMICS

She said she'd gone to Gotham City disguised as an old woman to ask The Outsider about her father, and she'd been overcome and forced to obey him. Nope, it doesn't make much more sense now than it did then.

And, yes, it's true: They actually went back and changed some basic part of an earlier adventure just to fit the whim of a story they were doing right then. Amazing! Fortunately, today's creators have more respect for readers than to do something like that. At least, they wouldn't do it more than once a month unless it was really important, like inside a comic they were writing. But I digress yet another time.

The combined might of our heroes allowed Zatanna to conquer her foes and free her father! And, as Zatanna finished her story, she conjured up her pop, who got to meet the heroes and everyone was happy.

At least, everyone was happy except for those few of us who still were trying to figure out how Zatanna had escaped from the jail where The Dynamic Duo had landed her butt after they captured her in that funky witch disguise. Not to mention those of us who were wondering why Zatanna kept calling on Earth-1 heroes, when her dad had been established as living on Earth-2. Fortunately, a few years after Zatanna's own "Zero Hour," there was a second one that cleared all that stuff up once and for all. You bet.

Mister Silver Age Recommends...

Hawkman Vol. 1, #4

DC Comics
Nov 1964

Cover artist:
Murphy Anderson

"story title"
Writer: Gardner Fox
Penciller: Murphy Anderson

Then **12¢**
Now **$140**

Reprints of Zatanna's introduction appear in...
• Hawkman Archives Vol. 1
• Supergirl (1st Series) #5 (in severely edited form)

Following in Daddy's Footsteps

Superman was only one of several characters to be introduced in *Action Comics* #1 (Jun 38). Granted, he may have been far and away the biggest, but that would be true no matter *who* else appeared in the issue.

Zatara, the World's Greatest Magician, first appeared just seven pages after The Man of Steel's debut in *Action* #1. Fred Guardineer wrote and drew the first adventure of the magical crime fighter and his faithful assistant Tong, with Gardner Fox scripting after that.

THE FIGURE OF A WOMAN STEALTHILY CREEPS UP BEHIND ZATARA – IT IS "THE TIGRESS"!

In that first adventure, the magical duo solved "The Mystery of the Freight Train Robberies," battling Zatara's "arch enemy," the beautiful Tigress. The 12-page adventure (a mere two shorter than Supes) featured only a few minor backward-spoken spells and a couple of hand gestures, emphasizing adventure over magic. (That Zatara owed a debt to the famous comic-strip hero Mandrake the Magician is pretty hard to ignore.)

Zatara went on to a 127-issue run in *Action Comics* as well as the first 51 issues of *World's Finest*. Those lasted through April-May 1951, when he disappeared. Amazingly, only his first adventure has been widely reprinted, in *Famous First Edition* #26 (1974), the tabloid reprint of *Action Comics* #1, with a second reprinting in the *Millennium Edition* of that issue.

The only other reprints I know about were in Alan Light's black & white *Flashback* series: #12 (*New York World's Fair Comics 1939*), #20 (*New York World's Fair Comics 1940*), #28 (*World's Finest #7*), and #38 (*World's Finest #8*). Those reprints are almost as tough to find as the originals, although they're a heck of a lot cheaper.

Both Zatara and Zatanna received spiffed-up secret origins in *Secret Origins* #27 (Jun 88). That's easily the most accessible option for readers interested in learning more about Superman's magical pal.

TRIVIA CHALLENGE I
Category: **SPIES**

Who did the **CRIMINAL ALLIANCE** of the **WORLD** first battle?

Answer on page 81

Answer from page 77
AGENT 13

ENTER: THE RELATIONSHIP!

Thor and Sif, Sitting in a Tree!

"How did The Mighty Thor first meet Sif? I say Nurse Jane Foster became Sif the same way Dr. Don Blake became Thor: by bashing a cane on the ground. My wife says they met on *The Dating Game*. Who's right?"

You two deserve each other. But frankly, I prefer either of your wrong-headed notions to the one that appeared in "To Become an Immortal!" in *Thor* #136 (Jan 67). It also can be found in *Marvel Spectacular* #7 (May 74), if you can't find the original.

Dating around can be tough when Norse mythology already has your girl picked out for you.

*A Silver Age moment to treasure, compliments of Mr. Silver Age: Thor meets Heimdall's little sister and they kinda hit it off in "To Become an Immortal!" in **Thor** #136.*
© 1967 Marvel

The Thunder God spent the bulk of the issue trying to acclimate Jane to Asgard. Thor's pop, Odin, the all-knowing, all-seeing (just like *my* pop!), had finally caved in and agreed to let the two lovebirds get hitched. So Thor took his honey home to meet the parents. Or, at least, Dad.

Jane and The All-Father shook hands, more or less. Then Odin outfitted her in raiment fit for a goddess, and a Kirby goddess at that. And he bestowed upon her the gift of unlimited flight. "Merely think of a destination," Thor told her, "and thou shalt fly there forthwith!" Maybe that's how it worked for Superman, too. It's at least as good as any explanation he ever gave us, and it sure beat following freeways.

After that, though, things headed downhill. After about six pages of screwing things up royally (to use a mythological term), Jane decided there was no place like home. Odin, never a big Jane fan, agreed heartily. So she clicked her heels together three times, Odin pointed his hand, and Jane went winging back to Earth. Meanwhile, Thor stood by, feeling mighty peeved.

> SIF, TOO, HAS BEEN NO STRANGER TO HEART-BREAK! EVER SINCE CHILDHOOD HAVE I SUFFERED THE ACHE OF *LOVE UNREQUITED!*

> --A *HOPELESS* LOVE --FOR ONE WHO EVER HAD EYES FOR *ANOTHER*--ONE TO WHOM *SIF* WAS NAUGHT BUT A FORGOTTEN MEMORY!

> MINE *EARS* HEAR THY WORDS--BUT MY *HEART* CAN-NOT BELIEVE THAT ANY COULD FORGET ONE SUCH AS *THEE!*

The All-Father tried to buck him up. "In thy heart of hearts," Odin assured him, "thou knowest godhood was not for one such as she!" Thor argued that his heart of hearts knew no such thing, but Big Daddy cut him off. "My power is beyond all measure, beyond all comprehension," Odin said modestly. "And yet, I cannot alter an emotion of the heart!" A glimmer of hope rose in Thor, because he thought that his all-knowing poppa was going to relent and suggest a way to make the marriage work.

Instead, his dad shrugged his shoulders. "But, we shall speak of this no more!" he said, deflating his son one final time. And he sent Thor off to Gundershelm to guard the Glade of Crystals. "Tis just as well!" The God of Self-Pity proclaimed. "If fortune looks upon me with favor, mayhap I shall fall in battle!" If I were you, Pop, I think I'd leave The Thunder God at home for a few days to stew in his room before I gave him the keys to the car or anything.

TRIVIA CHALLENGE I
Category: **SPIES**

Who fought OGRE (Organization for General Revenge & Enslavement)? Answer on page 82

Answer from page 75
AGENT DOUBLE-FIVE

But the All-You-Know-What Odin had a plan. For no sooner did T.M. Thor arrive in Gundershelm than The Unknown attacked! Just as the depressed immortal was about to be overwhelmed, another warrior arrived and saved his self-pitying butt.

When the dust cleared, the warrior stood revealed as Heimdall's younger sister, Sif. "Can it be?" Thor wondered. "The raven-tressed child whom once I dangled on my knee! But, by my mallet, thou art child no longer!" By my mallet, indeed.

Since there was only room for five more panels in this story, Sif quickly admitted that all her life she had loved this big blond galoot from a distance. It must've been all that knee-dangling that did it. Thor looked at the gorgeous, feisty, and most definitely nubile Sif for about one second and forgot he'd ever known Jane Foster. Heck, he was ready to order the rings!

"Verily, thou hast restored the lust for life to the smoldering soul of an errant thunder god!" he simpered. The lust for something else too, I daresay. Then the Mighty Thor and the Stunning Sif (Stan's adjective, not mine) walked off into the twilight of Gundershelm hand in hand. *Awwwww.*

Of course, Odin had been watching on his All-Seeing Color Monitor, which was tuned to Thor TV. His associate/lackey marveled at the miracle Odin had wrought. "Nay, not so!" Big Daddy argued modestly. "I did but provide the time, the setting. But only in the heart can be found the final enchanted ingredient men call love!"

And what of Jane, you might ask, if you were more sympathetic to her fate than our big Thunder Oaf appeared to be? Thor's one true love found herself back on Earth in the middle of a hospital, apparently with selective memories wiped out. "Are you the new resident nurse who was due to arrive today?" a nurse asked. "Why yes I am!" Jane agreed. (Odin must have filled out the forms for her.)

She was introduced to her new boss, a young, vivacious, near-lookalike for Don Blake. "He's so handsome!" she thought. "I feel as though I've known him before! Or is it that I've seen him so often in my dreams!" "I hope you'll be happy here with us, Nurse Foster!" the doc said, removing his oh-so-debonair pipe. "Oh I will, Doctor," Jane gushed. "I just know I will!" At least until you get lip cancer, pal.

So Jane Foster walked off happily into the sunset, without even a gold watch. At least she wasn't put out to pasture before today's comics got hold of her. She would have had to die a horrible death and then come back as a clone or an android or something. It could have happened.

In fact, gulp, it still could.

Odin attempted to give his thundering son some fatherly advice and then changed tactics and sent Thor on a mission to take the young god's mind off his broken heart in **Thor #136**.
© 1967 Marvel

Mister Silver Age Recommends...

Thor Vol. 1, #136

Marvel
Jan 1967

Cover artist:
Jack Kirby, Vince Colletta

"To Become an Immortal"
Writer: Stan Lee
Penciller: Jack Kirby
Inker: Vince Colletta

Then 12¢
Now $50

© 1967 Marvel

Reprints appear in...
• Marvel Spectacular #7
• Thor Vol. 2 #32

TRIVIA CHALLENGE I
Category: PETS   What's the real name of SUPER-HORSE?   Answer on page 83   Answer from page 79   HAWKMAN

ENTER: THE RELATIONSHIP!   **81**

Captain Stacy: Still Dead

"Mr. Silver Age, my all-time favorite *Spider-Man* character was Captain Stacy. I've always admired his courage, his intelligence, and his kindness. But mainly, I've always admired how he's manage to stay dead. How did he die on that one, solitary occasion?"

Staying dead after kicking the bucket in The Silver Age took real gumption, it's true. One of the few Marvel characters who hasn't been revived, replaced, or cloned (at least by press time), was Gwen Stacy's beloved dad, who started pushing up daisies in "And Death Shall Come!" in *Amazing Spider-Man* #90 (Nov 70).

> **Staying dead after kicking the bucket in the Silver Age took real gumption for a character.**

*Captain George Stacy met his maker in "And Death Shall Come!" in **Amazing Spider-Man** Vol. 1, #90.*

© 1970 Marvel

It also can be found in *Essential Spider-Man* #5, *Marvel Treasury Edition* #1 and *Spider-Man Comics Magazine* #13. But it's the same death each time, so it only counts once. With Stan Lee supplying the story and art handled by Gil Kane (pencils) and John Romita (inks), you knew this one would be a keeper!

Captain George Stacy always seemed to be in the right place at the right time to aid Peter Parker. Early in this issue, for instance, Spider-Man nearly got the beejeebers beat out of him by Doctor Octopus. The fight ended in a draw, and Petey retrieved his clothes from an alley. He stumbled out into the street, dead on his feet, where he fortuitously met the good captain. Pete collapsed into George's arms and was helped to the Stacy homestead, where Gwen nursed him back to health. *Mmmm, baby.*

Feeling much better (wouldn't you?), Peter went home to his lab and cooked up a way to beat Doc Ock. They met again and partook of the typical Marvel slugfest for a few pages. During the rooftop tussle, Ock's arms suddenly ran amok and smashed a chimney over the edge. The debris hurtled to the sidewalk below, where a little tow-headed boy stood paralyzed with fear.

TRIVIA CHALLENGE I
Category: **PETS**   What's the name of RAY PALMER's pet?   Answer on page 84   Answer from page 80 **AQUAMAN**

Captain Stacy appeared in the crowd. "Look out, son! Look out!" he yelled, throwing himself across the expanse. "Please God," he prayed. "Let me not be...too late! Let me—unhhhhhhh!" The boy was thrown free. Captain Stacy was not.

"He's got to be alive!" Spider-Man cried, throwing off huge chunks of masonry to reach him. "He's got to! He's got to!" "I'm done for, son," George told him. "No!" Spider-Man exclaimed, distraught. "You're not! You're not!" He carried the captain up the wall to seek a doctor.

Stacy begged to be put down, and asked Peter to take care of Gwen. Yes, that's right – *Peter*. Spider-Man suddenly realized something only a few sharp-eyed fans had suspected: that the pipe-chomping detective had figured out his greatest secret.

"You—you know who I am!" Spider-Man said to the deceased man. "You must have always known! But—you never told! You never gave me away!"

He hugged the captain. "First I lost Uncle Ben those long years ago. And now the second-best friend I've ever had! Rest easy, sir. Rest easy. I'll love Gwen, and cherish her, as long as I live! But what if she ever learns that you died because of me?"

Gwen did blame Spider-Man, of course, although that was hardly fair. And the rest of our star-crossed lovers' lives didn't work out exactly as they had hoped either, thanks to The Green Goblin (and Gerry Conway, John Romita, and a variety of other co-conspirators who killed Gwen in *Amazing Spider-Man* #121).

But let's face it, what a great death scene. Stan isn't called the Man for nothing.

George Stacy's demise in **Amazing Spider-Man** *Vol. 1, #90 was a classic scene, if only because the captain has managed to stay dead, lo, these many years.*

© 1970 Marvel

Mister Silver Age Recommends...

Amazing Spider-Man Vol. 1, #90

Marvel Comics Nov 1970

Cover artist: Gil Kane, John Romita

"And Death Shall Come!"
Writer: Stan Lee
Penciller: Gil Kane
Inker: John Romita

Then **15¢**
Now **$45**

© 1970 Marvel

Reprints appear in...
• Marvel Treasury Edition #1
• Spider-Man Comics Magazine #13
• Essential Spider-Man Vol. 5
• Spider-Man: The Death of Captain Stacy

TRIVIA CHALLENGE I
Category: PETS   **What's the name of DANE WHITMAN's horse?**   Answer on page 85   Answer from page 81   **BIRON THE CENTAUR**

ENTER: THE RELATIONSHIP!   **83**

Superman's Amazing Amazon Appeal

"So who do you think is the cooler hero, Superman or Batman?"

Ah, the eternal differentiator among DC super-hero fans. Much like Yankees-Mets or Cubs-White Sox debates, it would be possible for a fan to like both Superman and Batman equally—but it doesn't seem to work that way. Superman was the upstanding, moral guy with so many cool powers he would've forgotten some of them, if he hadn't had a super-memory. Batman, meanwhile, was the up-by-his-bootstraps dweller in the dark who did whatever needed to be done to come out ahead (within reason, of course).

Superman's cooler than Batman, of course. You didn't see Batsy hanging out will lots of Amazon princesses!

It's not a love-hate thing like those other opposites, but, in most cases, fans had a definite preference for one hero over the other. Frankly, I was always a Superman guy, if only because I had more in common with him. No, really, I did. Sure, Batman had that human thing going for him but, c'mon, he was the perfect physical and mental specimen! It didn't take many glances in the bathroom mirror or arithmetic tests for me to figure out that I wasn't going to become Batman any time soon.

*Oh, no! Superman became "The Super-Prisoner of Amazon Island" in **Action** #235! And those gorgeous, scantily clad babes intended to auction him off to the highest bidder! And Lois just got a raise!*

But could I be shot into space and land on another planet where I gained super-powers? Heck, yeah! In fact, there were days when I hoped that moment was just around the corner. On a few occasions, especially when I was marveling at one or another boneheaded moves by one of my brothers, it was pretty easy to pretend that's exactly what already had happened, except for that gaining-super-powers part.

But ultimately, whenever I find myself in an argument over whether Superman or Batman was cooler (and the topic comes up almost daily, when you're Mr. Silver Age), the discussion ends when I play my Superman trump card. Because Batman didn't make a habit out of being captured and married to gorgeous, scantily clad Amazons.

What was it about the Big Blue Boy Scout that made him so darned attractive to entire tribes of wild, beautiful women who apparently live all over the galaxy? His spit curl? His washboard stomach? His lack of potential in-laws? Whatever it was, Kal-El had it in spades. Sometimes it seemed as if he couldn't step out of The Fortress of Solitude without being captured by Amazons. Each time, he'd have to exploit every ounce of his manly wits to escape marrying some gorgeous, scantily clad Amazon queen.

These stories really appealed to me for some reason, and I'm guessing it was because they had such imaginative, finely honed plots. And lemme tell ya, these

TRIVIA CHALLENGE I
Category: **PETS**

What was the name of BOMBA's pet monkey?

Answer on page 86

Answer from page 82
MAJOR MINAH

plots were honed to a razor's edge. I still remember how my spine tingled, as I watched Supes try to wriggle out of the clutches of these enticing wenches. At least I *think* it was my spine tingling.

My introduction to this pulse-pounding side of Superman's career began when Elsha, Queen of the Amazons, turned The Man of Steel into "The Super-Prisoner of Amazon Island!" in *Action Comics* #235 (Dec 57). Before we even glimpsed those gorgeous, lightly clothed Amazons, we were treated to a meeting of Lois Lane's all-female Super Society. These were ladies who had banded together because they'd all been saved by Superman. After telling their tales, they headed out on their cabin cruiser for a three-hour tour (a threeee- hour tourrrrrr...).

Actually, the trip lasted until the next day. That's when the boat sank and marooned the girls on The Land Without Men. Catchy name, huh? Not as catchy as Elsha and her band of gorgeous cuties. Their costumes seemed to be patterned after Daisy Mae's line of fashionwear, except theirs were all white and skimpier, if you can imagine that.

It didn't take long for The Man of Steel to show up and show off. His manly performance dazzled Queenie, so she informed Kal-El about the Amazon law that proclaimed that any man who trespassed on the island became the Amazons' slave. She called for the chains, which made Superman laugh—until he noticed they were made of kryptonite.

As he started to flee, he realized the green K didn't affect him. To uncover the reason for this immunity, he let these gorgeous, hardly garbed Amazons sell him at a slave auction. Yeah. That's why he did it. Yeah.

Somehow, Lois outbid all these beautiful, lusty, half-naked Amazons who hadn't seen a man in donkey's years and didn't have much use for Lois' dollars under the best of circumstances. That made our little tart of a queen mighty peeved. She tore up the slavery law and decreed that any man caught trespassing must marry the first Amazon who gave him a task he couldn't perform. Ah, it's good to be the queen.

But, instead of all these Amazon babes lining up to give Superman an impossible task, for some bizarre reason the Super Society women got first crack. And that's gonna bring our story to a dead stop, of course, because these proper, civilized ladies no doubt will do the proper, civilized thing and give Superman easy tasks so he won't be forced to marry any them, right?

No way! They try to make him fail so they can become Mrs. Superman! That's the thanks Supes gets for saving the lives of these scheming vixens. But our boy in blue didn't seem all that fazed by this surprising attitude from the club of conniving cuties. "I'll take a chance," The Man of Steel decided, "that I can fulfill any tasks the girls think up and avoid the...er...penalty!"

I'm sure that the fact that every one of these Super Society babes was beautiful, smart, and talented didn't enter into his decision to hang around rather than use his X-ray vision to scope out his antidote. I'm sure.

Why the Amazons even let the Super Society babes participate in this contest, let alone go first, wasn't too clear to me. But, then, figuring out the nuances of Silver Age Superman plots often makes my head hurt, so I don't dwell on them. These points never seemed to come up when I was enthralled by the four-color wonders of these epic tales back when I was 11, and it's probably best to let that approach rule the day.

Mister Silver Age Recommends...

Action Comics #235

DC
Dec 1957

Cover artist:
Curt Swan, Stan Kaye

"The Super-Prisoner of Amazon Island"
Writer: Otto Binder
Penciller: Wayne Boring
Inker: Stan Kaye

Then 10¢
Now $240

© 1957 National Periodical Publications, Inc. (DC)

Reprints appear in...
• Superman's Girl Friend Lois Lane #104

Amazing Reprints

Here's where to catch some of these scantily clad Amazons in reprints:

Action #235 was reprinted for another generation of young, lusting male eyes in *Superman's Girl Friend Lois Lane* #104 (Sep-Oct 70).

Action #266 (Jul 60) was reprinted in *Superman* #207 (Jul 68) as part of Kal's 30th Anniversary *80-page Giant*, as well it should have been.

Green Lantern #16 was reprinted in *Green Lantern Archives* #3, *DC Blue-Ribbon Digest* #4 and *DC Special* #3.

Green Lantern #26 was reprinted in *Green Lantern Archives* #4.

That's all so far, but keep watching! Those other classics are bound to show up in a collection soon. They're too good to keep on the shelf.

Superman was a real pro at marriage avoidance.

Besides, I'd much rather focus on how our clever Kryptonian avoided marrying the beauteous Dr. Edna Blaine, scientist; the alluring Betty Dunn, swimming champ; the captivating Julia Johns, animal trainer; the bewitching Sonya Sophia, opera singer, and the ubiquitous Lois Lane, all-round pest.

Want to know how he does it? Want to know what the kryptonite antidote was? Then read the book! It's worth tracking this baby down just to see how artist Wayne Boring kept everything under wraps when Lois wound up with only a shirt-tail to retain her modesty. The other babes ended up in short-shorts, too. As I said, well worth tracking down.

Needless to say, it took a few years for that issue's excitement to wear off at the DC offices. When it did, Superman again found himself "The Captive of the Amazons" in *Action* #266 (Jul 60).

*Oh, no! Superman was ensnared as "The Captive of the Amazons" in **Action** #266!*
© 1960 National Periodical Publications, Inc. (DC)

And he drank a love potion and married the gorgeous and tightly clad Princess Jena of Adoria! He really did! Ooh, I could just barely watch!
© 1960 National Periodical Publications, Inc. (DC)

Just so we can skip to the good part, here's the basic set-up: Superman, as Clark Kent, was tricked into entering a spaceship that was part of a movie set where he was supposed to be interviewing a beautiful blonde actress. Once he entered, the ship took off and a bunch o' babes turned a kryptonite beam on him. He promised not to escape or hurt them if they released him from the deadly rays. That's good enough for our ship of shrews. They knew Supes would never break a promise, because he was a hero. (Don't be alarmed if that seems outlandish to you, kids — it's a Silver Age concept).

"I come from the distant planet Adoria, Superman!" explained Princess Jena, the group's gorgeous leader. "We have had you under telescopic observation for years! I came to Earth and became a movie star to capture you and take you back to Adoria with me!" Whew! Talk about long-term (not to mention roundabout) planning!

When they landed, Clark changed into his skin-tight Superman togs while our head hussy switched from her skin-tight spacesuit into a pair of skin-tight Capri pants. (Ask your mom, kids. Or, more likely—sigh—your grandma.) Jena told Kal, "Adoria's men are quite timid! Unlike us Amazon women, the men are not strong and courageous!" When her first five husbands didn't pass muster, they began pushing up daisies.

So Jena decided to rocket to Earth and spend a few years reading *Variety*, working menial jobs, going to auditions, hoping for a few breaks, making a few commercials, becoming noticed by producers, making some low-budget movies, getting some notoriety, landing a supporting role in a big movie, gaining a bigger role in another movie or two,

TRIVIA CHALLENGE I
Category: **PSEUDONYMS** What was the real name of MICKEY DEMEO?   Answer on page 88   Answer from page 84 **DOTO**

86   **BABY BOOMER COMICS**

becoming famous, and finally setting up an interview with Clark Kent. Boy, this cunning plan still leaves me dazzled.

The Man of Steel agreed to get hitched after Jena threatened to blow up Earth with her Master Destructo-Ray. "Don't look so miserable, Superman!" our Amazon babe cooed, spying Kal's long face. "There are worse fates than being married to a lovely princess! Kiss me — or Earth dies!" Boy, the choices you have to make when you're Earth's mightiest hero.

Supes surrendered to the inevitable and puckered up. But his smooch was somewhere on the short side of passionate, so Jena threw a hissy fit. She stomped off and ordered her royal wizard to mix up a love potion for The Man of Steel. The tonic turned the trick. "Jena!" he exclaimed after quaffing the brew. "You—you're supreme! A miracle of loveliness! I-I love you! What a fool I've been to give Lois Lane even a single thought!" Yes, it apparently also was a truth serum.

So the two lovebirds committed matrimony. "You're mine now!" Jena sighed. "Lucky me," Kal simpered back. Fortunately, this was one of those occasional 12-page epics and not a 9-pager. So Clark had three full pages to get his keister out of this mess. And — what a surprise — he did. I won't tell you how he wriggled free, but it involved his singing the song, "I'm so wild about Jena! I'm chasin' comets all the time!" So there was culture in this tale along with the rampant sex.

It took five years for the thrill of that Amazon adventure to wear off. When it did, Superman had the pleasure of meeting Orella, the trickiest little scamp of the bunch. She was better known as "The Girl Who Was Mightier than Superman" in *Superman* #180 (Oct 65). Orella and her gal pals, who mostly dressed in one-piece bathing suits with short skirts, tricked Superman into visiting their secret island in the South Pacific. When he arrived, Orella explained that he'd been brought there to marry her.

When he tried to leave, she threw a switch cleverly concealed inside the trunk of nearby palm tree. It turned on an artificial-kryptonite dome that surrounded the island. With Superman trapped, she explained that she and her sexy buds came from a race of warrior women on the distant planet Matron (quite a catchy name). Once each decade, their fiercest warriors mated with the bravest of their male captives. The female offspring who didn't measure up were banished into space. This particular batch landed on Earth, where they devised the cunning plan to let one of them marry Superman and start a race of super-women.

Frankly, I can think of better ways to start a new race of super-women than having Superman settle down with the chief Amazon. But that wouldn't do much for our plot. And our plot centered on Orella, who won the right to marry Superman through trickery and now was gloating at her prize. "Here you stay unless you marry me...or defeat me in a test of strength," she explained.

Naturally, rather than marry a gorgeous, scantily clad Amazon, The Man of Steel agreed to the contest. But thanks to even more trickery by that wily vamp, he lost. Dang!

I won't tell you how it ended, but let's face it: Do you ever remember reading a comic book called *Superman's Gorgeous and Scantily Clad Wife, Orella*? I think not.

Mister Silver Age Recommends...

Action Comics #266

DC
Jul 1960
Cover artist:
Curt Swan, Stan Kaye

"Captive of the Amazons"
Writer: Jerry Siegel
Penciller: Wayne Boring
Inker: Stan Kaye

Then 10¢
Now $80

Reprints appear in...
• Superman #207

© 1960 National Periodical Publications, Inc. (DC)

Oh, no! Superman had to marry the gorgeous and scantily clad Orella, better known as "The Girl Who Was Mightier Than Superman," in Superman #180, if she beat him in a tug of war! And guess who won?

© 1965 National Periodical Publications, Inc. (DC)

Mister Silver Age Recommends...

Superman Vol. 1, #180

DC
Oct 1965
Cover artist:
Curt Swan, George Klein

"The Girl Who Was Mightier than Superman"
Writer: Uncredited
Penciller: Curt Swan
Inker: George Klein

Then 12¢
Now $50

© 1965 National Periodical Publications, Inc. (DC)

TRIVIA CHALLENGE I
Category: **PSEUDONYMS**   *What was the real name of JAY GAVIN?*   Answer on page 89   Answer from page 85 **DENNY O'NEIL**

ENTER: THE RELATIONSHIP!    **87**

Oh, no! Superman was captured by three gorgeous and flimsily-clad babes who ripped his clothes off in "Half a Hero" in *Superman* #223! Why did these terrible things keep happening to our favorite Blue Boy Scout?

© 1960 National Periodical Publications, Inc. (DC)

Mister Silver Age Recommends...

Action Comics #395

DC
Dec 1970
Cover artist:
Curt Swan, Dick Giordano

"The Secrets of Superman's Fortress"
Writer: Leo Dorfman
Penciller: Curt Swan
Inker: Murphy Anderson

Then 15¢
Now $7

© 1970 National Periodical Publications, Inc. (DC)

Oh, no! Superman fell head over heels for a gorgeous and scantily clad Amazon slaver in *Action* #395. Clearly, his standards had dropped after so many years of being hounded by so many Amazon queens.

© 1970 National Periodical Publications, Inc. (DC)

Another five agonizingly long years later, Superman met three more cuties who had admired him from afar. In this case, though, Editor Mort Weisinger had something more elaborate in mind for "Half a Hero!" in *Superman* #223 (Jan 70). I won't tell you what went on, because that would take about a billion words. Besides, the convoluted plot was nowhere near as important as the opportunity to see Elura, Alena, and Nula wander around in their *I Dream of Jeannie* outfits after they beamed Supes aboard their saucer and ripped his clothes off (well, his Clark Kent suit).

Basically, our tantalizing trio were super-powered members of the Galactons, a club of super-heroines. Now they'd decided to admit their first male member (Hey! It's their term, not mine!), and Superman had been chosen. These gorgeous gals certainly were worthy club-mates for The Man of Steel. They explained how they'd each managed to meet Clark that day by taking temporary control of his mind via their long-range thought-implanters. "No wonder my mind's been jumbled today!" Big Blue exclaimed. It sounds like a gadget that Princess Jena should seriously have considered buying.

But all was not peachy with our three space sirens. And several pages later, The Last Son of Krypton was flying away from their saucer, sadder but wiser. "I let my curiosity sway my better judgment!" he thought ruefully. "I should have sent those girls on their way as soon as they drew me up here! Now I've paid an awful price for going along with them!"

And guys, at one time or another, haven't we all said exactly the same thing?

Less than one year later, in *Action* #395 (Dec 70), we learned that Superman had run into yet another gorgeous, hardly dressed Amazon some time in the past in an adventure we'd never heard about before! How could they have kept from revealing this for so long? For whatever reason, we finally learned of it when Superman played one of his memory tapes at his Fortress to remind himself of this special Amazon.

Their meeting began when Superman saved a group of alien male slaves being hunted down on another world. He rescued them, bringing him to the attention of Captain Althera, the Amazon warrior charged with finding new slaves for the Amazons' mines. Using his telescopic vision, The Man of Steel zeroed in on Althera and her warrior women, and— in a real switch from past meetings with Amazon women—immediately fell in love. Really!

TRIVIA CHALLENGE I
Category: **PSEUDONYMS**   What was the real name of **SCOTT EDWARD?**   Answer on page 90   Answer from page 86 **MIKE ESPOSITO**

88   **BABY BOOMER COMICS**

"Althera, their leader!" he said as she watched the Space-Amazons wiggle back to their space ship. "A beautiful goddess and incredibly strong. Yet her voice is melodious, like a bell, even when she commands!" But he was pulled away from his reverie when some of Althera's Amazons began hunting down more men-slaves.

Supes kept saving the slaves and falling more in love with Althera — and she did likewise, once she discovered he was behind the Amazon's failures. Finally, he saved Althera from an ambush and confronted her, where she used her womanly wiles to entice him into becoming her mate. "Althera, how can I resist you?" he replied. "After all these years, I've found the one woman fit for a Superman!"

Was this one of The Man of Steel's brilliantly cunning plans to play another gorgeous, incompletely costumed Amazon for a fool? Was he being mind-controlled and having to find a way to fight off this forceful manipulation? Um, no, he apparently really *was* in love with this slave-hunter and was devastated when Fate kept him from marrying his lady love. And so he kept her cape on display to remind him of "how beautiful it might have been!" *Ay, carumba!*

After all those years of avoiding some darned gorgeous and revealingly attired Amazons, it's hard to imagine he fell head of Kryptonian heels for an Amazon slaver! So let's just move on and get this one in the rear-view mirror.

There's one more Amazon story that really stuck out in my mind. In this adventure, our boy lost his memory and ended up on a remote island where Lola-La, the chief's beautiful and *extremely* scantily clad daughter, fell in love with him. After feeding him fruit while he was tied up, Lola released him and took him to a cave. She laid him down in the sleeping furs, kissed him, and then took him out to stand before her dad. There he was decorated with flower garlands and was about to unknowingly be married to this extremely nubile native girl when Mr. Z said...

What's that? You don't remember this story from back in The Silver Age? I'm not surprised. It was part of the epic "Blackout" story arc that ran through the Superman comics in 1991. These particular scenes were delineated (with loving care, I daresay) in "Mismatch" in *Superman: The Man of Steel* #6 (Dec 91).

To be truthful, I didn't get quite the same charge out of this tale that I received from those other stories of gorgeous, scantily clad Amazons. Those earlier ones appeared back in my own Golden Age, when long, hot summers were made for lying around in the shade slugging down sodas and reading comic books.

But that's all right. It's good to know that, through the years, no matter how often The Man of Steel is reinvented, updated, or even killed off, some things never change. And one of them is that Superman just cannot steer clear of gorgeous, scantily clad Amazons.

Oh, no! Superman had to marry a gorgeous and scantily clad Amazon in ... hey, wait a minute! That's not Superman! That's the star of **The Adventures of Bob Hope** *#65 (Oct-Nov 60)! How the heck did* **he** *get in here?*

Mister Silver Age Recommends...

Superman: The Man of Steel #6

DC
Dec 1991
Cover artist:
Jon Bogdanove, Dennis Janke

"Mismatch"
Writer: Louise Simonson
Penciller: Jon Bogdanove
Inker: Dennis Janke

Then $1
Now $2

TRIVIA CHALLENGE I
Category: **TEAMMATES**   What team included Awkwardman, Blimp, and Dumb Bunny?   Answer on page 91   Answer from page 87 **WERNER ROTH**

ENTER: THE RELATIONSHIP!

Green Lantern's Amazonian Adversary

"Besides Superman, Mr. Silver Age, has your crack research team (one person strong and counting) found any *other* super-heroes who regularly had to fend off the matrimonial advances of gorgeous, scantily clad Amazons?"

Sadly, pickings have proven slim. But we can report that at least one other super-hero found himself in that unusual position nearly as often as The Man of Steel himself did. But, in the case of Green Lantern, it was always the *same* Amazon: Star Sapphire, stubbornly returning to woo her man time after time. And, frankly, she wasn't all that scantily clad compared to Supes' bevy of beauties. But she was pretty *tightly* clad, so you take what you can get.

Even Green Lantern kissed the girls and ran away. Call him a costumed Georgie Porgie.

The matrimonial rubber really hit the road (so to speak), when Hal's boss/girlfriend Carol Ferris started living "The Double Life of Star Sapphire!" one more time in *Green Lantern* #41 (Dec 65). Carol had been replaced as Star Sapphire, which was actually the name given to the mortal warrior-leader of the Amazons of Zamaron. After offering the position to Carol and giving her a chance to live "The Secret Life of Star Sapphire!" in *GL* #16 (Oct 62), they had revoked her title in that issue when GL (a mere man, after all) defeated her in battle.

The new Star, who looked exactly like all the previous Stars (that is, exactly like Carol, which was how Carol snagged the offer in the first place) was otherwise known as Dela Pharon of Xanador. Dela had had an off-day while defending the Zamarons against an invader, so the tribe sent her to battle Carol (after reviving her knowledge of her Star identity) to decide once and for all who deserved to be Star.

Being the shrewd manager of Ferris Aircraft Co. (her dad's company) in her everyday guise, Carol, of course, had no problem outwitting her opponent and winning the battle of the identical Stars, which gave her a new perspective on her career plans. "I have decided that I shall be queen of the Zamarons!" she told Hal after a big victory smooch. "We'll be married on Zamaron! We could live as happy there as on Earth!"

Carol/Star was happy about the idea of marrying GL now that she was queen because she was under the impression that GL had agreed to marry her. She thought this because, well, he *had* agreed to marry her, in *GL* #26 (Jan 64). At the time, she was controlling his will power, and he wiggled out of an impending ceremony by saying that he would walk down the aisle with her— but only if she succeeded in unmasking him. So she promptly did that in the aptly titled, "Star Sapphire Unmasks Green Lantern!" The scheming minx.

Mister Silver Age Recommends...

Green Lantern (2nd series) #26

DC
Jan 1964
Cover artist:
Gil Kane, Murphy Anderson
"Star Sapphire Unmasks Green Lantern"
Writer: Gardner Fox
Penciller: Gil Kane
Inker: Joe Giella

Then 12¢
Now $115

© 1964 National Periodical Publications, Inc. (DC)

Reprints appear in...
• Green Lantern Archives #4

TRIVIA CHALLENGE I
Category: **TEAMMATES**   *What team included Hot Dog, Krypto, and Mammoth Mutt?*   Answer on page 92

Answer from page 88
GIL KANE

But before Star could pull the figurative trigger on her wedding day in that adventure, she reverted to Carol and lost her memory of the promise. I just loved Star Sapphire stories. Hal wasn't worried about fulfilling his promise when Carol regained her Star memories — and we all knew she would someday — since he wanted to marry Carol, anyway. He just hoped to do it as Hal rather than GL before that happened.

"It's all the same!" he mused, as he walked with Carol after she'd lost her memory. "She and I will be husband and wife — someday!" Well, um, except in one identity, she's your boss and in the other, she's queen of a planet of gorgeous and tightly clad Amazons! It may be a nuance to you, but I'd just as soon know which one of those two young ladies I was marrying.

Anyway, now in *GL* #41 (remember when we started this with *GL* #41?), Carol reclaimed her queenly title and wanted to redeem the emerald promise her soon-to-be hubby had made about getting hitched. But Green Lantern argued that, much as he'd like to become the husband of the leader of a tribe of gorgeous and tightly clad Amazons, and he *had* promised that he'd do that little thing, they would, alas, have to stay on Earth because of him being its protector and all. Star argued that if she was willing to give up her aircraft company, the least he could do was stop worrying about every little bit of danger to some dinky sector of the cosmos.

The Zamarons suggested a duel to decide where the newlyweds would live. (Being Amazons, they were big on duels.) The happy couple agreed. Green Lantern figured he'd beaten Star before and could do it again, while Star figured she could trick Green Lantern with an ambush, because she'd done *that* before, too. Guess who figured correctly? What a wily female.

GL admitted he'd lost and, since more amnesia didn't seem to be on the horizon, he agreed to marry the girl of his dreams (more or less) and live among a tribe of gorgeous and tightly clad Amazons. "After the wedding ceremony," he told her, "I'll make my last report to the Green Lantern Organization and tender my resignation." And so, a few panels later, GL and Star were standing in the Zamaron Hall of Honor getting hitched.

Obviously, since the comic book wasn't renamed *Green Lantern's Wife, The Gorgeous and Tightly Clad Star Sapphire*, Hal squirmed out of this one, too, and everyone agreed his promise was rescinded. (Whew!) But I won't tell you how he did it.

All things considered, he might've been better off biting the bullet and settling down with Star. After all, there are worse fates than marrying an Amazon queen, as Hal was to find out later in his career. But that's a story for another time.

*Star (Carol Ferris) Sapphire defeated Green (Hal Jordan) Lantern in combat in **Green Lantern** #41 (Dec 65). This forced GL to marry her and set up housekeeping on Zamaron when she became Queen of the Amazons! Oh, if only Superman were there to save him.*

TRIVIA CHALLENGE I
Category: **TEAMMATES**   What team included Big Anvil, Cannonball, and Long Rifle?   Answer on page 93

Answer from page 89
INFERIOR FIVE

ENTER: THE RELATIONSHIP!

The Batbabes of Gotham City!

"Mr. Silver Age, how can you say Superman is cooler than Batman? You overlooked all kinds of cool stuff that The Caped Crusader has going for him! You should re-evaluate that choice."

It's hard to imagine any argument that could counter the fact that Superman had an overpowering appeal to gorgeous, scantily clad Amazons across the galaxy. Whenever I lay out my supporting examples in detail — exacting, loving detail, I admit — bat-enthusiasts have a hard time disagreeing with my findings. But I have to agree that they have a persuasive counter-argument as to why Batman is the best.

Let's face it, Superman doesn't have many babes helping him in his daily crime-fighting duties. And the emphasis there is on *daily*. Superman's Amazonian tales, while pulse-pounding, were spaced at much too lengthy intervals, if you want to know the honest truth. Batman, on the other hand, had babes in skin-tight costumes patterned on his own running around every day of the year.

And it takes a special kind of gal to don cape and cowl to join a guy and his kid sidekick as they punch out crooks while running around amid really big props. But it seems there was a fairly substantial group of such women living in Gotham City. And if all those fabulous honeys weren't enough, Bruce and Dick even managed to find a dog to join in the fun!

Fabulous babes and a dog by your side. Not even The Man of Steel could top that! It's true, Supes did have Krypto, his boyhood pooch from Krypton, and that's a definite plus. But Krypto spent most of his time romping through outer space. And in the babe department, sadly, on a daily basis Kal-El was stuck with Lois Lane, everyone's favorite pest, and Supergirl, his first cousin! How much fun could *that* be? So I may have to rethink my position on who was coolest.

Batgirl wasn't the first batty female hanging from the roof of the cave.

Batman didn't spend much time rethinking his position on Kathy Kane, who was introduced in the cleverly titled "The Batwoman" in *Detective Comics* #233 (Jul 56). He talked her out of fighting crime at his side right after her debut and he did it again the *next* time she showed up, too. The guy apparently didn't know a good thing when he had it.

Batwoman kicked off her career of fighting bad guys among giant props by saving The Dynamic Duo from a giant robot in "The Batwoman" in **Detective** *#233. They convinced her to hang up her mask, but it didn't last long, thank goodness.*

Kathy didn't just put on a costume, hop on her Bat-cycle, and head out for the big prop factory. A circus acrobat who admired Batman, she inherited a fortune and decided to use it to fight evil. So she built a big mansion over an old mine tunnel and created a bat-cave beneath it. (Don't ask me how one creates a big bat-cave without *someone* knowing about it; we don't want to bog down in details here.) Then, she outfitted it with a crime lab and everything she needed for big-time crime-busting. Finally, she sewed her costume, modified her cycle, and put together her shoulder-bag utility case. Yep, her utility belt was a big ol' purse. Don't forget, I don't write 'em, I just read 'em.

Her first case was a major success. She swung down from the top of the new air terminal's giant plane props and caught the bad guys by blowing powder

TRIVIA CHALLENGE I
Category: **TEAMMATES**

Besides Black Canary, Dr. Fate, Hawkman, Atom, and Green Lantern, what two other JSA members fought the Crisis on Earth-One?

Answer on page 94

Answer from page 90
SPACE CANINE PATROL AGENTS

on their faces with her large powder puff. Then she used her charm bracelets, which were really steel handcuffs, to hold the crooks for the police. As I said, I don't write 'em.

But Batman was less than thrilled. "You can't crusade against crime!" he told her as she scooted out the door. "The law of Gotham City says that nobody can wear a Batman costume!" "You're wrong, Batman," Kathy replied for the first of no-doubt hundreds of times in her career. "The law says no 'man' can wear it! I'm a woman!" Mmm, baby, no argument with that.

Her success continued, but Batman wasn't convinced. "She doesn't realize that she's been successful thus far because of good luck!" he grumbled to Robin, not remembering all those stories where he'd survived primarily because his name was on the cover.

Being the world's greatest detective and having the world's greatest filing system, Bats uncovered Batwoman's real identity and convinced her that, if he could learn that detail, others more criminally inclined could do it, too. Even though Batman was the world's greatest at detecting this stuff and it still took a number of cases working with her closely for him to figure it out, Batwoman agreed she might be in danger.

But her feeling didn't last long. In "The Challenge of Batwoman" in *Batman* #105 (Feb 57), she wore her Batwoman costume to a Halloween party. Along the way, she spotted Robin chasing a crook down some train tracks, helped him catch the guy, became involved in a really convoluted story, and got to be Batwoman again. By the end, she again hung up her batarang for good. But this time, we knew it wouldn't last long.

In fact, by the time we'd read the cleverly named "Bat-Girl!" in *Batman* #139 (Apr 61), The Caped Crusaderette had become one of the gang. That's why it was so easy for the leader of the Cobra Gang to trap all three of them in his Electronic-Ring. As he did, a lithe, teen-age form swung through the window. "Don't worry, everybody! Bat-Girl will take care of him!" She turned off the ray, Batman slugged the bad guy, and Bat-Girl swung away. (Please note, only a trained writer like Mr. Silver Age should try to say "swung" twice in one paragraph.)

Back home, Kathy Kane discovered someone waiting in the Batwoman-Cave: Betty Kane, her niece. Betty had been staying with Kathy and discovered her secret identity. See? Batman was right about it being easy to figure out! Guys are always right about this stuff.

"If you can be Batwoman, I can certainly be Bat-Girl!" she argued, using dubious logic and a different spelling system all in one sentence. But Kathy still was reluctant. After talking it over with Batman, who was clearly the brains of this outfit, she agreed to allow Betty to remain Bat-Girl — but only after rigorous training that Kathy sneakily intended to continue until Betty was an old Bat-lady.

But Betty became antsy after only a few days of rigorous bat-training. So she followed Batwoman that night and joined in the fun. "How am I doing, Robin?" she cooed. "Not bad," he replied. "For a girl." Batwoman agreed. "Maybe we will go out as a team someday!" Kathy promised Betty. "Oh, I can hardly wait!" she exclaimed. "And perhaps Robin and I can work on a case together too! Well, Robin — is that a date?" "Ulp!" he replied. What a wit that Boy Wonder had. Robin kept many unplanned dates with Bat-Girl, of course. But there's no denying he became much more interested in general female bat-charms after "The Million Dollar Debut of Batgirl!" in *Detective* #359 (Jan 67). The key

Bat-Girl struck fear into the hearts of criminals with her scary balloon in the well-named tale "Bat-Girl!" in *Batman* #139. Kathy Kane's cousin Betty also struck fear into the heart of Robin, who tried playing hard to get.

Mister Silver Age Recommends...

***Batman* #139**

DC
Apr 1961

Cover artist:
Sheldon Moldoff

"Bat-Girl!"
Writer: Bill Finger
Penciller: Sheldon Moldoff
Inker: Sheldon Moldoff

Then **10¢**
Now **$140**

Reprints appear in...
• **Batman From the '30s to the '70s** (hardcover)

TRIVIA CHALLENGE I
Category: **GORILLAS** · *What was the name of the giant super-ape from Superman's homeworld?* Answer on page 95 · Answer from page 91 **TOMAHAWK'S RANGERS**

ENTER: THE RELATIONSHIP!

93

Now **this** is a Batgirl! Batman and Robin had to wait three long, lonely years after their New Look began for their crime-fighting sprees to be brightened by "The Million Dollar Debut of Batgirl!" in **Detective** #359.

© 1967 National Periodical Publications,Inc. (DC)

Finding reprints:

The debuts of Ace, Batwoman, Bat-Girl and Batgirl were gathered together in the *Batman: 1930s to 1970s* hardback collection.

Detective #233 was reprinted in *Batman Annual* #4.

Batman #105 was reprinted in *Batman Family* #3.

Batman #139 was reprinted in *Batman Annual* #7.

Detective #359 was reprinted in *Blue-Ribbon Digest* #9 and in a DC Millennium edition.

Detective #369 was reprinted in *Batman Family* #2.

Batman #197 was reprinted in the *Greatest Batman Stories* hard- and softcover collection.

Batman #92 was reprinted in *Batman Family* #5.

Batman #123 was reprinted in a Pizza Hut giveaway comic.

reason for this interest, besides his being six years older by then, was that Batgirl had a lot more female bat-charms to work with in this incarnation.

Batgirl, of course, was Barbara Gordon, daughter (yes, daughter) of Commissioner Gordon. "The whole world thinks I'm just a plain Jane," Barbara correctly stated while wearing her granny glasses and tightly wrapped hair. "I'll show them a far more imposing girl tonight!"

Babs was heading out to a Halloween party, for which she'd created a tight "Batgirl" costume. A really, really tight Batgirl costume. "This costume really does things for me!" she correctly stated again. She intended to unmask at the party and give her father a shock, but things didn't work out as planned. On the way, she happened upon Killer Moth trying to kidnap Bruce Wayne. She foiled the plot with Batman's help but refused to reveal her identity.

She gave this crime-fighting notion some thought, created a real Batgirl costume she could use, if the circumstances allowed, and started training. After a few days of rigorous training, she headed over to stately Wayne Manor to drop off a rare book just as Killer Moth made another stab at nabbing Bruce.

Babs quickly went into bat-action. Her beret flipped down into her mask, her skirt reversed to become a cape, her boots rolled up into longer boots, and her handbag transformed itself into a specially designed weapons belt! Whoa, baby, could we see all that in slow motion? Thank goodness I was a dumb kid (and a male one at that), or I might have thought about the plausibility of that convertible costume more than was good for me.

Batgirl didn't do as well at Wayne Manor, confirming The Caped Crusader's perennial macho attitude toward lady crime-fighters. "This is a case for Batman and Robin," he informed her, running off after the bad guys. "I'm sorry — but you must understand that we can't worry ourselves about a girl..."

The fact that the next caption described her as "a raging young tigress" sums up her reaction to that news. And, needless to say, she saved The Dynamic Duo from the death trap they managed to get caught in, although Batman claimed he could've gotten them out of it, anyway. Yeah, that's what he always says.

"Will the new Batgirl appear again?" the final caption asked, gesturing with one of those Infantino hands that I always loved. "That depends on you, dear readers! Write and let us know!" Well, of course she appeared again. Often. She was starring in a TV show by then! And I have to admit, her cases were some of my best-remembered issues of *Detective* from back then.

Take, for instance, "Batgirl Breaks up The Dynamic Duo!" in *Detective* #369 (Nov 67). "Wouldn't you rather go with me, Robin?" she asked sweetly on the splash page. "I have a sidecar with your own special insignia attached to my batbike!" I don't know about The Boy Wonder, Babs, but you talked *me* into it. Of course, maybe the story's ending had something to do with my liking this one, too. "Looks to me like Batgirl is making a play for Batman!" said a slinky, sultry vixen petting a cat. "She has her nerve — trying to cut herself in on my man! I've known Batman a lot longer than that Jill-come-lately! If he belongs to anybody, he belongs to...Catwoman!" That little speech led to a catfight between Selina and Babs in *Batman* #197 (Dec 67), as the two hissed and spit over Batman's affections. Ah, memories.

But my favorite Batgirl adventure came a mere two issues later, in "Batgirl's Costume Cut-Ups!" in *Detective* #371 (Jan 68). "Batgirl!" Batman yelled on the cover, as a bunch of hoods swarmed over him and Robin. "Get over here! Help

TRIVIA CHALLENGE I
Category: **GORILLAS**

What two substances made a poor little chimp into TITANO?

Answer on page 96

Answer from page 92
HOURMAN, FLASH

94

BABY BOOMER COMICS

us! We've got a problem!" "I have a bigger one," Batgirl said, sticking her well-rounded thigh right into the reader's face. "A run in my tights!" The best part was that the story actually lived up to the cover. Trust me, guys, you don't want show this one to any women you know. But to this day, it chokes me up to think about it. It must have been the Infantino/Anderson cover and the Kane art inside.

As noted, The Dynamic Duo had even more going for them than an array of curvaceous bat-babes following them around, not that they needed anything else. They also had their faithful canine companion and obedient partner, Ace The Bat-Hound!

In fact, they had Ace before the first Batwoman made the scene, even before the glorious Silver Age began! He'd shown up in the cleverly named story, "Ace, the Bat-Hound!" in *Batman* #92 (Jun 55). In it, Bruce and Dick rescued a stray dog drowning in the river and advertised for his owner.

When the Dynamic Duo next headed on a mission, Ace followed through the Bat-cave door, and they decided they had to let him into the Batmobile. Since his forehead mark gave him away as the dog Bruce Wayne had advertised, Robin created a cute little mask for him and made a bat-symbol for his collar — all while riding along in the Batmobile! It really paid off to take those arts and crafts classes at Gotham Elementary School.

When the new Bat-Hound helped collar the crooks (so to speak), Robin was saddened to think he'd have to give up his canine pal when they found his owner. And, indeed, that's what ultimately happened, with Ace returning home at story's end. "If you ever want to be a Bat-Hound again, Ace," Robin told him, "the position is open."

Well, heck, who *didn't* want to see Ace the Bat-Hound again? Sure, Krypto had super-powers and could think logically (and in English), but Ace could hang out with Bruce and Batman *both*! What a dog! So, in *Batman* #97 (Feb 56), Ace returned in a story cleverly named "The Return of the Bat-Hound!"

A bunch of crooks forced a dog trainer to use his prize pupil to help them rob factories. "That's bad," Robin opined. "Human criminals we can track down — but we wouldn't even know where to start with a dog!" "Robin," Batman decided, "we need the Bat-Hound to help us!"

So once again Bat-Hound saved the day and returned to his master at the end of the tale. By *Batman* #123 (Apr 59), Bat-hound's owner had conveniently gone to Europe and left the daring doggie in The Dynamic Duo's care. Unfortunately, in that issue Ace had to help Robin hunt down Batman, who had become a fugitive from justice. But it all worked out in the end, so don't worry.

Ace even got to sample the life of a super-dog, when Bat-Mite turned our poochy pal into "Ace — The Super Bat-Hound!" in *Batman* #158 (Sep 63). Ace not only could fly and bend steel with his bare paws, but he shot flames out of his mouth. Talk about dog breath! Of course, by story's end, Bat-Mite disappeared, thus ending Ace's powers.

In fact, Ace and Bat-Mite both vanished for good shortly after that. Batman's New Look was but five issues away, and it swept away Batwoman, Bat-Girl, Ace, *and* Bat-Mite. It took nearly three years for Batgirl to make her debut; three lonely years with no babes and no canine companion for our Caped Crusaders. Sob.

Ace the Bat-Hound was saved from the watery depths by the Caped Crusaders in **Batman** #92 and reappeared to help his costumed buddies with his K-9 IQ in **Batman** #97. Obviously, Ace got a little hungry and munched on my copy (below)!

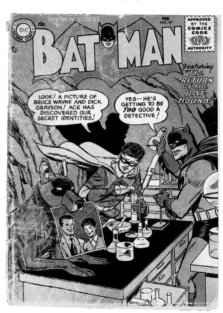

Police squads and crooks can't deduce Batman's identity, but a dog in a mask can crack it. That's the Silver Age!

TRIVIA CHALLENGE I
Category: **GORILLAS**   For what elective office did GRODD the Super-Gorilla run?   Answer on page 97   Answer from page 93   **KING KRYPTON**

ENTER: THE RELATIONSHIP!

95

RIP: S.C.P.A., 1966-1995

"I fondly remember Krypto's super-team, The Space Canine Patrol Agents! Are they still operating today, Mr. Silver Age?"

Sadly, I must pass along the word of their tragic (yet undetailed) demise, which was first revealed to fandom worldwide in *Legionnaires* #28 (Aug 95). You could almost see the sorrow dripping from each keystroke, as Assistant Editor Mike McAvennie answered reader John Kalb's impassioned plea to discover if The Space Canine Patrol Agents had survived Zero Hour, the 1994 follow-up cataclysm that cleaned up all the messy bits of continuity that the Crisis on Infinite Earths had left behind.

"Sorry, John," McAvennie wrote, in what undoubtedly was the last of many tries at putting it just right. "Tusky Husky no more. (Amen!)" Who?

"I'm Tusky Husky, and I can turn one of my teeth into a long tusk!" this canine marvel informed us in the first panel of "The Dog from S.C.P.A.!" in *Superboy* #131 (Jul 66). It was the first of three stirring adventures of Krypto and S.C.P.A., one of the finest dog teams ever to grace the DC Universe. Okay, they may be the *only* dog team to ever grace the DCU.

"Big Dog! Big Dog! Bow wow wow!"
— the Space Canine Patrol Agents chant

Other members included: Tail Terrier, who used his tail like a lariat; Hot Dog, who made himself red hot; Bull Dog, who grew horns; Mammoth Mutt, who blew himself up like a balloon; Chameleon Collie, who became any animal; and Paw Pooch, who changed into a many-legged centipede canine.

No one who ever heard it could forget their stirring battle cry: "Big Dog! Big Dog! Bow Wow Wow! We'll Crush Evil! Now! Now! Now!" Hey, they're dogs; what did you expect? Although I have to admit, apparently one of these dogs was fairly well educated, sincethe first half of that ditty sounds remarkably similar to the "Bulldog" ditty sung at Yale University. But, no matter where they found their inspiration, these heroic hounds intoned it every time they pledged allegiance to their flag, a map of the constellation Sirius, the dog star (of course).

Krypto met the heroic hounds of the Space Canine Patrol Agents in **Superboy** *#131. Readers would soon be goggling at the exploits of daring doggies like Tusky Husky, Mammoth Mutt, and Chameleon Collie.*

© 1966 National Periodical Publications, Inc. (DC)

Krypto first met these daring doggies one day while flying through space, where he saw the inflated Mammoth Mutt get punctured by a long-range missile. Before he died, MM told The Dog of Steel how the Canine Crime Caper Gang had captured his team. The Caped Canine rushed to the menacing mutts' headquarters planet, where he donned a spare pair of Clark Kent glasses to disguise himself. (Don't even ask.) He then allowed himself to be captured to join the other S.C.P.A.ers.

The peerless pooches broke loose and captured Top Dog and his gang of malignant mutts, who then were imprisoned on a world run by the Space *Cat* Patrol Agents. These courageous kitties included Atomic Tom, Power Puss, and Crab Tabby.

TRIVIA CHALLENGE I
Category: **GORILLAS**

What was the name of the BAT-APE?

Answer on page 98

Answer from page 94
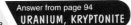
URANIUM, KRYPTONITE

96

BABY BOOMER COMICS

For his daring rescue, Krypto immediately became a proud S.C.P.A. member. So he was ready for action next issue (#132), when a glowing dog signal called him to his first meeting. The Mutt of Might quickly changed into his dashing all-blue S.C.P.A. togs and joined the group in considering a proposed member who could change himself into a cat (but unfortunately gained a craving for catnip, so he was nixed).

The team then faced down the dastardly Cat Crime Club, which was but one of the many evils the S.C.P.A. tracked in its Mutt & Meow Gallery. Other prominent members of this group included Fido Felon, Kid Kitty, Plunder Pooch, Gat-Cat, Hold-Up Hound, and Purring Pete. The names alone bring a shudder to my spine!

In their final (sob!) stirring adventure, in *Superboy* #136 (Mar 67), they rejected the membership proposals of Hoodoo Hound and Mammoth Miss (MM's sister). But they accepted Prophetic Pup after his prophesies helped the team save the home planet of their leader, Top Dog, from an invasion of giant fleas.

That calamity had been instigated by Tricky Tom and his army from the Black Cat World. He received sneaky help from The Phanty Cats, the pet cats of the Phantom Zone criminals. (Can't you just see General Zod and Jax-Ur relaxing by a phantom fireplace, stroking their little phantom kitties? Nope, me neither.)

During the battle, we learned of the heroic sacrifice of Beam Beagle, whose searchlight eyes saved the Seadog's Navy from disaster during a storm. Sadly, we were unable to read the plaques on the other depicted memorials to great doggie derring-do.

No further S.C.P.A. adventures ever were recorded, drat the luck. And none of these stirring tales has been reprinted (so far), either. Then, in 1995, we learned that this heroic team itself was (choke!) no more. We can only hope that somewhere in the Superman universe of today, there remains room for a cartoon show, an action-figure line, or perhaps a mere lunch box that will someday, somehow once again feature the proud image of the magnificent mutts of The Space Canine Patrol Agents! Bow Wow Wow!

A stirring rendition of the Space Canine Patrol Agents' battle cry reverberated through the team's headquarters in **Superboy** *#132, as they pledged allegiance to their flag, a map of the constellation Canis Major. Soon, they'd be battling the crafty Cat Crime Club!*
© 1966 National Periodical Publications, Inc. (DC)

Mister Silver Age Recommends...

Superboy Vol. 1, #131

DC
Jul 1966

Cover artist:
Curt Swan, George Klein

"The Dog from S.C.P.A.!"
Writer: Uncredited
Penciller: George Papp
Inker: George Papp

Then 12¢
Now $8

© 1966 National Periodical Publications, Inc. (DC)

TRIVIA CHALLENGE I
Category: **WEDDINGS II** — What was the real name of the person who married ELASTI-GIRL? Answer on page 99 — Answer from page 95 GOVERNOR

ENTER: THE RELATIONSHIP!

97

Herbie's Genetic Origin!

"With the good-looking parents he had, how the heck did Herbie Popnecker wind up looking like a fat little nothing (to coin a phrase)? What was going on with his genes, anyway?"

When the college roommate of Herbie's Dad revealed in **Herbie** #15 that Pincus Popnecker hadn't always had his current physique, it was obvious where Herbie got his own, um, distinctive looks.

© 1965 American Comics Group

Your confusion is understandable, although our hero's appearance makes perfect sense once you examine the (shudder) complete family tree for the Fat Little Nothing. Herbie, of course was the star of his own *Herbie* comic book from ACG Comics, a truly odd publication from that producer of "mystery" stories and a few mediocre attempts at super-heroes. Herbie was a homely, fat boy whose father coined the nickname mentioned above, in an effort to motivate the lad to achieve something—or at least shift his bulk out of his chair on occasion.

What Ma and Pa Popnecker didn't realize was that their son hid from them an amazing array of super-powers, which he used routinely to save the world from disasters of all types with little effort on his part. Fortunately, everyone else in the universe who mattered *did* know about Herbie, and that included the leaders of most nations, movie stars, major historical figures, alien invaders, and almost every real and mythological creature that ever existed.

Herbie could fly (although it mostly looked like he was walking without the benefit of having any ground underneath his feet), and he packed a mighty wallop thanks to a wide (and wild) array of lollipops he kept handy. Licking one gave him a specific power that handled whatever menace came his way, so he made sure he remained stocked with the best flavors. Herb also had a distinct way with pronouns—as in, he seldom used them — giving his speech a — shall we say? — *efficient* style that was unique to The Herbster.

His adventures made him well-respected in all the corridors of power, and he could make sexpots swoon at a distance of well over a mile, despite his ungainly appearance. That appearance was especially noteworthy since both his parents were normal-looking individuals, even if they were a bit dense in not figuring out how powerful their son really was.

One clue to how Herbie came by his distinct appearance came in "Popnecker the Pilgrim!" in *Herbie* #17 (Apr-May 66). In that epic adventure, we learned that Herbie's mom was a descendant of Myles Standish, which was causing her a problem in the present.

To make a long, hilarious (as always) story short, Herbie went back in time to Plymouth to straighten things out for his mom. There, he ran into Standish, who was his exact double. "My, but he's ugly," they both thought simultaneously. That kind of situation happened to Herbie a lot. Apparently, he saw something pretty different in the mirror than we saw on the page. Herbie also ran into historical characters who resembled him on occasion, but this one actually was a

TRIVIA CHALLENGE I
Category: **WEDDINGS II**

Who took out ATTUMA at Reed and Sue's wedding?

Answer on page 100

Answer from page 96
MOGO

relative. It's obvious his mother must have carried some pretty danged nasty recessive genes in her bod.

But in an ironic twist, his father also was at fault for his son's rotund stature and homely mug. Yes, Pincus Popnecker, that scourge of Herbie's life and his constant denigrator, had, in fact, been an exact physical duplicate of Herbie himself! This shocking revelation came to the fore in "Call Me Schlemiehl!" in *Herbie* #15 (Dec-Jan 65).

It all came out when Pincus' college roommate, Pud Bimbo, came to town and reminisced about their college days—when Pincus was, in Pud's words, "a real little fat nothing!" Sure enough, Herbie looked into the thought-balloon image Pud dreamed up and had to agree. "Golly," he mused. "Sure was ugly all right." Naturally, what Herbie saw was himself with a letter sweater and pipe.

So how did Pincus wind up looking (if not thinking) like a normal person? He revealed that, in order to win Herbie's mom away from Pud, he had dieted and exercised like crazy. But, most importantly, he had been stretched out, first by strongmen and then on a stretching machine. It's a hilarious panel.

Pud and Pincus naturally squared off in athletic competitions to prove who really deserved Herbie's Mom, and mayhem ensued. Finally, Mom revealed that she'd never liked Pud because he was a loudmouth and had always liked Pincus better, anyway. Whether Dad sacrificed any unknown Herbie-like super-powers by remaking his body wasn't addressed, but it'd have served him right.

Herbie meets his Mom's ancestor, Myles Standish, in **Herbie** *#17, showing that Herbie came by his fat little nothing looks honestly.*
© 1966 American Comics Group

Pincus Popnecker revealed how he changed from being a little fat nothing into the man he had become in **Herbie** *#15. You gotta love that stretching machine.*

© 1965 American Comics Group

Lollipop-loving Herbie was one of the strangest super-heroes of the Silver Age.

TRIVIA CHALLENGE I
Category: **WEDDINGS II**   *Whose engagement supposedly saddened Saturn Girl, Light Lass, and Duo Damsel?*   Answer on page 103   Answer from page 97 **STEVE DAYTON**

ENTER: THE RELATIONSHIP!

99

Patsy Walker's grand start in journalism

"Mr. Silver Age, I'm a big fan of that red-headed fireball, Patsy Walker! When did she become a full-fledged reporter?"

Honest, Mr. Silver Age has no idea how **Patsy & Hedy, Career Girls** #96 wound up in his collection. But, as long as it's there, he can tell you about Patsy's first foray into the dog-eat-dog world of big-time newspaper journalism. Lucky you.

© 1964 Marvel

By a weird coincidence, Mr. Silver Age just happens to have the issue that can answer that question here in the museum. How it wound up in his Marvel collection all by itself is a mystery for the ages. Ha, ha!

Patsy's grand introduction to the grueling world of journalism came about in *Patsy & Hedy, Career Girls* #96 (Oct 64). The tale was called "Patsy in Love!" which I believe was also the title of every other Patsy Walker story. But I wouldn't know for sure, since I didn't read these comics, so don't even bother asking such a funny thing. Ha ha!

Our two plucky leads, the red-headed Patsy and the raven-haired Hedy Wolfe, had been teen-age rivals for many years. By this issue, they'd become career rivals at *The Centerville Globe*, where Hedy was a reporter and Patsy was a secretary. Even so, Hedy was jealous of Patsy, because Patsy was far too happy working for Mr. Trent, her dreamy new boss. Patsy's ardor didn't even cool off when a letter arrived from her beau, Buzz, who was off in the Army.

"Dear Buzz!" she sighed. "His letters are so full of tenderness and warmth and feeling! I'll treasure them always! But how can I feel the way I do about Buzz and still have such a romantic crush on Mr. Trent?? How does a girl ever really know her own heart?" Based on this attitude, I'll bet you're not at all surprised to learn that the Buzz/Patsy marriage ultimately ended in divorce. But I digress.

Mr. Trent was so jazzed by Patsy's professional demeanor (oh, yeah) that he decided to send her on her first story. He asked Hedy to tell Patsy to cover a society tea at the Uptown Center. Hedy, that raven-haired minx, instead told Patsy the tea was at the *Downtown* Center. Then Hedy headed uptown. What cunning! What clever names for buildings in Centerville!

Patsy was perplexed when she found no society tea at the Downtown Center requiring her newly discovered journalistic talents. But as she puzzed and puzzed till her puzzler was sore, a nurse friend suddenly jumped out of an ambulance and ran for a nearby house. "Patsy!" she cried. "Am I glad to see you! There were no interns available, so I had to come here alone! Hurry!"

Needless to say, Patsy's scoop on how she helped a woman deliver quadruplets was front-page news, while Hedy's hot reportage on the society tea didn't make the cut. "When will I learn not to try any more sneaky schemes?" Hedy sighed. Not in this issue, as we were going to learn in the next story.

Take it from Mr. Silver Age, this is a must-have, double-bag item for all. You'll want it more once you learn this issue also included Patsy and Hedy Fashion Pages and Patsy's Heavenly Hair Styles. Frankly, the best feature was Patsy & Hedy's Hats. Mr. Silver Age would tell you that his favorite style was the Town 'N Country Top, but, of course, he would be joking about that. Ha ha!

Mister Silver Age Recommends...

Patsy and Hedy, Career Girls #96

Marvel
Oct 1964

Cover artist:
Al Hartley

"Patsy in Love!"
Writer: Stan Lee
Penciller: Al Hartley
Inker: Al Hartley

Then **12¢**
Now **$10**

© 1964 Marvel

TRIVIA CHALLENGE I
Category: **WEDDINGS II**

Who did CAROL FERRIS plan to marry rather than Hal Jordan?

Answer on page 104

Answer from page 98
DAREDEVIL

100

BABY BOOMER COMICS

IF THIS BE MY GIMMICK!

Silver Age Hot Spots

"Some things seem to make Silver Age comics stand out from all the rest. Mr. Silver Age, can you explain any of the key ingredients that make these comics so popular?"

In fact, I can tell you the three most critical elements in crafting any Silver Age comic book classic. Stan Lee and Jack Kirby knew them. John Broome and Gardner Fox knew them. Heck, even real estate agents know them.

Location, location, location.

What's that? Plot, script, and art? Deranged super-villains, unrequited love, and a sick aunt? Those all are important, too. But nothing beat an unusual, fascinating location to really add zing to your pulse-pounding, senses-shattering, epic Silver Age funny-book tale.

Not convinced that locations really made a difference to these stories? Then take this pop quiz to see how many of these distinctive, one-of-a-kind hot spots you remember from those glorious days...

1. Where was jewel kryptonite formed?
a. In Krypton's Jewel Mountains.
b. In the Phantom Zone.
c. In a gas cloud in space.
d. In Jimmy Olsen's disguise trunk.

*Boy, is Superman ever wrong! Besides X-kryptonite, kryptonite plus, anti-kryptonite and silver kryptonite, there's also jewel kryptonite, as shown in **Action Comics** #310. Where was it formed?*

© 1964 National Periodical Publicacations (DC)

2. Where do Peter Parker and his college buds hang out?
a. The Kozy Kampus Koffee Shop.
b. The E.S.U. Student Union.
c. The Coffee Bean Barn.
d. The Chok'lit Shoppe.

*There's a bigger feature in **Amazing Spider-Man King-Size Special #4** than his battle with The Human Torch! There's a two-page spread of the gang's watering hole! Where is it that Peter hangs out?*

© 1967 Marvel

TRIVIA CHALLENGE I
Category: **PETPOURRI**

What gives super-powers to STREAKY?

Answer on page 104

Answer from page 99
JIMMY OLSEN

3. Where do Captain Cold, The Top, Heat-Wave, and the rest of Flash's Rogues Gallery go as soon as they break out of prison?

    a. To a secret cave to pick up their weapons.
    b. To a tailor to have new costumes made.
    c. To a bank to steal money for more crimes.
    d. To the zoo to sneak a gorilla into the plot.

Wow! Look at all these dastardly villains ganging up on The Scarlet Speedster in **The Flash** *#174! Before they started beating on Barry each time they met, where did these big galoots always go first?*

© 1967 National Periodical Publicacations (DC)

4. Where was The Fantastic Four's planet-eating alien foe Galactus born?

    a. On Taa.
    b. On Zenn-La.
    c. In The Negative Zone.
    d. In the U.S.A.

You might think **Thor** *#169 was called "The Monster and the Man-God!" but it wasn't. It was entitled, "The Awesome Answer," because it told us where Galactus was born. Where was that hot spot?*

© 1969 Marvel

5. Where do Supergirl's parents live?

    a. In Midvale.
    b. In Smallville.
    c. In Kandor.
    d. In the Phantom Zone.

I don't know if The Maid of Steel actually won The Supergirl Game shown on **Action Comics** *#360, but I do know that you can get an answer to this quiz right, if you know where her parents live.*

© 1970 National Periodical Publicacations (DC)

6. Where does one super-hero or another invariably go every year on October 31?

    a. Sleepy Hollow, N.Y.
    b. Salem, Mass.
    c. Rutland, Vt.
    d. Amityville, N.Y.

A haunting Halloween novel right on time in the December **Batman** *(#237)! Full of chills, thrills, and familiar-looking guys who were much younger then! Where do heroes go to celebrate October 31?*

© 1971 National Periodical Publicacations (DC)

7. Where was Prof. Xavier when the Uncanny X-Men thought he was dead?

    a. In a prison on the Kree homeworld.
    b. In outer space with The Starjammers.
    c. In Tierra Del Fuego tracking down a dastardly villain.
    d. In the basement of the mansion.

Answers on the following page!

TRIVIA CHALLENGE I
Category: **PETPOURRI**   *What's the name of the pet for the Challengers of the Unknown?*   Answer on page 105   Answer from page 100   **JASON BELMORE**

Jax-Ur may not have been aware of the three "C"s of diamonds (cut, clarity, and carat weight), but he did know how to make a new form of kryptonite in the Jewel Mountains of Krypton, as shown in **Action Comics** #310.

Answers

1. Where was Jewel Kryptonite formed?
Answer a: In Krypton's Jewel Mountains.

Oh man! The Jewel Mountains! Where Krypton's prehistoric crystal birds went to die! Where Kal-El (aka Superman) romanced Lyla Lerrol! Where Lex Luthor asked Lara (aka Superman's mom) to marry him! How could we possibly have a locations quiz and not mention the Jewel Mountains, unless we mentioned, instead, the Rainbow Canyon? Oh man! The Rainbow Canyon!

I'm sorry. For a minute there, I was overcome by the smell of 40-year-old comics. Where was I? Oh, yeah. The Jewel Mountains! Where Jax-Ur, renegade scientist and well-known Phantom Zone criminal, created jewel kryptonite! At least, he's well known to those of us who love Superman comics and, in this case, "The Secret of Kryptonite Six!" in *Action Comics* #310 (Mar 64).

As that tale explained, Supes freed Jax from the Zone so they could return to Krypton's past to solve a crisis. While there, Jax slipped away from Kal and formed some of the jewel mineral into a giant gem. When Krypton exploded (choke!), the gem was transformed into jewel kryptonite (as, I have to think, were the rest of the Jewel Mountains, since all he did was shape this piece). When the two strange bedfellows returned to the present, Jax-Ur retrieved his giant jewelry. (He could do that because he was out of the Zone on 24-hour parole as part of the deal. Don't ask.)

Jax took a piece of his new kryptonite to Jimmy Olsen and hypnotized him into using it on Superman. The result was that any explosive material that Superman came near instantly detonated! The Man of Steel used his Zone-O-Phone (could I *make up* a name like that?) to scold Jax, who refused to cure Kal unless he freed every criminal in the Zone. Superman declined this offer and, instead, left Earth forever.

Nah, just kidding. But he did *consider* exile, until his super-brain realized how to solve his problem. I won't tell you what he did, but I will let you know that The Last Son of Krypton doesn't have to worry about jewel kryptonite any more, in case these things keep you awake at night. At least, he didn't have to worry about it during the Silver Age, and that's all that really matters here on Earth-Silver.

2. Where do Peter Parker and the gang hang out?
Answer c: The Coffee Bean Barn

It wasn't their first hang-out, but you know how fickle college kids are. The gang first met up at The Silver Spoon in *Amazing Spider-Man* #44 (Jan 67). But pretty soon—well, #53 (Oct 67), to be exact—they switched their allegiance to The Coffee Bean, also known as The Coffee Bean Barn. Maybe they had two-for-one sales.

To celebrate this momentous occasion, Jazzy Johnny Romita drew an impressive two-page spread of the place in *Amazing Spider-Man King Size Special* #4 (Nov 67). Tagged, "The Unofficial Cultural Center of Good Ol' E.S.U.," the Bean played host in the illo to the entire gang—including Aunt May and an unidentified friend.

While pondering yet again how to raise money, Peter Parker went sloshing towards his friends' favorite hangout, The Silver Spoon, in **Amazing Spider-Man** #44. The friends were fickle, however, and quickly moved to The Coffee Bean.

TRIVIA CHALLENGE II
Category: **PETPOURRI**
What's the name of LEX LUTHOR's dog?
Answer on page 102
Answer from page 106
X KRYPTONITE

104
BABY BOOMER COMICS

"So this is where it's happening, May!" exclaimed her friend, probably Anna Watson. "Cool it, sweetie," Aunt May whispered. "We don't want those cats to dig that we're hippies!" I don't know what she was drinking, but I'll have a double.

3. Where do Captain Cold, The Top, Heat-Wave, and the rest of Flash's Rogues Gallery go as soon as they break out of prison?
Answer b: To a tailor to have a new costume made.

Flash's famous bad guys were nothing without their spiffy costumes (literally). And, of course, they didn't go to just *any* old tailor shop. No, they went to the shop owned by Paul Gambi, tailor to the rogues! Gambi, by the way, was a tribute to long-time *Flash* letter-writer Paul Gambaccini, who now works for the BBC and remains a comics fan to this day.

Having a tailor design their duds made perfect sense to me. The only super-hero I ever saw with a needle in his hand was Spider-Man, and he wasn't very good with it. So where did all those spiffy super-hero and super-villain costumes come from? Flash's crew of no-goodniks pressed Mr. Gambi into service. The Scarlet Speedster unraveled their costume source in "The Mystery of Flash's Third Identity!" in *The Flash* #141 (Dec 63). He intercepted a delivery to the Top and went undercover to collar the criminals.

The Vizier of Velocity shut down this seamless operation, of course, but you can't keep a good tailor from bobbin to the surface. Or, at least, The Flash couldn't keep Gambi's apprentice, J.M. Leach, from opening another shop. That's where the usual suspects met in "The Gauntlet of Super-Villains" in *The Flash* #155 (Sep 65) before giving The Scarlet Speedster the needle one more time.

The Rogues held another reunion in "Stupendous Triumph of the Six Super-Villains!" in *The Flash* #174 (Nov 67), but this time they found Leach's services to be only sew-sew. "The chiseler jacked up his prices to meet the rise in the cost of living!" The Pied Piper exclaimed, venting his rage. Darn that guy! Can you believe a small businessman doing something like that — for a service that you've got to figure was pretty unusual? I tell ya, these super-villains were a real stitch!

The tailor shop also helped Jerry Lewis meet The Flash in an appropriately named story in *The Adventures of Jerry Lewis* #112 (May-Jun 69). Jerry dropped by to have his sweater cleaned just as "Pops" got hustled into a car by some rather sinister-looking guys. Jer promised to watch the shop until Pops returned (which I doubt happened) and promptly did a fitting for Captain Cold. The Flash showed up to investigate, Jerry hired The Scarlet Speedster as his delivery boy, and the story was a laff riot. Read more about it on page 149!

4. Where was The FF's planet-eating alien foe Galactus born?
Answer a: Taa.

"Taa! A planet so far advanced from any other that there are no words to do it justice! Taa! Among the simplest of its many miracles were the thought-spheres in which men lived and traveled! Taa! Ever changing — ever ancient — ever wondrous to behold! But not even fabled Taa could endure — forever!"

*Prof. Warren dropped Gwen and Peter off at the gang's new favorite hangout, The Coffee Bean, in **Amazing Spider-Man** #53.*
© 1967 Marvel

The Mirror Master was just one of The Flash's rogues who utilized the services of a crooked tailor when he needed a new uniform.

© 1967 National Periodical Publicacations (DC)

In the Marvel universe, "Taa!" was more than just a way to say good-bye.

TRIVIA CHALLENGE I
Category: **PETPOURRI**   Who owned REX THE WONDER DOG besides Paul Henley?   Answer on page 107   Answer from page 103
COSMO

IF THIS BE MY GIMMICK!   105

A Jack Kirby-rendered leviathan was just one of the wonders on Galactus' homeworld of Taa as shown in **Thor** #169.

© 1969 Marvel

Ever ancient? In any event, that's the way Galactus described his home world to The Mighty Thor in *Thor* #169 (Oct 69). And who was gonna argue with him? Especially when we were given two full pages of Taa scenes, including a full-pager and a half-pager drawn as only The King could draw them?

To make a long story short, Taa's entire population succumbed to the creeping plague. (I hate when that happens.) Galactus and the last survivors launched themselves into the heart of the sun, intending to make it their funeral pyre. As you may have guessed, Galactus didn't exactly start pushing up daisies. But he was put through a few Kosmic Kirby Changes, to say the least.

None of that will affect us here on Earth, of course. Unless his herald happens to notice us someday and signals the big galoot with a sudden burst of energy that travels through hyper-space instantaneously. And what are the chances of that? Actually, since that's the beginning of the cosmic plot that unfolded in *Fantastic Four* #48-50, one of the all-time best Fantastic Four stories, I'd have to say the chances are pretty good.

5. Where do Supergirl's parents live?
Answer c: In Kandor.

If you answered "Midvale," you probably thought we were talking about Fred and Edna Danvers, Linda Lee's step-parents. But we aren't. We're talking about Zor-El and Alura, Kara Zor-El's real-live, honest-to-goodness, flesh-and-blood Kryptonian parents. And they are, indeed, real, live, and with us today here on Earth-Silver. Just like Kara herself, now that I think about it. And there's no other Earth that can say that, since she was retroactively wiped out of existence, thanks to Superman's 1986 reboot (sob).

In "The Untold Story of Argo City!" in *Action Comics* #309 (Feb 64), we learned that by an amazing stroke of luck, Zor and Alura had escaped death from the deadly rays of kryptonite in the soil of Argo City, the Kryptonian town where Supergirl grew to teenhood after Krypton exploded.

(Technically, Argo City tragically had its soil turned into anti-kryptonite, which affected non-super Kryptonians. We learned this after the writer came up with a story in which Superman proved to be immune to kryptonite when he didn't have super-powers. It cleverly solved that story's scenario but created a problem for Supergirl. Hence, anti-kryptonite. You've just gotta love the fluidity of Silver Age mythologies.)

Supergirl's real parents tried to contact their daughter while she slept in **Action Comics** #309. You could say this story was not a dream even though parts of it happened in an apparent dream.

© 1964 National Periodical Publications (DC)

As meteors blew holes in the lead shielding that protected the citizens from their own soil, which had turned to kryptonite in the big boom, Kara's parents dematerialized into The Survival Zone. It was a delayed reaction to Zor's experimentation that didn't prove successful until the exact second that Argo City began to be destroyed, so nobody else was able to join them. Darn the luck! They finally managed to telepath a message to Kara, who learned of their existence just in time for the story to end.

Thus, in *Action Comics* #310, we learned of "Supergirl's Rival Parents!" Gasp! Hey, wait a minute! That's the same issue that introduced the world to jewel kryptonite! What a key Silver Age book! Grab it before all the guys at the all the price guides read this and jack up the price! Because, until then, it's a real steal! Oh, no, too late!

TRIVIA CHALLENGE II
Category: **FIRSTS**

Who was the first villain fought by the FLASH?

Answer on page 108

Answer from page 104
DESTRUCTO

106

BABY BOOMER COMICS

It's a real two-hankie tale, too. After a story too complex and heart-rending to relate here, Supergirl freed her parents from the Zone. Zor and Alura decided they couldn't possibly take their daughter away from the Danverses just because they were her parents. They also decided they wouldn't be happy living on Earth without Kryptonian customs to celebrate. So they moved to Kandor, and everybody lived happily ever after.

To be honest, I don't know that being stuck inside of a bottle has the same appeal as living with my daughter and being the strongest person in the world. But hey, these were two Kryptonians who'd had pretty darn interesting lives so far. So we'll cut them some slack. Sadly, we didn't get to see Kal's reaction to learning that his uncle and aunt were still alive, assuming Kara ever mentioned it to him. But I would imagine he was pretty thrilled. He had a lot of back birthday presents coming.

6. Where does one super-hero or another invariably go every year on October 31?
Answer c: Rutland, Vt.

Who could turn down an invitation from our genial host, Tom Fagan? Not most super-heroes, that's for sure, including some from both Marvel and DC. Rutland is a real town that, at least back in the Silver Age of the 1960s, staged a real Halloween parade that featured real people dressed up like real super-heroes (at least, as real as they got).

The appearances came at the tail-end of the Silver Age or a little later. The Avengers got the ball rolling when they participated in the parade in "Come on in, the Revolution's Fine!" in *Avengers* #83 (Dec 70). They wound up battling both the Masters of Evil (you know, Klaw, Melter, Whirlwind, and the gang) and the newly formed Liberators (The Valkyrie, Black Widow, Scarlet Witch, Medusa, and The Wasp). The latter formed their team because they were suddenly mad as heck about men being in charge and weren't going to take it any more. (Needless to say, they were being mind-controlled.) Not to be outdone, The Defenders (an Avengers wannabe team) made the trip the next year in "Nightmare on Bald Mountain!" in *Marvel Feature* #2 (Mar 72).

Not to be outdone, Batman and Robin made the trip that year, as well (albeit a few months earlier in comics dating) on the "Night of the Reaper" in *Batman* #237 (Dec 71). They prevented said reaper from slicing up some familiar-looking dudes who, on our Earth, just happened to write comic book stories. That trend had begun when Roy the Boy and his then-wife Jeannie had shown up for both of the earlier Marvel trips.

The next year featured an extravaganza of Halloween hooliganism when *three* interrelated adventures at the two companies took place in Rutland, with all of them featuring the comics quartet of Gerry Conway, Steve Englehart, and Len and Glynis Wein doing things that made slightly more sense if you read all three issues. It certainly explained why Glynis was wearing a "Powergirl" outfit that was an exact replica of Supergirl's outfit in the two Marvel entries — because she needed to be Supergirl in the middle DC entry.

The trio of stories began when the new, scary-looking Beast wound up in Rutland with our four comics pals just as the Juggernaut dropped in (literally) from another dimension in "...And the Juggernaut Will Get You if You Don't Watch Out!" in *Amazing Adventures* #16 (Jan 73). Juggy *did* get them, tearing

Rutland, Vt., parade and party host Tom Fagan usually made an appearance in comics stories set during the community's annual Halloween parade.
© 1970 Marvel

*A quartet of comics pros made a trio of Rutland, Vt., comics appearances in late 1972. Riding in Steve Englehart's car were Gerry Conway and Len and Glynis Wein. For this part of the adventure, from **Amazing Adventures** #16, they were joined by Hank McCoy (aka The Beast) and his ladyfriend, Vera.*
© 1973 Marvel

TRIVIA CHALLENGE II
Category: **FIRSTS**

Who was the first villain to learn the identity of IRON MAN?

Answer on page 109

Answer from page 105
DANNY DENNIS

IF THIS BE MY GIMMICK!

107

Batman's costume fit right into the annual Rutland, Vt., Halloween parade in **Batman** *#237.*

© 1971 National Periodical Publications (DC)

Marvel and DC both setting scenes in Rutland, Vt., was an early, if unofficial, inter-company phenomenon.

Professor X returned to lead his team of mutants just two issues before the original **X-Men** *series became a reprint series. Wouldn't it have just been easier to tell the team that he needed some privacy?*

© 1970 Marvel

up a bunch of parade floats in the process. Our comics quartet then segued over for "A Stranger Walks Among Us!" in *Justice League of America* #103 (Dec 72). The Leaguers and The Phantom Stranger ambled to Rutland to battle an evil that was, as PS put it, "so awesome, so overpowering, that I fear I cannot combat it alone!" I think Felix Faust was stealing UNICEF money or something. He definitely stole our pals' car to make his getaway, which wasn't the best idea.

For the finale, the mighty Thunder God, of all people, showed up in Rutland for "Firesword!" in *Thor* #207 (Jan 73). There was no real reason for him to be there, it just happened to be where he wound up fighting Crusher Creel and, oh, yeah, almost forgot, Loki. In this issue, too, "somebody" stole our pals' car, but we didn't get to see who it was. But we knew it was Felix, the rat!

Sadly, things calmed down on the Rutland front after that trio of tales. Only one trip was made the next Halloween, when Steve Englehart took us back for the "Night of the Collector" in *Avengers* #119 (Jan 74) just after the fabled Avengers-Defenders crossover had finished. No sooner had the team carted Loki off (again) than Mantis had a premonition of danger in Rutland. The Avengers scooted off, explaining the deal about Rutland to The Swordsman (at least, as well as it could be explained).

Rutland served as the scene of the crime several more times, unrelated to these Halloween hi-jinx. The first was in "The Carnival of Souls!" in *Justice League of America* #145 (Aug 77). As is obvious from the dating, Steve Englehart apparently just had a hankering to head back to Vermont (or maybe Rutland-Halloween stories had been banished by editorial fiat). In any event, The Justice League returned to save Superman, who had been sacrificed by a magician to gain power and now was in a deathly other-dimensional state. A second story that apparently occurred at the same time as this one showed up in *DC Super-Stars* #18 (Jan-Feb 78), featuring The Phantom Stranger along with Deadman and Doctor Thirteen.

As if that weren't enough appearances, Rutland was the location *du jour* in Gold Key's *The Occult Files of Dr. Spektor* #18 (Dec 75), although only the doc showed up in that one. The super-rabbit title character traveled to Rutland in WARP Graphics' *Thunderbunny* #5 (Feb 86) and met many real people in actual locations, thanks to photo references by writer Martin L. Greim. And, to cap things off, it made yet another appearance in *Animal Man* #50 (Aug 92).

Whew! Rutland was a pretty happening place, wasn't it? The main reason that Marvel and DC did their original Rutland stories, besides being able to draw out-of-shape guys in super costumes, was being able to write and draw comics creators into the stories. In addition to the four stooges noted above and Roy and Jeannie earlier, others who showed up included Berni Wrightson, Denny O'Neil, and Alan Weiss, amusing themselves no end, I'm sure.

7. Where was Prof. Xavier during the time that the Uncanny X-Men thought he was dead?
Answer d: In the basement of the mansion.

So, OK, not every Silver Age location was such a glamorous place. To tell you the truth, though, Prof. X's location was truly exotic compared to the explanation for why he wasn't stone-cold dead.

TRIVIA CHALLENGE II
Category: **FIRSTS**   Whose body was the first inhabited by **BOSTON BRAND?**   Answer on page 110   Answer from page 106 **THE TURTLE**

108   **BABY BOOMER COMICS**

As we all know, the prof began pining for the fjords after Grotesk blew him up in "If I Should Die" in *X-Men* #42 (Mar 68). But now, in "Before I'd Be Slave!" in *X-Men* #65 (Feb 70), it appeared that the report of his death had been a tad overstated.

But not really! You see, a few weeks before that explosion, Xavier was doing a little telepathic star-scanning. He had just learned of an alien invasion when who should walk in the door but The Changeling. Prof, you might want to check that security system. In any event, the former bad guy explained that he had just learned he was going to die in about six months. He wanted to go out in a blaze of glory, so to speak, so he offered to do the prof a favor. Just name it.

Charles asked him to take his place with The X-Men, so that the prof could remain in the mansion's sub-basement to prepare a counterattack to the aliens. Chuck used some of his telepathic powers to help The Changeling hide his true identity from the others. What a great teammate! So Prof. X *did* die, but it was really only someone who looked, acted, and sounded exactly like Prof. X, not the real one.

Only Jean Grey knew of the prof's true location. He had to keep secret the fact that he was still alive and living in the basement because his task was so critical he couldn't be interrupted. Right. "I know now how Hamlet felt when he saw his father's ghost!" Hank McCoy says, making an analogy so off-base I don't know where to begin making smart-aleck remarks about it.

It's a good thing this issue had such terrific Neal Adams art, including those fine caricatures of Chet Huntley and David Brinkley. It made it easier to forgive them for letting one more dead character get better in a really flimsy way.

Actually, it's a good thing Chuck managed to clamber out of that sub-basement when he did. Two issues later, all of the X-Men got banished to the cancellation sub-basement when the series started running reprints. New tales didn't return for more than four years. When they did, in #94 (Aug 75), they were about a bunch of new guys who had a hankering to be X-Men and called themselves stuff like Storm, Nightcrawler, and Wolverine. And who wanted to read stories about *them*?

Not only that, but it meant we weren't going to get to reread any more epic stories about those places I remember all my life, as the Beatles song goes. Those swinging hot spots, as the Joni Mitchell song goes. You know where I mean: those great locations dreamed up in the Silver Age of comics!

Scoring:

7: Excellent! You deserve a visit to the Batcave!

5-6: Really Good! You deserve a visit to Avengers Mansion!

3-4: Not Too Bad! You deserve a visit to Riverdale High School!

1-2: Not So Good! You deserve a visit to Camp Wack-A-Boy!

0: Pretty Awful! You deserve a visit to Prof. X down in the sub-basement!

> **Xavier had been whisked away by Marvel to give his students some time on their own — without the egghead prof psychically solving everything, as usually happened.**

Here's where you can visit these hot spots without going back to their original locations:

- "The Secret of Kryptonite Six" from *Action Comics* #310 was reprinted in *Superman* #227 and *The Best of DC Digest* #36.
- *Amazing Spider-Man* #44 was reprinted in *Marvel Tales* #32, *Marvel Masterworks* #22, and *Essential Spider-Man* #3.
- *Amazing Spider-Man* #53 was reprinted in *Marvel Tales* #38, *Spider-Man Comics Magazine* #1, and *Essential Spider-Man* #3.
- *The Flash* #141 was reprinted in *The Flash* #187.
- The saga of Supergirl's parents from *Action Comics* #309-310 was reprinted in *Adventure Comics* #416.
- Avengers #83 was reprinted in *Marvel Treasury Edition* #7 and *Avengers Marvel Illustrated Book* (in b&w).
- Batman #237 was reprinted in *The Best of DC Digest* #16 and *Limited Collectors' Edition* #52.
- *X-Men* #65 was reprinted in the *X-Men Visionaries* #2 trade paperback.

TRIVIA CHALLENGE I
Category: **FIRSTS**   *Who was the first METAL MAN created by Doctor Magnus?*   Answer on page 111   Answer from page 107 **THE ACTOR**

IF THIS BE MY GIMMICK!   109

The Men in the Iron Suit

"Mr. Silver Age, it seems to me that, while many super-heroes are powerful and wear a costume, a guy like Iron Man is powerful only because he wears a costume! He could quit and hand his armor to another person to take his place. Did he ever do that?"

Hey, have a heart! You have to realize that being a super-hero sometimes gets to be a real drag. Lots of heroes have decided to chuck it all at a low point in their careers, including Batman, The Flash, Green Lantern, The Fantastic Four, Spider-Man, Captain America, Giant-Man, and even Thor.

Iron Man's problem (or advantage, depending on how you look at it) was that, when he threw his suit in the trash can, somebody else could pick it up and be just as powerful as Tony had been. And Tony has been chucking his suit ever since he first put it on in the Silver Age. As you no doubt suspected, however, there's much more to being Iron Man than just a suit.

The first non-Tony to don the armor did so in the cleverly titled "When Titans Clash!" in *Tales of Suspense* #65 (May 65). A weaselly crook named Weasel Wills sneaked into Tony's factory one night while he was out of town. In an unlikely turn of events, Tony was so upset that his darn heart problems prevented him from courting his secretary, Pepper Potts, that he left town without his attaché case full of armor. Worse, he didn't activate any of the case's protective measures, either. Smooth moves, Tone.

Naturally, Wills found the case, put on the armor, and started robbing banks as Iron Man. He got away with this for awhile, because, in yet another astounding turn of events, Tony became so wrapped up in the rocket tests he was supervising that he didn't read a newspaper for several days. Right. And none of The Avengers stopped by to check out what the heck their pal was doing because they were "scattered around the country." Ooookay.

Tony finally splurged on a paper, returned home, and confronted his usurper by suiting up in his original, clunky armor. Good thing he never threw anything out. I won't give away how things turned out, but you haven't seen Weasel around much, have you?

His Starkness managed to keep a firmer grip on his briefcase until "The Other Man!" in *Tales of Suspense* #84 (Dec 66). Tony wound up in the hospital with heart problems, leading newspapers to speculate on why nobody ever saw Tony and his iron bodyguard together. No wonder Stark doesn't read much. Happy Hogan, who by then knew his boss's secret, convinced Tony to let him put on the armor to fool everybody.

You can't beat the classics! Tony donned the old armor for the first of many times when Weasel Wills stole the new version in "When Titans Clash!" in **Tales of Suspense** *#65.*
© 1965 Marvel

TRIVIA CHALLENGE II
Category: **RELATIVES**   Which LEGIONNAIRE has a twin brother?   Answer on page 112

Answer from page 108
TINY the STRONGMAN

That cunning plan would've wrapped things up in the usual half-issue available, but The Mandarin had been keeping tabs on things with his Tony TV. Seeing Happy enter the hospital room still dressed up in Tony's iron suit, Mandy pulled the switch and mistakenly teleported the *faux*-Iron Man to his castle, extending Happy's stint as Iron Man for another couple issues.

Fortunately, Tony sneaked out of the hospital, got to his lab, spent a few hours making a new suit of even-better armor (that could support his even-more-damaged heart), and shot himself near The Mandarin's castle in his one-man rocket to square things. Man, it must be nice to be that smart and that rich. I'm sure I'll never know.

Tony battled himself again in "The Beginning of the End!" in *Iron Man* #17 (Sep 69), this time in the form of a Tony Stark-like Life Model Decoy (L.M.D.). Tony created the realistic-looking L.M.D. in *IM* #11 to foil Mandarin's suspicions about Iron Man's real identity. Stark fooled Mandy (he had a habit of doing that) but, ever the packrat, Tony took his Tony-toy home to store it, and it accidentally reactivated. So, while Tony was again incapacitated, the L.M.D. took over his Tony life and learned to use the armor pretty well.

Fortunately, Tony's old flame Madame Masque helped him launch a sneak attack on the *faux* Iron Guy. And during that attack, guess what, Tony managed to sneak into his ever-growing storage room and don that original suit again. Needless to say, you don't want to mess with Tony when he's cranky enough to put on that old suit. Good thing he kept it oiled.

This all got to be a bit much for Tony by *Iron Man* #21 (Jan 70), so he went looking for "The Replacement" so he could retire. Happy volunteered, but Tony figured that wasn't fair, since Hap now had a wife (Pepper, the lucky guy).

Instead, Tony turned to Eddie March, a champion prize fighter nicknamed "Iron Man," who was retiring from the ring. Eddie accepted, so Tony trained him and sent him off to battle The Crimson Dynamo. What Stark didn't know was that Eddie had retired because he had a blood clot in his head and wasn't supposed to strain himself. Ed was willing to take the risk for the chance to be The Iron Dude. But, no matter how much of a chump The Crimson Dynamo was (and he was), it could still strain a guy to beat him up.

Stark learned the truth and put on a newer-but-still-old suit to save Eddie, but by then Ed had been pretty badly beaten. Tony decided he couldn't ask someone else to do his job and recommitted himself to the iron.

It's not as if that decision kept everybody out of the armor, of course, especially with so many copies floating around. But that at least covers us for the Silver Age, which I figure ended some time in late 1970. For you completists, Eddie donned the suit again in *IM* #65 (Dec 73), but he screwed things up so badly that Happy had to put on iron pants in *IM* #66. Then police detective Michael O'Brien wore the armor in *IM* #99-100.

James Rhodes took over for a drunk Tony in *IM* #170 and wound up making a nice little career for himself as IM and War Machine. Things got so out of hand that in *IM* #300, the *whole gang* put on armor, including Happy, Eddie, Michael, Rhodey, Carl "Force" Walker and Bethany Cable! Sheesh! Tony really ought to clean out his closet more often and get rid of some stuff.

Happy Hogan put on the ironware in **Tales of Suspense** #84 while in Washington, D.C., to make people (especially Congressmen) think the hospitalized Tony Stark and the high-flying Iron Man were two different people.
© 1966 National Periodical Publications

Suit-able Reprints

Want to read about the men in the iron suits but can't find or afford the originals? Sadly, only two of these stories have been reprinted so far. Keep in mind that, in some cases with Marvel reprint mags, pages were cut <choke!> out of the reprint. The savages!

• *Tales of Suspense* #65 was reprinted in *Marvel's Greatest Comics* #23 and *Essential Iron Man* #1.
• *Tales of Suspense* #84-85 were reprinted in *Marvel Double Feature* #1-2.

Special thanks to mad Marvel historian Kurt Busiek for tracking those post-Silver Age events.

TRIVIA CHALLENGE II
Category: **RELATIVES** What was the name of LANA LANG's uncle? Answer on page 113   Answer from page 109
URANIUM

IF THIS BE MY GIMMICK! **111**

Superman's Strategies

"I'm a great admirer of Superman's ability to plan ahead. What do you consider his greatest achievement in strategic planning?"

Krypto writing a giant "L" in the sky caused Lois to wriggle into a tight dress and start kissing super-heroes in "The Irresistible Lois Lane" in **Superman's Girl Friend, Lois Lane** #29. Trust me, she had a plan. Plan L, to be precise.

© 1961 National Periodical Publicacations (DC)

A cleverly worded communiqué from Big Blue made Perry White shackle The Man of Steel in "When Superman Goes Wild!" in **Action Comics** #295. Don't worry, it was part of Plan P, which you have to see to believe.

© 1962 National Periodical Publicacations (DC)

No doubt about it, I'd go with the series of plans he concocted with his *Daily Planet* buds to get him out of trouble should the need arise. Each was a monument to intricate (if not out-and-out confusing) strategy, and each was triggered by a code word or letter that was a masterpiece of mental gymnastics on its own.

We first learned of these cunning schemes when Plan L was triggered by "The Irresistible Lois Lane!" in *Lois Lane* #29 (Nov 61). We later learned it was activated when Superman's super-dog Krypto used a smoke flare to write a giant "L" in the sky outside the *Daily Planet* building. Subtle, huh? Upon seeing this, Lois suggested to Perry that she write a series of features on "Heroes I've Kissed." Oddly enough, Perry thought this was a good idea. No doubt, he'd glanced at the Good Idea jar on his desk and seen that it was empty.

To produce this ambitious (and no doubt Pulitzer Prize-winning) series, Lois squirmed into her tightest-fitting dress, "drenched" herself in perfume, draped herself in pearls, and headed out to corral some heroes. It didn't take long for her to find Green Arrow demonstrating his prowess at a national archery contest. She volunteered to help and found a good reason to plant a wet one right on his kisser.

"Gosh, Miss Lane!" the Emerald Bowman gushed. "That was terrific! May I kiss you again?" "Of course," Lois purred, as TV reporter Lana Lang, her Superman rival, simmered nearby. "As much as you like!"

Lana and Lois then ran into Aquaman, who saved passengers from a cruise-ship fire and was rewarded with several humongous Lois smooches. "Superman is a fool to neglect you!" effused The Sea King, as Lana stood by, mouth agape. "Kiss me again!"

"You've got more crust than a pie!" Lana meowed when Lois asked for a lift to find Batman. Another big buss ensued. "He's kissing Lois Lane!" a bystander exclaimed for the benefit of any blind passersby. "He can't tear his lips away!"

Once the lip-locking portion of our epic wrapped up, the heroes secretively gathered up the tissues on which they'd wiped Lois's lipstick and passed them to Batman. The Caped Crusader flew the tissues to the North Pole, where he dropped them from his plane onto Superman, who was surrounded by aliens watching him die from kryptonite poisoning. The Man of Steel wiped the lipstick-smeared tissue over his face and flew out of danger.

Afterward, Superman revealed that, when he'd found himself in the kryptonite death-trap, he'd used super-ventriloquism to order Krypto to write the "L" in the sky. That would have been enough of an accomplishment for most people, but that was only the beginning of Plan L.

As Lois expositorily reminded her super-boyfriend, "Plan`L' is to be carried out by me only when you're in dire peril from green kryptonite near The Fortress of Solitude!" Is that detailed planning or what? The key to Plan L was to sneak

TRIVIA CHALLENGE II
Category: **RELATIVES**   What is the name of NICK FURY's sister?   Answer on page 114   Answer from page 110   **FERRO LAD**

112   **BABY BOOMER COMICS**

Superman some red kryptonite grains that he knew would give him protection from green kryptonite. But Lois was being watched, so she put the red K in her lipstick and passed it around.

Lois explained the scheme to each JLAer, as she kissed him. "We're executing Plan L!" she'd whispered breathily to GA. "There's red kryptonite on my lip make-up! So kiss me hard!" To The Sea King, she'd murmured, "Aquaman, we're being monitored by Superman's enemies! Just kiss me again!" You'll be amazed at the reaction these lines have when you use them on your own sweetie, too! Try them tonight!

Naturally, Superman showed his gratitude to our plucky lass by getting a direct taste of that red K lipstick, right after explaining that there also were plans for Perry and Jimmy.

Sure enough, Plan P went into play a year later, when "Superman Goes Wild!" in *Action Comics* #295 (Dec 62). This time, The Man of Steel had to defeat the Superman Revenge Squad, which had discovered a way to hypnotize the Last Son of Krypton into doing mean, nasty, ugly things like rip up the *Daily Planet*'s office, smoosh Perry's cigar into his face, wreck Atlantis (oops!), and use his robots to smash world landmarks like the Sphinx.

Frustrated by his inability to overcome these goons on his own, Superman activated Plan P (although we anxious readers didn't realize it, of course). He told a police officer that he would surrender himself only to Editor Perry White, emphasizing that the cop must tell Perry those exact words. The words "Editor Perry White," we later learned, told Perry it was time to go to work on the plan. I won't tell you exactly what Plan P did, but it involved fake kryptonite and a whole heaping wad of Kandorians, each as super as our boy Kal himself. Simple, huh? Trust me, this situation was perfect for it.

Jimbo's turn came in "The Helmet of Hate!" in *Jimmy Olsen* #68 (Apr 63). This time, two members of Brainiac's gang started wreaking havoc. Supes couldn't stop them, because they had an impenetrable force field, as Brainiacs tended to have. They were keeping tabs on our Big Blue Boy Scout, so Superman was forced to activate Plan J. He found Jim and his fan club conveniently standing near a wrecked boat. The Man of Steel showed the club how strong he was by snapping off the right-hand side of the anchor to form a J. Clever, eh?

Even *more* clever were the details of Plan J. In fact, they were *so* clever, I can't explain why they worked in any logical fashion. But they involved The Helmet of Hate, and they got the job done. (Personally, I think Plan P might have worked better on these bozos, but Supes probably didn't want to overwork Perry.)

Fortunately, each of these imaginative plans was needed only once in The Man of Steel's career. And, for all we know, he had plans for all the other people in his life, too, depending on when he ran out of letters. Those could have included B for Beppo the Super Monkey, C for Comet the Super Horse, D for Krypto the Super Dog (leaving K open for Kandor, Bottle City of), E for Emergency Superman Squad, and on through the alphabet, *ad nauseam*. Sadly, he probably had a tough time involving any of his other girlfriends, since their names all began with "LL" just like Lois'. The man clearly had a fetish.

If Superman did have these other plans — and he was one darn super-planner, so I wouldn't bet against it — it's too bad we never saw them, especially those plans for the Legion of Super-Pets. I would've paid good money to see Superman activate Plan B with that stupid monkey.

Superman ripped the right side off an anchor, cleverly forming a "J" shape in front of his pal. This led our favorite red-head (well, after Lana Lang, of course) to don "The Helmet of Hate!" in **Superman's Pal, Jimmy Olsen** #68.

Tracking the Plans

Want to read these great stories but can't find the originals? Check these out:

- "The Irresistible Lois Lane" from *Lois Lane* #29 was reprinted in *World's Finest* #141 and *Superman Family* #171, a Giant of an issue.
- "The Helmet of Hate" from *Jimmy Olsen* #68 was reprinted in *Jimmy Olsen* #113 (Sep 68), another Giant. Mmm, love them Giants.
- Sadly, "Superman Goes Wild!" from *Action Comics* #295 has not been reprinted to my knowledge. I don't see much chance of it coming soon. That's just one more good reason to get going on those volumes of the *Silver Age Superman Archives*!

TRIVIA CHALLENGE II
Category: **RELATIVES**   **What are the names of PROFESSOR X's real parents?**   Answer on page 115   Answer from page 111   **PROF. POTTER**

IF THIS BE MY GIMMICK!

S.H.I.E.L.D.'s Energizer Bunny

"How did Sgt. Nick Fury wind up becoming the director of the secret-agent organization S.H.I.E.L.D. in the 1960s? How could he still be charging into firefights at his age? He was a commando in World War II, for cripes' sake! And he's still around doing the job in the 21st century!"

How Fury was selected to head S.H.I.E.L.D. (The Supreme Headquarters International Espionage Law-enforcement Division, at least in the Silver Age) is easy to answer, since the story was told at least twice in the 1960s. And the answer to how a guy from World War II remained so spry for so long takes us into the mid-1970s, a scary land that we try not to venture into too often, and you'll soon see why. But I knew this job was dangerous when I took it.

Fury first popped up in the 1960s' Marvel universe in *Fantastic Four* #21 (Dec 63) to enlist his war pal Reed's help in battling The Hate Monger. Fury explained he now was a colonel working for the C.I.A., although he didn't yet have his eye patch. But he had the patch by the time he was selected as "The Man for the Job!" in *Strange Tales* #135 (Aug 65). That story kicked off the new "Nick Fury, Agent of S.H.I.E.L.D." feature that replaced the Torch-Thing team-ups in the half of the issue not used by Doc Strange. Makes you wonder if maybe the patch symbolized Fury having to turn a "blind eye" to what his new organization sometimes had to do, doesn't it?

*Nick Fury switched from World War II action to the present-day Marvel universe in **Fantastic Four** #21, stopping by to see his old Army buddy, Reed Richards.*

© 1963 Marvel

(The story of how Nick gained an eyepatch some time after meeting The FF in 1963 but before starting work for S.H.I.E.L.D. in 1965 was told in *Sgt. Fury* #27 (Feb 66), no doubt after Stan Lee decided he'd better explain it. But rather than just say Fury had been poked in the eye with a pencil down at C.I.A. HQ, Stan explained it in Fury's companion mag, the World War II-era *Sgt. Fury*. Basically, the injury occurred during a rousing commando adventure during World War II, but it didn't actually affect Fury's vision until some time after that '63 meeting with The FF, necessitating an eyepatch 20 years after the fact. You've gotta hand it to Stan, he knew how to milk plot points for maximum productivity.)

Fury's first *Strange Tales* adventure opened with him stretched out in a mold for a Life Model Decoy (L.M.D.) wondering why he'd been called to the Pentagon. His curiosity really was piqued when the L.M.D.s were ready a half-hour (!) later and promptly were destroyed by assassins. Obviously, the bad guys were more in the know than Nick himself. I blame the media.

TRIVIA CHALLENGE II
Category: **TEAMMATES**   Who was the fourth person to join the already-formed JLA?   Answer on page 116   Answer from page 112
DAWN FURY

Fury and his driver avoided (and destroyed) a helicopter dropping napalm bombs on them and then lifted into the air to fly to S.H.I.E.L.D. HQ. There, Fury met Tony Stark, who moonlighted as the head of S.H.I.E.L.D.'s Special Weaponry Section. Stark led our favorite Howler into a large room populated with "some of the most famous joes from every nation." Whoever may qualify for that definition, it indicated this was big business.

Stark explained that the hordes of Hydra—the guys who had tried to destroy Fury on the way there—were scheming to take over the world, and S.H.I.E.L.D. had to stop them. But S.H.I.E.L.D.'s original director had died in battle, and the group decided Fury would be his replacement.

Fury was flabbergasted. "I'm outta my league!" he protested. "I'm just a bare-knuckles kinda guy! A bar room brawler! They made me a colonel, but I'm still a three-striper at heart! Where do I come off leadin' a hot-shot outfit like this? I'd fall flat on my ugly pan!" Stark didn't disagree with Fury's assessment of his looks, just of his capabilities.

Fury changed his mind after dealing with the chair he was sitting in, which he realized was boobytrapped. He quickly threw the bomb out the window, in a scene that always has nagged me. As the bomb exploded in air, we saw a

Above, Tony Stark was among those who welcomed Nick Fury to S.H.I.E.L.D.'s headquarters when the group decided Fury was "The Man for the Job!" in *Strange Tales* #135.

© 1965 Marvel

The S.H.I.E.L.D. helicarrier was revealed to Fury, when he threw a bomb out the window in *Strange Tales* #135 (left). The fact that it surprised him indicated he had a lot to learn as a spy. Virtually the same shot appeared when the story was retold in *Nick Fury, Agent of S.H.I.E.L.D.* #4.

TRIVIA CHALLENGE II
Category: TEAMMATES   Besides Rip Hunter, who are the other TIME MASTERS?   Answer on page 117   Answer from page 113 BRIAN & SHARON

IF THIS BE MY GIMMICK!

115

How Fury hooked up with S.H.I.E.L.D. was retold in greater detail (but with the basic story unchanged) in "And Now It Begins..." in **Nick Fury, Agent of S.H.I.E.L.D.** #4. © 1968 Marvel

dramatic Kirby full-page shot of the S.H.I.E.L.D. helicarrier. Stan's caption read, "And then, Nick Fury sees where he is—thousands of feet above Earth...as ever-vigilant military jets maintain a 24-hour patrol..."

It's impressive as all get-out, but how did Nick get there in the first place without realizing where he was? Did they make him promise to keep his right eye closed? Didn't he feel that he wasn't exactly coming back down after rising that high in his flying car in the first place? It makes me wonder if maybe Fury wasn't pretty accurate in assessing his spy capabilities. But I digress.

After the bomb went boom, Fury quickly took charge, chewing out security and then leading the efforts to capture the technician responsible for the bomb. That convinced him that he could lead S.H.I.E.L.D. When the story was retold by Roy Thomas and Frank Springer in "And Now It Begins..." in *Nick Fury, Agent of S.H.I.E.L.D.* #4 (Sep 68), he single-handedly uncovered the spy and disarmed him. (That was the one major addition that 20-page story made to the original 12-pager. It even duplicated that nagging heli-carrier caption, with Springer mimicking Kirby's original full-page panel.)

How Fury remained so youthful, albeit with gray at the temples, wasn't told until "Nick Fury—Assignment: The Infinity Formula!" in *Marvel Spotlight* #31 (Dec 76). That story revealed that Fury had had to take a special serum or else he instantly would age 60 years. When he was in his 20s after the war, that would have been darn inconvenient — but by now it would be really hard to live with, if you see what I mean. The upside was that if he took the

Spy School!

For his first two years as head of S.H.I.E.L.D., Fury was pretty busy keeping Hydra from conquering Earth. But, after he'd beaten them once and for all (yeah, right), he and the gang returned to New York City to meet new recruits going through "Spy School" in *Strange Tales* #159 (Aug 67).

As shown by the nigh-legendary Steranko, the group's special Underground Network Intelligence Training (U.N.I.T.) academy taught every type of fighting imaginable. While touring the place, Nick met S.H.I.E.L.D.'s technology whiz, Sidney E. Levine (aka The Gaff) and was talked into putting on a hand-to-hand combat demonstration with the help of

his now-much-younger pal, Captain America.

As you might expect of these two, the battle got a little out of hand, and Fury was dazed by one of his own maneuvers. He was seriously smacked around by a female recruit (left) with the massive monicker of Contessa Valentina Allegro De Fontaine. But mostly, Fury thereafter called her Val.

It proved to be the start of a beautiful friendship that became much more than that. They had rough times later on, as Fury's one good eye started to wander. But Val hung tough — and, in fact, helped him out big time in the aforementioned *Marvel Spotlight* #31. Fury always did take her for granted.

TRIVIA CHALLENGE II
Category: **TEAMMATES**   Batman, Gordon, Ralph Vern, and Kaye Daye founded which club?   Answer on page 118   Answer from page 114   **BLACK CANARY**

Nick discovered in **Marvel Spotlight** #31 that, without an annual inoculation with the Infinity Formula, he would age 60 years, which would make him even older than he really is.

© 1967 Marvel

serum, he might just live forever by aging at a much slower rate.

Slowing his aging wasn't Fury's idea. As told by writer Jim Starlin and artist Howard Chaykin, Nick had been torn up during one of his regular commutes behind enemy lines in France during The Big One. A French doctor sewed him back together but also used him as an unknowing guinea pig in an aging experiment. The result, after Fury returned home, was that the doc began blackmailing Fury for the required annual inoculation.

Does that sound like something Fury would put up with? I don't think so. But Fury reflected, "The doc stayed well out of my reach," an odd conclusion from a guy who didn't limit his adventures to Earth (and for a doctor apparently still living in France). But then the doc was murdered by a Las Vegas gangster, who demanded Fury use S.H.I.E.L.D. to aid the crook's schemes or he'd cut off the juice. Fury decided 30 years of blackmail was enough. Presumably, he took over his own injections after that so he could keep on going and going.

Debriefings

Early S.H.I.E.L.D. tales were reprinted as indicated:

- *Strange Tales* #136-138 were reprinted in *Nick Fury, Agent of S.H.I.E.L.D.* #16.
- *Strange Tales* #139-141 were reprinted in *Nick Fury, Agent of S.H.I.E.L.D.* #17.
- *Strange Tales* #142-144 were reprinted in *Nick Fury, Agent of S.H.I.E.L.D.* #18.
- *Strange Tales* #146-147 were reprinted in *Nick Fury and His Agents of S.H.I.E.L.D.* #1.
- *Strange Tales* #148-149 were reprinted in *Nick Fury and His Agents of S.H.I.E.L.D.* #2.
- *Strange Tales* #150-151 were reprinted in *Nick Fury and His Agents of S.H.I.E.L.D.* #3.
- *Strange Tales* #152-153 were reprinted in *Nick Fury and His Agents of S.H.I.E.L.D.* #4.
- *Strange Tales* #154-155 were reprinted in *Nick Fury and His Agents of S.H.I.E.L.D.* #5.
- Steranko's amazing contributions to the series were reprinted in two paperbacks, *Strange Tales* and *Nick Fury, Agent of S.H.I.E.L.D.*
- *Fantastic Four* #21 can be found in *Marvel's Collectors' Item Classics* #15, *Giant-Size Fantastic Four* #3, *Essential Fantastic Four* #2, and *Marvel Masterworks* #13.

Age considerations were already a factor in Fury's planning when President Lyndon Johnson approached the aging Howler to reassemble his team for a covert mission to Vietnam in **Sgt. Fury Annual** #3.

© 1969 Marvel

TRIVIA CHALLENGE II
Category: **TEAMMATES**   *Silver Shannon, Pack Rat, Flip, and Jangle made up what group?*   Answer on page 119   Answer from page 115   **JEFF, BONNIE, CORKY**

Batman's New Look

"Mr. Silver Age, what was so great about Batman's 'New Look' in 1964 that fans talk about it as a turning point in The Caped Crusader's career? So he added a yellow oval behind the black bat on his chest! Lots of Silver Age super-heroes changed their costume a little bit and it was no big deal."

Gee, how could readers find Batman's New Look more interesting than riveting adventures like "Captives of the Alien Zoo" in *Detective Comics* #326, the issue before the changes?

© 1964 National Periodical Publications, Inc. (DC)

Mister Silver Age Recommends...

Batman #164

DC
Jun 1964
Cover artist:
Sheldon Moldoff, Joe Giella

"Two-Way Gem Caper!"
Writer: France Herron
Penciller: Sheldon Moldoff
Inker: Joe Giella

Then 12¢
Now $70

Reprints appear in...
• *Batman: The Dynamic Duo Archives* Vol. 1

© 1964 National Periodical Publications, Inc. (DC)

The big deal came from more than that yellow oval behind the bat, pal. The oval was just the most prominent indicator of the changes introduced by Julius Schwartz when he became Batman editor with *Detective* #327 (May 64), which more than anything else began a new emphasis on The Dynamic Duo's detective side.

But, as the oval indicated, there were more changes happening to The Caped Crusader than a shift from battling aliens and other action-oriented tales to deductive-oriented adventures. The oval, in fact, was only part of the New Look cosmetic changes. Most of the good stuff appeared in "Two-Way Gem Caper!" in *Batman* #164 (Jun 64). The tale opened with Dick Grayson involved in his latest hobby, hootenanny folksinging. Please remember, I don't write 'em, I just read 'em. "If you can spare a little time from your hootenannying," Bruce told Dick, "I'd like to clear up that 'secret business' I've been on."

He led Dick into a room where a secret panel in the wall revealed an automatic elevator to the Batcave! "Boy," Dick gushed, "That beats taking the long stairway down!" Goodbye, secret entrance through the grandfather clock!

At the bottom of the stairs, Bruce unveiled another surprise: the Batmobile sports car! "The original Batmobile has had its day!" Bruce explained. "The trend now is toward sports cars — small, maneuverable jobs!"

We see the next surprise in a cutaway of the Batcave. "We're no long using the old barn exit!" Bruce explained, as the Batmobile was winched to the surface through a tunnel. At the top, an automatic door let them out onto a hillside that led to a highway.

The final surprise came as they drove into town. Seeing the Bat-signal flash overhead, Batman flipped open a dashboard compartment on his new compact Batmobile to reveal "a hot-line phone directly to Commissioner Gordon's office!" That call led to a caper that involved a jewel robber, the Hootenanny Hotshots, and, of course, lots of detective work.

Too bad Robin hadn't use his finely honed detective instincts to realize that Bruce had been adding secret doors and digging tunnels through the Batcave. And, if not Bruce, who dug those tunnels anyway, Superman? But I digress.

That *Batman* issue also introduced readers to a group that would pop up on a number of occasions and helped solidify Batman's detective status (as well as

TRIVIA CHALLENGE II
Category: EVIL GROUPS   What group had Emerald Empress, Mano, Persuader, Tharok, and Validus? Answer on page 120

Answer from page 116
MYSTERY ANALYSTS

his gregarious, Silver Age club-joining attitude). The Mystery Analysts of Gotham City consisted of detectives who met to discuss baffling mysteries and comprised Batman; Prof. Ralph Vern, a lab sleuth; Art Saddows, a crime reporter; Kaye Daye, a crime novelist; and Police Commissioner Gordon.

At their first meeting, private eye Hugh Rankin tried to join by solving Gotham City's greatest mystery: Batman's true identity. With Batman's permission, Rankin dramatically unveiled a dummy that didn't look a bit like Bruce Wayne. He was bald, his nose was too big, he weighed too much, *etc*. The club-members looked to Batman for confirmation or denial. In response, Batman walked to the dummy and, without a word, removed his cowl. And he looked exactly like the dummy!

You've gotta figure that was a tad more fun than our Dynamic Duo becoming "Captives of the Alien Zoo!" which had happened in the previous issue of *Detective*, #326 (Apr 64). Our heroes were spirited off to said zoo, which said aliens believed contained only dumb animals. Gee, I wonder where that story was going?

The back-up in #326 related "The Death of John Jones, Detective!" In the tale, Jones (aka The Martian Manhunter) fought the glowing menace of the Idol-Head of Diabolu. While battling said head surrounded by witnesses, Jones was swallowed up by the menace, which escaped. So The Manhunter headed off to star in *House of Mystery*, vowing to track down Diabolu and eventually establish a new identity. Even though he was a detective, he was moved out of the way so he could be replaced in *Detective* by the even-more detective-like Elongated Man. It was a jungle out there in Silver Age comicbookland.

Meanwhile, the previous issue of *Batman*, #163 (May 64), had featured "The Joker Jury!" In that epic, The Joker captured Batman and Robin and put them on trial before a jury of his henchmen dressed like him.

As if that wasn't enough excitement (and it wasn't), we also got to read "Bat-Girl: Batwoman II!" It was to be the final chapter in Alfred's make-believe series about what would happen when Dick Grayson grew up to become Batman II and work alongside Bruce Wayne Jr., the son of Bruce and Kathy Kane, as Robin II. That certainly wasn't a major loss.

If you'd like to read these pivotal moments in Bat-history in other locations, you've got a bunch of options, at least for *Detective* #327. It was reprinted in *DC Special* #1 and, along with its Elongated Man back-up feature, also was reprinted as *DC Silver Age Classic* #5, in a *Millennium Edition* reprint and in *Batman: The Dynamic Duo Archives* #1. That latter reprint volume is where you can also find the pivotal Hootenanny new-look story from *Batman* #164 and the Mystery Analysts back-up feature, which also appeared in *Batman* #240. Meanwhile, that goofy "Joker Jury" story from *Batman* #163 has shown up in both the *Greatest Joker Stories Ever Told* and the *Joker: Stacked Deck* collections. A Joker, apparently can trump a New Look in the reprint sweepstakes.

Batman's New Look may have made its debut in *Detective* #327, but all the cool stuff, like the new Batmobile, Batcave entrance, and the hot-line, appeared in **Batman** #164.
© 1964 National Periodical Publications, Inc. (DC)

Ironically, Batman's mask stayed the same when his New Look was introduced in **Detective Comics** #327. It was his bat-emblem that got revamped, with the addition of a yellow oval.
© 1964 National Periodical Publications, Inc. (DC)

TRIVIA CHALLENGE II
Category: **EVIL GROUPS**   Who brought together Cat Man, Ape Man, Frog Man, and Bird Man?   Answer on page 121   Answer from page 117   **THE MANIAKS**

IF THIS BE MY GIMMICK!   119

Karen Page, Super Detective

"Please settle an argument about how Karen Page learned Daredevil's secret identity. I say she deduced it from clues she uncovered, my pal Moe thinks she saw him change clothes, Curly bets she found his costume in Matt Murdock's attaché case, and Shemp guesses that a villain revealed it to her. Who's right?"

Oh, I really hate to break it to you, but all four of you are wrong. In truth, she just walked up to him and took off his mask while he stood and let her do it, something just about any stooge could've accomplished. That doesn't mean it wasn't dramatic as all get-out, though. Heck, this was a Marvel Silver Age comic, after all!

Karen Page, master detective, deduced the secret identity of The Man Without Fear in Daredevil *#57 by removing his mask. It may not have been difficult, but it was dramatic as all get-out.*
© 1969 Marvel

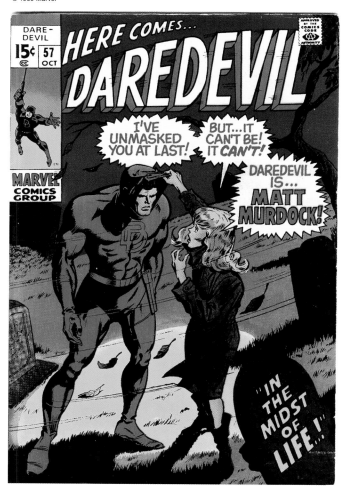

Karen's discovery of DD's secret identity began in "And Death Came Riding!" in *Daredevil* #56 (Sept 69). Karen had returned to her parent's home in Fagan Corners, Vt., to recuperate from her recent travails. (The town, as close observers will realize, is a sly reference by writer Roy Thomas to his pal Tom Fagan and his Vermontian hometown, site of an annual Halloween parade and party. Stick with Mr. Silver Age, and you can learn all kinds of things you could get along just fine without knowing.)

Karen was recovering from the shock of Matt Murdock's alleged death a couple issues earlier. That occurred (but not really) as part of a scheme to trap Starr Saxon, aka Mr. Fear II, who had kidnapped Ms. Page. DD followed her with the intent of leaving Matt deceased, conjuring a new identity, and marrying her in that new guise.

He ran into a few problems, to put it mildly, and wound up tangling with Death's Head. In the course of that two-issue battle, Karen's dad, Dr. Paxton Page, bit the big one.

In the two-page epilogue in #57, Karen was seen standing alone at her father's graveside, as Daredevil approached. "Even mother doesn't know I've lost two men that I loved," she said to herself. "First Matt, only a few weeks ago, and now..."

"Karen!" DD called. "Daredevil!" she replied. "I...I don't mean to be rude, but I'd like to be alone right now! You only remind me...remind me of..." "Karen," Matt interrupted. "Take off my mask." "Your...mask?" she asked. Tearfully, she reached out. She grabbed the corner. She pulled it off.

TRIVIA CHALLENGE II
Category: **EVIL GROUPS** — Who were the other two original members of **BATROC's BRIGADE?** Answer on page 122

Answer from page 118
THE FATAL FIVE

"It...it can't be!" she exclaimed. "You're dead—Dead!" "No, Karen, I'm not," he assured her, rather convincingly. "Matt Murdock is alive! And, what is more, my darling, Matt Murdock is Daredevil!"

In ish #58, after fainting into the arms of the Man Without Fear, Karen learned the wonderful things that radiation had done to her sweetie's super-sensitive senses. "Taste, touch, smell, hearing, all my senses were heightened!" he explained. "Except perhaps for that secret ingredient called common sense! Why else would I never have told you before that I love you?" A bunch of us readers had been wondering about that for a number of years, Matt.

They returned to the Big Apple and made plans to marry. DD decided to leave Matt dead and planned to announce his retirement as a super-hero at a parade in his honor the next day. And that was the end of this comics title.

At least it *would* have been, except, wouldn't you know it, The Stunt-Master showed up. After whaling the tar out of this loser, DD realized he couldn't turn his back on the city despite its having more super-heroes per capita than the rest of the Marvel universe combined. So he reneged on making his special announcement. He revived Matt Murdock. He didn't marry Karen.

And she was left with knowledge that, in the long run, she really would have been better off not having, considering she ultimately leaked it to The Kingpin, who didn't use it to Mr. Murdock's best advantage. But that's another story, written by Frank Miller in the 1980s...

*After Karen Page learned DD's secret ID in **Daredevil** #57, she gave up her plan to wed the big lug when he reneged on his promise to retire in **DD** #58.*
© 1969 Marvel

TRIVIA CHALLENGE II
Category: **EVIL GROUPS**   *Whose members had these first names: Otto, Ludwig, Fritz, and Ernst?* Answer on page 123   Answer from page 119 **THE ORGANIZER**

IF THIS BE MY GIMMICK!   **121**

Captain Atom's New Look

"Why did the Charlton Comics hero Captain Atom suddenly change his costume after so many years? There aren't too many Silver Age heroes who switched their looks *that* dramatically!"

No, it didn't happen often, although Iron Man, Daredevil, Green Arrow, Kid Flash, and Elongated Man come to mind as having changed their looks pretty substantially. But Capt. Nathaniel Adam's change involved more than a new wardrobe. It also brought a change in how his costume worked and how he operated.

The change began in "Finally Falls the Mighty!" in *Captain Atom* #83 (Nov 66) and was the handiwork of a renegade scientist named Professor Koste. Cap had been having a bad time of it even before Koste showed up, because his protective suit had ripped during a battle, causing nearby crowds to panic over possible radioactive contamination. That led them to worry that Cap was a danger to society and question why he wore a mask—a theme artist Steve Ditko had visited earlier during his years working on his co-creation Spider-Man over at Marvel Comics.

In order to cause confusion so he could steal some secrets, Koste sabotaged the nuclear reactor at the base where Capt. Adam/Captain Atom was stationed. Yeah, go ahead and laugh at that hokey Silver Age Adam/Atom name

Captain Atom's face was unmasked on national TV in **Captain Atom** *#84, making the evil Prof. Koste one of the most accomplished villains in the Bad Guy Union. Amazingly enough, no one recognized his alter ego.*

TRIVIA CHALLENGE II
Category: **FIRST WORDS**   Who said, "It all seemed so strange, Professor, and so mysterious." Answer on page 124

Answer from page 120
SWORDSMAN, LIVING LASER

coincidence, if you want. But before you do, I'd like to point out that, in DC's 1997 series of stories taking place in the "Tangent Universe," The Atom was really Arthur Thompson, which the Army abbreviated "A. Thom." So the Silver Age didn't have a monopoly on way-too-coincidental code names. But I digress.

Captain Atom discovered that the reactor was about to explode, so he absorbed all its radiation, which left him powerless. Don't ask me how that happened, I'm Mr. Silver Age not Albert Einstein (let alone a radiation-loving Silver Age comics writer). In his weakened state, our hero was easily overpowered by Koste and his goonboys, and they took him to their hideout.

Then, on the first page of #84, in one of the most amazing scenes in Silver Age comics, Prof. Koste did what few super-villains ever managed to do. He pirated a TV broadcast and unmasked our hero on live TV! Then, he demanded $10 million in gold for Cap's release. Why everybody was ready to believe this was the real atomic deal wasn't explained, but apparently they all did. Hey, it was on TV, it must be true!

Capt. Adam certainly thought it was being believed. "This is the end for Captain Atom!" he glumly thought. "My secret is gone!" As if that Adam/Atom thing didn't pretty well do the job, anyway. But I digress again.

Despite the homonyms in their names, Koste, unbelievably, didn't recognize Captain Atom as Capt. Adam, even though he knew him from the base. Captain Atom decided it was because, in his nuclear state, he sported white hair instead of brown. So maybe Clark Kent has been going a little overboard in disguising his identity.

While imprisoned, Cap recovered his powers, escaped, and flew back to the base, only to learn the ransom already had been paid. Oops. Before returning to battle Koste and his pals (including a souped-up strong man), Cap decided to try an experimental coating that would give him more control over his powers. He figured this was necessary because a new look would help his public image — which was in dire need of an uptick after he'd leaked radioactivity, been unmasked on TV, and lost $10 million in federal gold. Not his best day.

Cap was sprayed with a liquid protective metal in a base coat followed by several layers using different colors to create a new "suit" that was radiation-proof. When it took effect, he could turn it on and off with a power surge, allowing him to retain his civilian guise if he wanted. Thus, his former look of gold fabric costume with red mask and boots was gone. In its place were metallic silver arms, red leggings, a blue torso and boots and an unmasked face. This was an improvement only by the standards of 1966. (The story was reprinted by Modern Comics in 1977, when the company republished the original issues #83-85, but the design didn't improve with age.)

Needless to say, Captain Atom beat the beejeebers out of the baddies and recovered the gold, and his new look was a media smash. The ladies in particular seemed to enjoy seeing that handsome face.

And, of course, that hair-color change kept inquisitive types like nosy reporter Abby Ladd from realizing that Captain Atom and Capt. Adam were one and the same. The only difference was, Abby couldn't care less about Atom and admired Adam. Clark Kent should've only had such problems. Maybe if he'd ditched the glasses.

Captain Atom's new look resulted from spraying his body with a special protective metal coating in different colors in **Captain Atom** #84. He even thought far enough ahead to spray-paint a logo onto his chest.

TRIVIA CHALLENGE II
Category: **FIRST WORDS**   Who said, "The lady has a name, Flash!"   Answer on page 125

Answer from page 121
BLITZKRIEG SQUAD

IF THIS BE MY GIMMICK!   123

Oh Wasp, Where Is Thy Sting?

"To paraphrase the *Batman* movie, where did The Wasp get those wonderful toys?"

You really shouldn't go around quoting old super-villains, my friend, but we'll let it slide this time. As to the point of your question, I assume you're talking about those Wasp stingers she wore on her wrists.

Amazingly enough, Janet Van Dyne made it through 14 adventures by using readily available sewing needles and sharp sticks before she finally received a real weapon to battle super-villains, thanks to her partner and sweetie, Ant-Man. That happened in *Tales to Astonish* #57 (Jul 64) when our two insecty super-pals were "On The Trail of The Amazing Spider-Man!" That astonishing tale also can be found in *Essential Ant-Man* #1. That may be a misleading title for the collection, but it's still a fun book.

Hank (Ant-Man) Pym saw the need to give his main squeeze something more intrinsic with which to battle their foes besides her devastating one-liners. So he created two highly-compressed-air guns that strapped to the backs of her arms just above her wrist. She slipped her finger through a special ring that attached to the stingers and ran along the back of her hand, similar to what Spider-Man did with his web-spinners on the underside of his arm. With a tug, the sting-gun shot a blast of compressed air, and, by bending her finger down, she could send out one continuous burst or a series of short ones.

Fortunately, Hank thought to make the stings of the same molecular substances as the couple's costumes, so the weapons would shrink with her. That unstable-molecule material was darned handy stuff. And it came in so many textures and fabrics, too.

Considering our story's title, it won't surprise you to learn that the first person the Wasp used her stingers against turned out to be another denizen of the bug world, Spider-Man. Except at this point in his career, Spidey was still thought to be evil even by Avenger-type heroes. So it was easy for the villainous Egghead to plant a

Hank unveiled the Wasp's new stingers and taught her how to use them in Tales to Astonish #57. Unfortunately, he didn't mention how soon they'd run out of power.

Who said, "My magnetic eyes will slow down that criminal getaway rocket!" Answer on page 126

Answer from page 122
JEAN GREY

false message from one of Hank's ant scouts warning that the web-swinger was going to attack our two insect pals. I mean, how could you not intrinsically trust the word of a faithful ant?

Hank sent Janet out to search for the web-slinger, warning her not to take him on once she found him. Oh, like that was gonna work. Sure enough, she found Spidey swinging around the city and shot him with her sting to test it out. But she used too hard a blast, and it knocked him off his web. He recovered and trapped Jan, bringing Hank to the scene. Mayhem, as they say, ensued. This distraction gave Jan a chance to zap Spidey with her stinger again, using a more-controlled blast, proving to herself that she could make it work.

Egghead used this carefully concocted and executed plan to hold up an armored truck. What a criminal genius! Needless to say, you can imagine how well this worked out, once Spidey, Giant-Man, and The Wonderful Wasp figured out what was going on. This time, the Wasp got to try her stinger on some real bad guys, albeit the usual inept underlings and henchmen. She also got to learn that her sting only had so many charges, something Hank might've mentioned in that earlier six-panel training session.

Because of this introduction, The Wasp and The Spider didn't exactly wind up buggy pals. Hank found that reasonable, since the two creatures were such natural enemies. That makes sense to me, too, but I've clearly read way too many old comic books. Hank pointed out that Spider-Man did seem to be a handy guy in a pinch, though.

That didn't sway Jan's opinion, since she still was voting against Spidey on that natural-antagonism thing two years later when the web-swinger tried to join The Avengers in *Amazing Spider-Man King-Size Special* #3. She was one stubborn, albeit wonderful, wasp.

*Right: Aw, c'mon Janet, why don't you just send Spidey on a snipe hunt or after a left-handed monkey wrench? After all, that's about what The Avengers' real challenge to ol' webhead turned out to be in **Amazing Spider-Man King-Size Special** #3.*

© 1967 Marvel

*Above, The Wasp gives her stingers their first tryout against her natural (yeah, right) enemy, Spider-Man, in **Tales to Astonish** #57.*
© 1964 Marvel

TRIVIA CHALLENGE II
Category: **FIRST WORDS**   Who said, "A few seconds more, and we'll know whether we have succeeded or not!" Answer on page 127   Answer from page 123 **GWEN STACY**

IF THIS BE MY GIMMICK!   125

Doctor Strange's Strange Disguise

"With that funky costume, Doctor Strange is one hep cat! Why doesn't he have a secret identity like most super-heroes?"

Dr. Strange begins his short, strange trip into wearing snazzy super suits in "The Cult and the Curse" in **Doctor Strange** *#177, courtesy of Rascally Roy and Gene the Dean.*
© 1969 Marvel

octor Strange pretty much is Doctor Strange — literally, since his real identity was Doctor Stephen Strange, one of those fortuitous naming deals that Silver Age comics found way, way too handy. Since he was so darned all-seeing (not to mention bottom-line strange), he didn't need to hide his identity as much as some of the other heroes did. But he got closer to the super-hero norm for a while in the late 1960s, when he donned a traditional union suit and a face-covering mask. If you blinked, you missed it and, frankly, you didn't miss much.

The doc's costume change took place in "The Cult and the Curse" in *Doctor Strange* #177 (Feb 69). In a nutshell, Doc was banished to another dimension and then was attacked by minions of Azmodeus. (Not *Azmodus* — he was off bedeviling The Spectre somewhere. This guy had an "e" in his name and sported a nifty all-red outfit that looked as if it had been designed by Irving Forbush.)

After capturing our hero, Azmodeus took Steve's face and form and then went to Earth to take his place. So, even after Doc retrieved his cloak of levitation and called on the wisdom of Oshtur and the curse of Watoomb to free himself, he couldn't return to Earth, because there was only one Doctor Strange allowed per planet. Or, at least, that was the rule in this story.

Doctor Strange's mask was one of the more misguided ideas to come from The House of Ideas.

Right: He may have had more than one type of mystical weapon in **Doctor Strange** *#178, but fashion sense wasn't one of them. Perhaps Doc needed a visit from* **Queer Eye for the Straight Guy**. *"Oh, that hood just has to go!"*

© 1969 Marvel

TRIVIA CHALLENGE II
Category: **WAR IS HELL**   What was CAPTAIN STORM's distinguishing physical feature?   Answer on page 128

Answer from page 124
COSMIC BOY

"But, if yon shield affects me as I am," he told the fetching Clea, his main squeeze, who was along for the ride, "It shall not long prevail! For, many can be the forms, and many the faces, of The Man Called Doctor Strange!"

This little speech took four panels, the final one a full-pager. And when fans turned the page to glimpse that lovingly rendered panel by Gene the Dean Colan, there stood Doc with a smooth navy-blue face. His cool robe had become a typical super-hero costume, with light-blue gloves and boots along with the standard trunks in navy.

The alien dimension took one look at this new outfit and spit Doctor Strange back out onto Earth, along with the still-fetching Clea. So Steve skedaddled home, beat the snot out of Azmodeus, and began a career as a real top-of-the-line, state-of-the-art, super-duper super-hero!

Said career lasted all of six issues, not counting his last-gasp guest appearances in *Sub-Mariner* #22 (Feb 70), *Avengers* #61 (Feb 70) and *The Incredible Hulk* #126 (Apr 70). Surprisingly, The Avengers didn't even mention how dashing the doc looked in his new getup. But they were having a hard time dealing with him in his Casper the Ghost form, so they can be excused.

Doc got his cool suit back again in the back-up adventure in *Marvel Feature* #1 (Dec 71), when he decided to start The Defenders with his new buddies Subby and The Hulk. Picking those two guys with whom to start a club was just one more indication of why he was aptly named. That tale featured another guy impersonating our Strange pal, giving the Doc an excuse to change back into the garb he wore so well. But that's a story for another time.

Doctor Strange changed back into his traditional costume in **Marvel Feature** *#1 in a flashback story that showed him confronting an imposter wearing his new masked outfit.*

© 1971 Marvel

The Hulk described Doc's new look perfectly, calling him "Weird One" instead of "Magician" in **Incredible Hulk** *#126.*

© 1970 Marvel

TRIVIA CHALLENGE II
Category: **WAR IS HELL**   Who was the orderly to HANS VON HAMMER?   Answer on page 129   Answer from page 125   BRUCE BANNER

IF THIS BE MY GIMMICK!   127

Abin Sur's Space Ship Conundrum

"So if Green Lantern's power ring can fly him anywhere in the universe, how did his predecessor, Abin Sur, wind up piloting a space ship that crashed on Earth? And why did he have his lantern with him ready to give to Hal Jordan when he died?"

That's a question that has bedeviled fans for many, many years. Or, at least, it's bedeviled those fans who never got around to reading the back-up story in *Green Lantern* #16 (Oct 62), called "Earth's First Green Lantern!" And there apparently are quite a few.

Not having Mr. Silver Age available, Hal Jordan asked his ring to explain why Abin Sur was flying a spaceship when he crashed on Earth in "Earth's First Green Lantern!" in **Green Lantern** *#16. But neither one of us could adequately explain why the power battery came along for the ride.*

© 1962 National Periodical Publications (DC)

"AFTER I HAD WILLED MY *POWER RING* IN THAT STORY TO TELL ME ABOUT *BEVERLY BLANDING,* I REALIZED IT COULD ALSO EXPLAIN *ABIN SUR* AND HIS SPACESHIP...

POWER RING, TELL ME WHY *ABIN SUR* WAS IN A SPACESHIP WHEN HE CAME TO EARTH!

In that epic 10-pager, Hal admitted to his sidekick Pieface that he had always wondered why Abin had been flying in a spaceship. But earlier (in "Prisoner of the Power Ring!" in *Green Lantern* #10, to be exact), Hal discovered that he could communicate with the ring and let it tell him things about past adventures that Hal didn't know directly. So he asked it what the heck that spaceship deal had been all about.

To make a typical Silver Age 10-page story short, Mr. Sur had captured all but one of a bunch of energy beings who had done mean, nasty, ugly things to other aliens. The fugitive being tracked down Abin in his civilian identity (since Abin didn't wear a mask as Green Lantern) and took over his body while he was sleeping. Abin could have fought him off mentally, but he wouldn't have been able to use his ring to capture him, because its charge had run out while he'd slept. Darn.

Realizing the alien didn't know the ins and outs of power-ringdom, Abin cunningly explained that, by the time he flew across space to release the other creatures, his ring would be too weak to operate. So the energy being let Abin take a space ship to conserve power.

As they left, Abin surreptitiously picked up his invisible power battery and took it along. Why he didn't just tell the being he needed to charge his ring but take the spaceship anyway is hard to say, except that otherwise the battery stayed at home and Hal would've become GL for less than a day, until the charge wore out, and then he'd have been stuck.

Once on the ship, the alien figured he had Abin under his control and left his body, which was what Abin had hoped would happen when he suggested they take the ship rather than just fly. That gave our GL buddy the chance to lunge at his invisible battery, recharge his ring, prevent the alien from re-entering his body and then capture the energy dude.

With that done, Abin headed home. But on his way, he ran into that darn yellow radiation band that surrounds Earth, causing him to crash. We know the rest — although Green Lantern mentioned that Abin's fatal accident was

TRIVIA CHALLENGE II
Category: **WAR IS HELL**   **Who was the African-American member of EASY COMPANY?**   Answer on page 130   Answer from page 126   **A WOODEN LEG**

"A FEW NIGHTS LATER, HAVING TRACKED DOWN *ABIN SUR* BY MEANS OF HIS CIVILIAN IDENTITY, *BALZONA* APPEARED.."

WHILE HE SLEEPS, I SHALL ENTER HIS BODY-- AS WE ENTER HUMAN BODIES TO ROB OF THEIR *I-FACTOR*, AND SO GAIN CONTROL OVER HIM!

why he always used a narrow, radiation-free corridor to leave Earth, which never seemed to come up much in practice. Hal also mentioned that the being's ability to track down Abin in his civilian identity was the reason Hal Jordan wore a mask. But since he actually was doing that since Day One, let's not hang too many secret origins on this tale.

The story has been reprinted a few times, including *GL #87*, *DC Blue-Ribbon Digest #5*, and *Green Lantern Archives #3*, so there's no excuse for not knowing this vital tidbit.

On the other hand, at a 1998 San Diego Comic-Con panel, Green Lantern's Silver Age editor, Julius Schwartz, admitted in response to a question that he couldn't remember if they'd ever solved the conundrum of Abin Sur's spaceship. He had to be reminded that he had, indeed, done just that. So you're in good company.

Abin Sur's tricky scheme to defeat an alien who had kidnapped him ...

*...involved flying a spaceship to their destination rather than flying, leading him to later crash-land on Earth and pass his powers to Hal Jordan, we learned in **Green Lantern #16**.*

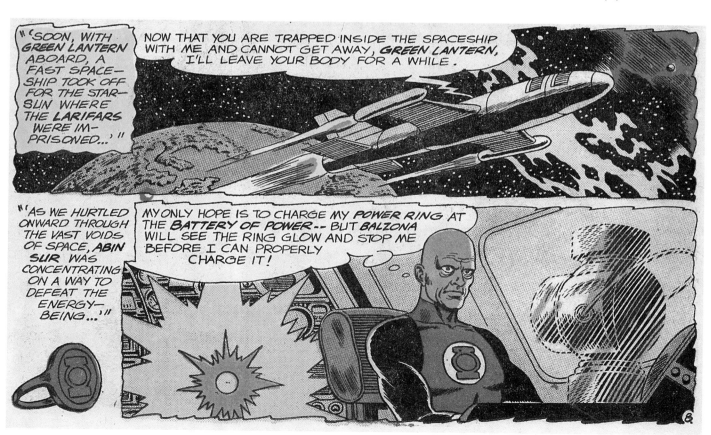

"'SOON, WITH *GREEN LANTERN* ABOARD, A FAST SPACE-SHIP TOOK OFF FOR THE STAR-SUN WHERE THE *LARIFARS* WERE IMPRISONED...'"

NOW THAT YOU ARE TRAPPED INSIDE THE SPACESHIP WITH ME AND CANNOT GET AWAY, *GREEN LANTERN*, I'LL LEAVE YOUR BODY FOR A WHILE.

"'AS WE HURTLED ONWARD THROUGH THE VAST VOIDS OF SPACE, *ABIN SUR* WAS CONCENTRATING ON A WAY TO DEFEAT THE ENERGY-BEING...'"

MY ONLY HOPE IS TO CHARGE MY *POWER RING* AT THE *BATTERY OF POWER* -- BUT BALZONA WILL SEE THE RING GLOW AND STOP ME BEFORE I CAN PROPERLY CHARGE IT!

TRIVIA CHALLENGE II
Category: **WAR IS HELL**   Where did SGT. FURY go on his very first mission?   Answer on page 133   Answer from page 127 **SCHMIDT**

IF THIS BE MY GIMMICK!   **129**

Adam Strange's Hot Foot

"Mr. Silver Age, how come when Adam Strange, the hero of Rann, flies with his rocket belt, he doesn't burn his tootsies?"

AS THEY JET TOWARD THE CAPITAL CITY OF RANAGAR...

ON THIS VISIT, IS THERE ANYTHING SPECIAL YOU'D LIKE TO DO ON RANN, ADAM?

ON EARTH I AM AN ARCHEOLOGIST! I'M CURIOUS TO SEE THIS PLANET'S REMNANTS OF EARLIER CIVILIZATIONS!

Adam Strange did some nifty jetting around to save Alanna from the "Attack of the Underworld Giants!" in **Mystery in Space** *#86. To learn why Adam didn't fear singeing his tootsies, just ask Mr. Silver Age. Or, more accurately, Murphy Anderson.*
© 1962 National Periodical Publications (DC)

That's a very good question, mostly because I can answer it. After all, you might think that strapping a couple of flaming jets onto their backs while they battled alien invasion after alien invasion during their adventures in *Mystery in Space* would have made Adam or Alanna, his even-more graceful sweetie, think twice about kicking their feet backward in those elegant Carmine Infantino poses. But neither of them seemed to give much thought to scorching their ankle bones.

Inker Murphy Anderson revealed the reason in the letters page of *Mystery In Space* #77 (Aug 62). That issue featured plenty of jet-pack roaming as our two Rann romantics faced the "Ray-Gun in the Sky!"

Murphy first explained the history of jet belts, tracing them to the science-fiction story "Armageddon — 2419 A.D." in the August 1928 issue of *Amazing Stories*.

That tale, by Phil Nowlan, was illustrated by Frank R. Paul and showed the hero, Anthony Rogers, using a flying belt. Nowlan later adapted the story to comic-strip form, changing the hero's first name to Buck. Sound familiar?

The reason the Rann jet-pack design doesn't leave our heroes with a nasty ouchie on their footsies can be credited to the planet's scientists, no doubt led by Alanna's pop, Saradath.

The pack's design, Anderson explained, included "a cooling device which eliminates the heat of the flaming gases as they rush out from the jets of Adam's flying belt."

Nice trick if you can do it. So now all we have to figure out is how they steered the darn things and came in for those nifty swooping landings.

TRIVIA CHALLENGE II
Category: **TEAM-UPS**

Who teamed with Green Arrow in the first **BRAVE & BOLD** team-up? Answer on page 134

Answer from page 128
JACKIE JOHNSON

PERIL on the PLANET of POP CULTURE!

Meet The Beatles, Silver-Age Style

"Mr. Silver Age, my favorite band from the 1960s was The Beatles. Did they make a big splash in Silver Age comics, too?"

Nothing in popular culture has ever compared to Beatlemania. For you kids out there, try to imagine a pop act bigger than Britney Spears with more media hype than for *Harry Potter.* If you can. After the Beatles—John, Paul, George, and Ringo — appeared on *The Ed Sullivan Show* in February 1964, U.S. teen-agers became obsessed with the group. That March, five of their songs ranked one after another at the top of *Billboard*'s Top 100 listing. Later, they registered 12 hits in the top 100 at one time. Not too shabby.

The centerpiece of Beatle paraphernalia was the Beatle wig. You needed one to look like a Beatle, of course, because hairstyles were somewhat shorter then. *If* you can call what we were wearing back then a hair "style." Today, it's hard to believe those early Beatles coiffures were considered way out.

No question about it, The Fab Four's impact was greater than any other group, including The Rolling Stones, The Animals, The Who, and even Freddie and the Dreamers. If you don't believe me, just look at comics. You knew we'd get back to them sooner or later, didn't you? Yes, as just one measure of The Beatles' impact, look at all the Silver Age comics where The Fab Four made appearances.

Comic-book editors in those days probably were not major Beatle fans, to put it charitably. But they knew what their readers wanted, and their readers wanted The Beatles! The mop tops could show up anywhere — love comics, teen-age humor comics, even super-hero comics. Yes, that's right, even in our very own pulse-pounding, senses-shattering super-hero comics!

Do you remember those ginchy days when The Fab Four had the entire comics world buzzing — including our boys and girls in the Spandex suits? I hope so, because you're about to take a pop quiz on those meetings.

Let your mind flash back to Earth-Silver, where the local drugstore's spinner is filled to bursting with comics like *Tales to Astonish*, *Thirteen (Going on Eighteen)*, *T.H.U.N.D.E.R. Agents*, *Dennis the Menace in Mexico*, *Beware the Creeper*, and *Archie's Pals 'N' Gals*. Makes me giddy just thinking about it. While I calm down, see if you can answer this handful of questions about The Beatles, culled strictly from their appearances and mentions in Marvel and DC comics:

POP QUIZ

1. Why did Jimmy Olsen become "The Red-Headed Beatle of 1,000 B.C.?"
a. To woo a B.C. Lucy Lane.
b. To trap a dangerous criminal.
c. To earn money.
d. Somebody had to do it.

2. What did Ringo want The Metal Men to do?
a. Sign his drum.
b. Sing with him.
c. Join his fan club.
d. Let him date Tina.

3. What was the reaction of Ben (the Thing) Grimm of The Fantastic Four to hearing that The Beatles were in town?
a. "They're the greatest!"
b. "We're better than those mopheads!"
c. "I'd rather go bowling than go to their concert."
d. "I wonder if Alicia would like to go to their concert?"

Doc Strange looked distraught over not being able to meet The Beatles in **Strange Tales** *#130, but it was up to The Thing and The Torch to actually interact with The Fab Four. What did The Thing think of the Lads from Liverpool?*

© 1965 Marvel

4. What did Kid Flash of The Teen Titans think of The Beatles?
a. "They're the greatest!"
b. "We're better than those mopheads!"
c. "I'd rather go bowling than go to one of their concerts."
d. "I wonder if Wonder Chick would like to go to their concert?"

Although some female fans may have wanted to call one or more of The Beatles "Honey Bun," it wasn't one of The Fab Four that The Teen Titans fought in **Teen Titans** *#8. What was Kid Flash's opinion of the quartet?*

© 1967 National Periodical Publications (DC)

5. Why did The Beatles show up at Kamp Karefree?
a. They were big fans of Jerry Lewis.
b. They were putting on a concert for the kids.
c. It was a hoax, a dream, or an Imaginary Story.
d. They'd lost their way to Albuquerque.

6. What did The Beatles want Forbush-Man to do?
a. Join the group.
b. Sign their autograph books.
c. Become their manager.
d. Take the last train to Clarksville.

7. Which one of The Oliver Twists did Batman fear was dead?
a. Glennan.
b. Saul.
c. Benji.
d. Fagin.

DC had its own take on the whole "Paul is dead" controversy with "Dead … Until Proven Alive!" in **Batman** *#222. Which one of the near-Beatles did Batman think was pushing up daisies?*

© 1970 National Periodical Publications (DC)

TRIVIA CHALLENGE II
Category: **TEAM-UPS** Who did the Golden Age Hourman, Dr. Fate, and Green Lantern fight in **SHOWCASE?** Answer on page 135

Answer from page 129
PARIS

Jimbo shook it up, baby, as the Red-Headed Beatle of 1000 BC in **Superman's Pal Jimmy Olsen** #79. What caused him to undertake this odd (even for Jim) behavior?

© 1964 National Periodical Publications (DC)

Would you have thought anyone could have started a Beatles craze in 1,000 B.C.? Jimmy Olsen did!

Mister Silver Age Recommends...

Superman's Pal, Jimmy Olsen #79

DC
Sep 1964
Cover artist:
Curt Swan, George Klein

"The Red-Headed Beatle of 1,000 B.C.!"
Writer: Leo Dorfman
Penciller: George Papp
Inker: George Papp

Then **12¢**
Now **$25**

© 1964 National Periodical Publications, Inc. (DC)

ANSWERS

1. Why did Jimmy Olsen become "The Red-Headed Beatle of 1,000 B.C.?
Answer c: To earn money.

"Great Krypton!" Superman said to himself while cruising through 1000 B.C. on the cover of *Jimmy Olsen* #79 (Sep 64). "Jimmy has started a Beatle craze here in the ancient past. He's become as popular as Ringo!" Sure enough, there was Superman's Pal in his orange Beatle wig, playing a shell-like horn and beating on a tom-tom, while a mob of (well, nine) B.C. beauties in Beatle bobs wigged out and screamed, "Yeah! Yeah! Yeah!"

Our epic (actually, a typical eight-page story) began with Jimbo grooving to The Fab Four in his apartment. "Man! Those Beatles are a blast!" he thought. "And I always seem to enjoy their music more when I wear my personal Beatle wig!" Don't we all? "Actually, it's Jimmy Olsen!" the caption revealed, in case we hadn't figured this out from the cover logo, folio line, splash logo, or drawing of Jim in his suit and bow tie. They didn't take chances with us dim kids back in the Silver Age.

The plot involved a 30th century villain who tricked our hero into helping him escape into the past via a Legion time bubble. They wound up in 1000 B.C., where a boy with fantastic strength beat the beejeebers out of our villain but not until said villain wrecked the time bubble. Did our favorite cub reporter bemoan his fate? Wail to the gods? Try to figure a way to signal The Legion or Superman?

Nah. He prevailed on Mighty Youth, the catchy name our historical hero was using, to lend him clothes and get him a job herding sheep. The Jimster conveniently had visited this time period before, he informed us, so he understood the language. Just like that time I went to France for a week. Works for me.

Anyway, when Jim made 5¢ for his day's work, he decided, much as the lads from Liverpool would do many years later, that there had to be an easier way to make your daily shekels. He fashioned a dozen Beatle wigs out of old wool, put on his own red Beatle wig (which he fortuitously had stuffed in his pocket), picked up his shepherd's horn, and started pounding on a homemade drum.

"Who is this strange fellow who twists and twitches like a beetle on a hot stove?" a boy prophetically wondered aloud. "That catchy drumbeat!" a young cutie exclaimed. "I can't keep my own feet from twitching!" "Hold everything, kids!" Jimmy announced, no doubt making them look around for the baby goats. "You can't do the Beatle dance without a Beatle wig! Get 'em while they last. A silver piece each!"

"Presently," we're told, "the market-place is rocking." "Yeah! Yeah! Yeah!" Jimmy sang, of course. "Crazy, man!" he thought. "Imagine, starting a Beatle craze thousands of years back in the past!" Crazy, man?

TRIVIA CHALLENGE II
Category: **TEAM-UPS**
Who did Spider-Man have to fight in his initiation for The Avengers? Answer on page 136
Answer from page 130
MARTIAN MANHUNTER

Now that we had our cover taken care of, the plot could heat up. The villain escaped, Jimmy got arrested, Mighty Youth turned out to be Someone We Knew From History, Superman showed up, and Jimmy gave a farewell concert. Yeah! Yeah! Yeah!

This isn't the only time Jimmy became a rock 'n' roll star, either. If you ask real nice, maybe someday I'll tell you the tale of Chip O'Doole, or about the invention of the Krypton Crawl, as danced to the music of Jimmy Olsen & The Carrot-Top Cut-Ups. (And you just know I'm not making these up.) Heck, we could do an entire quiz on great Jimmy Olsen rock 'n' roll stories! Consider yourself warned.

2. What did Ringo want The Metal Men to do?
Answer a: Sign his drum.

It happened in "Shake the Stars!" in *Metal Men* #12 (Feb-Mar 65), in what was called "The latest giant novel starring the original Metal Men — the only robots with their hearts where their 'responsometers' should be!"

We didn't have to read far into the story to meet The Beatles. They showed up in the story's first panel, below. "Wherever the unique Metal Men appear in person," the caption explained, "eager fans stampede toward them." At the edge of the crowd stood, left to right, George, John, Ringo, and Paul (the caricatures were courtesy of artists Andru and Esposito). "I say," Ringo sighed. "We haven't a chawnce of getting the Metal Men to sign my drum!" "Yeh! Yeh!" George and John chimed in. Paul withheld his own "yeh," no doubt distraught. Not to worry: The Metal Men were eager to comply.

Unfortunately, The Fab Four weren't the "Stars" referred to in the title. It alluded to what would happen when the dreaded Missile Men attacked our metal band in a huge armada. Sad to say, the lads from Liverpool had already made their entire contribution to this issue's story. At least, unless you count the "Metal Facts & Fancies" page, where they're drawn as golden robots singing to a bunch of swooning female robots to illustrate that gold is a great conductor of heat.

I don't get it, either.

Writers commonly portrayed their super-heroes as just as popular, in their own worlds, as The Beatles were in ours.

The Beatles and The Metal Men exchanged compliments (with The Mop Tops apparently unable to draw their own crowd), when the two groups met in **Metal Men** #12.

© 1965 National Periodical Publications (DC)

TRIVIA CHALLENGE II
Category: TEAM-UPS   What code-word helped the JLA and JSA beat the Crime Syndicate? Answer on page 137

Answer from page 133
SOLOMON GRUNDY

PERIL ON THE PLANET OF POP CULTURE!   **135**

Johnny and Ben got to "Meet The Beatles!" in **Strange Tales** #130, but they nearly ran past them on the stairs. What was The Thing's initial reaction to hearing the lads were in town?

© 1965 Marvel

The Beatles weren't the Big-Band-era fun that The Thing had in mind.

3. What was the reaction of Ben Grimm of The Fantastic Four to hearing The Beatles were in town?
Answer c: "I'd rather go bowling than go to their concert."

What can you expect from a man who fought in World War II? Ben's heyday had been 20 years earlier! I know just how he felt when I hear the latest catchy tune by Avril Lavigne booming out of the car next to mine. Time is not on my side, lemme tell ya.

You'll be glad to hear that Ben quickly changed his mind and got to "Meet The Beatles!" in *Strange Tales* #130 (Mar 65). No sooner had the blasphemous words in our answer left his mouth than his girlfriend, Alicia Masters, walked in behind him. "I'd just love to hear The Beatles tonight, Ben, dear," she cooed. So what's a Thing gonna do? "Now ain't that funny?" he agreed readily. "I was thinkin' the same thing!" "Sure you were, you big phony!" Johnny guffawed in the background.

Ben did become a little overwhelmed when he actually came face to face with The Fabs, though. Our own foursome (The Torch's gal pal Dorrie got the ducats) ran into the lads on the stairway, nearly plowing right through them. "It's them!" Ben sputtered. "My ever-lovin' idols! Be still, my patterin' heart!" Just then, the manager came running out yelling for help because three hoods had stolen the payroll! Our heroes certainly couldn't turn down a plea like that, especially when their arrival at the theater had caused the distraction that let the crooks escape.

I won't tell you what happened, but, when Ben returned the money (oops!), he put on one of the crook's Beatle wigs for one panel. The only place we got to see The Human Torch wear his wig was on the cover. Bummer.

4. What did Kid Flash of the Teen Titans think of The Beatles?
Answer b: "We're better than those mopheads."

Wally West never was known as a shrinking violet. This time, he reacted to a fan letter that The Fab Four (the Titans, that is) received in "A Killer Called Honey Bun!" in *Teen Titans* #8 (Mar-Apr 67).

Robin read that one fan liked The Beatles better than The Titans in **Teen Titans** #8, setting off a big letters column debate that could have taken place only in the Silver Age. What did Kid Flash think of The Beatles?

© 1967 National Periodical Publications (DC)

"Dig this letter, characters!" Robin exclaimed in the story's first panel. "Dear Titans: Next to The Beatles, you are my favorite four people." "Huh? I like that!" KF snorted. "We're better than those mopheads!" To show his contempt, he grabbed a handy acoustic guitar and sang, "All I wanna do is hold your foooot! Yeeeah! Yeh! Yeah!" "Listening to you, Twinkletoes," Wonder Girl complained, "all I wanna do is hold my ears!" Wally was unapologetic. "Yeaah! Yeah! And yeaah!" he wailed.

Naturally, this caused a big brouhaha on The TT's letter page from angry fans. Angry Teen Titans fans, that is. "Dear Editor," began a missive in #10. "Why mention those (CENSORED) [sic], The Beatles, in such a high-class mag as *TT*? I agree with Kid Flash: 'We're better than those mopheads!' The Teen Titans are the grooviest!"

TRIVIA CHALLENGE II
Category: **LOST LOVES**   Who was BARRY ALLEN's high school sweetheart?   Answer on page 138   Answer from page 134 **THE HULK**

136   **BABY BOOMER COMICS**

"Hmm," Editor George Kashdan (presumably) replied. "Wonder if John Lennon would like to match his group's popularity with the TT?" Sadly, John's reply was never printed.

But, no doubt in an effort to defuse this red-hot situation, the alleged mopheads sent a nice card to The Titans, which was posted on the bulletin board in the secret Titan Lair in #11. Under a sketch of the lads was the message, "From One Fab Foursome To Another — The Beatles!" You can't miss the note. It's right above a thank-you card from President Lyndon B. Johnson and a message to Wonder Girl that says, "Your mother called! You wore too much lipstick in our last adventure! Please correct!" What a time.

Alas, The Beatles' well-intentioned effort wasn't enough to calm things down. In #12, one fan wrote to say he was "disgusted" by the earlier letter and called the writer "a jerk." "The Beatles are just as good as the Titans!" he proclaimed, adding new meaning to the term "damning with faint praise. "I mean, the Titans are all right and I like them," he went on, "but The Beatles are good too." He suggested a popularity contest, which the editor nixed. "Too many feelings might be hurt!" he explained.

But the controversy was just too pulse-pounding to die! In #13, another Beatle fan rephrased the original line to ask, "Why mention such a high-class group as The Beatles in such a third-rate mag as TT?...The Beatles are far more popular than the Titans!" Another writer used such terms as "stupid idea" and "idiot-fiction Titans" before calling the editor "a fool to print any such thing."

Actually, it was refreshing to have such reasoned discussion on The Titans' letters page for a change. In #12, for example, one writer suggested that the team should add Aquachick to be with Wonder Chick (the editor's terms, I hasten to add). Another exclaimed that Robin was "so, so cute." A third boldly came out in favor of Wonder Girl switching from shorts to a mini-skirt. But, then, what could you expect from an issue with an outer-space story entitled, "Large Trouble in Space-Ville?" Cool, Daddy-o! Excuse me, I mean — crazy, man!

The Titans had lots of fans, as evidenced by the card at the top of their bulletin board in **Teen Titans** #11.

© 1967 National Periodical Publications (DC)

5. Why did The Beatles show up at Kamp Karefree?
Answer c: It was a hoax, a dream, or an Imaginary Story.

DC loved producing stories that turned out to be one of those three possibilities (so much so that they often trumpeted incredible stories as *not* being any of that trio). In this case, I'm afraid, it was the dream variation, much to the dismay of all of Renfrew's female buddies. But, since The Fab Four were drawn by Neal Adams, you didn't hear any of us readers complaining. The caricatures were dead-on, even if they did seem to have particularly pronounced high cheekbones.

The Fabs made their appearance during one of Jerry and his gang's annual treks to summer camp in "The Hound Dog from Mars" in *Adventures of Jerry Lewis* #102 (Sep-Oct 67). The girls went to Kamp Karefree, while the boys got to attend Uncle Hal's always delightful Camp Wack-a-Boy.

*The fun-loving inmates of Camp Wack-A Boy and Kamp Karefree got their chance to meet The Beatles in **Adventures of Jerry Lewis** #102.*

© 1967 National Periodical Publications (DC)

TRIVIA CHALLENGE II
Category: **LOST LOVES**   What name did SUPERMAN use to court Sally Selwyn?   Answer on page 139   Answer from page 135   **VOLTHOOM**

PERIL ON THE PLANET OF POP CULTURE!   **137**

Reprints Miss The Beatles

Sadly, only one of these fab and groovy issues has ever been reprinted, as far as I know: *Teen Titans* #11 was reprinted in *DC Superstars* #1. It's not really worth picking up for that bulletin-board note, but it's classic 1960s Titans, so keep an eye out!

*True, Forbush-Man flopped again in **Not Brand Echh** #8. But he still had four fans at the end of the ish — who sported costumes that could put The X-Men to shame.*

© 1968 Marvel

To make a long, hilarious story somewhat shorter, Rbrthny and Rnldrk, Jerry's Martian buddies, turned their Hallucina-Ray on the camp. It let each camper believe a personal dream had come true. So one sweet little pony-tailed lass was able to meet The Beatles. "It's been a hard day's night," they sang, eschewing their trademark "yeahs" on this rare comic-book occasion. "I may die!" she exclaimed. "Truly I may!" Truly, wouldn't we all?

6. What did The Beatles want Forbush-Man to do?
Answer a: Join the group.

"I say, luv — you get a nice sound out of that helmet!" John told Forbush-Man as our hero walked off dejectedly in the final panel of *Not Brand Echh* #8 (Jun 68), Marvel's short-lived parody comic with the bizarre name. But the Liverpudlian couldn't get the slouching super-hero to become the fifth Beatle.

Stan Lee in his letter columns had occasionally referred to other publishers' comics as "Brand Ecch" — a play on the "Brand X" commercials of the time — and *Not Brand Ecch* gave Marvel a chance to send up comics in general. And Forbush-Man, *Non Brand Ecch*'s pot-wearing mascot, had just spent the entirety of #8 trying to join the Revengers, S.H.E.E.S.H., and the Echhs-Men and had flopped with each. So he was certain no famous group would want him.

Get it? Famous group? He turned them down? What a knee-slapper. Just in case we couldn't figure out the caricatures, Tom Sutton drew The Fab Four in their Sgt. Pepper suits standing in front of the Sgt. Pepper drum.

And just in case parody wasn't the readers' cup of tea, Gary Friedrich hit us with a truly awful pun in his final line. "Moral: The Byrds in the hand are worth the Who in the bush!" I tell ya, with a little more practice, he might have been up to writing for *The Many Loves of Dobie Gillis*. High praise, indeed.

That was just the first of a trilogy of Beatles appearances in this title, the closest humor book fans had to the early *Mad* issues. The series was filled with parodies and gags about Marvel and DC super-heroes, and it was made all the funnier because it was written and drawn by the same guys who did the serious versions of the characters. Many of the issues were double-sized, 25¢ comics, and the humor still stands up in large part today — at least, if you're as warped as I am.

Friedrich wrote all three Beatle gigs to appear in *NBE*. The other two weren't anything to write home about, though. In #9 (Aug 68), John Verpoorten drew The Fabs as the hillbilly band that supplied background music every time "Boney & Claude" made their getaway.

In #13 (May 69), they appeared in a postage-stamp sized drawing as part of a one-page parody of the *Cheap Thrills* album cover drawn by R. Crumb for Big Brother & The Holding Co. The "Turtle

TRIVIA CHALLENGE II
Category: **LOST LOVES** **NATASHA** left Hawkeye to sabotage what device for S.H.I.E.L.D.? Answer on page 140 | Answer from page 136 **DAPHNE DEAN**

138 **BABY BOOMER COMICS**

Blues" slot was changed to "Beatle Blues," showing our Liverpool boys crying over BB&THC sitting at #1 in the charts.

Actually, it was a pretty clever redoing of the album cover with new names and illustrations (by Herb Trimpe) using Marvel heroes. For instance, the group's name became "Big Benjy & the Clobbering Co." Well, *I* liked it.

7. Which one of The Oliver Twists did Batman fear was dead?
Answer b: Saul.

Talk about your way-out plot lines! A rumor persisted that The Twists' lead singer, Saul Cartwright, died in a motorcycle accident in London, leading the three other band members — Glennan, Hal and Benji — to take a year off and go to the Himalayas. Clues were said to appear in the group's songs and on their album covers. Now, in "Dead...Till Proven Alive!" in *Batman* #222 (Jun 70), The Dynamic Duo had to uncover the truth!

What does this have to do with The Beatles, you ask? Sigh. I was afraid you'd ask, you young whippersnapper. This stuff can really make a guy feel old. Let's just say that it was inspired by a similar incident in The Fab Four's career, all right? Please don't ask for details. I can still cite at least 10 clues to Paul's death just off the top of my head, and you don't want to get me going. I hate to admit it, but that's the way it is. I had a stunted adolescence.

I mean, even if you don't put any stock in the "I buried Paul" line, what about the hand over his head on *Sgt. Pepper's* and the symbolic outfits worn on the cover of *Abbey Road*? What about the plaque on the desk and the black carnation in the *Magical Mystery Tour* booklet? What about...oops, sorry, I'm getting carried away.

But, then, so did Batman and especially Robin. When The Twists announce a concert in Gotham City, Dick returned from Hudson University and Bruce reopened Wayne Manor to take them in. Yeah, it was during that period. Then, our crusaders against crime undertook such cunning sleuthing activities as stealing Saul's personal tape-recorder, bugging the chandelier and the seats at the dinner table to compare voice prints, sneaking into The Twists' studio to tape them, and finally just confronting them. We don't call him The World's Greatest Detective for nothing!

It turned out that Saul was actually Saul, but the *rest* of them were phonies! They left Saul at home when they went off to groove in the mountains, and their plane crashed. So Saul hired doubles of everyone else! What a twist!

Sorry about that last pun. I can't take — nor do I want — credit for it. I stole that little *bon mot* from the last panel of the story. Blame it on writer Frank Robbins or Editor Julius Schwartz. Or even Editorial Director Carmine Infantino. But don't blame me. Or John, Paul, George, or Ringo, for that matter. None of us can help how wacky everybody got about The Fab Four during comics' Silver Age.

Comics figured out which Beatle was dead, but had nothing to say about who the Walrus was. (Walrus-man came much later...)

Scoring:

7: Fab! You've passed the audition! You have a memory longer than the road that stretches out ahead!

4-6: All right! You say you missed only a few? Well you know that can't be bad!

1-3: Help! It's been a hard day's night, hasn't it? That's OK, we can work it out.

0: You're a loser! Or, worse, you're a Stones fan. And from a quiz like this, you can't get no satisfaction.

The Oliver Twists (from left, Benji, Glennan, Hal and Saul) warble a tune for Alfred, leaving a clue for Batman in determining if one of the Twists was an imposter.

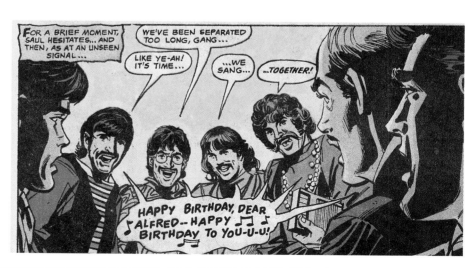

TRIVIA CHALLENGE II
Category: **LOST LOVES** Who killed Iron Man's gal-pal, **JANICE CORD?** Answer on page 141 Answer from page 137 **JIM WHITE**

How *Mad* Became a Magazine

"*Mad* became the only E.C. Comics title to survive the Comics Code crackdown by turning into a magazine. Didn't it take a change in approach to go from parodies like 'Superduperman' to cartoons by guys like Don Martin and Dave Berg?"

Norman Mingo's familiar rendition of Alfred E. Neuman first appeared on #30. The back cover showed the view from behind Alfred's head, with a bunch of famous people caricatured by Jack Davis laughing at Al.
© 1956 E.C.

Really, it wasn't as big a change as you would think, if you're comparing the early comic-book version of *Mad* and the version that exists today. The shift was more of an evolution during the first magazine-sized issues, thanks in part to *Mad*'s original comics style, which was easier to adapt to a magazine format than it would seem.

The transition occurred for two key reasons, as explained by Frank Jacobs in his 1972 book, *The Mad World of William M. Gaines*. First, *Mad*'s editor, the brilliant Harvey Kurtzman, was itching to move up to the more prestigious world of newsstand magazines — and he was getting some attractive offers. By allowing Kurtzman to change *Mad* to magazine size, publisher Bill Gaines kept Kurtzman satisfied where he was (at least, for a little while).

Converting *Mad* also avoided the tight restrictions imposed by the new Comics Code, which, among many other limitations, specifically forbade a number of the key words Gaines used in his comics' titles. It was almost as if the Code had been custom-designed to put his popular horror line out of business — and many people claim that was exactly one of its goals. If so, it succeeded admirably, since, shortly after the Code was introduced, Gaines folded his entire comics line, except for *Mad*.

In truth, Gaines had good reason to be concerned that *Mad* would not survive if exposed to the Comics Code's restrictions, because the comic books already weren't being received well by conservative authorities (and there were a lot of them then). As early as 1953, *Mad*'s sister comic, *Panic #1*, had been banned in Massachusetts because it featured a Will Elder-drawn parody of "The Night before Christmas." Authorities said the story "desecrated Christmas," and the distributor refused to handle it.

So, in the last comic-book sized issue, #23 (May 55), E.C. announced, "We're expanding *Mad* into a regular big 25¢ magazine with pictures, printed lettering, covers, and everything, gang. Boy, what exciting plans. Are we excited." And with *Mad #24* (Jul 55), it switched to the magazine size it still uses today.

The shift was not as dramatic editorially as you might think today. For one thing, the comic had begun adding variety to its content in later issues. For instance, *Mad #22* (Apr 55) was the "Special Art Issue," a satiric look at Will Elder's career from cradle to grave. Five of the six stories were laid out with b&w photos in the typical E.C. style of a paragraph of copy above each panel.

TRIVIA CHALLENGE II
Category: **TITLES**

Which character died in "Gotham Gang Line-Up"?

Answer on page 142

Answer from page 138
THE PSYCHOTRON

It also featured several parody ads Elder supposedly did, predating a feature the magazine version would become well known for doing.

In the magazine-sized *Mad* #24 two issues later, many of the features bore a striking similarity to the comic's old layout style: a paragraph of type above a panel of cartoon art. Kurtzman retained his three key comic-book artists — Jack Davis, Will Elder, and Wally Wood — and gave them features about wrestling, a parody of the TV show *This Is Your Life* called "Is This Your Life?" and a satiric look at the possibilities of a flight to the moon, respectively. He also began what would be a recurring theme: two pages of comic-strip-style parodies by Elder that made the connection to *Mad*'s former comic-book-style features.

But there were differences in the layouts, too. For instance, Davis's wrestling article opened with a full-page shot of a screaming, frantic crowd of fans (including parodies of Charles Addams' Gomez and Morticia) facing a page with the headline and intro, a spot illustration, and a half-page of type. That magazine-style layout then led into the more-typical *Mad* comic-book layout for the remaining eight pages.

The front cover featured an intricate border resembling a woodcut, with Alfred E. Neuman and his now-famous "What? Me Worry?" line in an oval at the top middle. The remainder showed vignettes of famous folks, including Beethoven, Pasteur, Columbus, Rembrandt, Galileo, and, um, Lassie, reading *Mad*.

Kurtzman also received contributions from high-profile comedic writers of the time to supplement his own scripts. These were led by Ernie Kovacs, one of the biggest TV comedians of the 1950s, who did a satire of Tom Swift books and contributed other features in later issues. Also writing were Roger Price, the creator of the popular game Droodles, and Bernard Shir-Cliff, an editor at Ballantine Books, where the *Mad* comics were being reprinted in paperbacks. Writer Ira Wallach also contributed a two-page humorous short story.

Kurtzman put the magazine format to good use with a number of ad parodies, spotlighting "Bofforin" pain-killer, "Bind-Aig" bandages, and "Jell-Y" gelatin on the covers. Additional interior ads featured "Pund's Cold Cream" and "Anasprin." This created an interesting situation in #27, when *Mad* did something real magazines do all the time but it had never done before in its magazine format: It accepted a real ad. The editorial explained that up to then, *Mad* hadn't accepted advertising — not because the magazine was editorially pure, but because it couldn't get any.

"On page 7 is our first real advertisement," the editorial said. "Please do what it asks." The one-third-page vertical ad promoted Bogen High Fidelity record players. A few more ads followed in later issues, notably full-page ads for the Dollar Mystery Guild in #31 and the Famous Artists School in #32. These soon stopped, however, and Gaines became proud that *Mad* didn't rely on advertising for revenues.

(That changed a second time in 2001, when the periodical once again began accepting ads, this time on a regular basis. The ad revenue helped pay for *Mad*'s conversion to all-color interiors, which, ironically, helped it look more like its original comic-book version but less like the black-and-white magazine version that had made it famous.)

The new magazine edition of the 1950s clearly was targeted to a more adult

In **Mad** #22, Editor Harvey Kurtzman replaced the usual line art with photos and featured several pages of ad parodies, producing a decidedly different look for the comic that reflected the style **Mad** would use in its early magazine format.
© 1955 E.C.

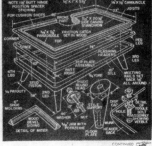

Pages 2 and 3 of Jack Davis' "how-to" article in the magazine-style **Mad** #24 don't look much different from the comic book's style, with captions below the art rather than above it. But the opening right page has a magazine style.
© 1956 E.C.

TRIVIA CHALLENGE II
Category: **TITLES**　　**What team title featured the "Menace of the 'Atom' Bomb"?**　Answer on page 143　Answer from page 139　**TITANIUM MAN**

PERIL ON THE PLANET OF POP CULTURE!　　　**141**

The cover of **Mad** #25 made it clear the magazine targeted adults. A joke relying on a cartoon from the 1870s Tammany Hall scandals in New York City seldom has 12-year-olds rolling on the floor.
© 1955 E.C.

audience than the comic book had been, and this continued with later issues. For instance, the cover of #25 (Sep 55) featured a joke using an 1870s-era political cartoon by Thomas Nast about New York City's mayor, Boss Tweed — not exactly humor designed to have 12-year-olds rolling in the aisles.

Contributors in these later issues included Stan Freberg, a well-known humorist with popular LP records on the charts; writer and TV celebrity Steve Allen; and Doodles Weaver, a cast member of the popular Spike Jones TV show. These line-ups would be akin to having people like Jerry Seinfeld, Dave Barry, and Dennis Miller contributing today.

Subject themes, too, began to settle into place. In #26 (Nov 55), *Mad* parodied the ways different magazines would treat the same story and satirized suburban highways, boxing, and golf. Issue #27 kicked off Phil Interlandi's "Scenes We'd Like to See" recurring strip and Will Elder's Norman Rockwell-style back cover parodies. Russ Heath illustrated a satiric "Sea Chanty," and other features included a humorous essay on bullfighting, a parody of *The Ed Sullivan Show*, and a reprint of cartoons from the turn of the century, which also was a recurring (and, no doubt, cheap) feature.

Layouts soon began to diverge from the original E.C. look. Two-page spreads dragged graphics across the gutter, and the designs offered more variety in panel sizes and type placement. The format continued to evolve, and by issue #28, Kurtzman and his crew had set both the humor tone and design style that left behind the magazine's roots as a comic book.

Then, Kurtzman quit. Feeling his efforts deserved more reward, he asked for part ownership in E.C., Jacobs wrote. Gaines refused and Kurtzman left, taking with him Davis and Elder. (Davis returned to *Mad* in 1965.) Frantic, Gaines quickly rehired his former comic-book editor, Al Feldstein, got Production Editor John Putnam to agree to stay on, and hoped for the best. A few days after Feldstein started, he was visited by an aspiring cartoonist who was hired immediately. Don Martin's contributions began appearing in #29, as one-page gags called "Alfred E. Neuman Answers Your Questions." Feldstein also added Basil Wolverton, Jack Kamen, and several other comics artists to the mix.

Issue #30 (Dec 56) kicked off with the first painted cover featuring Alfred E. Neuman, as portrayed by Norman Mingo. His version of the character — and his many-year run of covers featuring Alfred — became the standard. The issue also added Bob Clarke, who became another perennial.

*Mort Drucker's inimitable caricaturing style isn't apparent in his first **Mad** contribution in #32, but the one-page ad spoof he illustrated was a standard for many years, even after he moved to other features.*
© 1956 E.C.

TRIVIA CHALLENGE II
Category: **TITLES**   "The Long Journey Home" was the title of what series' 100th issue? Answer on page 144

Answer from page 140
ALFRED

In #31, Feldstein eliminated the cover border, giving Mingo's cover art more room.

In #32, he added Mort Drucker, who became renowned for his dead-on caricatures.

Dave Berg illustrated his first article, on "modern furniture," in #34 (Aug 57). It wasn't too close to the style he became known for in his "The Lighter Side Of..." features, but his fascination with suburban fashions and lifestyles was clear. Feldstein added other artists, too, including renowned science-fiction cover artist Frank Kelly Freas and former E.C.-er Joe Orlando. He also began expanding his writers' list, with names like Bob and Ray, the radio comedians; Orson Bean, a popular comedian and game-show panelist; and E. Nelson Bridwell, who went on to become a DC editor.

By its "Special 5th Anniversary Issue" in #35 (Oct 57), *Mad* was a magazine that today's readers would recognize easily, by design if not by its topics.

As the 1960s began and changed the cultural norm from cocktail parties and beatniks to love-ins and hippies, the topics began to shift away from the adult humor and name-brand authors to subjects of interest to the continually younger age bracket that bought the magazine. Baby Boomers became the target, and that youth trend continues today.

It's kind of ironic that as Mr. Silver Age grew older, *Mad* downshifted its focus from humor about cocktail parties, buying new cars, and advertising and began featuring jokes about report cards, barfing, and zits. I don't know when exactly we passed each other on the scale of interests. But I think it's a shame that most of *Mad*'s humor now is something you grow out of rather than grow into.

There's not much of Dave Berg's later style evident in the first article he illustrated for **Mad***, in #34. But his interest in all things suburban already was apparent.*

© 1956 E.C.

TRIVIA CHALLENGE II
Category: **TITLES**   **Who revealed his identity to his girlfriend in "In the Midst of Life"?** Answer on page 145

Answer from page 141
JUSTICE LEAGUE

ERIL ON THE PLANET OF POP CULTURE!

143

Silver Age Marvel Movie Stars!

"Marvel sure seems to be making a lot of movies these days. Why didn't more super-heroes star in movies during the Silver Age?"

Tinsel Town was interested, but one of two situations usually prevented the movies from being finished. Either a super-villain attacked during filming or the movie was merely a ploy by some dastardly villain to defeat our heroic buddy. At least, that's what happened within the Marvel comics themselves, which is where Mr. Silver Age gets all his information about how life works.

Probably the most agreeable hero to this type of chicanery was Spider-Man. After all, the guy was appearing on TV four pages after that radioactive spider bit him! Plus two of his early villains were connected to the movies: Mysterio, a special-effects wizard turned bad guy introduced in #13 (Jun 64), and Joe Smith, a boxer turned actor who gained super-strength and a mad-on while making a movie in "Just a Guy Named Joe!" in #38 (Jul 66).

Spidey's desire for stardom bit him in the butt several times during his Silver Age career. The first came right after he beat Mysterio, which should have had his finely honed spider-sense buzzing. In "The Grotesque Adventure of The Green Goblin" in #14 (Jul 64), we got our first glimpse of Gobby, as he convinced a producer to make a movie starring his own green self and the wall-crawler.

The Green Goblin talked Spidey into starring in a movie in *Amazing Spider-Man* #14. Needless to say, this was Gobby's first appearance.
© 1964 Marvel

TRIVIA CHALLENGE II
Category: **THE FUTURE**   Who was the secretary to Star Hawkins?   Answer on page 146   Answer from page 142 **FANTASTIC FOUR**

144   BABY BOOMER COMICS

The producer agreed, not knowing this guy was going to become Spidey's most hated foe. Gobby flew off to find Spider-Man, and his presence quickly was mentioned on the radio. "It sounds like someone's imagining things," Petey said, running off to check. Oh, if only they had been. Spidey agreed to do the flick but, at rehearsals, he discovered the other actors weren't amazing simulations of The Enforcers but were, in fact, the real deal. Fortunately, Spidey avoided their first attack and hid in a cave. Unfortunately, the Hulk was hiding there, too. Things went downhill from there, The Goblin escaped, and Spidey's movie went on hiatus.

The wall-crawler was more careful the next time, not that it did him any good. This time, he teamed with The Human Torch, in "The Web and the Flame!" in *Amazing Spider-Man King Size Special #3* (Nov 67). Spidey saw The Torch acting out of control, so he intervened. But it turned out that Johnny was starring in a government-funded short feature called, "The Torch Goes Wild!" It's hard to imagine the exact nature of the government's interest in The Torch's wildness, but nothing the government did should really surprise us, I guess. In any event, the next day, the radio announced Paragon Productions had been inspired by this dust-up to sign Spider-Man to star in a movie with The Torch, who already had agreed. Spidey flew to Hollywood (by plane), he met up with the Torch, and they started filming.

The only problem was that Paragon Productions was owned by The Wizard and Mysterio. Spidey's movie mishap had inspired The Wizard to spend his previous ill-gotten gains to set up a studio (overnight, it should be noted) to lure our pals into a trap rather than fly to Rio and live like a king. And this guy was the brains of the outfit. Needless to say, the web and the flame figured things out. But our dastardly villains had a back-up plan that had our heroes battling a King Kong-sized gorilla, no doubt boosting sales through the stratosphere. At least, it always worked that way for DC.

Movie reruns

Here's where to find these first-run thrillers at second-run prices:

- *King-Size Spider-Man #3* was reprinted in *Marvel Tales #129-130*, *Marvel Masterworks #22*, and *Essential Spider-Man #3*.
- *Fantastic Four #9* was reprinted in *Marvel's Collectors Item Classic #6*, *Marvel Masterworks #2*, and *Essential Fantastic Four #1*.
- *Thor #128* was reprinted in *Marvel Special Edition #1*, and *Marvel Treasury Edition #3*.

Spidey went West to star in a movie with the Human Torch in "The Web and The Flame!" in **Amazing Spider-Man King-Size Special** *#3. As usual, things didn't work out.*
© 1967 Marvel

HE'S RIGHT ON CUE!

HE'S SUPPOSED TO *ATTACK* THEM BEFORE I CAN *STOP* HIM -- THUS MAKING THEM DECIDE TO *BATTLE US!*

HOLD IT!! GIVE THEM A *CHANCE* FIRST!

WHEN I START TAKIN' ORDERS FROM A WOBBLY WALL-CRAWLER, *THAT'LL* BE THE DAY!

EVERYTHING'S GOING ACCORDING TO THE *SCRIPT* --

SO WHY IS MY *SPIDEY SENSE* STILL *TINGLING??*

TRIVIA CHALLENGE II
Category: **THE FUTURE**   *Where did Tommy Tomorrow go to school?*   Answer on page 147   Answer from page 143
DAREDEVIL

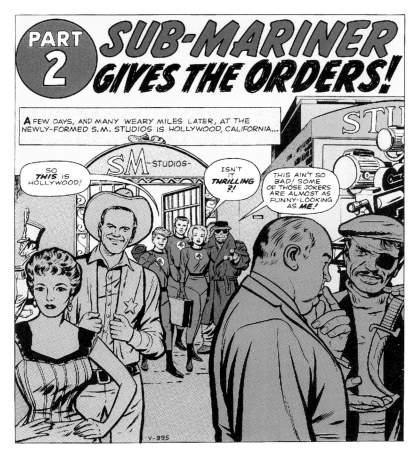

Bankruptcy led to a Fantastic Four movie in **FF** #9 (Dec 62). OK, it was the FF who were bankrupt, and The Sub-Mariner produced the movie, but it still gave me hope for our Earth's version.
© 1962 Marvel

The acting bug bit DD while helping The Stunt-Master on his TV pilot during The Man Without Fear's visit to Karen Page in Hollywood in **Daredevil** #67 (Aug 70).
© 1970 Marvel

Spidey wasn't even the first Marvel hero to be wooed by stardom. The Fantastic Four got hornswoggled into a fake flick in "The End of The Fantastic Four" in *FF* #9 (Dec 62). You'd have thought that might have made Johnny a little more curious before signing on with The Wizard and Mysterio, but caution was never his strong suit.

Our fantastic heroes got roped into this deal the same way Spidey always did — they needed money. Much as would happen to their comics company some years later, their bills mounted too fast, so they declared bankruptcy. Namor the Sub-Mariner heard this tidbit on his underwater television. (He must have had cable.) He set up S.M Studios (get it?) and, without revealing his true identity, smooth-talked the needy team into starring in a movie for $1 million.

Naturally, our heroes overcame all the deadly traps Subby set for them, including his marriage proposal to Sue. But, as they were about to pound lumps on his head, Sue pointed out that the traps had been filmed, and it would make a lot more sense for Namor to live up to the contract, produce the movie, pay The FF the money they had coming, and go away. Showing unusual common sense, that's just what he did.

Too bad Sue wasn't on staff at Marvel, or we might have enjoyed a lot more movies a whole lot faster than we did.

Daredevil also got a chance to yell, "Hey, that's not in the script!" He went to La-La Land searching for his former secretary, Karen Page, in "Suddenly...The Stunt-Master!" in *DD* #64 (May 70). The Man Without Fear's former foe was being blackmailed into committing a crime by a shady producer, and DD helped him out of his jam. Daredevil then tracked down Karen and helped solve a murder mystery on her set in #65-66.

In #67, he was asked to guest-star in the pilot episode of the new TV series Stunt-Master had agreed to do. For some odd reason, The Stilt-Man decided that a really good way to seek revenge on Daredevil would be to disguise himself as Stunt-Master and attack DD during the filming. Why am I hearing the music to *Mission: Impossible* in the background?

Hercules also tried to get into pictures by signing a movie deal with a producer, Mr. Pluto, in *Thor* #128 (May 66). Unfortunately, this Pluto was, indeed, Pluto, aka Hades, the Olympian ruler of the Underworld, and the deal gave Pluto rights to Herc's soul. In other words, it was a standard Hollywood contract. In the next few issues, Thor acted as Herc's agent and literally went to Hell and back for his new client to set things straight. Since the book had changed from *Journey Into Mystery* to *Thor* with #126, Pluto didn't stand much chance.

TRIVIA CHALLENGE II
Category: **THE FUTURE**   What was the name of Space Ranger's girlfriend?   Answer on page 148   Answer from page 144   **ILDA**

A 1966 *Journey into Mystery* story arc sent Hercules off to Tinseltown. Good thing no one called him "The Mighty Hercules!"
© 1966 Marvel

This is not to say that DC heroes had a much better time of it. Some of my favorites are listed in the accompanying box. Check 'em out, and don't forget to bring popcorn. (And special thanks to Marvel's mad historian, Kurt Busiek, for (koff!) helping me remember a few of these movie appearances.)

Those wacky Bizarros made their version of a horror movie in **Adventure** #292, and I had to show it to you because I just love those Bizarros!
© 1962 National Periodical Publications (DC)

DC Movie Stars

DC had its own share of Silver Age movie and TV stars. Here are some of my favorites:

• Lois Lane went to Hollywood in *Lois Lane* #2 (May 58).

• "Neslo" (aka Jimmy Olsen — get it, Olsen-Neslo?) hosted the Midnight Scare Theatre in *Jimmy Olsen* #38 (Jul 59).

• Jimbo helped Mammoth Studios make a Superman movie in *Jimmy Olsen* #42 (Jan 60).

• Superman's Pal starred in another dimension's horror movie in *Jimmy Olsen* #43 (Mar 60).

• The Bizarros made a horror movie (with a handsome actor, of course) in *Adventure Comics* #292 (Jan 62).

• Our favorite cub reporter produced a monster movie in *Jimmy Olsen* #84 (Apr 65).

• Batman stayed home to watch himself on TV in *Batman* #183 (Aug 66).

• Clark Kent was caught changing to Superman by *Candid Camera* in *Action Comics* #345 (Jan 67).

• Roger Vickers, stand-in for the star of the Green Lantern television show, was killed on-screen in *Green Lantern* #55 (Sep 67).

• The Kents regained their youth as the result of another dimension's movie of them in *Superboy* #145 (Mar 68).

• Linda Danvers starred in a jungle epic in *Action Comics* #372 (Feb 69).

TRIVIA CHALLENGE II
Category: **THE FUTURE**   *Rick Purvis, Karel Sornson, and Homer Glint made up what team?*   Answer on page 149   Answer from page 145   **PLANETEER ACADEMY**

PERIL ON THE PLANET OF POP CULTURE!   **147**

Sacré Bleu! Jerry Lewis & The Justice League

"Zut alors! I am ze big fan of Jerry Lewis! M'sieu Silver Age, why was he nevair asked to join Ze Justice League?"

You wouldn't be French by any chance, would you? Well, no matter, many of us were big fans of Jerry Lewis back in the Silver Age—or, at least, we liked his comics, which were pretty big sellers into the mid-1960s. But in those days, Jerry didn't really offer what The Justice League was looking for. But that's not to say he wasn't pals with some of the members. In fact, he teamed up (more or less) with four of them.

It all started, as many of these things did, with a Batman team-up in 1966. Thanks to a certain TV show that was all the rage at the time, The Dynamic Duo managed to team up with lots of folks that year. So it's not really that surprising that "Batman Meets Jerry" in *Adventures of Jerry Lewis* #97 (Nov-Dec 1966).

In fact, the TV show played a role in the story. Batman and Robin were keeping really busy saving dads and kids who dressed up like super-heroes after being inspired by watching their show. Those duos included Jerry and his nephew Renfrew, who, at Renfrew's urging, outfitted themselves as Ratman and Rotten, The Boy Blunder. The big bat-meeting came when an odd super-villain called The Kangaroo kidnapped Renfrew, thinking he was a millionaire's son. That the size of Jerry's apartment didn't dissuade him from this notion indicates the caliber of villain we were dealing with.

Batman and Robin showed up to track down Renfrew, and Jer went along in his Ratman costume. "Imagine me, riding in the real, true, 100% genuine Batmobile!" Jerry enthused. "It's marvelous!" "It'll be more marvelous in three months," Batman said. "That's when we pay off the final note at the bank — and the Batmobile is finally ours."

Worn down from handling all those wanna-bes inspired by their TV show, the dynamic duo were exhausted by the time "Batman Meets Jerry" in **Adventures of Jerry Lewis** #97. Anybody remember that TV show?
© 1966 National Periodical Publications (DC)

"The Batman has to borrow money to buy a car?" Jerry asks. "But in real life, you are Bruce Wayne, famous and a wealthy rich man!" "Sure," Batman agreed, ignoring this astounding revelation from such a goof. "But as Batman, I haven't got a penny's worth of credit! It took me three years to get that bank loan! Did you ever try walking into a bank and borrowing money while wearing a mask?" So at least we know why he was so proud of that credit card in the movie.

The story also includes appearances by Penguin, Joker, and Riddler, who complained about The Kangaroo during a meeting of the American Society of Costumed Villains. They decided to teach Kangy a lesson, adding more fun to the festivities.

TRIVIA CHALLENGE II
Category: **LETTERCOLS**   "Mutant Mailbox" was once the name of what title's letter column? Answer on page 150

Answer from page 146
MYRA MASON

That team-up apparently worked so well that "Superman Meets Jerry" in *Adventures of Jerry Lewis* #105 (Mar-Apr 68). This time, Clark Kent visited Jerry to interview Renfrew, because Renfrew was picked as the "most typical pre-teen," which shows just how bad media information can be.

The only trouble was that, just before this assignment came up, Clark as Superman stopped Lex Luthor's robot monster from creating mayhem (darn that Lex). As the robot exploded, it coated The Man of Steel with kryptonite dust that slowly weakened him. So Clark was little help when, after being doused with water by Renfrew and having to take off his clothes (and costume) to dry out, Jerry discovered the super-suit in the wash and tried it on, just as Lex showed up, using his kryptonite detector to learn the secret identity of the man wearing Big Blue's suit. Did you follow that?

I think my favorite scene was when Clark, using his faltering super-breath to help Jerry perform a semi-super stunt to fool Lex, took a deep breath and sucked in a pigeon instead. You just never saw scenes like that in a Mort Weisinger Superman story.

That adventure proved such a laff riot that "The Flash Meets Jerry Lewis" in *Adventures of Jerry Lewis* #112 (May-Jun 69). This time, Jerry wandered into a tailor shop just as a couple of hoodlums were hustling the proprietor out the door. Jer volunteered to mind the store until the tailor returned, which the hoods admitted could be a while. The shop, of course, was the one where the members of Flash's Rogues Gallery had new costumes made when they got out of jail. And the proprietor was about to spend some time swimming with the fishes.

Soon, Captain Cold sauntered in to pick up his duds, followed by Abra Kadabra, who accidentally left his wand behind, where Renfrew found it. Oops. The Flash also happened to run by. Mistaking The Scarlet Speedster for the shop's delivery boy (it could happen), Jerry handed him a bunch of costumes to deliver. Flash delivered the costumes to the crooks — and delivered the crooks to jail.

Clark Kent made the mistake of hiding his super-suit at Jerry's house when he went to interview Renfrew, leading Jerry to find it (of course) and start the mayhem rolling in when "Superman Meets Jerry" in **Adventures of Jerry Lewis** *#105.*

© 1968 National Periodical Publications (DC)

Mister Silver Age Recommends...

Adventures of Jerry Lewis #112

DC
May 1969
Cover artist:
Bob Oksner

"The Flash Meets Jerry Lewis"
Writer: Arnold Drake
Penciller: Bob Oksner

Then 12¢
Now $14

© 1969 National Periodical Publications, Inc. (DC)

TRIVIA CHALLENGE II
Category: **LETTERCOLS**   What was the name of **CAPTAIN MARVEL**'s letter column?   Answer on page 151   Answer from page 147 **THE STAR ROVERS**

With help from Abra Kadabra's wand and the ring Barry Allen accidentally left in his pocket when he got his pants pressed at Jerry's store, our hero tried on a Flash-y suit when *"The Flash Meets Jerry Lewis"* in **Adventures of Jerry Lewis** #112.

© 1969 National Periodical Publications (DC)

Gloating at his easy triumph, Flash returned to the shop and accidentally left behind his Flash ring, which Jerry found. He tried on the costume that sprang out as Renfrew gave him a little jolt with Abra's wand. Just then, Abra returned looking for his wand, and we were off and running (so to speak).

Last but not least, "Jerry Meets The New Wonder Woman!" in *Adventures of Jerry Lewis* #117 (Mar-Apr 70). This time, in a break with tradition, Jerry went out looking for the Amazon Princess rather than just stumbling into her (if you know what I mean). Sadly, in what was *not* a break with tradition, Jerry wound up dressing up like her. Thankfully, that didn't involve wearing the famous star-spangled number, because at this point in her career, she was the New Improved Wonder Woman and was wearing the hip, happening clothes of 1970. Think Emma Peel.

As luck (and our story's needs) would have it, she hurt her leg while signing an autograph for Jerry, forcing her to return to Paradise Island to have it mended. Jerry and Renfrew got caught in her warp-drive and arrived with her, in time to hear that Wondie's mom had been kidnapped. Since Diana was hurt and Jerry just happened to be available, he dressed up like an Amazon and led the warriors in battle to retrieve Hippolyte. Oh, how I wish I were making this up.

That pretty much ended Jerry's adventures with The JLA. But, all things considered, it's a rather impressive resume. Sadly, the team members didn't seem to want to own up to these adventures, as Jerry's name never was forwarded for membership. And, let's face it, if Snapper Carr could find a way in the door, Jerry could've been right behind.

TRIVIA CHALLENGE II
Category: **LETTERCOLS**

"Listen to the Mockingbird" was the name of what series' lettercol? Answer on page 152

Answer from page 148
X-MEN

150

BABY BOOMER COMICS

Nice LAAA-DIE! More on Jerry Lewis' comics!

Looking for these great Silver Age issues? Don't forget: Jerry will be found under "A" for *Adventures of Jerry Lewis*, unless the dealer isn't paying attention and puts them under "J." Or maybe "D" to cover when it was *Adventures of Dean Martin and Jerry Lewis* in the early days. Readers of *Adventures of Bob Hope*, *Many Loves of Dobie Gillis*, and *Beware The Creeper* know full well the problems that I'm talking about.

As noted, Jerry started out as one-half of *Adventures of Dean Martin and Jerry Lewis*, which continued until Dino left the strip with #40. Those early issues usually had Dino's lust for some beautiful babe getting our two pals into hot water, which usually caused Jerry to do some heavy lifting and carrying before saving the day.

On his own, Jerry tended to get into trouble because he was a nice guy who helped out others (usually beautiful women) who had their own (often hidden) agenda or because he fell into jeopardy without even realizing it. He was aided by an occasional ability to talk to animals, which could get him both in and out of trouble.

In #85 (Nov-Dec 64), Jerry's nephew Renfrew came to live with him. Renfrew had all the trouble-making capability of Dennis The Menace without the (relative) cuteness. To handle Renfrew, Jerry hired a peculiar housekeeper in #88 (May-June 65). Witch Kraft turned out to be, well, a witch, and her spells usually kept Renfrew in line. Her niece, Zanyia, also joined in the fun on occasion.

Most of these later stories were written by Arnold Drake and drawn by Bob Oksner, a terrific team. Neal Adams also pitched in sometimes, such as with the pencils on #104 (Jan-Feb 68). Although Adams was uncredited, Mr. Silver Age could spot his style from across the room, even on *Jerry Lewis*.

Jerry was coerced into helping Diana Prince and her Amazonian pals in a big battle after he accidentally injured her in "Jerry Meets Wonder Woman!" in **Adventures of Jerry Lewis** *#117. Who could say no to Wondie?*

TRIVIA CHALLENGE II
Category: **LETTERCOLS**   What was the letter column in TOMAHAWK called?   Answer on page 153   Answer from page 149 **MAIL IT TO MAR-VELL**

The Inferior Five Meets the Marvel Universe

"How come whenever anyone talks about the great series of crossovers between DC and Marvel characters, they never talk about those classic stories that appeared in *The Inferior Five?*"

ister Silver Age has to agree that it's a puzzler, because the quality certainly was there. That is, if your sense of humor was skewed enough to appreciate the under-appreciated work of writer E. Nelson Bridwell and a variety of such great Silver Age artists as Mike Sekowsky, Joe Orlando, Mike Esposito, and Win Mortimer.

And if you were among that number, you were howling along with me whenever you immersed yourself in the epic adventures of Merry Man, The Blimp, The White Feather, Awkwardman, and, of course, Dumb Bunny. But then, I was a pretty dumb kid.

The problem is that The Inferior Five never *really* crossed over with Marvel characters. The heroes they were cavorting with were simply amazing simulations of the heroes from The House of Ideas. These homages were a continuing theme through *IF*'s incredible 12-issue run, the last two of which reprint our queasy quintet's first two *Showcase* adventures in #62 and #63. In fact, eliminating the reprints, it's probably not surprising to learn that our little dusty troupe suffered through 13 unlucky adventures in all.

Editor Jack Miller's original notion was to create a super-team parodying four of Marvel's fantastic super-heroes. But by the time they were launched, The Inferior Five wound up having too many members and roaming further afield than that. A key element was that they were the offspring of far-more-successful super-parents, the members of The Freedom Brigade.

Forget about Marvel: Only in *The Inferior Five* could you find Dean Egghead and his students, The Eggs Men.

The first parody team to face The Inferior 5 were The Vendetta (left to right): The Masked Swastika, Silver Sorceress, Sparrow, and Speed Demon in **Showcase** *#63.*
© 1966 National Periodical Publications (DC)

Their skewering of the competition began with "Conquer Man-Mountain — Because He's There!" in *Showcase* #63 (Jul-Aug 1966), their second adventure. Our fearful five fought a super-villain team called The Vendetta: the bow-wielding Sparrow, the super-fast Speed Demon, the Germanic Masked Swastika, and the magical Silver Sorceress. I'll spare you most of the alleged jokes this avenging team made in trying to outdo our humble

TRIVIA CHALLENGE II
Category: **FIRST WORDS**   *Who said, "This pilot trainer wasn't meant to fly, it has no wings!"* Answer on page 154

Answer from page 150
SECRET SIX

heroes in screwing up. But I did like their battle cry: "Vendetta, get togedder!" It had a certain ring to it.

The edge in their all-out slugfest shifted back and forth, until The Blimp deflected The Masked Swastika's Phi Beta Kappa bomb through an open window. There, it exploded next to a lousy boxer. He grew very large and green, became Man-Mountain, and joined the bad guys. Needless to say, the battle royale between Merryman and Man-Mountain is not to be missed! 'Nuff said!

Their next visit with slightly skewed super-heroes came in "Agony at the Academy or A Scrap'll Floor the Teacher!" in *Showcase* #65 (Nov-Dec 66). This time, Dean Egghead of The Academy of Super-Heroes hired our semi-heroes to teach his new students, known as the Eggs Men. (Just remember, I don't write 'em, I just read 'em.) When our pals arrived, they met the intellectual Ape; Basilisk, whose eyes turned creatures to stone; the winged Icarus; the icy Winter Wonderland; and Levitation Lass. After a quick trip to the Danger Ro...I mean gymnasium, they all went off to meet their FAN club — that is, the Fraternity of Atavistic No-goodniks. It was composed of Dr. Dinosaur, Frog Man, Angel Fish, Mr. Amoeba, and Pterano Don Juan.

Naturally, justice prevailed. And our gawky group decided to turn its teaching duties over to a more experienced group: their parents! The Freedom Brigade featured the older and wiser Patriot, Lady Liberty, Capt. Swift, The Bowman, Princess Power, Mr. Might, and the Mermaid. We can only hope The JLA ages better.

Merryman faced Man Mountain all by his lonesome in **Showcase** *#63. Why? Because he was there.*
© 1966 National Periodical Publications (DC)

The Inferior Five met the somewhat-familiar Eggs Men in **Showcase** *#65, one of a number of satires that set the tone for this series about the sons and daughters of older heroes who had been just a tad more successful.*
© 1966 National Periodical Publications (DC)

TRIVIA CHALLENGE II Category: **FIRST WORDS** Who said, "No, no! Take the fish away! Take them away! They'll kill me!" Answer on page 155

Answer from page 151
THE SADDLE BAG

H.U.R.R.I.C.A.N.E. Agents' The Missing Fink and Mr. Mental's exchange almost devolved into a "Who's on First?" routine in **Inferior Five** #1. Thank goodness they weren't trying to get to Niagara Falls.
© 1967 National Periodical Publications (DC)

With laffs just pouring off the page, it wasn't long before The IF graduated to their own book. To celebrate their first issue (Mar-Apr 67), they shifted gears and focused their parodic sights on a different company's characters. This time, the heroes were designed as the villainous group H.U.R.R.I.C.A.N.E., no relation at all to the stars of Tower Comics' *T.H.U.N.D.E.R. Agents*, I'm sure. The group included Powerhouse, who drank a super serum; The Missing Fink, an android who could make himself invisible; Mr. Mental; the super-fast Yellow Streak; the winged Blackbird; and a team of H.U.R.R.I.C.A.N.E. Agents. Nah, not even close to *T.H.U.N.D.E.R. Agents*.

Fortunately, The IF teamed up with secret agents Mr. Ivanhoe, Caesar Single, and Kwitcha Belliakin of C.O.U.S.I.N.F.R.E.D. to stop H.U.R.R.I.C.A.N.E. Needless to say, they did.

Another vaguely familiar group showed up in "The House-Hunting Heroes!" in *Inferior Five* #2 (May-Jun 67). This time, after a barrage of Bridwell's patented parody songs, we met Rod Rickard, his wife Sophie, her brother Jerry Drizzle, and Rod's assistant, Bjorn Anderson. One of Rod's experiments went boom, and the four discovered they'd been transformed into The Kookie Quartet: The Matchstick Kid, the Vanishing Queen, Mr. Manplastic, and The Whatchamaycallit.

We learned the secret origin of The Kookie Quartet in **Inferior Five** #2, after which they all trooped off to the costume store as good heroes always do.
© 1967 National Periodical Publications (DC)

But, since they decided to become heroes, our story still needed a villain. I mean, how could one heroic group ever end up fighting another in a comic? It just wouldn't be believable! Fortunately, that conflict was resolved by bad-guy Hector Prynne and his girlfriend Janice. Hector invented size-control belts that turned him into a giant named King-Size and Jan into The Terrible Tse-Tse Fly. Doesn't sound like anybody I know, nope.

In #4 (Sep-Oct 67), our pals 'n' gals met up with Thor, Sif, Balder, and Loki. Isn't it amazing what we can get away with when we all steal from the same (public domain) sources? The name of this classic was "Valhallaballoo!" Stop it, my sides are splitting.

In #7 (Mar-Apr 68), pencilled by Win Mortimer, Thor returned. But this time, he was accompanied by Prince Nabob, Iron Pants, and The Cobweb Kid. Well, and Ed Norton, if you want the full lineup.

TRIVIA CHALLENGE II
Category: **FIRST WORDS** Who said, "So it has happened at last! I must be true to my vow." Answer on page 156

Answer from page 152
HAL JORDAN

For once, our hapless heroes did themselves proud. At least, they did until right near the end, when they mistakenly beat up on The Cobweb Kid's Aunt Meg and had to do a fast fade into the sunset.

Last but not least, many of our favorites returned to help end "A Monster Rally!" in *IF* #10 (Sep-Oct 68). This time, the returnees were the Submoron (aka Prince Nabob), The Kookie Quartet, and The Cobweb Kid, who helped battle some outer-space dudes. Good thing Superman also showed up, or these guys might still be fighting those darn aliens.

I gotta admit, as good as these issues were, my favorite IF story would have to be "How to Make a Bomb!" in *IF* #6 (Jan-Feb 68). No super-heroes showed up, but they came darned close, when our grungy group showed its absolute fearlessness by visiting the offices of DC Comics.

The best page showed DC editors Julius Schwartz, Joe Orlando, Mort Weisinger, Jack Miller, E. Nelson Bridwell, Sol Harrison, Carmine Infantino, and Murray Boltinoff fighting tooth and claw to beat each other to the buffet table. Boy, they sure don't make comics like that any more.

Mayhem ensued, when the DC editors learned there was a traitor in their midst in **Inferior Five** *#6! Well, actually, they were trying to beat the other guys to the buffet table, but that doesn't sound quite as heroic.*
© 1968 National Periodical Publications (DC)

To stop an alien invasion, our super-pals tried to team up with The Kookie Quartet, The Submoron, and The Cobweb Kid in **Inferior Five** *#10. That was an impressive group, but, if Big Blue hadn't showed up, we'd probably all be speaking an alien language now.*
© 1968 National Periodical Publications (DC)

TRIVIA CHALLENGE II
Category: **FIRST WORKS** Who said, "If the Destructo beam from the Eternal's space ship hits us, we're done for!" Answer on page 157

Answer from page 153
AQUALAD

PERIL ON THE PLANET OF POP CULTURE!   155

Missing: 206 issues of 'Tarzan'!

"I'm a big fan of Joe Kubert's *Tarzan* series for DC Comics. But I can't find any issues before #207. Why are those so hard to find?"

*DC's **Tarzan** #207 picked up the numbering from Gold Key's title but helped readers figure out the switch with its own "1st DC Issue" tag.*
© 1972 Edgar Rice Burroughs Inc.

Because they don't exist, my friend. When DC picked up the license to publish comic books about Tarzan (and his son Korak) from the Edgar Rice Burroughs estate, it did so by continuing the ongoing numbering from the Dell/Gold Key series that preceded it. Thus, DC's *Tarzan* #207 (Apr 72) followed almost seamlessly after Gold Key's *Tarzan* #206 (Feb 72).

It was an unusual situation, made possible by the title being licensed from an outside source that no doubt wanted to maintain continuity. It happened a few other times but not often. (See the sidebar for examples). Just to be safe, DC slapped a big "1st DC Issue!" tag on *Tarzan* #207 that was hard to miss, and it continued this added numbering for several issues.

In truth, DC's title followed "seamlessly" only in the publishing sense, because Kubert's *Tarzan* was a revelation to fans. As the new editor, Kubert made the best possible editorial decision: He assigned the writing and pencilling duties to himself. And Kubert the writer took the series back to basics, producing a series that was faithful to the original novels.

"I've heard that my work was one of the reasons the Burroughs people brought the characters to DC, but I'm not really sure about that," Kubert told me. (Mr. Silver Age's Rolodex is a thing of wonder.) "Regardless, I was tickled pink to do it. One of the reasons I got into the business was because of the influence that Hal Foster's *Tarzan* [newspaper strip of the 1930s] had on me as a kid. I thought that if I could inject that feeling into my stories, it might stimulate the readers the same way it stimulated me back in the Stone Age."

Kubert's first step was to reread all 25 *Tarzan* books. "After reading them, I decided the best thing to do was to start right from the beginning and adhere as closely as possible to the books themselves." He supplemented his research with examples of Foster's *Tarzan* strip, obtained from the Burroughs estate. "I tried to follow Foster's

TRIVIA CHALLENGE II
Category: **FIRSTS**

What comic featured the first "Imaginary Story"?

Answer on page 158

Answer from page 154
SUE RICHARDS

delineation and interpretation of the character, and it really was a pleasure to do," he said. "I analyzed how it should be done, which meant simplifying my work as much as I could while still maintaining the momentum that Burroughs had achieved in the storytelling aspects and in the characteristics of the character itself."

That meant reintroducing a jungle man who educated himself to speak both French and English (and read English) and who could operate in society but preferred the more-civilized jungle. DC readers met Tarzan in "Origin of the Ape-Man," which ran through the first four issues. It fairly faithfully adapted *Tarzan of the Apes*, the first Tarzan novel from 1912.

The first issue (*i.e.*, #207) explained how Lord and Lady Greystoke wound up marooned on the African coast and how their newborn baby was carried off by a female ape whose own baby had died. It also showed Tarz coming of age and learning to use a knife to even the odds in an ape-fight. Issue #208 explained how he found his parent's abandoned cabin, used their books to learn to read, and discovered he was a "man." The issue also revealed that when a native killed his mother, he killed the man in return, taking his lion-skin loincloth, bow, and poison arrows. *Ooh*, the secret origin of his costume and gadgets! A key issue by any measure.

In #209, he met William Clayton, his cousin who had become Lord Greystoke in Tarzan's stead. He also met Clayton's fiancée, Jane Porter, whom he later saved from a raging bull ape. And we all knew where that was headed. Sure enough, in #210, Jane returned to America, Tarzan learned his real identity, and he went after her.

"My favorite issues are the origin, which came from the first book," Kubert said. He later adapted *Return of Tarzan* (#219-223), *Tarzan & The Lion Man* (#231-234), *Tarzan & The Castaways* (#240-243), *Jungle Murders* (#245-246) and *Tarzan & the Champion* (#248-249). He also remade three stories from *The Jungle Tales of Tarzan* short-story collection: "Captive" (#212), "Balu of the Great Apes" (#213) and "Nightmare" (#214). After he left the book, *Tarzan the Untamed* was adapted as #250-256.

"I loved creating new stories, but I also enjoyed adapting the novels," Kubert said. "The only disappointing part was that, ultimately, my responsibilities for editing and for drawing covers cut my time terribly with the Tarzan character. I would have loved to continue to do it." Instead, he began working with a group of artists based in the Philippines, including Nestor

Tarzan met Jane in #209 when she and her fiancé (and Tarzan's cousin) William Clayton, aka the new Lord Greystoke, landed in Africa and wound up in trouble.
© 1972 Edgar Rice Burroughs Inc.

Comics Shifts

Comics don't usually shift companies, much less retain their numbering in the process. But back in the day, having a higher number could result in better sales, so any rationale would be used. A few examples of this approach include:

Quality's *Blackhawk* #107 (Dec 56) moved to DC with #108 (Jan 57).
Little Audrey moved from St. John Publishing with #24 (May 52) to Harvey with #25 (Aug 52).
Casper, the Friendly Ghost moved from St. John with #5 (Aug 51) to Harvey with *Harvey's Comics Hits* #61 (Oct 52) and then became *Casper the Friendly Ghost* #7 (Dec 52). Just imagine all those fans who tried to find issue #6.
Harvey's *Dick Tracy* #25 (Mar 50) followed Dell's *Dick Tracy* #24 (Dec 49).
And, of course, DC's *Korak, Son of Tarzan* #46 (May-Jun 72) followed Gold Key's issue #45 (Jan 72).

Special thanks to Jerry Beck for his impeccable research!

TRIVIA CHALLENGE II
Category: FIRSTS   Who was SPIDER-MAN fighting the first time Aunt May was hospitalized? Answer on page 159   Answer from page 155   ADAM STRANGE

PERIL ON THE PLANET OF POP CULTURE!   157

Joe Kubert said drawing Tarzan was like getting a piece of his childhood back.

*In **Tarzan** #210, The Ape Man went to Baltimore to make Jane Porter his mate, learning upon his arrival that he was the true Lord Greystoke.*
© 1972 Edgar Rice Burroughs Inc.

Tarzan Treats

The first three issues of *Tarzan* (and first *Korak* issue) were published during DC's flirtation with the 52-page 25¢ size. That allowed space for the main 26-page feature plus lots of other goodies. These included a John Carter of Mars back-up strip with art by Murphy Anderson (and by Gray Morrow in #208) and illustrated text stories taken from Hal Foster's Sunday comic strips in 1931 and 1932. There also were text features, such as a review of "Tarzan of the Movies" in #209.

The extras were cut when the series was reduced to standard size with #210, but fans had one more surprise coming when the comic re-expanded to 100 pages with #230. What a collection of stuff! Running through #235, the expanded page count featured Kubert lead stories and Russ Manning reprints from Gold Key. Various issues also offered Congo Bill, Detective Chimp, Rex the Wonder Dog, Bomba (reprinted as "Simba" for copyright reasons), and text features.

Those issues make a great sampler of offbeat DC strips—Carmine Infantino has said that Detective Chimp was his all-time favorite strip to draw. So check 'em out! You can't go wrong with a 100-pager.

Redondo, Franc Reyes, and Rudy Florese. He supplied them with detailed thumbnail layouts on 8½ x 11-inch paper, but it didn't work to his satisfaction.

"They did a pretty good job; they're marvelous artists," he said. "But it turned out quite different from what I had in mind when I laid out the pages. That was very disappointing. It proved my point that it's important for an artist to do the complete job — even coloring and lettering, if possible — or else it results in an amalgam that's an entirely different work."

The title still holds good memories for him. "It was a very pleasurable time, and I loved doing it," he said. "It was great for me. It was like revisiting my childhood and getting a piece of it back." Mr. Silver Age can relate to that.

*Joe Kubert tipped his hat to his inspiration, Hal Foster's Tarzan comic strip, by reprinting several strips, including "The Baby of the Apes" from Jan. 23, 1932 in **Tarzan** #208.*
© 1972 Edgar Rice Burroughs Inc.

TRIVIA CHALLENGE II
Category: **FIRSTS**

Where did CAPTAIN AMERICA confront the very first Sleeper?

Answer on page 160

Answer from page 156
LOIS LANE #19

158

BABY BOOMER COMICS

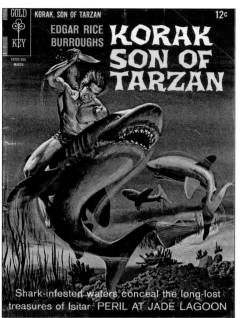

When they made the move to DC, both **Tarzan** and **Korak**'s numbering was retained from their earlier incarnations at Dell and later, Gold Key. The **Tarzan** issue shown above was the last of the Gold Key series and adapted a portion of Burroughs' **Tarzan and the Lion Man** before Kubert started the adaptations all over again at DC with the original **Tarzan of the Apes.**
© 1969 Edgar Rice Burroughs Inc.

Korak's Saga

One month after Tarzan began his bimonthly adventures at DC, his son Korak joined the line-up. As with the *Tarzan* title, *Korak, Son of Tarzan* picked up from the old Gold Key numbering with Vol. 9 #46 (May-Jun 72).

The Son of Tarzan's DC adventures kicked off with a rousing Done in One tale. Written by Len Wein, with art by Frank Thorne and edited by Joe Orlando, it featured a sexy woman searching for her father in the lost city of Opar, and loaded on the scheming helpers, dungeons filled with skeletons, treasure vaults filled with gold, and, of course, The Beast Men of Opar!

In #49, we learned Kor's origin, which the book's name pretty well already summed up. The title also featured Wein and Michael Kaluta's cool Carson of Venus strip through #56 (and a final one in *Tarzan* #230).

Korak's adventures took a winding but relentless path. He lasted through 12 issues of his own title, moving after #56 (Feb-Mar 74) to the new *Tarzan* 100-page book with #230 (Apr-May 74). He stayed there until #234 (Feb-Mar 75), gave his own book one more try with #57 (May-Jun 75), and then kept with it when it became *Tarzan Family* with #60 (Nov-Dec 75). Whew!

Fans were in for a real treat when DC's **Tarzan** comic expanded to 100 pages for six issues beginning with #230. In addition to new adventures of The Ape Man, there was room to present material from the Dell and Gold Key runs, as well as stories of Detective Chimp, Congo Bill, and Rex the Wonder Dog, among others.
© 1974 Edgar Rice Burroughs Inc.

Korak, Son of Tarzan joined the DC line-up one month after The Ape Man himself. The book also featured Carson of Venus and (for one issue) Pellucidar. When **Tarzan** and **Korak** were reduced in page count, those back-up Burroughs stories, which also included John Carter of Mars, moved over to **Weird Worlds**.
© 1972 Edgar Rice Burroughs Inc.

TRIVIA CHALLENGE II
Category: **FIRSTS**

Who was the JLA fighting when they revealed their identities to each other? Answer on page 161

Answer from page 157
ELECTRO

PERIL ON THE PLANET OF POP CULTURE!

159

Wham-O's Giant of a Comic

"Mr. Silver Age, you seem to know so much about old comics, especially back before they were really hyped the way they are today. So what was the *biggest* comic book of the Silver Age?"

Wham-O Giant Comics #1 offered truth in packaging, measuring 14 by 21 inches—nearly four times the size of a regular comic. It featured a bunch of famous creators, including Wally Wood, Lou Fine, John Stanley, and Virgil Partch.
© 1967 Wham-O

Wally Wood's Radian led off Wham-O Giant Comics, featuring the super-hero's battle with the Steel Skull. Most strips in the book ran three pages at most, but that was as many panels as 12 pages in a regular comic.
© 1967 Wham-O

There can be many arguments about which Silver Age comic was most important, but when it comes to the one that really stood out above all the others, I'd have to go with *Wham-O Giant Comics* #1 (Apr 67). It stood out primarily because it measured 14 by 21 inches—nearly four times the size of most of today's comics! When the guys at Wham-O said Giant, they meant it.

Touted as "The World's Largest Comic Book!" with more than 1,500 "action-packed" panels, it featured 48 pulse-pounding pages of features. All the key stars were shown on the wrap-around cover by W.T. Vinson (who also did a one-page strip inside), and it was a darned eclectic group, too, covering virtually every genre. None of the features ran more than three pages, but remembering our Wham-O Conversion Scale, that equated to about 12 regular comics pages.

This wasn't just cheesy stuff, either (although there was a certain amount of that, too). The lead story featured Radian by Wally Wood. Bearing a resemblance to his Dynamo stories for Tower Comics, the story introduced Gilman Graves, who was exposed to radiation

TRIVIA CHALLENGE II
Category: **REAL NAMES** What were the real names of SANDRA and MAGI? Answer on page 162

Answer from page 158
BAVARIA

160

BABY BOOMER COMICS

and became as dense as metal and extremely strong. He battled The Steel Skull and tried to cozy up to Barbara Scott, the world's foremost woman physicist. Too bad she wasn't into chemistry.

The second story highlighted Lou Fine's Tor, a two-pager about a stone-age charm that turned into a prehistoric caveman to help a Jonny Quest-like kid and some undersea explorers.

Other highlights included a three-page adventure about World War I fighting aces; a two-page "Goody Bumpkin" elf tale by Wood; single-panel gags by Virgil Partch (aka VIP); a one-page "Bridget & Her Little Brother Newton the Nuisance" by John Stanley, drawn in the style of his *Thirteen (Going on Eighteen)* comic; and "The Wooden Sword," a three-pager about a young boy facing combat in the Roman coliseum. None of it was exactly classic, but it was nice-looking stuff.

*A number of strips look to have been drawn by animators, which Wham-O had access to from its California base. This "Clyde" strip bears a striking resemblance to the **George of the Jungle** cartoon, for instance.*
© 1967 Wham-O

There were 24 strips in all, not counting the panel gags and various puzzles and games. The intro said that if you placed all the panels end to end, they would stretch the length of a football field, but I never actually tried it.

Needless to say, this comic book is a bear to store, and don't even think about bagging it. So it doesn't show up much at conventions. When it came out, it cost 98¢ and sold primarily through five-and-dime stores, who also didn't know what to do with it.

So this really weird — but really big — experiment never appeared again.

*The hand of John Stanley of **Little Lulu** and **Thirteen (Going on Eighteen)** fame was evident in Bridget & Her Little Brother Newton The Nuisance in this one-pager. The use of balloons to indicate sound effects, a Stanley trademark, is a good indication that he wrote as well as drew the strip.*
© 1967 Wham-O

TRIVIA CHALLENGE II
Category: **REAL NAMES** What was the real name of THE MASTER PLANNER? Answer on page 165

Answer from page 159
DR. DESTINY

PERIL ON THE PLANET OF POP CULTURE!

161

Super Team-Up!

"Mr. Silver Age, there were a lot of classic team-ups during the Silver Age. My favorite was when Superboy teamed up with Super Turtle. I've misplaced my copy, and the price guides shockingly don't annotate this key first meeting. Do you remember it?"

Sadly, I must confess, I don't remember it. But now that my entire Silver Age collection has been computerized in a format similar to the one Batman used to store all the information in the world, I can pull up that tidbit with a couple of keystrokes.

Ah, yes, here it is. That momentous meeting of the titans occurred in *Superboy* #130 (Jun 66). Surprisingly enough, this special Silver Age moment wasn't even mentioned on the cover, making it that much more difficult for the average fan to find.

*Another collector's item, double-bag comics moment, compliments of Mr. Silver Age: Superboy and Super-Turtle meet for the first time in **Superboy** #130. Rumor has it the unofficial name of this untitled story is "When Titans Clash!"*

© 1966 National Periodical Publications (DC)

That could be because it was one of those charming half-page filler cartoons that featured some truly exceptional Silver Age characters. They included Cora the Car Hop, Chief Hot Foot, Jerry the Jitterbug, Varsity Vic, Casey the Cop, and, of course, Super Turtle. And they all were written and drawn by Henry Boltinoff, the man who most likely has more art in more Silver Age comics than anybody else.

His Superboy team-up strip was jam-packed with plot and characterization. Today's writers could do worse than study some of these old masterpieces to learn about pacing and personality.

It was head and shoulders above all those other Superman-teams-with-a-tortoise stories that DC was running back then, even the superb Giant Turtle Olsen stories that are classics of the period. As you well know!

TRIVIA CHALLENGE II
Category: **REAL NAMES**

What was the real name of THE GIRL WITH THE GREEN HAIR? Answer on page 166

Answer from page 160
LUCY LANE, JIMMY OLSEN

Spidey's Almost-Secret Origin!

"I've heard that when Peter Parker was in high school, Liz Allen thought he was a creep. But I've heard that Liz made a play for Peter that made Mary Jane Watson mad — but I didn't think Pete met MJ until college! I hoped the Spider-Man movie would help me figure this out, but it didn't even mention Liz. So I'm very confused. What's the deal?"

that there are a whole mess of versions of Spidey's early days available for our reading enjoyment, if you want to know the unvarnished truth — and I assume you do or you wouldn't be here. And no two of those origins use the details in the same way. Who could've ever imagined that happening?

In addition to the current *Ultimate Spider-Man* comic on the newsstands, written by Brian Michael Bendis, which the movie most closely followed (except for that part about Liz putting the moves on Petey, which she did in *Ultimate*), there also was the quickly forgotten *Spider-Man: Chapter One* by John Byrne in 1998-1999 (where Liz thought Pete was a jerk). And even earlier, Kurt Busiek wove stories around the original early tales (without altering the existing stories, a masterful performance) in *Amazing Fantasy* #16-18 (1995-1996) and *Untold Tales of Spider-Man* (1995-1997).

Here at stately the Silver Age Museum, of course, we prefer the original recipe, since it was so tasty. But some of the details have gotten a bit muddled in fans' minds with the passing of time and the new incarnations. So let's see just how much you remember from 40 (gulp) years ago about the true origins of the web-swinger. Here's a helpful hint: Not only are all the "d" answers wrong as usual, but they all come from the movie.

From **Amazing Fantasy** #15 (Aug 1962) to **Spider-Man: The Official Movie Adaptation** (2002), the wallcrawler's origins have been tinkered with, "improved upon," and otherwise revised several times.

POP QUIZ

1. What was responsible for giving Spider-Man his powers?

a. A spider irradiated by Dr. Octopus.
b. A spider irradiated by atomic energy.
c. A mutant spider created by Norman Osborn.
d. A mutant spider bred from other mutant spiders.

*Peter Parker's amazing transformation took place right smack dab on the street in **Amazing Fantasy** #15. But what gave him those powers?*
© 1962 Marvel

2. What was the name of the wrestler the masked Peter Parker defeated?

a. The Invincible Crusher.
b. Crusher Hogan.
c. Crusher Creel.
d. Bonesaw McGraw.

*While Peter hadn't come up with a name for his costumed alter-ego yet, he did don a mask to wrestle in **Amazing Fantasy** #15. Who was on the ticket in that first outing?*
© 1962 Marvel

3. Why did J. Jonah Jameson proclaim Spider-Man a menace?

a. He thought Spidey was a bad influence on kids.
b. He thought Spidey tried to wreck his son's space flight.
c. He hated all super-heroes.
d. He wanted to sell more papers.

*Spidey's troubles with JJJ began in **Amazing Spider-Man** #1, but why did The Bugle's publisher target him?*

4. Who was the first super-villain Spider-Man faced?

a. Dr. Octopus.
b. The Vulture.
c. The Chameleon.
d. The Green Goblin.

*Yeah, yeah, Spidey faced the burglar that killed Uncle Ben in **Amazing Fantasy** #15, but he was hardly a super-villain. Who was the first super-villain the wallcrawler fought?*
© 1962 Marvel

5. To what publication did Peter Parker sell his first photos?

a. *The Daily Globe.*
b. *Now magazine.*
c. *Today magazine.*
d. *The Daily Bugle.*

*By **Amazing Spider-Man** #3, Peter's relationship with J. Jonah Jameson and The Daily Bugle was firmly established and not hanging by a thread. What publication did he first sell photos to in The Silver Age?*
© 1963 Marvel

6. Who gave Peter his first job?

a. Prof. Cobbwell, an electronics expert.
b. Mr. Petty, a computer scientist.
c. Prof. Newton, a scientist with the Defense Department.
d. Dr. Connors, a herpetologist.

In his Silver Age career, Peter Parker's first after-school job wasn't with Dr. Connors, as the movie told us. For whom did he work?
© 1963 Marvel

TRIVIA CHALLENGE II
Category: **REAL NAMES**   What was the real name of THE LIVING MONOLITH?   Answer on page 167   Answer from page 161 OTTO OCTAVIUS

THE CURIOUS CASE OF THE QUIRKY COMICS!

165

ANSWERS

As a result of a mutated spider's bite, Peter gained his spider powers (and lost his need for glasses) overnight in the new movie (and the movie adaptation by Stan Lee).
© 2002 Marvel

The Crusher left the world of Warner Bros. cartoons and came to the Marvel universe in **Amazing Fantasy** #15. He kept changing his last name for later retellings of Spidey's origin, but the end result was always the same.
© 1962 Marvel

1. What was responsible for giving Spider-Man his powers?
Answer b: A spider irradiated by atomic energy.

You wouldn't think this basic bit of business would be so open to fiddling, would you? And yet, each supplied answer has been used in a version of Spider-Man's origin. In truth, Stan has only himself to blame for everyone trying to improve on his original brainstorm, because, as quick and to the point as it was, Spidey's moment of truth is just so danged loony.

The fact is that Stan never met a radiation particle (or wave) that he didn't like. He had cosmic rays bombard four people who had more courage than brains, blasted a frail scientist with gamma rays, and then zapped a high school kid with "atomic energy." (He later had radiation literally fall off the back of a truck to hand out some super-powers, too). In those first two instances, the radiation was a feared energy source that ran amok. But in *Amazing Fantasy* #15 (Aug 62), it simply required Peter to attend a demonstration in "the fascinating world of atomic science!"

In this world, "fantastic amounts of radioactivity" leaped from one energy ball on a floor-mounted machine to another one attached to the wall — and nobody noticed that a spider slid into the way! Or that said spider continued down its web and somehow crawled all the way over to bite Peter before dying. The powers didn't have to build up, either — Peter was climbing walls and winning money for wrestling before he went to bed that first night. With only 10 pages for the story, Stan had to work fast.

It's not really surprising that John Byrne (answer a.), Brian Michael Bendis (c.) and the movie (including, of course, the comic-book adaptation by Stan the Man himself) tried to make it more plausible and overwhelming a change. None of them are too believable, either, but given that a danged powerful spider has to bite a high-school mope without causing a full federal investigation, they gave it their best shot. We dopey 1960s kids were way more accepting of this stuff than today's youngsters. I'm not sure if that's a good thing or not.

2. What was the name of the wrestler the masked Peter Parker defeated?
Answer b. Crusher Hogan.

Mr. Hogan had the privilege of being the first guy to battle Spidey, although he didn't know who was pounding on him in the original version, which he did in the movie. In the Silver Age, Peter didn't come up with his fancy name until he convinced himself he could beat guys like Crusher. That's how the other two comic-book versions handled it too (with Byrne sticking with the Crusher Hogan name and *Ultimate* shortening it to Crusher). But they both draw out the time between Peter gaining his power and taking on Crusher. Stan just had Peter see the sign about winning money, run home to put on a sweatshirt, and charge off to the arena.

TRIVIA CHALLENGE II
Category: **IMPS**

What imp bedeviled AQUAMAN?

Answer on page 168

Answer from page 162
KARA ZOR-EL

166

BABY BOOMER COMICS

In a sign of the times, Peter originally won $100 by beating Crusher. By 1998's *Chapter One*, the price had risen to $1,000. But by 2001's *Ultimate*, it had dropped back to $500. In all three cases, Parker got all the prize money, probably because he was smart (or lucky) enough to keep his mask on. In the movie, he should've pulled down a whopping $3,000 (movie budgets are always huge), but he took off his mask and was paid only 50 bucks because he was a kid. That was a nice touch, because it gave him more motivation to screw the promoter when he was robbed just moments later by Uncle Ben's killer.

In the original, Spider-Man became a show-biz sensation after beating Crusher and before Uncle Ben's death. Although depicted in only one (double-wide) panel in *AF* #15, Spidey's appearances were numerous and sold many papers during this span. In fact, one front-page headline shouted "Spider-Man Wins Showbiz Award!" That had to have taken a few weeks, at least. Both *Chapter One* and *Ultimate* allude to this period, but the movie condensed it to one event.

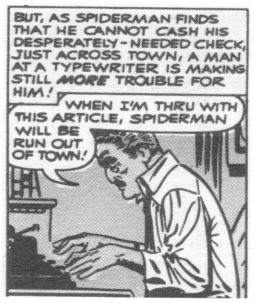

None of JJJ's bluster was lost for the 2002 movie adaptation and actor J.K. Simmons captured the character perfectly on screen.
© 2002 Marvel

3. Why did J. Jonah Jameson proclaim Spider-Man a menace?
a. He thought Spidey was a bad influence on kids.

Jameson's first pronouncements labeled Spidey a vigilante and a bad influence on youngsters. "Think what would happen if they make a hero out of this lawless, inhuman monster!" he thundered in *Amazing Spider-Man* #1 (Mar 63). "We must not permit it!" That bit of selflessness got lost along the way to making Jameson a self-promoter, to where the movie quoted him as making Spider-Man a menace because "Fear sells newspapers."

Of course, Jameson wasn't *entirely* self-effacing about his anti-Spidey crusade, even in the Silver Age. There's a strong implication that he was afraid Spider-Man would steal the spotlight from his astronaut son, John, who was about to be launched into space. Sure enough, Spidey saved John when his capsule malfunctioned, Jameson assumed Spidey caused the problem so he could steal the glory, and a life-long feud began — which, incidentally, sold a whopping load of newspapers.

Later on, J. Jonah Jameson actually aided super-villains against Spider-Man. He eventually came clean about that — on his own editorial page, of course!

Plenty o' reprints

These early Spider-stories have been reprinted many times, so pick them up and relive the way things really were:

All these stories are in *Essential Spider-Man* #1 and *Marvel Masterworks* #1, one of which you really outta have. They also appear in *Amazing Spider-Man Pocket Comics* #1 (1977 from Pocket Books), and *Spider-Man Megazine* #1.

Amazing Fantasy #15 appears alone in *Marvel Tales* #1 and #137, *Origins of Marvel Comics*, *Marvel Milestone* edition, *Spider-Man Classic* #1, *Best of Spider-Man*, and *Fantastic Firsts* paperback.

Amazing Spider-Man #1 was reprinted in *ASM Annual* #2 (Jameson story) and *ASM Annual* #7 (Chameleon story), *Marvel Tales* #138, *Spider-Man Classic* #2, and a Golden Record comic.

Amazing Spider-Man #2 was reprinted in *Marvel Tales* #139, *Spider-Man Classic* #3, and *Spider-Man Annual* #2 (Tinkerer story).

TRIVIA CHALLENGE II
Category: **IMPS**
What was the first thing THE IMPOSSIBLE MAN turned into?   Answer on page 169

Answer from page 165
AHMET ABDOL

THE CURIOUS CASE OF THE QUIRKY COMICS!

167

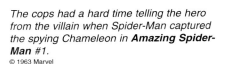

The cops had a hard time telling the hero from the villain when Spider-Man captured the spying Chameleon in *Amazing Spider-Man #1*.
© 1963 Marvel

4. Who was the first super-villain Spider-Man faced?
Answer c. The Chameleon.

This bit of bad luck was the true catalyst for Spidey's disreputable reputation with the law. In *ASM #1*'s second story, The Chameleon read about the wall-crawler's attempt to join The Fantastic Four earlier in the tale. He reasoned, correctly, that Spidey needed money, so he dressed up like Spidey and used a fake web gun to make the wall-crawler the fall guy for his scheme to steal missile-defense documents.

The Chameleon's plan was uncovered and he was captured by police, but that didn't seem to clear Spidey as well as it should have. But he was just a high-school kid in his first big-time battle, so he didn't think to go back to put things right as the cops hauled The Chameleon away. "Nothing turns out right…<sob>" he bemoaned as he ran off down the street. Running off in tears rather than helping to march Chameleon to the slammer was probably one of the biggest mistakes of Spidey's career.

Dreams of avarice danced through Peter Parker's head when he saw *Now* magazine's offer to purchase photos of The Vulture in *Amazing Spider-Man #3*.
© 1963 Marvel

5. To what publication did Peter Parker sell his first photos?
Answer b. Now magazine.

Surprised to see *The Bugle* down there in the "d" slot? In fact, Jameson also was publishing a feature magazine and needed photos of Spider-Man for the cover feature.

The kids at school mused that a magazine like *Now* would probably pay a fortune for pictures, and a light bulb went off over Peter's head, even though he was hard at work on a chemistry experiment. Jameson was still the buyer, but it was in his role as publisher of that glossy magazine, not the newspaper. But that didn't last long.

Petey did sell photos to *The Daily Globe* once, in *Amazing Spider-Man M #27* (Aug 65), as he was frustrated by Jameson's attitude and penny-pinching ways. But photo editor Barney Bushkin asked too many questions, putting Parker on the defensive. Pete decided he'd take the non-inquisitive Jonah despite his flaws.

TRIVIA CHALLENGE II
Category: **IMPS**

What was SUPERBOY doing when he met MR. MXYZPTLK?

Answer on page 170

Answer from page 166
QUISP

168

BABY BOOMER COMICS

6. Who was Peter's first after-school job with?
Answer a. Prof. Cobbwell, an electronics expert.

The movie's Dr. Connors was a nice tip of the hat to the great Silver Age villain The Lizard, but Prof. Cobbwell takes home the real prize in *ASM* #2 (May 63). Parker was recommended for the job, which involved weekend research, by his chemistry teacher. In Stan's world, since Peter was good in "science," that meant he was a genius in chemistry, biology, electronics, physics, engineering and even fashion design.

Pete's first task was to stop at The Tinkerer Repair Shop and pick up the doc's radio, which needed new tubes. Remember when radios had tubes? No, don't answer that, I'd rather not know. But darn the luck, The Tinkerer turned out to be an alien — the outer-space type, I mean — and Spider-Man ultimately shut down the shop. *Chapter One* kept Cobbwell and Tink, but tied the villain to The Vulture and made the aliens a hoax. *Ultimate* left these guys on the cutting-room floor, and I'm betting the movie sequel won't have much room for them, either.

Peter's science background turned him into a glorified errand boy for Professor Cobbwell in **Amazing Spider-Man** *#2. Thank goodness, Doctor Connors had better tasks for Peter to do!*

© 1963 Marvel

But that's all right by me. Spider-Man's origin is so intrinsic to his character that in any retelling of his early days, the really key events always rise to the surface. The details may change, sometimes for the better and sometimes not, but those are just the seasonings that flavor the dish. All of these sources learned the wall-crawler's most important lesson: That with the great power to tell Spidey's resonating story comes the great responsibility to tell it in a way that keeps the message clear and his reasons for being a hero from becoming lost in the shuffle.

Other versions of Spider-Man's origin appeared in **Spider-Man: Chapter One** *#1,* **Untold Tales of Spider-Man** *#1, and* **Ultimate Spider-Man** *#1.*

Scoring:

6: Excellent! You've probably been following the wallcrawler's adventures for most of the past 40 years and weren't a bit confused by the movie!

4-5: Pretty darn good! So one or two stumped you. Hey, even Mr. Silver Age has his off-days.

2-3: Less than good! Your spider-knowledge came from one of the later revamps, didn't it?

0-1: Not good at all! You just heard about this guy who can cling to walls and shoot webs to immobilize his foes, right?

TRIVIA CHALLENGE II
Category: **IMPS**

In his first trick on Batman, BAT-MITE turned what into rubber? Answer on page 171

Answer from page 167
A JET

THE CURIOUS CASE OF THE QUIRKY COMICS!

169

Superman: Everything You Know Is Wrong

"When they rebooted *Superman* in 1986, the new story said that Martha Kent not only didn't die when Clark was a boy, but she was married to a rich department-store owner before she married Jonathan Kent! That's blasphemy! Why didn't later creators and editors leave well enough alone?"

Although I sympathize with your feelings — and I agree with the spirit of your rant — when it comes to the actual specifics, I'm afraid we may have some problems. If there's one motto DC didn't follow with the Man of Steel during the Silver Age, it was "Let's leave well enough alone."

In fact, I'm betting that many, many bits of business you accept as gospel about the Silver Age Superman aren't really the way they wound up happening by the time everybody got done fiddling with things. At some point, especially late in the 1960s as the Idea Barrel was apparently emptying out, some basic plot points were altered for the sake of that month's story.

Since nobody later went to the trouble of wiping away those plot points, it was up to us readers to act as if those stories had never existed. That's a useful attitude to keep handy while reading Silver Age comics because, much as we love them, those tales are riddled with revisions that can make a fan's hair stand on edge. Superman comics alone account for, by my rough estimate, seven billion.

Fortunately, each of the problems was buried inside one issue that can be ignored or forgotten. Unfortunately, I've got a lot of those comics, and I'm not shy about exhuming them. So here's your chance to take a really easy Silver Age True or False pop quiz about Superman's life, focusing just on events until he was adopted. It's an easy quiz because every statement below, hard as it may be to believe, is False.

Mister Silver Age Recommends...

Superman (1st series) #205

DC
Apr 1968

Cover artist:
Neal Adams

"The Man Who Destroyed Krypton"
Writer: Otto Binder
Penciller: Al Plastino
Inker: Al Plastino

Then **12¢**
Now **$20**

© 1968 National Periodical Publications, Inc. (DC)

Black Zero learned that Jor-El's warnings about Krypton were wrong, so he ensured the planet would blow up anyway in **Superman** *#205.*

© 1968 National Periodical Publications, Inc. (DC)

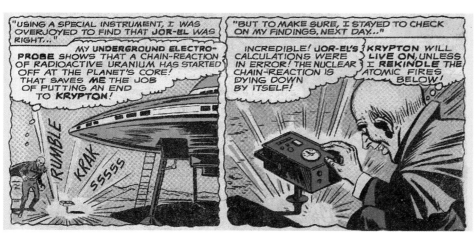

1. Jor-El correctly predicted that Krypton would explode due to a chain reaction in the planet's uranium core.

Sadly, Jor-El was mistaken, according to "The Man Who Destroyed Krypton!" in *Superman* #205 (Apr 68). In that tale, a sinister alien called Black Zero confronted the Man of Steel, speaking Kryptonese. The villain shocked Supes by explaining that he had been a saboteur assigned

TRIVIA CHALLENGE II
Category: **SIDEKICKS**

Who was the sidekick to **MARTIAN MANHUNTER?**

Answer on page 168

Answer from page 172
CARRYING A WHALE

170

BABY BOOMER COMICS

by space pirates to destroy Krypton before it entered the space age and threatened their rule.

Black Zero learned that Krypton's Science Council didn't believe Zor-El's warning of imminent destruction. So he checked the core himself and found the Council was right — the chain reaction was dying down. So the dastardly villain shot a nuclear rocket into the core to reignite it. "I'm doing Jor-El a favor!" he chortled. "Making his prediction come true!" As he flew away, Krypton went boom.

2. Jor-El and Lara perished on Krypton after sending Kal-El's rocket into space.

Pretty basic, right? Unfortunately, pretty basically wrong, according to "Superboy's Darkest Secret!" in *Superboy* #158 (Jul 69). In that tale, Superboy was shocked to intercept a deep-space message being broadcast by his parents. Tracking it to its source, he found his parents entombed in a rocket that had turned to kryptonite.

To make a long story short, a prerecorded message from Jor-El explained that Jor suspected a scientist working with the Els during Krypton's final moments might try to save the couple by shooting them away in an experimental rocket, even though Kal's parents had declined his offer.

The tape revealed that the reason they had refused to go was that Jor had been fatally contaminated with kryptonite radiation while exploring Krypton's core, and he had infected Lara before finding an antidote that saved Kal. He asked that their bodies not be revived if someday they were found in space, because they would die anyway. Kal honored their request, so Jor and Lara continued floating around in outer space. Brrr.

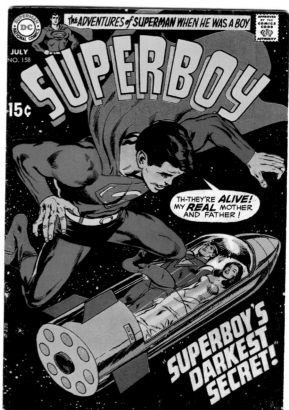

Not a hoax, dream or Imaginary Story! Jor-El and Lara really were floating in space forgotten until Superboy grew to be a teen, as revealed in **Superboy** *#158.*
© 1969 National Periodical Publications, Inc. (DC)

3. Kal-El was a couple years old when he landed on Earth.

Kal learned he was in fact at least 102 years old when he landed on Earth, according to "100 Years — Lost, Strayed or Stolen!" in *Action Comics* #370 (Dec 68). Vivid nightmares of his rocket landing in a weird civilization led him to analyze the age of his Kryptonian spaceship. He learned that it was pretty danged old, even though he knew it had been built just before he was placed in it.

"Will I ever solve this mystery?" he pondered. "No!" the caption told us, before the story explained what the Man of Steel would never learn. And that was that the blast that destroyed Krypton opened a space warp in the cosmos' fabric that pushed Kal-El's ship into another dimension. There he grew to adulthood, married, and had all kinds of adventures for the next 100 years before being de-aged into a baby again and returning through the space warp for reasons I won't spoil here. Aren't you glad you know?

4. Clark was the Kent's only child.

Superboy learned about "The Kent's First Super-Son!" in *Superboy* #108 (Oct. 63). He tracked a blonde teen villain, Mighto, to his other-worldly lair, where

Superman never figured out why his rocket was more than 100 years old, but we learned the details — even if we didn't want to — in **Action Comics** *#370.*
© 1968 National Periodical Publications, Inc. (DC)

TRIVIA CHALLENGE II
Category: **SIDEKICKS**   Who was the sidekick to **SPACE RANGER**?   Answer on page 173   Answer from page 169 **A BRIDGE**

THE CURIOUS CASE OF THE QUIRKY COMICS!   **171**

NO, SON...WE KNOW NOTHING ABOUT A SUPER-CHILD CALLED *MIGHTO!* THIS PHOTO YOU FOUND IN THE ATTIC TRUNK, WHICH SHOWS HIM FLYING OUR SLED, IS A *FAKE!*

Revealed! THE SENSATIONAL TRUE STORY OF... "The KENTS' FIRST SUPER-SON!"

BOTH MY FOSTER-PARENTS ARE STARING BLANKLY! THEY MUST BE UNDER THE POST-HYPNOTIC CONTROL OF *MIGHTO*, THE SUPERBABY THEY SECRETLY ADOPTED MANY YEARS BEFORE ME!

The Kents never got around to telling Clark that he wasn't an only child, as revealed in **Superboy** #108. But they had a good excuse: They'd been told to forget. (You can see I forgot to keep my copy in better shape, too.)
© 1963 National Periodical Publications, Inc. (DC)

USING FALSE CREDENTIALS, "REVEREND BLAKE," ALIAS "DEACON" DUGAN, FILLS OUT ADOPTION PAPERS, AND...

WE NEEDN'T CHECK UP ON THE MINISTER OF THE RECTORY IN WATERTOWN! HE'S YOURS, FOLKS!

JONATHAN,..LOOK! THEY GAVE OUR BABY TO---- SOMEONE ELSE!

THAT FELLOW'S A PHONEY, MARTHA! I KNOW THE REAL WATERTOWN MINISTER!

Adopting a baby you leave on the doorstep the previous night takes pinpoint precision, as the Kents learned when someone else adopted Kal-El in **Superboy** #133.
© 1966 National Periodical Publications, Inc. (DC)

Superboy was shocked to discover an array of photos and memorabilia indicating Mighto previously had lived with the Kents, his very own foster-parents. But Ma and Pa denied any knowledge of this bozo.

So Superboy super-hypnotized them, and they spilled their guts. It turned out Mighto was the son of the Kent's handyman, who apparently died in an accident. They adopted him, only to discover he had amazing super powers. After living with the Kents until he was a teen-ager, events turned Mighto evil.

I won't tell you what's really going on, but I will tell you that my favorite part came when we learned that, in order to ensure his plans weren't uncovered, Mighto not only hypnotized the Kents into forgetting that he'd lived with them for many years, but he also "mass-hypnotized" everyone in Smallville and destroyed his adoption papers and all newspaper records of his existence! Man, do I love the Silver Age!

5. After Kal-El landed on Earth, he was immediately adopted by the Kents.

To return the favor for Clark's foster-parents adopting a baby before him, it turned out that he also was adopted by another family before the Kents laid claim to him. It was all revealed in "Superboy's First Foster-Parents!" in *Superboy* #133 (Oct 66), in which the Kents found Kal and dropped him on the doorstep of the Smallville Orphanage as usual. But before they could return to officially adopt him, he was adopted by "Deacon" Dugan, a con man who masqueraded as a minister so he could win approval for adopting the little tyke. It turned out that Superbaby was a dead ringer for the richest baby alive, and the Deacon planned to make a switch.

I don't think we need to drop a spoiler warning in here if I reveal that his plan didn't quite work out and that Superbaby wound up back in the orphanage, where the Kents quickly applied to adopt him. Whew.

6. OK, they did some dumb things, but at least Superman didn't have some stupid clone created long after the fact that came back to haunt him for a long time the way that dumb Spider-clone did for Spider-Man in the early 1990s.

Sadly, I wouldn't bet money on that. And I'm not even talking about that weird sand creature from Qarrm who siphoned off Supe's powers in *Superman* #233 (Jan 71). He only lasted 10 issues or so, which was a few weeks of Superman's life in comic-book terms. No, we're talking about a super-clone who lasted years. And years and years and years.

In the three-part novel "The Two Faces of Superman!" in *Superman* #137 (May 60), we learn that after Jor-El and Lara shot Kal's rocket into space (and

TRIVIA CHALLENGE II
Category: **SIDEKICKS**   Who was the canine sidekick to **BOB HOPE**?   Answer on page 174   Answer from page 170 **ZOOK**

172   **BABY BOOMER COMICS**

apparently after it returned from that 100-year space warp), it glanced off a giant alien space ship. The blow jarred a ray gun into operation, which created "a duplicate of the rocket and everything inside it, including the tiny infant!"

One rocket landed on the Kent's farm, yadda yadda yadda. The other landed at the mountain retreat of criminal "Wolf" Derek and his wife, Bonnie. Wolf's reaction to seeing a tiny baby crawl out of the rocket was to shoot the kid with a tommy gun. That probably was our first clue that Wolf was not going to be named "Parent of the Year." When that failed to make much impact, the pair decided to raise the kid as their own. Thus, while the Kents were teaching Clark not to cross against the light, the Dereks were teaching Super-Brat to punch out cops.

The criminals used Super-Brat to help with robberies. He grew to become the teenage Super-Bully, who caused Superboy problems such as creating hurricanes in Smallville with his super-breath and (gasp!) trying to steal his dog. But still, Super-Bully kept his presence a secret and didn't try to, oh, take over the world or anything. Not until he became the grown-up Super-Menace did he reveal himself to Superman and lure him into a kryptonite trap. Fortunately, Superman prevailed and Super-Menace, um, went away (read it to find out how).

But this doesn't negate the fact that throughout Superman's life from the day he landed on Earth until he was that 29-year-old adult he always was back then, he had a clone wandering around pulling robberies and dissing Krypto. Scary thought, huh?

There remains only one saving grace to this "Untold Story" (oh, if only it were), and it is one today's comics creators might keep in mind: The whole thing took place in one issue. So if you missed it or didn't care for it — and that was probably most of us who stopped to think about what it meant for every Superboy story we were ever going to read — another story was coming next issue. And it, no doubt, was going to be much cooler.

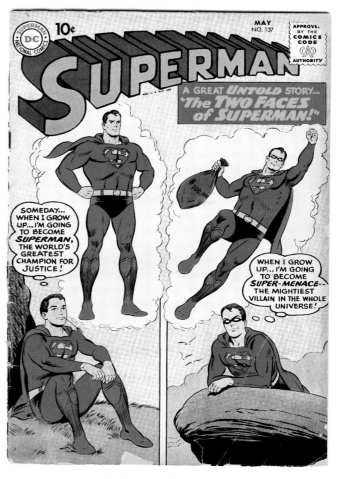

Unknown to Superman, he had an exact clone that grew up alongside him and waited many years before confronting him, as shown in **Superman** #137. It kinda puts a new spin on all those Superboy stories.

Reprint Warning!

Are you for some unknown reason feeling like you want to read these better-forgotten stories but can't find the originals? Not too surprisingly, they don't lead the list of most-reprinted tales. But amazingly enough, three of the six have reappeared, like the bad pennies they are.

Superman #137 was reprinted in *80-Page Giant* #1, which supposedly presented Imaginary Stories, but that's only wishful thinking in this case.

"Superboy's First Foster Parents!" from *Superboy* #133 was reprinted in *Superman Family* #165.

"Superboy's Darkest Secret!" from *Superboy* #158, perhaps the most amazing one to reprint of all, reared its head again in the *Superboy-Legion* paperback from Tempo. So at least it isn't easy to find even in reprint.

Mister Silver Age Recommends...

80-Page Giant Magazine #1

DC
Aug 1964
Cover artists:
Curt Swan, George Klein

"The Two Faces of Superman"
Writer: Jerry Siegel
Penciller: Curt Swan
Inker: John Forte

Then 25¢
Now $165

TRIVIA CHALLENGE II
Category: **SIDEKICKS**   **Who was the sidekick to the Silver Age PLASTIC MAN?**   Answer on page 175   Answer from page 171 **CRYLL**

Beware The Futuremen of 2000!

"Comics often tell stories about the future. How well did Silver Age comics from 40 years ago predict what the future would be like?"

That's an easy one to answer, especially now that we're living in the 21st Century ourselves. And we didn't even need a time bubble, fancy equipment or all those spinning effects with dates swirling around to get here. What a deal! And now that we're here, we can put on our jumpsuits, climb into our flying space cars, and peel off for Jupiter.

At least, we can do all that according to Silver Age comic books. Comics have always projected a pretty nifty-looking if sometimes dangerous future. But judging by the ubiquitous personal spaceships and video-phones, they had a lot more faith in automakers and the phone company than they really should've had. And for as much as comics artists loved to show our descendants living in bizarro fashions, the next time jumpsuits or ascots catch on as the height of style for the rising executive on the go, it'll be the first time. Of course, sometimes they forgot to update everything around their heroes, leading to the odd image of guys in fedoras shooting at each other with ray guns.

In most cases, writers and artists played it safe by showing us the future 1,000 or more years from the present or they set their stories in an indeterminate time. It's always less dangerous (and way more wacky) to show how we'll be living in the 30th Century than in the 21st Century.

Because here we are in the 21st Century, and we can check out those comics where creators didn't play it quite so safe and showed us what our life would be like. Granted, parts of this century are still nearly 100 years off, so anything could still happen. But a few daring comic creators presented life right here in 2001. How well did they do? Let's just take a look:

Superman: My all-time favorite near-future vision appeared in "Superman Versus The Futuremen," a two-part epic in *Superman* #128 (Apr 59), which sadly has never been reprinted. Of course, that may be because the Futuremen were from the year 2000 (or "2,000," as they call it, as if it ever would've occurred to them to say "1,959). Alleged members of the Earth Bureau of Investigation returned to 1959 in their time-machine and claimed that Superman was an escaped crook from the future. Citizens were shocked, but even more shockingly, they seemed willing to believe this dubious claim from these goofy guys nobody had seen before.

The year 2,000 fell a little short of being able to confront the Man of Steel with space ships shooting power bands as shown in "Superman Versus the Futuremen" in **Superman** *#128 (Apr 59).*

TRIVIA CHALLENGE II
Category: **RELATIVES**

Which relative of the real deal is thought by some to be GREEN LANTERN? Answer on page 176

Answer from page 172
HARVARD HARVARD III

174

BABY BOOMER COMICS

To prove his innocence (using Kryptonian logic too subtle and complex for me to understand), Superman tape-recorded his origin, giving all the details of the Kents finding him, but giving us the Golden Age version of the story, which didn't include Superboy. Supes gave the tape to Perry White to listen to only if the Man of Steel was taken to the future to pay for his "crimes." Sure enough, the EBI boys, armed with several kinds of red kryptonite that conveniently did just what they needed it to do, captured Big Blue, and took him back to the future.

And what a future it was! The Futuremen of 2,000 live in a world of rocketships, the Mars Terminal, space stations, and women who dressed in hot pants. Woo-hoo! Sadly, they also lived on a world with no oceans, as they had been dissolved by a failed atomic experiment. Oops! That, in fact, was the real reason Supes was dragged back to the future by these guys, who had an evil scheme in mind, of course. Did the Man of Tomorrow foil this dastardly plan and return to the present in time to stop Perry (and Lois) from listening to his tape? What do you think?

Frankly, these creators conjuring the world of 2000 had a lot of optimism for only 41 years' worth of advances. Considering Superman forgot he'd ever been Superboy, maybe this was Earth-2's Superman and its 21st Century. Yeah, that's the ticket.

The uniforms worn by the police in the year 2000, as predicted by **Superman** #128 (Apr 59), may have been designed to scare criminals into giving up. (On fashion critics, it might have worked.)

The other prime Superman forecast came in "Superman 2001!" in *Superman* #300 (Jun 76). For that anniversary, DC supposed what would happen if Superman had come to Earth in 1976 rather than, um, whenever he at that point was supposed to have done it. In this version, space around Earth was so well monitored that his rocket was noticed on its arrival and claimed by America, just beating out those dirty Commies. Thus Kal-El grew up as a ward of the military as "Skyboy."

By 1990, the story informed us, "The New Empire State Building has reclaimed the title of the world's tallest skyscraper, stabbing a full mile into the sky! Supersonic aircraft no longer harm the ecology of the land, departing and arriving at floating seaports instead! The hallowed White House remains unchanged—except that it is covered by an impenetrable dome, protected from all who might do the president harm!"

Of all the wondrous changes to point out in 1990, I wonder how they picked those three? The closest they got was on the White House, which has some wimpy concrete blocks around it instead of a bubble over it. Fortunately, they also missed out on fashions, as everyone was decked out in spiffy Curt Swan-style future clothes of shiny lapels, ascots and knee-high boots. That's a fashion trend I'm glad we skipped.

Most optimistically of all, the President was a woman. Quite a stunning amount of progress for 24 years, considering a woman hadn't even been a vice-presidential candidate by then in real life. Sadly, President Wiener (no really) had an itchy trigger finger, as did her Soviet counterpart. And after Superman's presence on Earth finally was revealed to the world, the two leaders were tricked into firing atomic weapons at each other and releasing poison gas. Supes saved both countries and then vowed never to use his powers again, although they'd been pretty handy this time out.

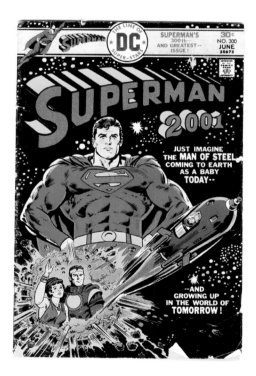

Warning: If you think Jor-El and Lara dress a little funny, don't open this copy of **Superman** #300 from 1976. You always know you're in the future if people are wearing ascots to work.

TRIVIA CHALLENGE II
Category: **RELATIVES**   *What is the name of HAWKEYE's brother?*   Answer on page 177   Answer from page 173 **GORDON K. TRUEBLOOD**

THE CURIOUS CASE OF THE QUIRKY COMICS!   **175**

As the digital clock turned 2001 in Times Square, hundreds of thousands celebrated the new century as space ships flew overhead. So they missed the celebration by one year (mistakenly figuring we'd still remember how to count) and the space-ship thing by quite a few. The three-dimensional, life-sized television, watched by people sitting in their floating armchairs, hasn't come along yet either. But I'm betting that'll make it before those space ships do (or, I'm praying, those ascots).

*Back in 1976, they foolishly thought we'd be able to count correctly, so they figured we'd celebrate the beginning of the new century in 2001, according to **Superman** #300.*
© 1976 National Periodical Publications (DC).

*Any similarity between your life and the one depicted in Marvel's **2001: A Space Odyssey** in 1976 would be truly scary. Jack Kirby used Stanley Kubrick's movie as a jumping off point, and that combination led to some really wacky comics.*
© 1976 Marvel Characters Inc.

2001: Another great comic dealing with the new century was Marvel's *2001: A Space Odyssey*, which produced 10 issues in 1976-1977. Based on concepts from the MGM/Stanley Kubrick production (it said so right on the cover), the book was less about the wonders of 2000 and more about extending ideas from the movie into new adventures.

Considering the movie was made in 1968, it didn't do too badly with its predictions. For instance, two key concepts were the existence of huge space stations and computers that refused to do what we wanted them to do. A version of the former is being built right now, and I've got one of the latter sitting on my desk, although it doesn't actually talk to me before it refuses to work.

Jack Kirby wrote and drew the series, unleashing an imagination that both astounded and horrified fans. Either way, it definitely mystified them. The first few issues dealt with similar (some fans said exactly the same) plots revolving around the movie's Black Monolith. Each time, it changed the protagonist, with a later descendant running into the Monolith and being put into a clear membrane that turned him into an embryo, which was shot into space.

With #5, the book shot forward to 2040 for no apparent reason to bring us the two-part story of "Harvey Norton, comic freak and astronaut!" With #8, it presented a tale in a more-recent but unspecified year, although I'd have to guess it was 1977. It revealed the origin of X-51, aka Mr. Machine, later known as Machine Man. (I'm betting Marvel's editors discovered that Hasbro still held a copyright to its toy name, something most Baby Boomers could've told them.)

The letters column ran from very hot to very cold, with #6, for instance, featuring one letter that said, simply, "Kirby is a genius" and one that said, "Please stop your regular-sized book before any damage is done." Kirby unleashed can be a wacky thing.

TRIVIA CHALLENGE II
Category: **RELATIVES** — What is the name of Challenger RED RYAN's kid brother? — Answer on page 178 — Answer from page 174 **JIM JORDAN**

176

BABY BOOMER COMICS

Morlock 2001: This one may have slipped by you altogether. Produced by the short-lived Atlas Comics in 1975, it told the sad tale of a weird pod-grown guy who became a fugitive and learned to kill anyone who got in his way by turning them into shrubbery. Hey, whatever worked.

He was born into 2001, "a time when life was we know it has become hideously transformed," the first caption told us. You can argue over the closeness of that resemblance if you like but not the details, which explained that "A rigid totalitarian regime holds the people in an iron grip, and mankind's greatest truths have been declared 'inoperative.'" One of those inoperative truths probably was, "You can set your futuristic comics story 25 years in the future because no fans will be reading comics for that long."

The world of 2040 will feature guys dressing up as superheroes to act out adventures, according to Jack Kirby and **2001: A Space Odyssey** #5 (Apr 77). That's kind of like comics conventions in 2001, only with somewhat less hitting.
© 1976 Marvel

Morlock became a fugitive after his father/scientist was shot and killed by the Thought Police as a deviant because he read books, which had been outlawed. The cops took the pod they found back to HQ, where Morlock hatched (already wearing a nifty light- and dark-blue uniform) and then broke loose.

By issue #3, Morlock's potential apparently had played itself out, as the book changed its name to *Morlock and the Midnight Men*. In the story, Morlock met a group of underground dissenters led by said Midnight Man. He was caught reading books, a crime punishable by death, and he was scorched with a flame-thrower on the spot. Ouchies. Rather than dying, he hooked up with Morlock to fight back.

But at the book's conclusion, Morlock was shot by the Midnight Man, and then Mr. Man tried to destroy everything with the push of a button. Was that the end of them all? "Don't bet your last two bits on it!" the final caption exclaimed. Actually, it would've been a strong bet, because we never saw them again. It's too bad, as it wasn't the worst book ever, and the last issue featured Steve Ditko-Bernie Wrightson artwork. But any revival would probably have to move that 2001 dating.

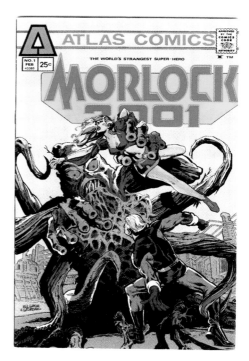

In **Morlock 2001** #1 (Feb 75), thought police acted as cops, jury and judge, meting out death to anyone caught owning books. It didn't actually turn out that way, but try putting "Huckleberry Finn" on a high-school class's reading list and see how close you get.
© 1975 Atlas Comics.

E.C.s: Back before the Silver Age, in the early 1950s, E.C. set many of its fantasy stories in centuries to come, and on occasion it would date them to times in the far-flung future, like 1970. Here are some of my favorite near-misses:

• "The Origin of the Species!" in *Weird Fantasy* #8 (Jul-Aug 51) tells a time-travel paradox story about the Solar Brothers in the year 1997, "when space-travel is a past conquest of man!" The scariest part of the story is seeing the tight bathing suits and long-sleeved shirts that apparently were to become the fashion. Whew! Another fashion-bullet dodged!

• "The End!" in *Weird Fantasy* #13 (May-Jun 52) explained how a comet passing Earth on Dec. 8, 1952, sterilized the entire population. In 2003,

TRIVIA CHALLENGE II
Category: **RELATIVES**   What are the names of LORI LEMARIS' kid sisters?   Answer on page 179   Answer from page 175   **BARNEY BARTON**

THE CURIOUS CASE OF THE QUIRKY COMICS!

For the beginning of our story, let us move ahead a number of years into the future, to a time when space-travel is a past conquest of mankind! The year is 1997! The place...the solar-apartment of the Revere brothers, the famous archaeologists! As we look in, Ernest is packing a small suitcase, while Stanley paces the floor, angrily...

All right, Ernest! Go on your crazy trip! It's going to be two valuable years wasted! You'll never find what we're looking for up there in the stars...

And I maintain...you'll never find it digging here on Earth!

Weird Fantasy #8 (Jul-Aug 51) predicted regular space travel and many other wondrous things for the year 1997. Fortunately, those bizarre bathing trunks and long-sleeved shirts were among the ideas that didn't quite make the cut.
© 1951 E.C. Publications.

"TV became of age! Its roving eye was everywhere! In 1983, it recorded the landing of the first earth-men on the moon..."

We are only the pilgrims of space! Others will follow us!

Man's landing on the moon in 1983 was broadcast back to Earth, according to "The Last Television Broadcast on Earth!" in **Mystery in Space** *#22 (Nov 55). Not a bad prediction, if only they'd been able to factor in Sputnik and President Kennedy.*
© 1955 National Periodical Publications Inc. (DC).

scientists began experimenting with temporal-travel to pull people from the past to reproduce in the future. By 2012, they perfected their equipment, and this being E.C., it was pretty darn ironic why it didn't work.

• "Punishment Without Crime!" in *Weird Science* #21 (Sep-Oct 53) told how George Hill, a few years after 1997, purchased the services of Marionettes Inc. to gain revenge on his cheating wife. The company built an exact duplicate of his wife, complete with blood and thought patterns. Then he killed it, only to be charged with his wife's murder, because making and killing such creatures was a crime—punishable by death, even though the real person was still alive.

Strange Adventures: DC was no slouch at predicting the future in its various science-fiction stories, either. Again, it often left open exactly when the story took place. But on occasion, for that extra smidgen of verisimilitude, it nailed it down:

• In "The Mad Planet" in *Mystery in Space* #19 (Apr-May 54), the year 1989 saw tourists traveling to the stars for sightseeing thrills and a couple landing on a planet that instruments showed was habitable. "It's not on the star maps, Harry!" said Doris. "But land anyway — maybe we'll discover something new!" That's a lot of progress for 35 years, isn't it? On the other hand, with millionaires buying their way onto space launches these days, they may not have missed it by so much after all.

• In "The Last Television Broadcast on Earth!" in *Mystery in Space* #22 (Nov 55), television was shown as outmoded as of April 8, 2065. The announcer signing off the final broadcast presented TV's history, including the introduction of wide-screen TV in 1970, with its first telecast showing the opening of the super-skyway that linked the East and West Coasts. He also reminded us how TV showed the landing of men on the moon in 1983, the landing on Mars in 2001 (and our greeting to the Martians), and the use of TV to present the underwater creatures we discovered on Venus. It also kept us up to date when Pluto invaded Earth in 2026. And we watched in 2029 as Saturn's rings suddenly hurtled off the planet and … oh, now, this is just getting silly! The reason TV was going away was even sillier, trust me. Still, it's a notable story in that it was one of the few stories to *underestimate* how quickly we'd reach the moon, which wasn't the way these stories tended to miss the mark.

• *Real Fact Comics* did considerably better predicting our broadcast future in "How Television Will Change Your Future!" in #15 (Jul-Aug 48). It showed how TV could be used in the classroom (although it didn't mention those pesky ads that seem to be included). It also expected broadcasts would help hunt down escaped criminals, which we mostly do through scheduled prime-time shows, although some cities are using TV to help find missing children, nearly mimicking this prediction. Using TVs to explore caves and deep seas also came darned close. Also dead on were the predictions for televising sporting events (although maybe not chess finals), showcasing products for purchase and even showing us the first man on the moon! OK, it missed on having that emergency "video" light blink to warn us when a hot news story was being broadcast, but the story has an amazingly good batting average.

TRIVIA CHALLENGE II
Category: **REAL NAMES**   What's the real name of the **COMPOSITE SUPERMAN?**   Answer on page 180   Answer from page 175 **TINO MANARRY**

178   **BABY BOOMER COMICS**

How various comics predicted the 21st Century...	FASHION FAUX PAS	TRAVEL UPDATES	MOST ACCURATE PREDICTION	LEAST ACCURATE PREDICTION
Superman #128 Apr 59 "Superman Vs. The Futuremen"	Police dressed in capes and finned helmets.	Time machines, personal spaceships	Superman will forget he was Superboy	Oceans will evaporate
Superman #300 Jun 76 "Superman 2001"	Waist-length capes for men and women.	Rocket ships landing at seaports.	Separate TV channels for news, finance, sports	Soviet Union still exists
2001: A Space Odyssey #1-10 1976-77	Tunics, space suits like Major Matt Mason's	Manned space travel to asteroids	Comics fans will be obsessive (#5)	Oh, just pick one
Morlock 2001 Feb 75 "The Coming of Morlock!"	Long sleeveless tunics	None; cars and trains still around	Trains still run through downtown	Thought police can kill you for owning books.
Weird Fantasy #8 Jul 51 "The Origin of the Species!"	Tight Speedos and long-sleeved shirts	Everyone travels in outer space	Archeologists still dig up the past	Uranium-vapor street lights
Weird Science #21 Oct 53 "Punishment Without Crime!"	Ascots, belted waist-length jackets, fedoras	NA	People argue over death penalty	Thinking robots

TRIVIA CHALLENGE II
Category: **REAL NAMES**   What's the real name of POISON IVY?   Answer on page 181

Answer on page 181

Answer from page 177
LENORA, INA

A CALL IN A LANGUAGE THAT IS UNDERSTOOD ONLY BY CHRIS KL-99, THE COLUMBUS OF SPACE ...

NYALA! NYALA DI LOND!

I'VE HEARD STAR-LANGUAGES MUCH LIKE THAT! IT'S A CALL FOR HELP!

WE CAN'T ANSWER IT UNLESS WE KNOW WHERE IT COMES FROM!

Chris KL-99 was one of DC's many space heroes of the 1950s.

© 1959 National Periodical Publications Inc. (DC).

• Many of DC's key space characters had adventures that took place in the "21st Century." They included private eye Star Hawkins and his secretary Ilda; Chris KL-99, the Columbus of the 21st Century; and Tommy Tomorrow, the Super-Planeteer. Since those adventures could still be 100 years off — Tommy's adventures were said to take place 100 years in the future — a lot could still happen in that time to make them accurate. But unless they dig some soon, I doubt Tommy's going to have to worry about floods in the Martian canals, as he was shown doing in *Action Comics* #238 (Mar 58).

Technically, Tommy began his adventures in "The Columbus of Space" (not to be confused with Chris KL-99) in *Real Fact Comics* #6 (Feb 47). The story presented what the future would be like "based on authentic modern forecasts." This optimistic scenario told us that "schoolboys of the year 2000 will be as familiar with [Tommy's] hop to Mars as they are with Columbus's voyage to America." Sadly, with the beating Columbus has taken these days, they may be right.

THUS, WHEN THE NEXT HOT-JET RACE FROM EARTH TO THE MOON BEGINS, TOMMY TOMORROW'S SWIFT "SPACE-ACE" IS WAITING...

COLONEL TOMORROW CALLING ALL PATROL SHIPS! HERE THEY COME-- GET THOSE SPACE-BLOCKS UP TO CLEAR THE LANES, AND THEN STAND BY!

I HOPE THIS WORKS, SO WE CAN GET BACK ON OUR OTHER ASSIGNMENT.

Tommy Tomorrow was another one of DC's many space heroes of the 1950s, but he was more "Silver Age" than Chris: His initials were the same.

© 1959 National Periodical Publications Inc. (DC).

Tommy went to Rocket College in 1954 and was chosen to be the first man on Mars in 1958. He dug up Martian dinosaur bones under a flowering tree (based on authentic forecasts!) and returned to a ticker-tape parade on Earth, as well he should. His next adventure, in *Real Fact* #8 (May 47), took us up to 1967, when Colonel Tommy mined uranium on the moon. By *Real Fact* #13 (Mar-Apr 48), we'd skipped ahead to 1998 and Tommy was flying off to Venus. *Real Fact* did better when it stuck to TV predictions.

Just because we're now in the 21st Century doesn't mean that comics' days of predicting our specific futures are past, of course. Lots of old comics pushed things ahead 100 years. So we still can look forward to Killraven's Martian-conquered world in 2018, as vividly brought to life in *Amazing Adventures*' "War of the Worlds" extrapolation beginning with #18 (May 73). There also will be "The Future Blackhawks" from *Blackhawk* #147 (Apr 60) showing up in 2060, with their nifty headbands with the keystone-shaped decorations at their center and some nifty disintegrator guns.

And let's not forget all those Imaginary Stories, such as "Lana Lang's Romance With Superman III!" in *Lois Lane* #36 (Oct 62), in which Lana traveled into the future and fell in love with Superman's grandson. If Supes got married in 1962, his grandson could be coming along any time now, so we'd better start building those robot police the story showed. The same is true of "Lois Lane's Outlaw Son!" who appeared in *Lois Lane* #46 (Jan 64) after Lois married Lex Luthor and they had a son. He in turn grew up to cruise through space and wear one of those ascots that always tells us we're in DC's future.

OK, OK, I know. Those are only Imaginary stories. Heck, aren't they all? We certainly better hope they are. I'm not wearing an ascot unless I get a spaceship.

TRIVIA CHALLENGE II
Category: **REAL NAMES**

What's the real name of THE TRAPSTER?

Answer on page 182

Answer from page 178
JOE MEACH

Missed It By That Much

Sometimes when comics went back to the future, they targeted a date we've already been to. Here's how well they did:

@ "Martian Infiltration!" from *Weird Fantasy* #3 (marked #15, Sep-Oct 50) related the dramatic events of June 20, 1960, when we first learned that Martians were on Earth preparing for an invasion. (In fact, they were actually Venusians, but let's not get into it.)

@ "The Mysterious Ray From Another Dimension!" in *Weird Fantasy* #4 (marked #16, Nov-Dec 50) looks 20 years ahead to 1970, when "skirts are now back to above the knee" and TV is driving radio out of existence. Pretty good so far, but then we learned that the radiation given off by TVs was making everyone disappear.

@ "Child of Tomorrow!" in *Weird Fantasy* #5 (marked #17, Jan-Feb 51) began with atomic bombs destroying most of the country on July 4, 1971. I think I'd remember that.

@ "By George!" in *Weird Fantasy* #15 (Sep-Oct 52) predicted that two archeologists would find a cube with alien languages on it from a crashed spaceship in Beirut, Lebanon, in October 1972. I can't prove they didn't, but I'm betting the truth is out there.

"The Mysterious Ray From Another Dimension!" was actually the radiation from the cathode ray tube of early televisions as shown in **Weird Fantasy** *#4.*

@ In "The Comet Peril!" in *Mystery In Space* #2 (Jun-Jul 51), Halley's Comet pulled Earth out of its orbit when it shot by in 1986. That didn't come about, but there will always be the next time to worry about.

@ *Space: 1999*, produced by Charlton for eight issues in 1975-76, showed what life would be like on Moonbase Alpha. Since this was an extrapolation from the TV show, it's not really fair to blame the comic for getting us so far in only 24 years.

@ My favorite, and maybe the most famous miss: *Strange Adventures* #117 (Jun 60) showed how World War III, the Atomic War, began on October 9, 1986, killing all plants and most animals and leading to chaos. Fortunately, Sgt. Gardner Grayle and a handful of others banded together to prevent thugs from taking over, thanks to a set of knights' armor that was atomically strengthened to resist radiation. Thus was formed the Atomic Knights, who battled evilness to help devastated America through *SA* #160 and in reprints in *SA* #217-231. It was a fun series, even if they did miss it by that much.

Gardner Grayle was one of the lucky ones, surviving the October 1986 atomic war that devastated America. You don't remember that one? Gee, it was in all the papers, not to mention **Strange Adventures** *#117 (Jun 60).*

TRIVIA CHALLENGE II
Category: **REAL NAMES**   *What's the real name of MR. HYDE?*   Answer on page 183   Answer from page 179
PAMELA ISLEY

THE CURIOUS CASE OF THE QUIRKY COMICS!   **181**

Twice-Told Tales!

"I really loved the story, 'The Last Days of Superman' in *Superman* #156 (Oct 62), especially the part where Supergirl grieved as Superman was dying. But my brother said Supergirl wasn't even in the story! I know he's wrong — heck, Supergirl was right there on the cover! But why would he argue?"

A special issue focusing on the physically handicapped had similar themes (and nearly identical final pages) in **All-Star Comics** #27 (above) and **Justice League of America** #36 (below).

He argued because in fact, you're both right. "The Last Days of Superman" is one of a number of stories from early in Superman's career that were rewritten and redrawn, sometimes in expanded form, and republished during the Silver Age. And we're not talking a handful of stories, either. A group of dedicated fans have identified more than *50* Superman Family stories that were updated and reused during the Silver Age.

The rewrites mostly were the work of Superman editor Mort Weisinger, but they didn't affect just Superman. In fact, several members of the fan-favorite Legion of Super-Heroes team were introduced to the DC universe in stories that originally featured other characters in those roles.

Several other editors redid stories in interesting ways, too. For instance, Julius Schwartz had Gardner Fox rewrite *All-Star Comics* #27 (Fall 45) for use as *Justice League of America* #36 (Jun 65). He changed the details but picked up the main theme of teaming with handicapped boys and included a redrawn version of *All Star*'s final-page salute to FDR, Helen Keller, Beethoven, John Milton, and Demosthenes. He also has said he used Golden Age Hawkman stories featuring The Raven and The Ghost as the basis for Silver Age Hawkman stories.

His most quirky rewrite, however, came in the Silver Age *Flash* only two issues apart (#159 and #161), when he showed how two writers would address the same cover idea in different ways. (For more on this quirk, see page 196.)

Romance and funny-animal editor Lawrence Nadle also was said to redo stories during his tenure. The Superman reruns began while Weisinger was serving as story editor under Executive Editor Whitney Ellsworth. But once Weisinger became full editor of the Superman line in 1959, the remakes came faster and faster.

Michael L. Fleisher, author of *The Great Superman Book* encyclopedia, noted some of these repeats. But he didn't catch them all, because his book was limited in the titles and time period it documented. The *Overstreet Comic Book Price Guide* even commented on the trend, noting that the story in which Superboy meets Jor-El's robot Metalman in *Adventure Comics* #276 (Sep 60) was "similar" to *Superboy* #49 (Jun 56).

Even now, there no doubt are more that haven't been found because of the age of the original comics and the need to know both stories to find a match. It takes a devoted fan to notice when a Tommy Tomorrow story in *Action Comics* is redone eight years later as a Jimmy Olsen story in his own mag!

© 1945 National Periodical Publications Inc. (DC)

© 1965 National Periodical Publications Inc. (DC)

TRIVIA CHALLENGE II
Category: **TITLES**

"The Man Who Broke the Time Barrier" was the back-up in what issue? Answer on page 184

Answer from page 180
PETER PETRUSKI

Fortunately, comics fandom has such devoted historians. The late comics fan Rich Morrissey collected many of the duplications, based on his own research plus help from Edwin Murray, Bob Hughes, Jon Ingersoll, and Paul Levitz. That's a true Hall of Fame of comics fandom! In all, the group has found 53 duplicated stories so far (see the chart).

These aren't just stories with similar themes, like Superman hiding the effects Red K has had on him or creating a hoax to confuse people about his secret identity. A list like that would fill this book and a sequel. No, these stories replicate major plot points or complete storylines, often using the same scenes if not the exact pacing.

There are three basic types of twice-told tales. Basic plot ideas often were recycled with new specifics, such as a new ending, changes in key events, or substituting key cast members. An example, which also added plenty of new material, is "The Last Days of Superman." In the first version, a 13-pager in *Superman* #66 (Sep-Oct 50), Clark Kent became ill and decided he had only one month to live thanks to his repeated exposure to kryptonite.

Dr. Superman didn't share that expert diagnosis with his friends, but they learned that Clark wasn't long for this world. He spent his time performing super-stunts to aid humanity (while Clark's friends hid from him their knowledge that he was dying), and he burned a final message for Earth into the face of the moon that revealed his secret identity.

In the 25-page version in *Superman* #156 (Oct 62), it was Superman who became ill and from his deathbed directed more elaborate activities, carried out by Supergirl, The Legion, and Lori Lemaris. He again burned (the same) message into the moon's face. Ultimately, his recovery in both stories came from the same source, with Jimmy Olsen substituting for a generic character the first time around. Both stories ended with Supes wiping his secret identity off his moon message.

The second type of remake occurred when the original plot was left intact but was expanded to add new developments or different twists. The introduction of (gasp!) Legionnaire Mon-El fell into this category. In "Superman's Lost Brother" in *Superman* #80 (Jan-Feb 53), Supes discovered a man had crashed-landed on Earth with a star map from Jor-El that called the man, "my son." Halk Kar had amnesia, but ultimately, he and Superman discovered that Halk had simply visited Krypton and received the chart Jor-El intended to use to soon send his only son to Earth.

When that 10-pager was rewritten into a 19-pager to introduce Mon-El in "Superboy's Big Brother" in *Superboy* #89 (Jun 61), Mon replaced Halk and added some adventures. He took on a secret identity and accompanied Clark to school, and Superman's concern over Halk's fading powers was replaced with Superboy's suspicions that Mon-El was scamming him. The ending changed, too, since Halk wound up leaving in his spaceship while Mon landed in the Phantom Zone for a thousand years.

In "The Last Days of Superman!" in **Superman** #66, Clark Kent thought he was dying and set out as Superman to make his final mark on humanity. In **Superman** #156, it was Superman who was dying, and he received deathbed help from all his super-pals.

TRIVIA CHALLENGE II
Category: **TITLES**
What's the name of the first story featuring GREEN LANTERN?
Answer on page 185
Answer from page 181
CALVIN ZABO

THE CURIOUS CASE OF THE QUIRKY COMICS!
183

It's everybody's worst nightmare — not only did Superman owe a billion dollars in taxes, but he owed it twice! Dueling splash pages appeared in "Superman's Billion-Dollar Debt" in **Superman** #114 and "Superman Owes a Billion Dollars" in **Superman** #148.

Other Legionnaires also were introduced in remade stories. When "Lana Lang's Romance on Mars," in *Adventure* #195 (Dec 53) was redone as "Lana Lang and the Legion of Super-Heroes" in *Adventure* #282 (Mar 61), Lana's pretend crush to make Superboy jealous shifted from Marsboy to the new Legionnaire, Star Boy. A similar reworking came when "The Two Clark Kents" from *Adventure* #191 (Aug 53) was rewritten as "Secret of the Seventh Super-Hero" in *Adventure* #290 (Nov 61) with Sun Boy, not Clark Kent, impersonated by a criminal.

The final category of redone tales consists of basic rewrites, in which the story is essentially retold with some minor updates, mostly to supporting characters or with a few new replacement scenes. An example is "Superman's Billion-Dollar Debt" in *Superman* #114 (Jul 57), which was redone as "Superman Owes a Billion Dollars" in *Superman* #148 (Oct 61). In both, an IRS man wanted Superman to pay back taxes. The individual ways Superman made money differed — and in the second version included Bizarro, Aquaman, and Lori Lemaris — but the resolution was identical.

A related situation arose even more often when key scenes inspired scenes in later stories. A prime example is "The Babe of Steel" in *Superman* #66 (Sep-Oct 50). Two scenes feature baby Superman demolishing a police sergeant's desk and then using his X-ray vision while being pushed in a baby stroller by Lois Lane. They were redone (as the covers no less) for "The Babe of Steel" in *Action* #284 (Jan 62) and "Lois Lane's Revenge on Superman" in *Lois Lane* #32 (Apr 62) — just three months apart.

Morrissey suggested that the repeats can be considered to be adventures of the Earth-1 Superman that mimic earlier adventures of the Earth-2 Superman. But since there was no Earth-2 Superboy, about the only explanation for his repeats is Hypertime, DC's latest attempt at claiming all the stories it ever published really "happened" without having to find a way to fit them into its hopelessly disconnected and continually revamped continuity. That never seems to satisfy anyone, Earth-2 advocates or post-*Crisis* fans.

A key question to ask is, why would Weisinger recycle these stories? The best answer is, why not? They weren't plagiarized, since DC owned the originals. And they weren't being done to save money, since Weisinger reassigned the stories to be rewritten rather than simply handing the old script to an artist.

Updating old stories probably wouldn't be noticed by readers, since the conventional wisdom was that the comics readership turned over about every five years as kids lost interest in comics and new ones grew into them. The need to create so many short, punchy stories for titles that often featured three tales per issue generated a demand that might have been hard to meet some months.

Of course, it's possible Weisinger had ulterior motives in reusing these plots. According to research that identifies story writers, led by fan Martin O'Hearn, it appears Weisinger seldom gave the rewrite to the original's author. Writers from that time say it was Weisinger's style to disparage his writers' story ideas and then suggest those ideas to another writer as if they were his own creations, to show the writers that he was more creative than they were. There's no doubt that Weisinger had a pretty overbearing attitude toward the creators he worked with and often belittled them.

But Weisinger didn't hide the rewrites, either, often using similar if not duplicated titles. One rewrite even was acknowledged on a letters page when a fan wrote in to point it out, and some early house ads for 80-page Giants mention "updated" stories. Sometimes, the rewrites were done surprisingly quickly — a story from *Lois Lane* #7 (Feb 59) was rewritten with virtually the same title only one year and 12 issues later. Most rewrites came five to 15 years later.

To be sure, giving the same plotline to a different writer was certain to produce a different spin on the original idea, no matter how specific the plot synopsis. And in some cases, the artist who did the original was given the rewrite, and he easily could have remembered doing the earlier story. In some cases, similar character or prop designs indicate the artists definitely saw the original and replicated some scenes while doing the rerun.

A number of Superman comics stories also were rewritten for use in the newspaper strip and vice versa. Morrissey and friends have identified at least six newspaper sequences that were redone as comics stories and eight comics stories redone as newspaper sequences.

Think such concepts are the product of a bygone era? Think again. When John Byrne restarted Superman in 1986, he took several key themes from the original Bizarro story in *Superboy* #68 (Oct-Nov 58) for his "The Mirror, Crack'd" in *Man of Steel* #5 (Aug 86) mini-series. And to reintroduce Lori Lemaris, Byrne essentially combined "The Girl in Superman's Past" from *Superman* #129 (May 59) with "Superman's Mermaid Sweetheart" in *Superman* #135 (Feb 60) to create "Lost Love" in *Superman* (second series) #12 (Dec 87).

Later on, Byrne created the 13-part *Spider-Man Chapter One* series, which offered a late-1990s version of Spider-Man's earliest stories for new audiences. Even more recently, Marvel's *Ultimate Spider-Man* comic has told Spider-Man's history yet again, changing some parts and keepings others intact. In that case, at least, the character was said to be an entirely different entity, so there was no attempt to suggest that this hero's history was the official version — at least, not yet there hasn't been.

Ironically, many Silver Age fans are up in arms over Byrne remaking 30-year-old stories, yet they loved the five- to 15-year-old Superman stories that were redone into Silver Age classics. No doubt, that's at least in part because those fans didn't know they were reading remakes, since the originals weren't as readily available as the Spidey comics now are. It just shows that it's a different kind of comics world out there today.

*"The Babe of Steel!" in **Superman** #66 featured a number of fun scenes, including Superbaby smashing a police sergeant's desk and Lois wheeling him in a baby carriage. They were so good, they were reused as the covers to **Action** #284 and **Lois Lane** #32.*

TRIVIA CHALLENGE II
Category: **TITLES**   **What character debuted in "The Creature from Kosmos"?**   Answer on page 187   Answer from page 183
"SOS GREEN LANTERN"

THE CURIOUS CASE OF THE QUIRKY COMICS!   **185**

Twice-Told Superman Tales

This list was compiled by Rich Morrissey, with help from Edwin Murray, Michael L. Fleisher, Paul Levitz, Bob Hughes, and Jon Ingersoll. The stories are listed in chronological order of their second version, to show how frequently those Silver Age favorites relied on earlier stories.

"The Man Who Could See Tomorrow" *Superboy* #1 [Mar-Apr 49]	...reuses the **PLOT from...**	**"That Old Class of Superboy's"** *Superman* #46 [May-Jun 47]
"The Statues That Came To Life" *Action* #146 [Jul 50]	...reuses the **PLOT from...**	**"Superman's Super-Self"** *World's Finest* #28 [May-Jun 47]
"Superman's Hunt for Clark Kent" *Superman* #126 [Jan 59]	...**EXPANDS** the story...	**"Superman's Search for Clark Kent"** *Superman* #32 [Jan-Feb 45]
"The Super-Servant of Crime" *Superman* #130 [Jul 59]	...reuses the **PLOT from...**	**"The Man Who Bossed Superman"** *Superman* #51 [Mar-Apr 48]
"The Super-Clown of Metropolis" *Superman* #136 [Apr 60]	...reuses the **PLOT from...**	**"The Man Who Couldn't Laugh"** *Superman* #56 [Jan-Feb 49]
"The Day Lois Forgot Superman" *Lois Lane* #19 [Aug 60]	...reuses the **PLOT from...**	**"When Lois Lane Forgot Superman"** *Lois Lane* #7 [Feb 59]

Our Super pal thought he had a big brother when he found someone crash-landed on Earth with a map from Jor-El. In "Superman's Big Brother" in **Superman** #80, Halk Kar had the map...

...while in "Superboy's Big Brother" in **Superboy** #89, it was Mon-El.

"Superman's Flight from Lois Lane" *Lois Lane* #20 [Oct 60]	...is a **REWRITE of...**	**"Superman's Other Life"** *Superman* #84 [Sep-Oct 53]
"Voyage to Dimension X" *Action* #271 [Dec 60]	...reuses the **PLOT from...**	**"Destination X"** *Superman* #83 [Jul-Aug 53]
"The Mystery of Mighty Boy" *Superboy* #85 [Dec 60]	...is a **REWRITE of...**	**"The Power-Boy from Earth"** *Superboy* #52 [Oct 56]
"The Flame-Dragon from Krypton" *Superman* #142 [Jan 61]	...reuses the **PLOT from...**	**"The Beast from Krypton"** *Superman* #78 [Sep-Oct 52]
"Lois Lane's X-Ray Vision" *Lois Lane* #22 [Jan 61]	...**EXPANDS** the story...	**"Lois Lane's X-Ray Vision"** *Action* #202 [Mar 55]
"Superman's Rival, Mental Man" *Action* #272 [Jan 61]	...**EXPANDS** the story...	**"The Adventures of Mental-Man"** *Action* #196 [Sep 54]
"The Great Superman Hoax" *Superman* #143 [Feb 61]	...is a **REWRITE of...**	**"Paul Paxton Alias Superman"** *Action* #213 [Feb 56]

TRIVIA CHALLENGE II
Category: **POTPOURRI** — What forms the mask for FORBUSH MAN?
Answer on page 188

Answer from page 184
GROTESQUE

"Lana Lang & the Legion of Super-Heroes" *Adventure* #282 [Mar 61]	**...is a REWRITE of...**	**"Lana Lang's Romance on Mars"** *Adventure* #195 [Dec 53]
"The War Between Supergirl and the Supermen Emergency Squad" *Action* #276 [May 61]	**...reuses the PLOT from...**	**"Superman's Exposed Identity"** *Action* #237 [Feb 58]
"Superboy's Big Brother" *Superboy* #89 [Jun 61]	**...EXPANDS the story...**	**"Superboy's Big Brother"** *Superman* #80 [Jan-Feb 53]
"The Rejected Super-Tot" *Superboy* #90 [Jul 61]	**...reuses the PLOT from...**	**"The Mighty Mite"** *Superman* #73 [Nov-Dec 51]
"The Great Mento" *Superman* #147 [Aug 61]	**...is a REWRITE of...**	**"The Man Who Could Read Superman's Mind"** *Superman* #103 [Feb 56]
"The Monster That Loved Aqua-Jimmy" *Jimmy Olsen* #55 [Sep 61]	**...is a REWRITE of...**	**"The Copy-Cat Creature"** *Adventure* #244 [Jan 58]
"The 20th-Century Achilles" *Superman* #148 [Oct 61]	**...reuses the PLOT from...**	**"Achilles versus Superman"** *Superman* #63 [Mar-Apr 50]
"Superman Owes a Billion Dollars" *Superman* #148 [Oct 61]	**...is a REWRITE of...**	**"Superman's Billion-Dollar Debt"** *Superman* #114 [Jul 57]
"Lois Lane's Super-Lesson" *Lois Lane* #28 [Oct 61]	**...is a REWRITE of...**	**"Lois Lane's Royal Romance"** *Superman* #68 [Jan-Feb 51]

In **Superman** (second series) #12, John Byrne continued a Silver Age tradition when he let Lori Lemaris dump the new Superman...

... pretty much the same way she dumped the Earth-1 Superman in **Superman** (first series) #135. Fortunately, the Earth-2 Superman didn't have a Lori Lemaris to dump him.

"The Man Who Saved Kal-El's Life" *Action* #281 [Oct 61]	**...EXPANDS the story...**	**"The Man Who Went to Krypton"** *Superman* #77 [Jul-Aug 52]
"Secret of the Seventh Super-Hero" *Adventure* #290 [Nov 61]	**...EXPANDS the story...**	**"The Two Clark Kents"** *Adventure* #191 [Aug 53]
"The Great Super-Hunt" *Superboy* #93 [Dec 61]	**...is a REWRITE of...**	**"The Man of Steel's Super-Manhunt"** *Superman* #59 [Jul-Aug 49]
"Superboy's Romance with Cleopatra" *Adventure* #291 [Dec 61]	**...is a REWRITE of...**	**"Superboy and Cleopatra"** *Adventure* #183 [Dec 52]
"When the World Forgot Superman" *Superman* #150 [Jan 62]	**...is a REWRITE of...**	**"The City That Forgot Superman"** *Superman* #59 [Jul-Aug 49]

TRIVIA CHALLENGE II
 Category: **POTPOURRI** | What's the more familiar name of Able Company's First Attack Squad? Answer on page 189 | Answer from page 185
 THE WASP

Faithful readers of "There Is No Superboy!" in **Superboy** #50 probably experienced déjà vu all over again...

© 1956 National Periodical Publications Inc. (DC)

"The Laughingstock of Smallville" *Adventure* #292 (Jan 62) — *...is a* **REWRITE of...** — **"The Six Elements of Crime"** *Superman* #68 (Jan-Feb 51)

"The Duel of the Superboys" *Adventure* #295 (Apr 62) — *...is a* **REWRITE of...** — **"The Duel of the Superboys"** *Adventure* #175 (Apr 52)

"The Secret of the Superman Stamp" *Superman* #153 (May 62) — *...is a* **REWRITE of...** — **"The Superman Stamp"** *Superman* #91 (Aug 54)

"The Super-Practical Joker" *Action* #289 (Jun 62) — *...is a* **REWRITE of...** — **"The Practical Joker"** *Superman* #95 (Feb 55)

"The Fat Boy of Steel" *Adventure* #298 (Jul 62) — *...is a* **REWRITE of...** — **""The Super-Fat Boy of Steel"** *Superboy* #24 (Feb-Mar 53)

"The New Superman" *Action* #291 (Aug 62) — *...EXPANDS the story...* — **"The New Superman"** *Action* #181 (Jun 53)

"The Man Who Owned Superboy's Costume" *Superboy* #99 (Sep 62) — *...reuses the* **PLOT from...** — **"The Amazing Adventures of Superboy's Costume"** *Superboy* #44 (Oct 55)

"The Doom that Destroyed Clark Kent" *Superboy* #99 (Sep 62) — *...is a* **REWRITE of...** — **"The Death of Young Clark Kent"** *Superboy* #19 (Apr-May 52)

"The Last Days of Superman" *Superman* #156 (Oct 62) — *...reuses the* **PLOT from...** — **"The Last Days of Superman"** *Superman* #66 (Sep-Oct 50)

"Superboy Meets Steelboy" *Adventure* #302 (Nov 62) — *...is a* **REWRITE of...** — **"Superboy Meets Superlad"** *Adventure* #199 (Apr 54)

"The Kryptonian Courtship" *Lois Lane* #39 (Feb 63) — *...reuses the* **PLOT from...** — **"The Courtship on Krypton"** *Action* #149 (Oct 50)

"Clark Kent, Coward" *Action* #298 (Mar 63) — *...is a* **REWRITE of...** — **"The City Under the Sea"** *Superman* #67 (Nov-Dec 50)

"The Trial of Superman" *Action* #301 (Jun 63) — *...is a* **REWRITE of...** — **"The People vs. Superman"** *Superman* #62 (Jan-Feb 50)

TRIVIA CHALLENGE II
Category: **POTPOURRI** — Who spoke at PETER PARKER's high school graduation? — Answer on page 190

Answer from page 186
A POT

STILL UNAWARE OF **SUPERBOY'S** TRUE POWERS, THE MOBSTERS ALL GANG UP ON HIM AT ONCE...TO THEIR SORROW...

CHINS READY? WHY WASTE TIME? **ONE** ROUNDHOUSE PUNCH AND YOU **ALL** KISS THE CANVAS!

YEOWWW! SOMEBODY DROPPED A BOMB ON US!

...when they read "There Is No Superboy!" in **Superboy** #123 and saw the Boy of Steel take on a bunch of hoods in the boxing ring.

"The Amazing Confession of Super-Perry White" *Action* #302 (Jul 63)	...is a **REWRITE** of...	**"The Two Identities of Superman"** *Superman* #60 (Sep-Oct 49)
"The Interplanetary Olympics" *Action* #304 (Sep 63)	...reuses the **PLOT** from...	**"The Interplanetary Olympics"** *Action* #220 (Sep 56)
"Lana Lang, Movie Star" *Adventure* #312 (Sep 63)	...is a **REWRITE** of...	**"Lana Lang, Movie Star"** *Superboy* #18 (Feb-Mar 52)
"The Mystery of Sorcery Boy" *Superboy* #108 (Oct 63)	...reuses the **PLOT** from...	**"The Secret of the Golden Coins"** *Superboy* #15 (Jul-Aug 51)
"The Superboy of 800 Years Ago" *Superboy* #113 (Jun 64)	...is a **REWRITE** of...	**"Superboy's Double"** *Superboy* #17 (Nov-Dec 51)
"Super-Mxyzptlk-Hero" *Superman* #174 (Jan 65)	...reuses the **PLOT** from...	**"Mr. Mxyztplk, Hero"** *Superman* #62 (Jan-Feb 50)
"The Millionaire of Smallville" *Superboy* #119 (Mar 65)	...is a **REWRITE** of...	**"Superboy, Millionaire"** *Adventure* #159 (Dec 50)
"The Menace Called 'It' " *Superman* #172 (May 65)	...is a **REWRITE** of...	**"It"** *Action* #162 (Nov 51)
"Clark Kent's Butler" *Superboy* #122 (Jul 65)	...reuses the **PLOT** from...	**"Clark Kent's Private Butler"** *Adventure* #169 (Oct 51)
"There Is No Superboy" *Superboy* #123 (Sep 65)	...reuses the **PLOT** from...	**"There Is No Superboy"** *Superboy* #50 (Jul 56)
"Clark Kent's Masquerade as Superman" *Action* #331 (Dec 65)	...is a **REWRITE** of...	**"Superman's Secret Revealed"** *Superman* #20 (Jan-Feb 43)
"Jimmy Olsen's Journey to Nowhere" *Jimmy Olsen* #92 (Apr 66)	...is a **REWRITE** of...	**"Destination Unknown"** with Tommy Tomorrow in *Action* #246 (Nov 58)
"Clark Kent, Assassin" *Superman* #229 (Aug 70)	...is a **REWRITE** of...	**"Clark Kent, Man of Mystery"** *Superman* #117 (Nov 57)

TRIVIA CHALLENGE II
Category: **POTPOURRI**   **What did MA and PA KENT die of?**   Answer on page 191

Answer from page 187
HOWLING COMMANDOS

The Mopee Awards!

"You've got to admit that not every single Silver Age comic was a classic, right? I mean, there had to be a couple of losers in there somewhere. Didn't there?"

Curses! You've found me out. It's true that a heckuva lot of Silver Age comics featured stories that were true classics —heck, sometimes there were two or three in an issue! But I have to admit that, on occasion, in their haste to tell those great tales and ship those incredible mags to us eager kids, the creators let something slip past them that they might not have let go by if they'd had another night to sleep on it.

Should we linger on these sometimes embarrassing, sometimes hilarious missteps in classic comics history? Nah. Mr. Silver Age is very, very aware that nobody is great every time out. But should we perhaps mention some of the all-time laughers, the stories that left us with a tear in our eye, a lump in our throat, and a throbbing pain in our temple as we tried to figure out what the heck was going on? Oh, yeah.

Never one to pass up a chance to sing the praises of Silver Age stories or laugh at a favorite funny book when the opportunity presents itself, Mr. Silver Age hereby announces the winners of the first-ever Mopee Awards. Named for the dweeby little elf from *The Flash* #167 (Feb 67) who claimed to be the source of the lightning bolt that gave Barry Allen his powers, these honors go to those stories that made us readers roll on the floor in laughter or shake our heads and say, "No way!"

We're not talking about the obvious losers out there, the off-brand jokers put out by publishers who didn't quite get it or about Marvel or DC's second- (or seventh-) tier B'wana Beast wannabes. Nor are we talking about the "Bob Banner" kind of misstatements that Stan Lee notoriously committed. No, we're saving our Mopees for the big cheeses, the all-time flameouts.

And the following cheeses are pretty flaming, if you know what I mean. But don't take my word for it. Here are the first six winners of the coveted Mopee Award. These half dozen were selected primarily because they were the first ones that came to mind and because they had Mr. Silver Age rolling on the floor in laughter again when he reread them. You can't beat a 12¢ value like that.

*Mopee, who billed himself as a Heavenly Helpmate, was introduced in "The Real Origin of The Flash," in **The Flash** #167 (Feb 67). The little nebbish has never been written out of continuity since.*

THE NAME'S MOPEE-- INITIATE TENTH CLASS OF THE HEAVENLY HELP-MATES!

THEN--YOU ARE RE-SPONSIBLE FOR RE-MOVING MY AURA?! BUT WHY'D YOU WANT TO DO THAT?

?...TY!

TRIVIA CHALLENGE II
Category: **POTPOURRI**

Whose house did SUE and REED move into after they were married? Answer on page 192

Answer from page 188
J. JONAH JAMESON

190   BABY BOOMER COMICS

The **"By Jove, Holmes, You've Done It Again!"** **Award** to: "The Two Boys of Steel!" in *Superboy* #63 (Mar 58). I'm a big believer in conventions. You say Batman can create a rubber mask that perfectly resembles some two-bit hood and hides his pointy ears so he can wear his cowl underneath? No problemo. Wally (Kid Flash) West has a ring with a nozzle on it with such pinpoint accuracy that it can alternately dye his hair brown to red to brown to disguise his identity every time he opens the ring (which also holds his uniform in a compressed form)? I'm with ya all the way. Just don't make it the pivotal point of the story, okay? Because this stuff just doesn't hold up to a lot of scrutiny.

And thus we have the key reason I was spitting Nehi across the room as I read this titanic (in more ways than one) tale. The basic setup was this: Clark was on the Kent's roof working on a kryptonite experiment during a thunderstorm, wearing a coat his Uncle Frank left after his last visit. The experiment went bad, Clark got knocked to the ground, and he lost both his glasses and his memory. Dazed, he ran off into the stormy night.

Hours later, a soaked, amnesiac Clark knocked on his next-door neighbor's door, and Lana Lang opened it. Did she say, "Clark, why are you all wet and not wearing your glasses?" I'm afraid not. Did she say, "Superboy, why are you all wet and wearing an old coat?" Nope. She said, "Ma, there's a boy out here in trouble!"

They opened their door to this mysterious stranger, who didn't even know who he was himself. Lana was puzzled. "I know everyone in town! No one wears a jacket like that! Who can he be?"

That Lana, a whiz with jackets but a little dim with faces. How big is this burg that she's catalogued the coats? A page later, after the lad lifted a piano and took off his wet sweatshirt to reveal Superboy's costume (including a cape stuffed down his pants, padding out Clark's butt), Lana deduced one of the stranger's identities. She helped the Boy of Steel create a new civilian disguise, which included a pencil-thin mustache that must've looked dashing on a 15-year-old boy. (Fortunately, she didn't think to add glasses.)

Does it really matter where this story went from here? Not to me. Lana, it's my pleasure to present you with the first-ever Mopee Award. It'll look just grand sitting on your desk, right next to your Smallville Outerwear flash cards.

The **"Goldilocks Is My Real Estate Agent"** **Award** to: "A House There Was!" in *Fantastic Four* #88 (Jul 69). I should've known this story would be a little loopy when the splash page featured Mr. Fantastic reaching out to the reader with his right arm, to which was attached his left hand. Full-page drawings of impossible anatomy are sure signs that a tale is heading south.

Reed actually was reaching out to his newborn son Franklin, whose birth spurred the Fantastic Four to go house-hunting. The house they found was secluded, which was good, but it was kind of weird, which was bad. So ol'

Lana "Sherlock" Lang didn't recognize Clark without his glasses or Superboy in a sweatshirt, leading to mayhem and wackiness in **Superboy** #63. And the Silver Age was just getting started!

Mister Silver Age Reluctantly Recommends...

Fantastic Four (1st series) #88

Marvel Jul 1969

Cover artists: Jack Kirby, Joe Sinnott

"A House There Was!" **Writer:** Stan Lee **Penciller:** Jack Kirby **Inker:** Joe Sinnott

Then 12¢ Now $22

Reprints appear in... • Marvel's Greatest Comics #70

TRIVIA CHALLENGE II Category: **POTPOURRI** *Who joined the JLA in "Doom of the Star Diamond"?* Answer on page 193 Answer from page 189 **FEVER PLAGUE**

THE CURIOUS CASE OF THE QUIRKY COMICS! 191

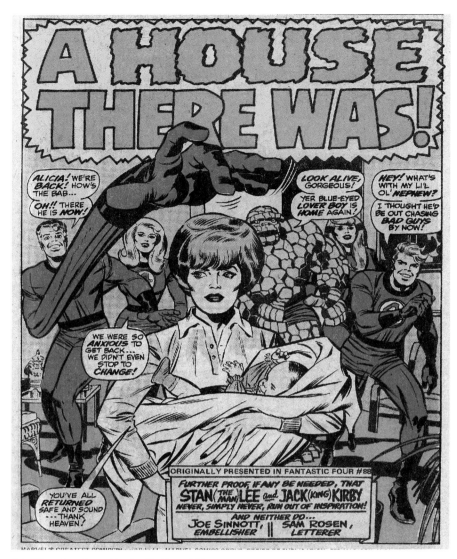

*Mr. Silver Age knew **Fantastic Four** #88 was gonna be a little loopy when Reed stuck his left hand on his right arm on the splash page. But nothing prepared him for how the FF "bought" their new house!*
© 1969 Marvel

suspicious Reed asked Sue how she found it. She explained "an ordinary real estate agent" told her of it. "He said it's been here for months! No one knows who built it or why! Let's go in, Reed! He said we could see it any time!"

How do "ordinary real estate agents" in the Marvel universe get their listings? By waiting outside a home for several months until there's no sign of activity and then jimmying the lock? This house definitely was not for sale, as it was owned by (what a coincidence) a long-time Marvel villain, who definitely did not want The FF moving in. Yet, somehow, Mr. & Mrs. Fantastic bought it! And moved in! And after it started attacking them, Reed decided to stay and solve the mystery! It was solved when the bad guy suddenly appeared (in his own house) and started pounding on them. I don't think that's even against the law.

Congratulations on winning a Mopee, guys. I'm sure you'll find the perfect spot for it in your house. Just don't forget to take it with you when the home's real owner returns!

The "Another Cunning Plan Gone Awry" Award to: "In The Coils of Copperhead!" in *The Brave & The Bold* #78 (Jun-Jul 68). To catch the Copperhead, the toughest, most baffling foe Batman had ever faced (he said), the World's Greatest Detective devised a cunning plan: He talked both Wonder Woman and Batgirl into pretending to be in love with him. Their continued catfights over the right to be his solo honey would appear to be so distracting to Bats that Copperhead would feel free to go on a crime spree—at which point, the Caped Crusader would nab him. Or so the theory went.

Thus we were treated to dueling sky-written love proclamations, contests to give Batman the best present, and such deathless dialogue as when Batgirl overtook Batman's whirlybat in her Batgirl-plane and purred, "Hi, there lover! The plane's on automatic, and I'm on the smooch beam!" Which was countered by Diana's memorable, "Let me show you how an Amazon kisses the one she adores!"

Holy hormones, where did Batman buy his cunning plans, Riverdale High School? But the true high point came when the crafty Copperhead fell for this brilliant scheme. Batman dropped his paramours to charge after him—and Wonder Woman and Batgirl grabbed him! They both had fallen in love with him for real and couldn't let him go! "What'd I do?" Batman moaned as two luscious ladies wrestled him to the ground. "It seemed such a foolproof plan!"

TRIVIA CHALLENGE II
Category: **POTPOURRI**

What is MILLIE THE MODEL's last name?

Answer on page 194

Answer from page 190
THE MOLE MAN's

192

BABY BOOMER COMICS

Cheer up, Caped Crusader. There are worse fates than having two super-heroines panting after your Bat-bod. And here's a Mopee Award to prove it.

The "Science Says You're Wrong If You Think This Makes Sense" Award

to: "Fate of the Flattened-Out Atom!" in *The Atom* #16 (Dec 64-Jan 65). Editor Julius Schwartz loved to use detailed pseudo-science to make his heroes' adventures seem more plausible. But sometimes that science didn't really get the job done.

In this story, a crook found he could use the "ato-energy" The Atom gave off when he was tiny to see a few minutes into the future. He captured the Mighty Mite to ensure a steady flow of energy to help with his crimes. And to release as much ato-energy as possible, he ironed the Atom flat! With an iron! The sole explanation given for this amazing feat was our crooked scientist saying, "This iron will not harm you in the least! It is designed to rearrange the atoms of your body in such a way that it will increase your outflow of ato-energy!"

Now, when it comes to Silver Age comics, I don't need a lot of mumbo-jumbo to be able to go with the flow. But geez, even dumb kids need *something* to work with! Especially since, after The Atom was sandwiched between two plates of glass to hold him still, we were treated to seven panels and 266 words (I counted) of our hero figuring out how to escape using his major internal (albeit flattened) organs! This featured him ruminating on lactose acid, the endocrine glands, and the adrenal glands (located on top of the kidneys, he helpfully pointed out) and how he could manipulate them all to cut off that darned ato-energy.

Frankly, I would have preferred a little less exploration of the wonders of the human body and a little more discussion of that nifty atomic appliance — which gave us our cover image, after all. But thanks to The Atom, I now know how to activate my adrenal glands. And if that's not worth a Mopee, then this comic grabs one for those scenes of our six-inch, paper-thin hero rolling himself up like a tube and then battling the villain with a hammer! (How'd he un-iron himself? He just did. Now, back to our adrenal glands…)

The "Stand Back! He's Got A Garden Hose!" Award

to: "Prisoner of the Plant Man!" in *Strange Tales* #121 (Jun 64). Sadly, "Strange Tales" is the perfect name for a book featuring The Human Torch's solo adventures. Mark Waid did a masterful job of summing up the series' goofiness in *Captain America: Sentinel of Liberty* #11 (Jul 99). In Waid's tale, based on *ST* #114 (Nov 63), Johnny Storm gleefully related to Cap the story of how the Torch battled a Cap imposter and the amount of money the guy must've lost even though he was robbing banks because of the huge cost for such handy equipment as an asbestos-lined truck.

Sadly, when the Torch's foes weren't clearing out the Asbestos "R" Us store in preparation for their battles, they were neutralizing this hero — who could

*Wonder Woman and Batgirl vied for Batman's affections in **The Brave & The Bold** #78 after Batman's cunning plan of having them both pretend to love him went awry — because they both fell in love with him for real. No, really.*

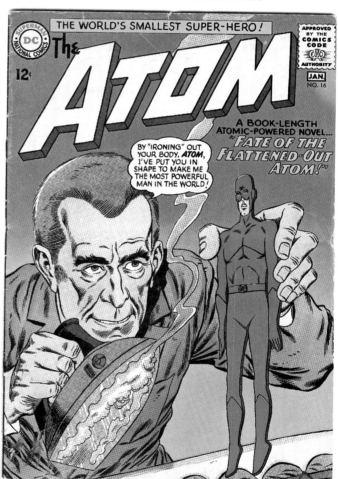

*Wanna know how this guy managed to iron the Tiny Titan flat in **The Atom** #16? Science says you're never gonna find out inside! But you do learn lots of fascinating facts about your adrenal glands.*

TRIVIA CHALLENGE II
Category: **POTPOURRI**   Who went to the Phantom Zone for destroying one of Krypton's moons? Answer on page 195   Answer from page 191 **GREEN ARROW**

THE CURIOUS CASE OF THE QUIRKY COMICS!

Darn! Just when Johnny Storm had Plantman cornered in **Strange Tales** *#121, Planty pulled out that old wet-stingy-acorn death trap and defeated The Torch! And you just knew our dastardly villain had a garden hose handy to finish him off.*

© 1964 Marvel

Mister Silver Age Reluctantly Recommends...

Strange Tales #121

**Marvel
Jun 1964**

Cover artists:
Jack Kirby, Steve Ditko

"Prisoner of the Plantman"
Writer: Stan Lee
Penciller: Dick Ayers
Inker: Dick Ayers

**Then 12¢
Now $45**

Reprints appear in...
• Marvel Tales #23
• Essential Human Torch Vol. 1

© 1964 Marvel

create the heat and light of a supernova, remember — with a convenient sprinkler or wet dishrag. And I'm not exaggerating, as his epic second battle with The Plantman showed.

Vowing revenge for his earlier defeat, Plantman visited Johnny one night while he was sleeping. Planty's vines crept in the open window and threw a bucket of water on the Torch, neutralizing him. Plantman then locked Johnny in the closet while he robbed the hotel across the street. Ooh, the dastardly fiend!

After extracting vows that the other FF members wouldn't interfere, The Torch tracked down Plantman. But alas, Johnny was drawn into a trap where he was pelted with wet acorns. No, really! And they didn't just sting a bunch, either. "Too many of them! Covered with dew! So moist — putting out my flame!"

Oh man, I'm dying here! Regrettably, that's not the end of the damp doings. No sooner had Torch recovered from that death trap than Plantman turned on a nearby sprinkler, neutralizing Johnny yet again. Our hero finally found a stray sprayer filled with weed killer and turned the tide of battle. Whew! Here's your Mopee, Johnny. Try not to get it moist!

The "Mommy, Make It Go Away!" Award to: "Return of the Black Flame!" in *Adventure Comics* #400 (Dec 70). There's a lot of talk among fans about the value of continuity. Should writers worry about whether a story's details gel with bits of business from older stories or just focus on telling a fun story for this issue?

I think creators have to play fair with readers. If last year the Flash circled the globe 10 times in a second to escape a dastardly death trap, he shouldn't have difficulty catching a crook fleeing in a car this month. If so many details change that I can't anticipate what a hero may do, I lose interest. But I don't particularly care if the Flash has a broken leg in his title and is fine in *Justice League*. Just because both issues have the same cover date doesn't mean they happened the same day.

Before anyone argues that continuity is the hobgoblin of little minds, consider the Supergirl series in *Adventure Comics*. It was bad enough when, in issue #397, Supergirl used her mind-reading powers on an unconscious henchman to learn the name of a criminal mastermind. But #400 took disregard for details to a new level.

Our story began with Zora, aka Black Flame, escaping from the Kandorian prison where she'd been sentenced for past crimes against Supergirl. She stunned the guard and stole a space flyer, using it to fly to the Phantom Zone planet, "where the criminals of many galaxies are kept."

Yikes! As we all know, the Phantom Zone is a, um, zone — that is, a dimension (not a planet) where Superman's Kryptonian foes were sent before Krypton exploded. But Zora didn't know that, apparently, so she flew there in her space ship.

TRIVIA CHALLENGE II
Category: **POTPOURRI**   **What planet is known as the World of Doomed Olsens?**   Answer on page 196   Answer from page 192 **COLLINS**

Once she arrived, she overcame the guard and gathered the phantoms together. Holding a ray gun on the rest to keep them back — and how a ray gun was going to hurt the phantoms wasn't explained — she ushered three forward and escaped with them in her rocket.

The three became non-phantoms (but didn't gain superpowers, as they should have), and they joined BF in trapping Supergirl in a series of green-kryptonite traps. But Kara escaped each and chased them down.

To stop her once and for all, one villain cast a magic spell on Supergirl, giving Black Flame time to douse her with gold kryptonite. Yikes! As we all know, exposure to gold kryptonite immediately and permanently removes any Kryptonian's powers! In this case, the gold k worked slowly to steal the Maid of Steel's powers, and they returned after she escaped some time later.

Capturing the villains, Kara returned them to the Phantom Zone planet in the space flyer and dropped off BF in Kandor. Then Supergirl headed for home, and readers headed for the aspirin bottle.

What a special story to celebrate a 35th anniversary issue! It makes you wonder if they'd read any of the stories in those first 34 years, doesn't it?

Needless to say, they had plenty of letters for the letters column after that. And even without all those weird continuity gaffes, I frankly am willing to give this series a Mopee just for getting Kara started wearing all those silly-looking costumes she used in the early 1970s.

Does that clean out the closet of all-time goofiness? Heck no! We haven't even mentioned the Legion or the Avengers, let alone Lois and Jimmy, whose every random story probably deserves a Mopee! Uatu knows, there are gems as good as this half-dozen scattered all through the Silver Age, waiting to pop up and make you spit Pepsi onto the page. I purposely steered clear of some of the obvious wackiness just to show how wide and deep this streak really ran.

Mister Silver Age Reluctantly Recommends...

Adventure Comics #400

DC
Dec 1970

Cover artists:
Mike Sekowsky, Dick Giordano

"Return of the Black Flame"
Writer: Mike Sekowsky
Penciller: Mike Sekowsky
Inker: Jack Abel

Then 15¢
Now $8.50

A MOMENT LATER, A SHOWER OF GOLDEN FLAKES POUR OVER THE MAID OF STEEL, AND...

*Supergirl was doused with gold kryptonite while captured by Black Flame and her Phantom Zone planet escapees in **Adventure Comics** #400. Don't worry, her powers returned when she moved away from the gold k. No, really. Don't they always?*

Tracking The Turkeys

Want to read these all-time gems but can't find the originals? Amazingly enough, some of them have been reprinted. Don't ask me why:

"The Two Boys of Steel!" in *Superboy* #63 was reprinted in *Superboy* #129.
Fantastic Four #88 was reprinted in *Marvel's Greatest Comics* #70.
The Brave & The Bold #78 was reprinted in *B&B* #116.
"Prisoner of the Plant Man!" in *Strange Tales* #121 was reprinted in *Marvel Tales* #23.

Sadly for you cheapskates out there, the Supergirl and Atom stories haven't yet been republished. The Atom's story should make volume #2 of *The Atom Archives*, but if they have any decency at all, they'll stop the *Supergirl Archives* series before they reach this story.

TRIVIA CHALLENGE II
Category: **POTPOURRI**   **What is MR. MXYZPTLK's first name?**   Answer on page 197   Answer from page 193 **JAX-UR**

Flash Dejà Vu

"Why did Julius Schwartz commission two Flash stories based on the same cover, as you mentioned in discussing Superman's twice-told tales? And how different were the two stories?"

Julie did indeed use the same Flash cover to generate two story ideas, as I mentioned on page 182. That took place in *Flash* #159 (Mar 66) and #161 (May 66), separated only by an *80-Page Giant*. And he didn't try to sneak it by readers, as he promoted the second use on the issue's cover as "A Comic Mag First!" and showed the previous cover.

Why would he do that? "It was just pure inspiration," he told Mr. Silver Age. "I'm an editor, and I try to come up with ideas that readers haven't seen before." To be sure, using covers to inspire story ideas was an old trick Schwartz had used many times. "We used to look at the artwork on a story to find a scene that made a good cover," he explained. "But after awhile, there weren't any new ideas in the stories and no scenes stood out as making a really good cover. So I decided to turn it around."

That idea, in turn, had come from his pal Mort Weisinger, the editor of the Superman family books. "He'd created stories based on covers all the time when he worked as an editor for the science-fiction pulp magazines," Julie related. "I didn't originate the idea, I just picked it up."

Julie was trying to think up an idea for the lead story in *The Flash* #161 when the concept hit him. "I realized that once you have a cover, you can come up with any type of story from it. I decided why not try it?" The original story had been written by Flash stalwart Gardner Fox. Schwartz didn't have to go far to find a writer to give him a new take.

"Bob Kanigher shared an office with me [as editor of other DC titles], so I asked him if he'd give it a try." Kanigher was familiar with Barry Allen, as he'd written the first Flash story in *Showcase* #4 as well as the lead stories for the character's other *Showcase* appearances (backups were by John Broome). "I didn't even let him read the earlier story, I just showed him the cover."

As expected, the stories were entirely different. Fox used the cover scene as a small part of a bigger tale, as he often did. Aliens hypnotized Barry into making him think he was unappreciated as the Flash, which made him decide to quit. They'd done this to prevent

The actual story scene created to go with the cover to **Flash** #159 was even more dramatic than the cover image, with Kid Flash watching in amazement. But that's what sometimes happens when you create a cover first and then make up the story to go with it.

Answer from page 194
GION-EL

him from using his super-speed, which would trigger a bomb planted by an evil alien guy. They admitted that Flash would have agreed not to use his speed if they'd asked, "but our method is a safeguard to stop you from it using it voluntarily — or involuntarily," they later explained.

Admittedly, that's not the most cunning of plans, but it achieved the goal of fitting the cover into the story. That was the downside to using a cover as a story catalyst. Some stories had totally different agendas than readers could infer from the cover, wedging the cover scene in on the periphery.

That happened most dramatically in *Flash* #167 (Feb 67), the notorious introduction of Mopee. That cover showed Flash advertising his availability for employment as a superhero with no mention of Mopee (except for the title, "The Real Origin of the Flash!"). While the scene does appear, it wasn't the strongest story element considering Mopee was claiming credit for creating the Flash.

Kanigher's version of the costume story, on the other hand, focused directly on the ramifications of Barry abandoning his uniform. It included the Kanigher trademark of giving the costume its own thoughts. After an adventure, Barry thanked his costume for helping him, and it "thought" back, "I'd never leave you, Barry! I'm your second skin!" But several days later, on his way to his wedding to Iris West, Barry was waylaid into an adventure in another dimension.

When he returned, he discovered he had been gone five hours rather than returning the moment after he'd left as he'd anticipated, and he'd missed his wedding. Iris was ticked, Barry became fed up with his Flash identity interfering with his life, and he nailed the costume to the tree. As he left, his eyes teared up—and moisture appeared on the eye holes of the costume, too. Its ability to think (and move) on its own played a role in Barry putting it back on again, as you knew he was gonna.

The obvious next question is: Why didn't Julie try this trick one more time, giving the same cover to his other favorite Flash writer, Broome? "It was something I only wanted to try once," said the man nicknamed B.O. (Be Original). "If you take an idea and do it over and over, it loses impact." I have to agree a third try might have been more than readers would've wanted. But I can't help wishing I'd had a chance to see how all three Flash writers would have handled the same cover inspiration.

*Robert Kanigher's story in **Flash** #161 focused more closely on Barry abandoning his Flash identity, giving the uniform its own thoughts and making it a key player in the plot about Barry giving up on superheroing in order to win back Iris.*

Answer from page 195
MXYZPTLK

*Julie Schwartz's favorite **Flash** cover, #163, features a concept that a writer could take just about anywhere he wanted and writer John Broome did.*

Julie's Favorite

Of all the *Flash* covers that Julie used to generate stories, the one that stands out as his favorite was *Flash* #163 (Aug 66). It featured a solid black background on which the Flash, shown chest-high, is holding up his hand at the reader to grab attention.

"Stop!" his balloon said in huge letters using a red outline around red and white striped interiors. "Don't pass up this issue! My life depends on it!" The copy at the bottom added, "Is this the last stand of the Fastest Man Alive? 'The Flash stakes his life on—you!'"

"I took that cover to John Broome, and he came up with a really beautiful story," Schwartz says. "That's my prize example of a cover that really grabs a reader."

The story featured the Flash, Tinkerbell-style, losing his tangibility when a villain made everyone in Central City forget who he was. "Since our own belief in ourselves is based on how others feel about us," he chortled, "you began at once to lose your identity!"

That's not the greatest of scientific explanations, but the story indeed was a real wowser, showing the power of a child's belief in heroes. (Just don't try not believing in Mr. Silver Age to see if he'll go away, because he won't.)

The (Sob!) End Of The Silver Age

"Mr. Silver Age, my head is filled to bursting with all the fascinating information and four-color wonder that makes up the Silver Age! So I just have one final question: When did the Silver Age finally end? Has it ended yet?"

Unfortunately, it ended long ago, just as all good things must. Sustaining that level of excellence — and creating new characters who had that new-hero smell to them — couldn't continue forever. But deciding when the final act played out exactly has become a significant sticking point for comics fans of all ages.

A key complication for carbon-dating the end to the Silver Age comes from the fact that most readers really love the comics they read when they were 10 to 12 years old — no matter when that took place. That "Golden Age" of comics reading affects their perspective when dating the Silver Age. Readers in their teens by the mid-1960s view the first changes as the Age's death, since they were losing interest anyway as they tired of super-heroes and found girls were much more fascinating. Whereas fans who didn't reach the magical age of 12 until 1970 rave about Julie's Superman (by Curt Swan and Murphy Anderson) as a Silver Age high point.

Did the coming of Go-Go Checks and the "camp" attitude spurred by the **Batman** TV show end the Silver Age? Nope. It wasn't an especially pretty picture, but it was way too early to bring down the curtain completely.

© 1966 National Peroidical Publications Inc. (DC)

It makes sense to fans that their favorite comics came out during a great Age, and when they lost interest, other fans must have as well. Thus, some fans are ready to call it quits early while others see the Silver Age extending well into the 1970s and beyond.

The other problem with finding the end of the Age is that it's often hard to determine when the last bit of something that is fading away has truly vanished. Major events often begin with a bang, a true catalyst from which more events spring, but then they peter out little by little. So in finding an endpoint, do you pick that point at which things first began to peter out, or do you use the point at which the last small flicker was finally extinguished? Different perspectives will result in different answers, even if everyone agrees on the impact of each event — and they of course don't.

But in the final analysis, there's only one solid, satisfying spot to mark the closing of the Silver Age's greatness. It's *Fantastic Four* #102 (Sep 70), Jack Kirby's last regular-run Marvel issue (#108 was published well after Kirby left) before he left to join DC. That issue combines with *Superman* #229 (Aug 70), Mort Weisinger's last issue before he retired and the title shifted to Julius Schwartz. Those two events, happening nearly simultaneously to two of the biggest titles of the age, is too major of an occurrence to pass by.

The loss of Kirby from Marvel was a shock to comics fans. He'd been instrumental in virtually all of the company's key characters, and his run of 100-plus *FF* issues with Stan Lee still stands as one of the best long-run series of comics stories in history. Fans knew that a true era had ended when DC began publishing ads touting the arrival of Jack Kirby. They just didn't know that the era they saw ending later would become known as the Silver Age.

Similarly, but not quite as dramatically, Superman shifted away from Weisinger's quirky plotting to Schwartz. He attempted to modernize Supes by eliminating an unspecified amount of his powers (which quickly returned), updating his look with a flashy wardrobe, and giving him a high-profile TV-news job. These changes indicated that the 1960s version was being left behind, for better or worse.

DC trivia geek Mark Waid agrees with this cut-off, picking *Jimmy Olsen* #132 (Sep 70), the issue before Kirby arrived at DC, as the official end from DC's standpoint. "It feels right," he says. "By that time, a lot of the silver had been badly tarnished." But, as noted, not everyone agrees with this rational and entirely reasonable perspective. Here are some other suggestions that have been proposed, along with my explanation of why they're just dead wrong:

Kryptonite would come back. What the cover of **Superman** #233 (Jan 71) should have said was "Silver Age Nevermore!" The one-two punch of Jack Kirby leaving Marvel and Mort Weisinger retiring from Superman with September 1970-dated issues meant key comics would never be the same.

- **Go-Go Checks:** The introduction of that wacky checkerboard stripe on DC's March 1966 covers corresponded roughly to the infatuation with "camp," generated by the Batman TV show that started in January. The combination killed the Silver Age, say some fans, especially those older ones who had been reading comics since the 1950s and weren't dazzled by a bunch of revamped super-heroes. But that's way too early for me, who *was* dazzled by all those heroes. It means all but the first dozen or so issues of *Daredevil* and all of Thor's eponymous title occurred after the Silver Age was over. No way. (I've also heard people argue Batman didn't truly *enter* the Silver Age until his New Look began in May 1964. Put these two ideas together, and Bats had a pretty short Silver Age.)

- **Captain America #100 (Apr 68) and Secret Six #1 (Apr-May 68):** The argument is that the fading popularity of super-heroes led to a rash of new DC titles in various genres that were abandoned quickly, making fans lose more interest. Meanwhile, Marvel's distribution deal finally let it expand its output, but that weakened the quality and pushed the number of titles too high for a fan to keep up with everything. I think this period marked the beginning of the end, but there was still too much excitement going to end it here.

Did Gwen Stacy's death in **Amazing Spider-Man** #121 (Jun 73) bring down the Silver Age curtain? Nope. The curtain was down. Gwen's death maybe turned out the lights and locked the door, but the audience was already over at the parking garage paying the cashier, if you know what I mean.

- **The (shudder) 15-cent cover price in 1969:** Fans had plenty of advance warning on this calamity, as one of the first comics to jack up its price by (gasp!) three full cents was *Adventure Comics* #381 (Jun 69), the first issue to give Supergirl the lead feature (replacing the Legion after many years). The issue was featured in a lot of house ads, so we all knew Supergirl was taking over — and that her comic was gonna cost us three more shiny pennies. It was pretty shocking, but it wasn't enough to end an era, just as the two-cent price rise in 1962 didn't have an effect on dating.

- **Amazing Spider-Man #121 (Jun 73):** No question about it, Gwen Stacy's death shocked Spider-Man readers. Such a tragedy makes a strong symbolic ending. This theory gained adherents when Kurt Busiek and Alex Ross' *Marvels* mini-series in 1994 ended with Gwen's death, but I'm not buying it. It's too late. Too many new directions — especially Conan and monsters — were on firm ground by this time.

Busiek told me, "I pick the death of Gwen Stacy as the Silver Age's end simply because it works as a coda, a sign of lost innocence, of bittersweet ending. I don't really argue with anyone who picks one of the others, but Gwen's death simply works as a milestone for me." Like me, he sees three periods: a build-up from *Showcase* #4 to *Daredevil* #1, a

Did **Superman** #423, along with **Action Comics** #583 (Sep 86), the last issues before Superman was rebooted, work with the earlier **Crisis on Infinite Earths** maxi-series to signal the end of the Silver Age? Nope. Unlike Paleolithic ages, comics ages are special periods and don't last for millions of years.

© 1986 DC Comics

flourishing from 1964 to 1968 and a fading as Marvel expanded and DC began experimenting. He just holds off the final curtain longer than I can do it, because Marvel losing Kirby provided a far greater loss of innocence for us fans than the events in any one comic could supply.

• **Crisis on Infinite Earths #12 (Mar 86):** This mini-series, coupled with the reboot of Superman after Alan Moore's "Whatever Happened To The Man of Tomorrow?" in *Superman* #423 and *Action* #583 (both Sep 86), created a new starting point, say this theory's supporters. Baloney, say I. Creating an Age with that many peaks and valleys, covering nearly 30 years of comics, dilutes the reason for naming it at all — which is to call attention to the overall excitement and quality of a focused period of creativity.

Some fans have tried to carbon-date when each title precisely "left" the Silver Age, based on a major change in the book during the 1968-1972 period. But so many changes were occurring to try to boost sales as interest faded overall that there are lots of arbitrary options to choose among in some titles, making it hard to find a consensus. Still, it can be a fun exercise and fits with my slow-fading concept. But I believe the Silver Age ended in 1970, so comics that faded or changed after that did so after the Silver Age officially ended.

I have to admit, all my reasoning and rationales are slightly tainted by one key fact. I was 10 to 12 years old in 1964-1966, during what I consider the absolute peak of the Silver Age's greatness. And I was 16 and becoming far more interested in other things besides the adventures of some faltering super-heroes in 1970, when the Silver Age ended. Coincidence? I think so. I mean, no matter how old I was personally, those comics were some of the greatest ever and represent the best years of the Silver Age! You can look it up.

Golden Age Good-Bye

So if the Silver Age started with *Showcase* #4 and ended with *Fantastic Four* #102, how about the Golden Age? It started with Superman's first appearance in *Action Comics* #1 (Jun 38). Please don't argue, I'm not listening, and neither is anyone else. It's one of the few dates that virtually everyone can agree on.

Some fans claim the Golden Age ended along with World War II in 1945, which eliminated both a large, captive audience and the key villains that gave the era lots of drama. Others say it ran through the end of the E.C. Comics boom and the institution of the Comics Code in 1954, when comics content was eviscerated, giving the comics no chance to progress beyond kiddie fare.

A strong case can be made for its end coming in 1949, when *Captain America* became *Captain America's Weird Tales* and *Flash Comics* died with #104. Those changes to such basic icons pretty much say the bloom was off the Golden Age rose. That creates an age of 11 years, as opposed to about 14 for the Silver Age. Others say it ended when *All-Star Comics*, home to the first and greatest super-hero

team, The Justice Society, became *All-Star Western* with #58 (Apr-May 51). That works too and makes the Golden Age nearly as long as the Silver Age. Maybe if I were Mr. Golden Age, I'd feel more strongly one way or the other.

Are there other options for the ending of the Ages? Of course there are. Just a little while ago, I saw someone argue that the Silver Age ended when Snapper Carr betrayed the JLA to the Joker in *Justice League of America* #77 (Dec 69). That's roughly the right period, but it's not a big enough reason, even with the intro of the team's satellite headquarters. Maybe that was the JLA's "last Silver Age" issue. But others say that occurred when Gardner Fox left with #66.

These undoubtedly are arguments that can never be resolved to everyone's satisfaction, especially for the people who were there, reading the comics while drinking their soda pop and lazing around on a summer's day. Comics read in a situation like that were truly great, no matter the time period. Those comics will always represent the true Golden Age of Comics.

Silver Age Comics PRICE GUIDE

Prices in this section are from *The Standard Catalog of Comic Books 2nd Edition*, the world's largest comics reference work!
Order your own copy at (888) 457-2873.

What's it worth? Comics are worth their weight in gold as far as sentiment goes, but some are also worth some big bucks. Here's what you could expect to pay (in U.S. dollars) for Near Mint copies of U.S. comics published between 1956 and 1971!

Abbott & Costello (Charlton)

1 30
2-3 20
4-10 14
11-16 12

Action Comics

221-240 240
241 250
242 1,200
243-251 185
252 1,100
253 400
254 300
255 225
256-261 100
262 90
263 100
264-266 80
267 250
268-270 80
271-275 65
276 125
277-284 60
285 100
286-287 55
288-290 52
291-292 30
293 35
294-299 30
300 55
301-304 25
305-309 18
310 24
311-333 16
334 36
335-340 14
341-346 10
347 22
348-359 9
360 18
361-372 8
373 18
374-392 7

Adventure Comics

228-246 170
247 4,400
248-255 130
256 525
257-259 125
260 500
261-266 80
267 740
268 80
269 225
270 80
271 225
272-274 65
275 145
276-280 65
281 60
282 95
283 100
284 60
285-286 110
287-289 60
290 100
291-292 45
293 100
294 90
295-298 45
299 55
300 200
301 70
302-305 55
306-310 45
311-312 40
313-316 30
317 35
318-320 30
321 45
322-340 25
341 16
342-345 14
346 16
347 14
348 16
349-351 14
352 12
353 15
354-360 10
361-372 9
373-380 8
381 9
382-397 7

Adventures of Bob Hope, The

40-50 55
51-60 40
61-70 35
71-80 30
81-90 25
91-105 15
106-109 25

Adventures of Dean Martin & Jerry Lewis

32-40 40

Adventures of Jerry Lewis

41 40
42-50 36
51-60 34
61-80 28
81-91 25
92 30
93-96 25
97 35
98-100 25
101 32
102 55
103-105 32
106-116 14
117 20
118-119 14
120-121 12

Adventures of the Fly

1 180
2 120
3 100
4-5 80
6-10 70
11-15 50
16-20 40
21-31 30

Adventures of the Jaguar

1 125
2 75
3 50
4-5 40
6-10 30
11-15 22

Air War Stories

1 22
2-8 14

Alarming Adventures

1 40
2 25
3 20

Alvin

1 25
2 18
3-10 15
11-20 12

Amazing Adult Fantasy

7 600
8 475
9-13 425
14 525

Amazing Fantasy

15 32,000

Amazing Spider-Man (Vol. 1)

1 25,000
1/Golden Record reprint ... 240
2 3,200
3 2,500
4 1,900
5 1,600
6 1,250
7-8 900
9 1,000
10 900
11-12 550
13 700
14 2,000
15 900
16 425
17 600
18 385
19 325
20 425
21 300
22 265
23 440
24 210
25 300
26 285
27 275
28 325
29 175
30 150
31 175
32-36 150
37-38 140
39 250
40 350
41-42 150
43-49 100
50 450
51 150
52-57 85
58 70
59-60 75
61-69 70
70-74 55
75-80 48
81-88 45
Annual 1 ... 650
Annual 2 ... 250
Annual 3-5 ... 90
Annua 6 26

America's Best TV Comics

1 55

Angel and the Ape

1 25
2 20
3-7 15

Anthro

1 24
2-6 18

Aquaman (1st Series)

1 475
2 250
3 140
4-5 110
6-10 80
11 65
12-20 58
21-30 42
31-32 32
33 60
34-40 26
41-47 20
48 22
49 12
50-52 20

Archie

82-90 44
91-99 34
100 55
101-120 22
121-140 16
141-150 13
151-180 9
181-200 5
201-203 3
Annual 8 ... 135
Annual 9 ... 120
Annual 10 .. 110
Annual 11 ... 70
Annual 12 ... 60
Annual 13 ... 58
Annual 14-15 . 50
Annual 16-17 . 26
Annual 18-19 . 22
Annual 20 ... 14
Annual 21 9

Archie and Me

1 125
2 75
3 45
4-5 34
6-10 20
11-20 12
21-30 8
31-38 6

Archie As Pureheart the Powerful

1 55
2 35
3-6 25

Archie Giant Series Magazine

4 325
5-6 275
7-8 200
9-10 185
11 140
12 125
13 140
14-15 110
16 125
17 110
18 125
19 110
20 100
21 85
22 60
23 80
24-25 60
26 80
27 60
28 80
29-30 60
31-141 40
142 45
143-160 20
161-175 12

Archie's Girls Betty & Veronica

26-29 165
30-39 115
40-50 85
51-60 55
61-70 45
71-90 32
91-110 24
111-140 16
141-160 13
161-177 10
Annual 5 ... 250
Annual 6 ... 175
Annual 7 ... 150
Annual 8 ... 100

Archie's Jokebook Magazine

24-30 100
31-40 75
41 135
42-43 65
44-48 70
49-60 35
61-70 24
71-80 16
81-90 12
91-100 8
101-120 5
121-152 3

Archie's Madhouse

1 175
2 95
3 68
4-5 50
6-10 38
11-15 26
16-20 23
21 18
22 100
23-25 18
26-30 14
31-40 9
41-50 6
51-66 4
Annual 1 65
Annual 2 25
Annual 3 15
Annual 4-6 ... 10

Archie's Pals 'n' Gals

6-7 135
8-10 80
11-20 45
21-28 22
29 45
30 22
31-40 13
41-50 9
51-60 7

Archie's TV Laugh-Out

1 42
2 24
3-5 16
6 12
7 22
8 12

Around the World Under the Sea

1 20

Astonishing Tales

1 30

Atom

1 400
2 200
3 150
4-5 110
6 85
7 125
8-10 85
11-15 70
16-20 40
21-25 30
26-28 25
29 85
30-35 25
36 35
37-38 25

Atom and Hawkman

39-45 20

Atom Ant

1 85

Attack (3rd Series)

1 25
2 15
3-4 12

Aurora Comic Scenes

181-193 25

Avengers

1 2300
2 575
3 400
4 1450
4/Golden Record reprint 75
5 210
6-8 165
9 175
10 155
11 140
12-16 90
17-18 70
19 75
20-30 40
31-40 26
41-51 20
52 28
53 35
54-56 18
57 90
58 65
59-60 22
61-67 18
68-70 15
71 24
72-74 12
75 14
76-80 12
Annual 1 55
Annual 2-3 ... 26
Annual 4 10

Baby Huey The Baby Giant

1 150
2 85
3 48
4-5 36
6-10 20
11-20 15
21-30 12
31-40 9
41-50 6
51-70 4
71-91 3

Baby Snoots

1 12

Bamm-Bamm & Pebbles

1 75

Banana Splits

1 30
2 18
3-4 14

Barbie and Ken

1 200
2-4 150
5 165

Bat Lash

1 25
2-7 15

Batman

102-104 360
105 475
106-109 360
110 375
111-120 265
121 350
122 195
123 220
124-126 195
127 240
128 195
129 250
130 195
131 145
132-135 130
136 215
137-145 140
146-147 110
148 140
149-150 110
151 80
152 90
153-154 70
155 285
156-158 70
159 80
160-162 70
163 80
164-168 70
169 75
170 70
171 425
172-175 48
176 70
177-178 48
179 100
180 48
181 155
182-186 48
187 55
188 28
189 100
190 35
191-192 28
193 40
194-196 28
197 45
198 75
199 28
200 110
201 35
202-203 20
204-207 18
208 35
209-211 18
212 16
213 45
214-217 16
218-219 28
220-221 14
222 45
223 30
225 14
Annual 1 ... 540
Annual 2 ... 275
Annual 3 ... 215
Annual 4-5 .. 110
Annual 6-7 ... 85
Annual 8 7

Battlefield Action

16 28
17 13
18-20 10
21-30 9
31-40 7
41-50 6
51-62 5

Beatles (Dell)

1 440

Beep Beep (Dell)

4-9 24
10-14 16

Beep Beep Road Runner (Gold Key)

1 28
2 26
3-5 20
6-15 15
16-19 10

Beetle Bailey (Vol. 1)

7-10 24
11-20 18
21-30 14
31-40 10
41-50 8
51-60 7
61-70 6
77-100 4

Ben Casey Film Stories

1 55

Betty & Me

1 65
2 40
3-5 24
6-10 15
11-20 10
21-30 7

Beverly Hillbillies

1 60
2 38
3 28
4-5 24
6-10 18
11-17 15
18-21 12

Beware the Creeper

1 50
2-4 30
5-6 25

Bewitched

1 85
2 50
3-10 40
11-14 30

Big Valley

1 40
2-6 25

Billy the Kid

9 58
10 35
11 40
12 30
13 40
14 30
15-16 40
17-19 30
20-22 35
23 20
24-26 35
27-30 20
31-40 14
41-50 8
51-60 7
61-70 5
71-80 4

Binky

72-74 7

Binky's Buddies

1 26
2 16
3 12
4-11 10

Blackhawk (Vol. 1)

104-107 105
108 325
109 130
110-117 110
118 135
119-130 85
131-140 65
141-149 50
150-163 48

164 60
165-166 48
167-180 22
181-190 12
191-197 10
198 12
199-200 10
201-243 8

Blazing Combat

1 90
2-4 30
Annual 1 45

Blondie Comics

94-99 9
100 10
101-124 8
125 9
126-130 8
131-140 7
141-167 8
168-180 5
181-187 4

Blue Beetle (Vol. 2)

1 45
2 30
3-5 20

Blue Beetle (Vol. 3)

1 55
2 24
3-5 18

Bobby Sherman

1 15
2-7 10

Bomba

1 16
2-7 8

Bonanza

1 110
2 75
3-5 50
6-10 32
11-20 22
21-30 15
31-37 12

Boris Karloff Tales of Mystery

3 25
4-6 20
7-8 18
9 30
10 15
11 22
12 15
13-14 12
15 15
16-20 12
21 18
22-31 10

Boris Karloff Thriller

1 55
2 40

Brady Bunch

1 45
2 30

Brain Boy

2 65
3 50
4-6 45

Brave and the Bold

8-10 425
11-22 340
23 390
24 340
25 425
26-27 330
28 5,300
29 2,300
30 2,000
31 350
32-33 200
34 2,000
35 550
36 415
37 250
38-39 225
40-41 140
42 300
43 350
44 260
45-49 60
50 175
51 225
52-53 125
54 275
55-56 45
57 145
58 65
59 75
60-62 85
63 32
64 55
65-66 22
67 35
68 50
69-71 25
72 22
73-78 20
79 40
80-82 35
83 45
84-86 32
87-90 20
91 18

Brenda Lee's Life Story

1 50

Brother Power the Geek

1 30
2 20

Buck Rogers (Gold Key)

1 36

Bugs Bunny and Porky Pig

1 26

Bugs Bunny Winter Fun

1 30

Bullwinkle

1 100

Bullwinkle and Rocky (Charlton)

1 30
2 18
3 15
4-7 12

Bullwinkle and Rocky (Gold Key)

1 90
2 68

Bullwinkle Mother Moose Nursery Pomes

1 85

Burke's Law

1 24
2-3 20

Captain Action (DC)

1 58
2-5 35

Captain America (Vol. 1)

100 285
101 55
102-109 35
110-111 35
112 25
113 38
114-116 15
117 35
118-120 14
121 10
122-129 9

Captain Atom (Charlton)

78 40
79-80 25
81-82 20
83-84 25
85-89 20

Captain Marvel (1st Series)

1 60
2 24
3-4 20
5 15
6-9 10
10-11 9
12-21 7

Captain Nice

1 35

Capt. Storm

1 28
2-5 18
6 14
7-15 12
16-18 9

Captain Venture and the Land Beneath the Sea

1 26
2 18

Car 54 Where Are You?

2 75
3 45
4-5 40
6-7 35

Cat, T.H.E. (Dell)

1 18
2-4 12

Cave Kids

1 35
2 18
3-5 15
6-12 12
13-16 9

Challengers of the Unknown

1 1,850
2 725
3 600
4-5 500
6-8 475
9-10 275
11-15 185
16-20 110
21-30 65
31 75
32-40 40
41-50 24
51-60 20
61-73 7
74 14
75 7

Chamber of Darkness

1 15
2-3 6
4 9
5-6 4
7 8
8 4

Charlton Sport Library: Professional Football

1 35

Clyde Crashcup

1 90
2 65
3-5 48

Daredevil

1 1685
2 425
3 300
4 250
5 200
6 145
7 200
8 135
9-10 130
11-15 85
16-17 90
18-19 50
20 45
21-26 34
27 38
28-30 34
31-42 28
43 24
44-49 20
50-52 22
53 25
54-59 15
60-68 12
Annual 1 25

Daring Adventures

9-10 20
11 20
12 40
13-14 20
15-16 20
17-18 20

Daring Comics

9 1100
10 950
11-12 875

Dark Shadows (Gold Key)

1 145
1/A 50
2 55
3 50
4-5 40
6 32

Date with Debbi

1 16
2 12
3-10 10

Davy Crockett

1 100
2 20

DC Special

1 25
2-8 12

Debbi's Dates

1 30
2-5 18
6 30
7-9 18

Dennis the Menace (Fawcett)

23-30 35
31-40 25
41-50 18
51-70 14
71-90 10
91-100 6
101-110 4

Detective Comics

235 565
236 325
237-240 275
241-260 210
261-264 165
265 275
266 165
267 210
268-270 165
271 175
272 125
273 160
274-280 125
281-297 100
298 175
299-300 70
301 65
302-326 54
327 75
328 85
329-330 40
331 35
332 38
333-340 30
341 40
342 30
343-358 28
359 75
360-364 28
365 40
366-368 28
369 44
370-371 28
372-386 22
387 45
388 25
389-390 16
391-394 13
395 20
396 13
397 20
398-399 13
400 45
401 10
402 20
403 10

Dirty Dozen

1 25

Dr. Kildare

2 50
3-9 40

Doctor Solar, Man of the Atom

1 100
2 45
3-5 30
6-10 22
11-14 16
15 20
16-20 16
21-27 12

Doctor Strange (1st Series)

169 100
170 40
171-176 32
177-183 26

Doctor Tom Brent, Young Intern

1 15
2-5 10

Donald Duck

49-51 35
52 90
53-58 30
59-60 80
61-67 25
68 70
69-70 25
71-84 20
85-100 18
101-120 16
121-133 12

Donald Duck Album

1 45

Donald Duck Beach Party

1 100
2 65
3-6 55

Doom Patrol (1st Series)

86 70
87 48
88-90 40
91-98 38
99 45
100 50
101-120 25
121 45
122-124 2

Drag-Strip Hotrodders

1 40
2-16 25

Dudley Do-Right

1 25

80 Page Giant Magazine

1 165
2-3 100
4-5 75
6 65
7 75
8 100
9 65
10-15 55

Escapade in Florence

1 40

Espionage

1 18
2 15

Family Affair

1 24
2 20
3-4 14

Fantastic Four (Vol. 1)

1 16,000
1/Golden Record reprint ... 180
2 3,400
3 2,350
4 2,500
5 3,250
6 1,500
7 775
8 165
9-10 140
11 565
12 1,125
13 460
14-20 310
21 210
22 150
23-24 150
25-26 375
27 150
28 180
29-30 100
31-40 80
41-44 50
45 60
46 55
47 50
48 725
49 225
50 265
51 50
52 80
53 55
54 45
55 65
56-60 45
61-65 38
66 35
67 40
68-70 30
71 26
72 35
73 28
74-75 30
76-80 28
81-88 22
89-99 18
100 55
101-102 16
Annual 1 ... 425
Annual 2 ... 250
Annual 3 ... 100
Annual 4 55
Annual 5 70
Annual 6 45
Annual 7 18

Fantastic Voyage

1 25
2 16

Fantastic Voyages of Sindbad

1 18
2 12

Fantasy Masterpieces (Vol. 1)

1 18
2 15
3 14
4-7 12
8 13
9 12
10-11 10

Fatman Human Flying Saucer

1 35
2-3 25

Felix the Cat (2nd series)

1 35
2-12 24

Fightin' Air Force

3 32
4-5 20
6-10 15
11-20 12
21-53 8

Fight the Enemy

1 22
2-3 16

First Kiss

1 45
2 28
3 22
4-5 18
6-10 13
11-20 12
21-40 8

Flash (1st Series)

105 3,850
106 1,100
107 650
108 600
109 440
110 800
111 275
112 300
113 275
114 200
115-116 175
117 200
118-120 175
121-122 135
123 625
124 90
125-128 75
129 200
130-136 75
137 200
138 65
139 100
140 65
141-150 55
151 70
152-159 40
160 55
161-164 30
165 40
166-168 30
169 50
170-174 30
175 90
176-177 30
178 36
179-180 30
181-186 20
187 30
188-190 18
191-195 15
196 30
197-200 15
Annual 1 ... 400

Flash Gordon (Gold Key one-shot)

1 26

Flintstones at the New York World's Fair

1 48

Flintstones Bigger and Boulder

1 65
2 45

Flintstones with Pebbles and Bamm-Bamm

1 50

Flipper

1 25
2-3 18

Flying Nun

1 32
2-4 20

Flying Saucers (Dell)

1 26
2-5 15

Fly Man

32 18
33-39 16

Forbidden Worlds

57-60 45
61-70 40
71-72 35
73 275
74-80 35
81-85 24
86 30
87-90 24
91-93 20
94 55
95-100 20
101-109 16
110 35
111-113 16
114 35
115 16
116 30
117-120 16
121-124 12
125 25
126-127 12
128 14
129 12
130 14
131-140 12
141-145 10

Fox and the Crow

35-40 85
41-61 60
62-80 42
81-94 26
95 50
96-100 22
101-108 18

Fractured Fairy Tales

1 75

Frankenstein (Dell)

1 35
2 25
3-4 15

Frogmen

2 34
3 26
4 20
5 22
6 20
7-11 18

From Beyond the Unknown

1 35
2 18
3-5 13
6 10

F-Troop

1 50
2 40
3-5 36
6-7 32

Fury (Dell)

1 25

Gallegher Boy Reporter

1 15

Garrison's Gorillas

1 21
2-4 14
5 12

Gentle Ben

1 30
2-5 20

George of the Jungle

1 35
2 24

Get Smart

1 45
2 30
3-5 22
6-8 20

Ghost Manor (1st Series)

1 12
2-5 7
6-10 6
11-14 5

Ghost Rider

1 28
2-3 20
4-7 .... 12.50

Ghost Stories

1 36
2 20
3-5 14
6-10 10
11-16 7
17-20 6
21-25 5

G.I. Combat

40-43 75
44 350
45 225
46 115
47-50 100
51-60 85
61-66 70
67 110
68-86 70
87 260
88-100 55

101-110 45
111-113 38
114 75
115-120 28
121-140 22
141-143 8

Gidget

1 100

Girl from U.N.C.L.E.

1 36
2 24
3 20
4-5 15

Girls' Love Stories

42-49 38
50-71 30
72-94 25
95-105 20
106-111 17
112-123 15
124-143 14
144-153 9

Go-Go

1 40
2-9 30

Gomer Pyle

1 40
2-3 25

Great Society Comic Book

1 16
2 12

Green Hornet (Gold Key)

1 120
2-3 80

Green Lantern (2nd Series)

1 2750
2 750
3 450
4-5 340
6 275
7-10 245
11-12 170
13 185
14 145
15-16 140
17-20 130
21-28 115
29 120
30 110
31-39 90
40 340
41-44 55
45 80
46-50 55
51-58 38
59 100
60 24
61 35
62-70 24
71-75 18
76 150
77-78 75
79 58

Hanna-Barbera Bandwagon

1 70
2-3 50

Hanna-Barbera Super TV Heroes

1 58
2-3 36
4-5 30
6-7 35

Hardy Boys

1 28
2 18

Hawk & the Dove (1st Series)

1 30
2 20
3-6 18

Hawkman (1st Series)

1 350
2 140
3 85
4 140
5 85
6-10 65
11-15 50
16-19 36
20-27 32
Bk 1 ..... 19.95

Heart Throbs

49-50 60
51-60 48
61-70 38
71-80 27
81-90 20
91-100 16
101 60
102-110 13
111-127 10

Heckle and Jeckle (Dell)

1 25
2-3 13

Heckle and Jeckle (Gold Key)

1 36
2 18
3-4 16

Hector Heathcote

1 30

Help (Vol. 1)

1 45
2 28
3-12 20

Help (Vol. 2)

1 26
2-3 16

Herbie

1 95
2 60
3-5 48
6-7 40
8 50
9-10 38
11-23 30

Hercules (Charlton)

1 14
2 9
3-5 6
6-8 5
8/A 10
9-13 5

High Chaparral

1 40

Hogan's Heroes

1 50
2 40
3-5 32
6-9 26

Homer the Happy Ghost (2nd Series)

1 40
2-4 30

Honey West

1 25

Hot Rod Racers

1 30
2-15 20

Hot Stuff the Little Devil

1 150
2 80
3-5 60
6-10 52
11-20 40
21-30 28
31-40 16
41-50 12
51-70 10
71-100 6

Hot Wheels

1 45
2 30
3 24

House of Mystery

54-61 95
62 70
63 85
64 70
65 85
66-69 70
70 85
71-75 65
76 85
77-79 65
80-83 54
84-85 85
86-99 54
100 65
101-116 45
117-119 35
120 45
121-130 28
131-142 22
143 90
144 48
145-155 40
156 65
157-159 36
160 55
161-173 32
174-177 12
178 14
179 25
180-185 9
186 10
187 6

House of Secrets

1 1,385
2 540
3 420
4 325
5-7 195
8 230
9-12 195
13-15 120
16-20 100
21-22 80
23 100
24-30 80
31-50 65
51-60 52
61 80
62 60
63-65 50
66 65
67 40
68-79 36
80 45
81 12
82-87 9

How The West Was Won

1 18

Huey, Dewey, and Louie

1 36
2 20
3 16
4-6 12

I Dream of Jeannie (Dell)

1 60
2 40

Incredible Hulk

1 9200
2 2250
3 1525
4-5 1400
6 1500
102 175
103 60
104 50
105-110 40
111-120 25
121 15
122 40
123-125 15
126-131 12
Annual 1 75
Annual 2 40

Inferior Five

1 24
2 16
3-10 14
11-12 10

In Search of the Castaways

1 20

Invaders (Gold Key)

1 40
2-4 28

Iron Man & Sub-Mariner

1 120

Iron Man (Vol. 1)

1 325
2 90
3 55
4-5 50
6-7 42
8-10 36
11-15 28
16-20 18
21-29 15
Annual 1 22

I Spy

1 28
2 18
3-6 15

It's About Time

1 25

Jet Dream

1 18

Jetsons (Gold Key)

1 90
2 65
3-5 48
6-10 40
11-20 24
21-30 16
31-36 14

Jetsons (Charlton)

1 35
2 22
3-5 14
6-10 10
11-20 7

Jigsaw

1 16
2 10

Jim Hardy (2nd series)

1 100
2 60

John Carter of Mars

1 30
2-3 16

John F. Kennedy

1 45
1-2 30
1-3 22

Johnny Jason, Teen Reporter

2 20

Johnny Thunder

1 12
2-3 8

John Steele, Secret Agent

1 18

Joker

1 16
2 12
3-5 8
6-9 7

Jonny Quest (Gold Key)

1 85

Journey into Mystery (1st Series)

38-40 215
41 185
42 165
43-44 175
45 160
46 175
47 150
48 160
49 175
50 155
51-61 150
62 225
63-75 135
76-77 130
78 140
79-82 130
83 3100
83/Golden Record reprint 120
84 675
85 425
86 275
87 285
88 235
89 260
90 140
91-92 115
93 140
94-96 115
97 130
98-100 90
101 70
102-108 75
109 85
110-111 75
112 185
113-114 75
115 80
116 75
117-118 65
119 70
120-125 65
Annual 1 130

Jughead as Captain Hero

1 28
2 15
3 10
4-7 7

Jughead's Jokes

1 60
2 35
3 25
4-5 18
6-10 15
11-15 12
16-20 10
21-30 7
31-40 5
41-60 4
61-78 3

Jungle Book (Gold Key)

1 25

Jungle Jim (Charlton)

22 24
23-24 18
25-28 16

Jungle Jim (King)

5 9

Jungle Tales of Tarzan

1 45
2-4 35

Justice League of America

1 3,500
2 825
3 625
4 465
5 375
6-8 300
9 450
10 275
11-15 210
16-20 175
21 345
22 290
23-28 90
29-30 115
31 80
32 52
33 42
34 58
35-36 42
37-38 85
39 90
40-41 42
42-45 32
46 105
47 48
48 45
49-54 20
55 54
56 38
57 18
58 22
59-60 18
61-73 15
74-75 13
76 15
77-80 9
81-83 8

Kid Colt Outlaw

64-70 48
71-100 40
101-110 28
111-120 18
121-130 14
131-139 10
140-149 5

King Leonardo and His Short Subjects

1 35
2-4 25

King Louie and Mowgli

1 20

Kona

2 18
3-5 15
6-14 12
15-21 10

Konga

1 75
2 50
3-4 35
5-10 25
11-20 16
21-23 14

Konga's Revenge

1 10
2-3 7

Kong the Untamed

1 4
2-5 3

Korak, Son of Tarzan

1 35
2-5 25
6-11 20
12-20 16
21-30 13
31-40 8
41-45 6
46 4
47-59 2

Korg: 70,000 B.C.

1 8
2-9 5

Lancelot Link, Secret Chimp

1 22
2 14
3-8 10

Lancer

1 25
2-3 20

Land of the Giants

1 30
2 18
3-5 15

Laurel and Hardy (Gold Key)

1 24
2 18

Laurel and Hardy (DC)

1 40

Life with Millie

8 35
9-10 28
11-20 26

Li'l Kids

1 35
2-5 22
6-12 16

Linda Lark

1 15
2-8 10

Linda Carter, Student Nurse

1 60
2-5 40
6-9 30

Lippy the Lion and Hardy Har Har

1 60

Little Archie Mystery

1 60
2 42

Little Audrey TV Funtime

1 45
2 28
3 24
4-5 20
6-10 16
11-20 12
21-33 9

Little Dot Dotland

1 75
2-3 40
4-5 35
6-10 24
11-20 20
21-29 16
30-39 12
40-54 10
55-61 8
62-63 10

Little Dot in 3-D

1 ..... 2.50

Little Dot's Uncles and Aunts

1 70
2-3 42
4-5 36
6-10 28
11-35 22
36-52 14

Little Lotta (Vol. 1)

1 225
2 90
3 75
4-5 55
6-10 40
11-20 28
21-30 22
31-40 18
41-50 15
51-70 12
71-90 8
91-98 5
99-102 6
103-120 3

Little Lotta Foodland

1 45
2-3 35
4-5 30
6-10 24
11-15 16
16-20 12
21-29 8

Lone Ranger Golden West

1 45

Love and Romance

1 24
2 16
3-5 12
6-10 8
11-20 6
21-24 4

Lucy Show

1 65
2 40
3-5 32

Ludwig Von Drake

1 16
2 10
3-4 8

Magilla Gorilla (Gold Key)

1 30
2 15
3-5 12
6-10 10

Magnus, Robot Fighter (Gold Key)

1 110
2-3 65
4-10 30
11-20 18
21-28 12
29-46 5

Mandrake the Magician (King)

1 32
2 20
3 14
4-5 13
6-7 10
8 16
9 9
10 24

Man from U.N.C.L.E.

1 45
2 30
3-5 20
6-10 15
11-20 14
21-22 8

Marines Attack

1 16
2 12
3-5 9
6-9 6

M.A.R.S. Patrol Total War

3 12
4-5 9
6-10 ..... 7.50

Marvel Collectors' Item Classics

1 48
2 30
3-4 26
5-10 15
11-20 12
21-22 10

Marvel Super-Heroes (Vol. 1)

12 45
13 26
14 40
15-17 10
18 22
19-20 9
21-28 6
SE 1 40

Marvel Tales (2nd Series)

1 165
2 85
3 40
4-5 22
6-9 16
10 15
11-20 10
21-27 8

Masque of the Red Death

1 20

Maverick (Dell)

7-10 50
11-15 40
16-19 30

McHale's Navy

1 40
2 32
3 26

Melvin Monster (Dell)

1 60
2 45
3 40
4-5 32
6-10 26

Metal Men

1 350
2 175
3-5 110
6-10 80
11-20 55
21-26 45
27 80
28-30 42
31-41 24
42-44 12
45-56 6

Metamorpho

1 45
2 24
3 20
4-5 16
6-9 12
10 14
11-17 10

Mickey Mouse Surprise Party

1 18

Mickey Mouse
28-30 25
31-40 22
41-50 20
51-60 16
61-70 15
71-80 14
81-100 12
101-120 11
121-140 10
141-160 8
161-180 7
181-200 6
201-210 5
211-220 4
221-240 3
241-256 2

Microbots

1 10

Midnight
1 54
2 38
3-6 26

Mighty Atom (2nd Series)
1 22
2-6 18

Mighty Comics
40-50 15

Mighty Crusaders (1st Series)
1 24
2 15
3 12
4-7 10

Mighty Hercules
1-2 40

Mighty Heroes
1 50
2-4 35

Mighty Marvel Western
1 20
2 13
3-5 10
6-10 8

Mighty Samson
1 30
2-3 18
4-5 12
6-10 10
11-20 8

Mike Shayne Private Eye
1 16
2-3 10

Mission: Impossible
1 24
2-4 18
5 12

Mr. and Mrs. J. Evil Scientist
1 50
2 30
3-4 20

Monkees
1 45
2 30
3 24
4-5 20
6-10 18
11-17 12

Monsters on the Prowl
9 8
10-15 5
16 6
17-30 4

Mouse on the Moon
1 15

Mummy (Dell)
1 25

Munsters (Gold Key)
1 120
2 75
3-5 48
6-10 34
11-16 30

My Favorite Martian
1 55
2 35
3-4 30
5-9 24

My Greatest Adventure
11-15 110
16-18 125
19 110
20-21 125
22-27 85
28 90
29-30 85
31-40 70
41-61 55
62-79 35
80 300
81-85 150

Mysteries of Scotland Yard
1 50

Mysterious Suspense
1 35

Mystery in Space
34-40 235
41-52 195
53 1,100
54 425
55 250
56-60 175
61-71 120
72-74 95
75 140
76-80 80
81-86 60
87 125
88-90 90
91-103 26
104-110 12

Nanny and the Professor
1 16
2 10

National Velvet
1 12
2 9

National Velvet (Dell)
1-2 30

Navy War Heroes
1 12
2 8
3-7 6

Naza
1 15
2-9 6

Nick Fury, Agent of SHIELD (1st series)
1 50
2 32
3 28
4 35
5 30
6-7 18
8-11 12
12 13
13 12
14 8
15 35
16-18 6

Not Brand Echh
1 25
2 15
3-5 12
6-8 10
9-13 15

Nurses
1 50
2 40
3 30

Our Army at War
51-60 80
61-70 75
71-80 60
81 2,400
82 600
83 1,000
84 225
85 275
86-90 225
91 550
92-100 135
101-110 80
111-120 64
121-127 50
128 200
129-130 46
131-150 36
151 275
152 20
153 115
154 20
155 50
156-157 20
158 32
159-163 20
164 45
165-170 20
171-176 18
177 36
178-181 18
182-183 20
184-185 15
186 20
187-190 15
191-199 12
200 20
201-202 8
203 22
204-210 8
211-215 7
216 16
217-220 7
221-223 6

Our Fighting Forces
13-15 135
16-20 115
21-30 90
31-40 75
41 90
42-44 70
45 235
46 95
47 80
48-50 60
51-60 35
61-64 28
65-70 18
71-80 15
81-90 10
91-99 7
100-120 6
121-127 5

Outer Limits
1 55
2 30
3 24
4-10 20
11-18 10

Peanuts (Dell)
4 75
5-13 55

Peanuts (Gold Key)
1 125
2-4 75

Pebbles Flintstone
1 75

Pep
117-120 28
121-130 18
131-160 15
161-177 7
178-240 4

Perry Mason
1-2 40

Peter Pan (Gold Key)
1 20
2 12

Phantom Stranger (2nd Series)
1 65
2-4 28
5-8 15

Plastic Man
1 45
2 25
3-5 20
6-10 14

Quick Draw McGraw (Dell)
2 15
3-7 10
8-12 8
13-14 6
15 10

Raggedy Ann and Andy (2nd Series)
1 35
2-3 20

Rat Patrol
1-5 40
6 25

Rawhide (Dell)
1 200

Rawhide (Gold Key)
1 175
2 150

Rawhide Kid
11-16 105
17 325
18-19 82
20 8
21-22 76
23 175
24-30 76
31-35 60
36-44 55
45 85
46 55
47-60 30
61-70 22
71-79 14

Richie Rich (1st Series)
1 900
2 450
3 275
4-5 190
6-8 125
9-10 100
11-15 75
16-20 55
21-30 38
31-40 25
41-49 16
50-60 12
61-70 8
71-97 6

Richie Rich Dollars & Cents
1 85
2 45
3-5 24
6-10 16
11-20 12
21-30 9
31-38 7

Richie Rich Millions
1 90
2 50
3 35
4-5 28
6-7 20
8-10 16
11-20 13
21-30 9
31-40 7
41-43 5

Richie Rich Success Stories
1 100
2 45
3 35
4-5 28
6-10 20
11-20 14
21-30 10
31-33 8

Rifleman
2-3 85
4-10 70
11-20 55

Rin Tin Tin & Rusty
1 50

Rip Hunter: Time Master
1 350
2 140
3 115
4-5 95
6-7 85
8-15 70
16-20 58
21-25 48
26-29 40

Robin Hood (Dell)
1 20

Rocky and His Fiendish Friends
1 100
2-3 75
4-5 60

Ronald McDonald
1 52

Ruff and Reddy
4-8 40
9-12 30

Runaway
1 16

Sad Sack

62-70 8
71-90 6
91-100 4
101-150 3
151-215 2

Sad Sack & The Sarge
1 80
2 45
3-5 30
6-10 20
11-20 16
21-30 12
31-40 9
41-49 7
50-60 6
61-80 5
81-83 3

Sad Sack Army Life Parade
1 35
2 20
3 15
4-5 12
6-10 10
11-20 8
21-30 6

Sad Sack Laugh Special
1 90
2 45
3-10 25
11-20 20
21-30 15
31-40 12
41-55 10

Sad Sack's Funny Friends
5 20
6-10 16
11-20 12
21-30 10
31-40 8
41-50 5
51-75 3

Sad Sad Sack World
1 45
2-10 20
11-22 15

Scarecrow of Romney Marsh
1 30
2-3 20

Sea Devils
1 300
2 175
3 120
4-5 85
6-10 55
11-12 38
13 42
14-20 38
21-35 28

Sea Hunt
4-6 30
7-9 25
10-13 20

Secret Origins (1st Series)
Annual 1 400

Sgt. Fury
1 1,100
2 400
3-5 225
6-10 150
11-12 80
13 350
14-20 80
21-30 60
31-40 40
41-50 30
51-70 24
71-80 20
Annual 1 125
Annual 2 55
Annual 3 30
Annual 4 22
Annual 5-6 10

77 Sunset Strip (Dell)
1 150

77 Sunset Strip (Gold Key)
1-2 100

Shadow (1st Series)
1 30
2-8 18

Showcase
4 26,000
5 900
6 3,600
7 1,800
8 11,500
9 6,000
10 2,500
11-12 1,625
13-14 4,200
15 1,650
16 900
17 2,200
18-19 1,100
20 850
21 450
22 5,000
23 1,600
24 1,500
25-26 275
27 700
28-29 350
30 650
31-33 325
34 1,250
35 700
36 525
37 500
38 350
39-40 300
41-42 150
43 400
44 100
45 225
46-47 95
48-52 65
53-54 80
55 275
56 100
57-58 120
59 90
60 225
61 125
62 70
63 35
64 125
65 35
66-72 20
73 110
74 65
75 85
76 40
77 45
78 30
79 45
80 35
81 12
82 45
83-84 40
85-87 12
88-89 8
90-93 7

Silver Surfer (Vol. 1)
1 375
2 160
3 130
4 350
5-6 90
7 85
8-10 58
11-13 52
14 68
15-18 42

Sinister House of Secret Love
1 40
2-4 30

Six-Gun Heroes (Charlton)
46-50 48
51-60 32
61-70 22
71-83 16

Snagglepuss
1 65
2-4 42

Snooper and Blabber Detectives
1 100
2-3 75

Soupy Sales Comic Book
1 80

Space Adventures
23 100
24-32 70
33 325
34 150
35-40 125
41 25
42 75
43-50 25
51-60 18
61-67 12

Space Family Robinson
1 200
2 100
3-5 70
6-10 50
11-15 30
16-20 24
21-36 20

Space Ghost (Gold Key)
1 150

Spaceman
2 40
3 32
4-6 24
7-8 22

Space War
1 95
2-3 55
4-6 100
7 30
8 100
9 30
10 100
11-15 30
16-27 16

Spectacular Spider-Man (Magazine)
1 45
2 80

Spectre (1st Series)
1 100
2-5 65
6-10 38

Spooky (Vol. 1)
6-10 35
11-20 24
21-29 20
30-39 18
40-50 15
51-70 12
71-90 8
91-110 6
111-119 5

Spooky Spooktown
1 85
2 45
3-5 30
6-10 22
11-20 15
21-29 8
30-35 5

Star Spangled War Stories
49-70 60
71-83 55
84 125
85-87 80
88-89 65
90 325
91 45
92 110
93 45
94-99 110
100 145
101-133 75
134 80
135-138 75
139 60
140-143 35
144 40
145 35
146-150 24
151 130
152 25

Star Trek (Gold Key)

1 300
2 195
3-5 145
6-9 116
10-20 62
21-30 46
31-40 36
41-59 25
60-61 22
Bk 1-Bk 4 25

Steve Zodiak and the Fireball XL-5
1 65

Strange Adventures
72-80 90
81-90 80
91-99 72
100 100
101-110 56
111-116 50
117 525
118-119 70
120 250
121-130 62
131-134 54
135-150 40
151-160 34
161-179 22
180 110
181-183 15
184 75
185-189 15
190 80
191-194 12
195 50
196-200 12
201 35
202-204 10
205 75
206 50
207-210 36
211-216 32
217-221 8
222 12
223-225 8

Strange Tales (1st Series)
49-57 150
58 160
59 180
60 150
61 180
62-63 130
64 160
65-66 125
67 170
68 125

69 155
70-78 120
79 200
80 120
81-82 110
83 100
84 185
85-88 110
89 240
90-92 110
93-96 100
97 300
98-100 100
101 700
102 290
103-105 230
106 170
107 185
108-109 170
110 950
111 290
112-113 105
114 240
115 360
116 80
117-118 65
119 85
120 80
121-125 45
126 50
127-129 40
130 45
131-134 40
135 80
136-145 26
146 28
147 26
148 45
149 26
150 30
151 40
152-158 24
159 30
160-168 24
Annual 1 325
Annual 2 350

Sub-Mariner (Vol. 2)
1 75
2 25
3-4 15
5 16
6-8 15
8-2 .... 1.50
9-10 15
11-13 12
14 20
15 10
16-20 8
21-29 6

Sugar & Spike
3-5 450
6-10 300
11-20 230
21-30 145
31-40 110
41-50 75
51-60 58
61-80 48
81-91 34

Summer Love
46 95
47 70
48 15

Superboy (1st Series)
51-60 110
61-67 90
68 475
69-77 70
78 135
79 70
80 110
81-85 52
86 125
87-88 52
89 220
90-93 48
94-97 35
98 45
99 35
100 175
101-110 16
111-120 15
121-128 10
129 13
130-137 8
138 13
139-140 7
141-146 6
147 10
148-155 6
156 9
157-164 6
165 9
166-168 6
Annual 1 140

Supercar
1 250
2-4 200

Super DC Giant
13 75
14-16 30
17 125

Supergirl (1st Series)
1 15
2 10
3-10 8

Super Heroes Versus Super Villains
1 50

Superman (1st Series)
108-110 260
111-120 225
121-122 185
123 200
124-130 185
131-139 145
140 170
141-145 110
146 150
147 135
148 110
149 125
150-161 65
162-180 50
181-182 35
183 45
184-186 35
187 45
188-190 35
191-192 30
193 40
194-196 30
197 40
198 30
199 200
200 30
201 20
202 30
203-206 20
207 30
208-211 20
212 30
213-216 20
217 30
218-221 20
222 30
223-226 20
227 30
228-229 20
Annual 1 600
Annual 2 325
Annual 3 210
Annual 4 180
Annual 5 105
Annual 6 90
Annual 7 62
Annual 8 46

Superman's Girl Friend Lois Lane
1 2,600
2 625
3 415
4-5 300
6-10 220
11-18 125
19 215
20 125
21-29 86
30-50 48
51-67 34
68 44
69 34
70 175
71 105
72-73 15
74 34
75-76 15
77 24
78 15
79-85 10
86 16
87-94 10
95 16
96-103 8
104 16
Annual 1 75
Annual 2 50

Superman's Pal Jimmy Olsen
15-20 235
21-30 150
31-40 100
41-50 75
51-56 50
57-70 30
71 25
72-73 30
74-75 25
76 30
77-87 25
88-90 20
91-94 16
95 25
96-99 16
100 25
101-103 12
104 25
105-112 12
113 25
114-119 12
120-130 10
131-132 8

Swamp Thing (1st Series)
1 60
2 30
3-4 20
5-6 15
7 12
8-10 10
11-24 5

Tales of Suspense
1 1,400
2 540
3 475
4 450
5-10 325
11-20 240
21-32 150
33-38 135
39 3,500
40 1,100
41 650
42-45 325
46-47 210
48 265
49 210
50 155
51 105
52 140
53 120
54-56 62
57 170
58-59 210
60 120
61-62 82
63 180
64 72
65-66 125
67-70 52
71-80 42
81-99 32

Tales of the Unexpected
1 750
2 385
3 275
4-5 225
6-10 165
11-20 125
21-30 100
31-39 85
40 650
41-42 275
43 450
44-45 200
46-50 150
51-55 125
56-60 100
61-70 85
71-74 60
75-82 50
83-90 30
91-100 22
101-104 20

Tales to Astonish (Vol. 1)
1 2,000
2 635
3-5 440
6-10 355
11-20 265
21-26 200
27 3,600
28-34 175
35 1,900
36 625
37-40 350
41-43 230
44 290
45-48 150
49 205
50-56 95
57 125
58 95
59 150
60 175
61-65 75
66-69 70
70 100
71-81 55
82 78
83-90 55
91 52
92-93 75
94-99 50
100 75
101 85

Tarzan (Gold Key)
132-154 14
155 18
156-162 10
163-164 8
165 10
166-167 8
168 10
169-170 8
171 10
172-195 7

Tarzan, Lord of the Jungle (Gold Key)
1 40

Tasmanian Devil and His Tasty Friends
1 75

Teenage Hotrodders
1 35
2-10 20
11-24 15

Teen-Age Love
4 30
5 16
6-10 14
11-20 9
21-30 7
31-50 5
51-72 40

Teen Confessions
1 75
2 40
3-10 30
11-30 25
31 125
32-50 20
51-58 15
59 20
60-97 12

Teen Titans
1 175
2 100
3-5 60
6-10 40
11-17 30
18 32
19 30
20-22 32
23-25 18
26-29 14

Tender Love Stories
1 15
2-4 10

Thor
126 125
127-133 50
134 55
135-140 50
141-157 30
158 60
159-160 30
161 20
162 35
163-164 20
165 32
166 28
167 16
168-169 35
170-179 16
180 14
Annual 2 60

Those Magnificent Men In Their Flying Machines
1 25

THUNDER Agents
1 140
2 75
3-5 55
6-8 42
9-10 35
11-15 38
16-19 22
20 15

Thunderbolt
1 16
51 10
52-60 9

Time Tunnel
1 40
2 35

Timmy the Timid Ghost (1st Series)
3 36
4-10 20
11-20 18
21-45 10

Timmy the Timid Ghost (2nd Series)
1 10
2-10 6
11-26 4

Tomahawk
43-50 56
51-56 45
57 85
58-60 40
61-80 32
81-90 25
91-100 15
101-110 10
111-120 8
121-130 6

Tom & Jerry Comics
146-170 6
171-190 5
191-200 4
201-230 3
231-252 2

Top Cat (Dell)
1 60
2 35
3-5 25
6-10 20
11-20 15
21-31 12

Top Comics: Lassie
1 10

Top Eliminator
25-29 10

Total War
1 40
2 35

Tower of Shadows
1 20
2-3 12
4-8 10

Tuff Ghosts, Starring Spooky
1 35
2-5 18
6-10 12
11-30 10
31-39 8

Turok, Son of Stone
3 155
4-5 125
6-7 110
7/A 135
8-10 110
11-20 75
21-30 48
31-40 38
41-50 28
51-60 22
61-70 15
GS 1 85

TV Casper and Company
1 75
2-5 30
6-10 20
11-20 15
21-29 10

Twilight Zone (Vol. 1)
1 90
2 55
3 42
4-10 35
11-20 30
21-27 16
28-30 10
31-34 8

Two-Gun Kid
33-44 60
45-46 55
47 45
48 50
49-50 40
51 50
52 40
53-54 20
55 40
56 20
57 40
58-59 20
60 30
61-80 12
81-94 8

UFO Flying Saucers

1 25
2-4 15
5-13 10

Uncle Scrooge
15 100
16-20 80
21-30 65
31-40 55
41-50 45
51-70 40
71 38
72-88 32

Uncle Scrooge and Donald Duck
1 50

Uncle Scrooge Goes to Disneyland
1 275

Underdog (Charlton)
1 60
2 38

Undersea Agent
1 32
2 22
3-6 18

Unexpected
105 30
106-113 18
114-118 12
119 14
120 12

U.S. Fighting Men
10-11 15
12-18 12

Wacky Races
1 40

Wagon Train (Dell)
4-6 38
7-9 34
10-13 25

Wagon Train (Gold Key)
1 38
2-4 25

Walt Disney's Christmas Parade (Gold Key)
1 75
2-8 50
9 20

Walt Disney's Comics and Stories
192-200 80
201-240 75
241-260 60
261-283 50
284-285 25
286 28
287 25
288-289 28
290 25
291-293 28
294-296 25
297-308 28
309-311 25
312 28
313-334 14
335 25
336-341 14
342-359 25

Wendy Good Little Witch (Vol. 1)
1 60
2 40
3-5 28
6-10 22
11-15 14
16-20 12
21-25 8
26-30 6
31-40 5
41-50 4
51-62 3

Wendy Witch World
1 90
2-5 50
6-10 35
11-20 26
21-30 22
31-35 18

Wham-O Giant Comics
1 100

Wild West (Charlton)
58 10

Wild, Wild West (Gold Key)
1 70
2 45
3-7 35

Witching Hour
1 50
2 25
3 18
4 12
5 18
6-10 10

Wonder Woman (1st Series)
84-90 155
91-100 120
101-104 90
105 600
106-110 80
111-120 65
121-126 46
127-130 40
131-150 26
151-159 22
160-170 18
171-179 15
180 16
181-191 12

Woody Woodpecker
38-50 12
51-72 9
73-75 25
76-100 7
101-113 5

World's Finest Comics
84-90 235
91-93 175
94 525
95-99 175
100 260
101-110 95
111-121 75
122-142 42
143-150 28
151-155 22
156 80
157-161 22
162-165 15
166 20
167-169 14
170 20
171-174 14
175-177 20
178-187 8
188 10
189-190 8
191-196 6

Wyatt Earp
6-10 50
11-20 42
21-29 30

Wyatt Earp, Frontier Marshal

14-18 18
19 40
20-40 10
41-50 8
51-60 7
61-72 6

X-Men (1st Series)
1 6500
2 2000
3 825
4 725
5 500
6 375
7-10 315
11 275
12 375
13 260
14 300
15-16 250
17-20 140
21-27 120
28 175
29-30 120
31-34 85
35 120
36-37 85
38 110
39-40 85
41-48 75
49-51 80
52 55
53-57 65
58 85
59 60
60-62 65
63 65
64-65 65
66 70

Yellow Submarine
1 110

Young Lawyers
1-2 10

Young Love (DC)
39 30
40-50 24
51-70 20
71-82 14

Young Rebels
1 15

Zorro (Dell)
8-9 70
10-12 68
13-15 65

Zorro (Gold Key)
1 70
2-4 38
5-7 34
8-9 28